The Foundations of Ethology

The Principal Ideas and Discoveries in Animal Behavior

Konrad Z. Lorenz

Translated by Konrad Z. Lorenz
and Robert Warren Kickert

A TOUCHSTONE BOOK
Published by Simon and Schuster
NEW YORK

First Touchstone Edition, 1982

Published by Simon and Schuster
A Division of Gulf & Western Corporation
Simon & Schuster Building
Rockefeller Center
1230 Avenue of the Americas
New York, New York 10020

Published by arrangement with Springer-Verlag New York, Inc.

TOUCHSTONE and colophon are trademarks of Simon & Schuster

Manufactured in the United States of America

10 9 8 7 6 5 4 3 2 1 Pbk.

Library of Congress Cataloging in Publication Data

Lorenz, Konrad.
    The foundations of ethology.

    (A Touchstone book)
    Revised and enl. translation of: Vergleichende
Verhaltensforschung.
    Bibliography: p.
    Includes index.
    1. Animal behavior.   2. Human behavior.
3. Psychology, Comparative.   I. Title.
QL751.L7213   1982   156   82-10464

ISBN 0-671-44573-1 Pbk.

Frontispiece photo by Hans J. Böning, Wien

This English edition is a revised and enlarged version of *Vergleichende
Verhaltensforschung: Grundlagen der Ethologie,* first published in 1978 by Springer-
Verlag/Wien—New York.

To Nikolaas Tinbergen

Foreword

This book is a contribution to the history of ethology—not a definitive history, but the personal view of a major figure in that story. It is all the more welcome because such a grand theme as ethology calls for a range of perspectives. One reason is the overarching scope of the subject. Two great questions about life that constitute much of biology are "How does it work (structure and function)?" and "How did it get that way (evolution and ontogeny)?" Ethology addresses the antecedent of "it." Of what are we trying to explain the mechanism and development? Surely behavior, in all its wealth of detail, variation, causation, and control, is the main achievement of animal evolution, the essential consequence of animal structure and function, the raison d'etre of all the rest. Ethology thus spans between and overlaps with the ever-widening circles of ecology over the eons and the ever-narrowing focus of physiology of the neurons.

Another reason why the history of ethology needs perspectives is the recency of its acceptance. For such an obviously major aspect of animal biology, it is curious how short a time—less than three decades—has seen the excitement of an active field and a substantial fraternity of workers, the addition of professors and courses to departments and curricula in biology (still far from universal), and the normal complement of special journals, symposia, and sessions at congresses. Of course, animal behavior has been a subject of serious writings, usually called natural history, for centuries. However, for reasons that need historical perspectives to be evaluated, the dignity of a major discipline long escaped all but the facets embraced by psychologists.

Did the arrival and spread of acceptance of the modern study of free animal behavior await the impetus of a school, of advocates, of theories and models? Surely Konrad Lorenz was a major factor, through his thought-provoking approach, his eloquence, his inspiration to many students—and above all his intimate and wide familiarity with animals in nature.

When a figure so largely responsible for the emergence and development of a scientific approach chooses to summarize the field, as Konrad Lorenz does here for ethology, it is an historical document and worth attention. It is all the more important for a subject so bound up with concepts, conceptual methodology, and interpretation, and so dependent on accumulated experience in watching animals. It is Lorenz's perception that "fashion" and "ideological prejudice" have obscured our familiarity with some of the basic foundations of ethology, even on the part of knowledgeable authors, so that a main aim of this work is to remind us of the historical origins and of "how narrow that factual foundation is and hence how needful is thorough verification."

One cannot but wonder whether the brigades of workers who have followed Lorenz's lead have not provided either that verification or some modification. It is therefore an understandable hope of some readers to find Lorenz's evaluation of newer data and his position on the debates over concepts or terms. However, this would have meant virtually a full review of the accumulated literature and such is not Lorenz's aim within these covers. On the whole, apart from a few interesting admissions of changes in viewpoint and terminology, one has to look hard for changes in usage, definition, or concepts made as a result of the findings and reinterpretations of later workers.

It is only to be expected that such a document will be highly personal. Moreover, it is bound to sound familiar. But a close reader of Lorenz will note many new or refined positions. Of special interest to those who think of ethology as mainly concerned with unlearned, instinctive behavior of non-mammalian taxa will be two features. One is a series of chapters devoted to adaptive modification of behavior. In one of these Lorenz distinguishes between two forms of operant conditioning, a form which he believes is common in nature, and another that is quite uncommon. The other feature is an appendix devoted to *Homo sapiens*. Here he gives reason to claim that the science of human ethology has much to teach us, all the more so because the human species, while not outside the natural biological order, is very special indeed in cultural heritage and the elaboration of language.

Only a personal restatement of the foundations by one of the founders can have the poignancy this book has as the result of changes in the prevailing intellectual climate, such as the new respectability of discussions about animal consciousness and mental life. Not that such changes have an easily predictable effect, for example, in making Lorenz's viewpoint more persuasive or some ogres less like straw men. It is certainly one of the charms of this book to see for oneself what the arguments sound like in the light of all that has happened in science and society. Lorenz lets us reexamine not only the factual foundations but the methodological and even some philosophical bases. The reexamination may not always lead to greater sympathy for the Lorenzian alternative but should lead to better history and a greater motivation to broaden the base.

Appreciation of this book and the wealth of observation of nature it represents is enhanced if one adapts to Lorenz's methods of exposition. Each reader will no doubt develop his or her own approach. For example, I learned not to judge or even to try to absorb the sweeping induction that opens the paragraph, but to wait until the example unfolds that makes the key terms understandable. It is best not to be put off by expressions such as "explanatory monism," "atomism," "technomorphically," "teleonomy," or "relatively entirety-independent." But these are no doubt the limitations of a relatively example-dependent physiologist-reader! I could not expect every familiar term to be defined or strong language to be eschewed ("never," "any at all," "exploded"). And I learned that one road to understanding is to contrast the right view with a delineation of the bad guy's view.

There have been various images of scientists: bricklayers adding facts to erect an edifice of knowledge, revolutionaries putting together discrepancies to overturn established "paradigms," delvers uncovering nuggets of gold, and wise men avoiding the Baconian idols of the marketplace and idols of the tribe. This book conjures up the image of a slayer of dragons; the preferred form of exposition of scientific advance is to show how wrong was some previous view. Most authors cited are either protagonists or adversaries, and the latter are astonishingly bad. The list of bad guys is long: vitalists, monists, reflexologists, Pavlovists.

One reads on, captivated by the parade of striking examples. The enduring images are the vivid descriptions—of a shrike holding an object in its bill and searching for thorns, or performing impaling motions in vacuo; of a goose, satiated with corn but deprived of an opportunity to up-end and gather food from the pond bottom, so that when offered corn thrown into the pond at the right depth, began "feeding for the sake of up-ending instead of up-ending for the sake of feeding"; of the experienced male cichlid fish that is not fooled by the best fish-like dummy, in contrast to the male raised in isolation that gives a full male courtship response when the simplest dummy moves into view. While unusual for fish, this drives home both the nature of the evidence for innate releasing mechanisms and the possibility of refining both the sign stimuli and the recognition process by learning. These and scores of other graphic instances are mostly familiar to ethologists as classical examples; they form the solid empirical foundations of ethology. It is understandable how they invite categorization, concept formation, the induction of entities, and the attempt to interpret in some sort of crude mechanistic terms. It is too much to ask that the ethologist "stick to his last" and avoid wandering into physiology. We should expect and welcome such excursions, and judge their success not so much by the sophistication or modernity of the physiological model but by how heuristic it is in suggesting things to look for.

Rarely does a founder of a field give us his insider's view of it. Would that other participants in the founding of ethology were moved to emulate Dr. Lorenz in sharing their impressions of its development. In such a spectrum of memoirs, this book would have a key position.

Theodore Holmes Bullock
University of California, San Diego
La Jolla, California

Preface

In some respects, the development of a science resembles that of a coral colony. The more it thrives and the faster it grows, the quicker its first beginnings—the vestiges of the founders and the contributions of the early discoverers—become overgrown and obscured by their own progeny. There is one drawback to the strategy of growth pursued by the coral tree. The polyps at the end of its branches have a much better chance of further development than those situated near the foundation. The ends go on growing faster and faster without considering the necessity for strengthening, in proportion, the base that must carry the weight of the whole structure. Unlike an oak tree, the coral colony does nothing to solidify its support. Consequently, there is a lot of coral rubble detached from points of departure, and this is either dead or, if still partly alive, growing in indeterminate directions and getting nowhere.

Having myself grown very near the point from which ethology, as a new branch of biological science, had its origin, it may seem presumptuous if I compare the present state of our science to a coral colony whose branches, by losing contact with their foundation, are producing quite a lot of rubble. However, there is no doubt that they do, and I *am* presumptuous enough to criticize this. My justification lies in the fact that really important discoveries, such as those made by Charles Otis Whitman, Oskar Heinroth, Erich von Holst, Kenneth Roeder, and others, are being forgotten, and for reasons, I contend, which are partly to be found in mere fashion, and partly in ideological prejudices.

So this book is not an up-to-date textbook on ethology. It does not presume to include all the most recent developments within this science, not even those which mean very real advances. Its aim is to remind scientists in general of the basic facts on which ethology is founded, and to remind ethologists in particular of how narrow the factual foundation of our science really is, how completely our science relies on these facts being correct, and how much, therefore, their thorough verification remains necessary.

Contents

Introductory History

Ethology, the comparative study of behavior, is easy to define: it is the discipline which applies to the behavior of animals and humans all those questions asked and those methodologies used as a matter of course in all the other branches of biology since Charles Darwin's time.

When one considers with what rapidity the ideas of evolution, and particularly the Darwinian concept of natural selection, caught on in almost all branches of biology, one searches for an explanation as to why these ideas were so tardily accepted by the disciplines of psychology and behavioral science. The main reason that biological thinking and especially comparative methods were prevented from penetrating the study of behavior was an ideological dispute between two prominent schools of psychology.

The bitterness with which this dispute was pursued was nourished, above all, by the diverse philosophies of the antagonists. The school of purposive psychology, represented primarily by William MacDougall and later by Edward Chase Tolman, postulated an extranatural factor: "instinct" was regarded as an *agens* or agency neither in need of nor accessible to a natural explanation. "We consider an instinct but we do not explain it," wrote Bierens de Haan as late as 1940. To this conception of instinct was always also appended a belief in its infallibility. MacDougall rejected all mechanistic explanations of behavior. For example, he considered it a consequence of instinct when insects pressed forward purposively toward light; he conceded the possibility of a mechanistic explanation, through tropism, only in those cases where these animals, most unpurposively, flew into a burning lamp. According to MacDougall and his school, everything animals do is in pursuit of a purpose and this purpose is set by their extranatural and infallible instinct.

Those of the behaviorist school of psychology justifiably criticized the assumption of extranatural factors as unscientific. They demanded causal explanations. Through their methodology they sought to place themselves as much apart as possible from the purposive psychologists. They regarded the controlled experiment as the only legitimate source of knowledge. Empirical methods were to take the place of philosophical speculation.

With the exception of a certain lack of appreciation for simple observation, this program incorporated no methodological error, and yet it brought about an unfortunate consequence: all research interests were concentrated on those aspects of animal and human behavior which readily lent themselves to experimentation—and this led to explanatory monism.

A combination of William Wundt's (1922) association theory with the reflex theory (reflexology) that was then dominating the fields of physiology and psychology, as well as with the findings of I. P. Pavlov (1927), facilitated the abstraction of a behavior mechanism—the so-called *conditioned reflex*—the qualities of which marked it as ideal for experimental research.

At that time the corrective criticism made by the behaviorists concerning the opinions held by the purposive psychologists was salutary in every way. But, unobserved, a ruinous logical error crept into behaviorist thinking: because only learning processes could be examined experimentally and since all behavior must be examined experimentally, then, concluded those of the behaviorist school, all behavior must be learned—which, naturally, is not only logically false but also, factually, complete nonsense.

Knowing the views of those in the opposition, and having made a justifiable critique of those views, the purposive psychologists as well as the behaviorists were pushed into extreme positions which neither of them would otherwise have taken. While those of one group were imbued with a mystical veneration of "THE instinct" and attributed excessive capacities, even infallibility, to the inborn, those of the other group denied its very existence. The purposive psychologists, who were quite aware of innate behavior patterns, regarded everything instinctive as inexplicable and, just as Bierens de Haan (1940), refused even to attempt a causal analysis. Those others who certainly would have been capable and ready to undertake such analytical research denied the existence of anything inborn, and dogmatically declared that all behavior was learned. The truly tragic aspect of this historical situation is that the purposive psychologists, particularly MacDougall himself, knew animals well and possessed a good, general knowledge of animal behavior, something which is still lacking among the behaviorists even today, because they regard simple observation as unnecessary, in fact, as "unscientific." In this context, the truth of a statement of Faust's comes to mind: "What one does not know is exactly what one needs, and what one does know one cannot use."

This ideological dispute between these two schools of psychology was still being actively pursued when, completely unnoticed by both and independent of their influence, the scientific study of innate behavior patterns came into being. At the turn of the century Charles Otis Whitman and, a few years later, independently of him, Oskar Heinroth discovered the existence of *patterns of movement*, the similarities and differences of which, from species to species, from genus to genus, even from one large taxonomic group to another are retained with just as much constancy and in exactly the same way as comparable physical characters. In other words, these patterns of movement are just as reliably characteristic of a particular group as are tooth and feather formation and such other proven distinguishing physical attributes used in comparative morphology. For this fact there can be no other explanation than that the similarities and dissimilarities of these coordinated movements are to be traced back to a common origin in an ancestral form which also already had, as its very own, these same movements in a primeval form. In short, the concept of *homology* can be applied to them.

These facts alone prove that these movements originate phylogenetically and are imbedded in the genome. It is just this that is overlooked by those students of behavior who would like to explain away every conceptual distinction between innate and acquired characteristics. When the African black duck *(Anas sparsa)* living on tropical rivers, the mallard living on our own lakes, the many species of wild ducks living on the ponds of zoos, and the domesticated ducks living in the barnyards of our farms, in spite of the differences of their environments and despite all the possible influences of captivity, display courtship movements that are unmistakably similar in a countless number of characteristics, then the program for these movements must be anchored in the genome in a manner exactly identical with that in which the program of morphological characters is coded in the genes. If, after this discovery, theories concerned with the problem of "nature versus nurture" continue to be published, this is explainable only through the assumption that these authors are unaware of the discoveries made at the turn of the century, or that they have chosen to ignore them. That they indeed do this was soon clear to me. American psychologists often visited Karl Bühler's institute. I asked each and every one of them whether they knew the name Charles Otis Whitman. Not one of them knew the name.

The discovery that movement patterns are homologous is the Archimedean point from which ethology or the comparative study of behavior marks its origin. Paradoxically, even the work of authors who deny the essential difference between innate and acquired behavior mechanisms is built upon the same factual base.

I discovered for myself, independently of Whitman and Heinroth, that patterns of movement are homologous. When studying at the university under the Viennese anatomist, Ferdinand Hochstetter, and after I had become thoroughly conversant with the methodology and procedure of phylogenetic comparison, it became immediately clear that the methods employed in comparative morphology were just as applicable to the behavior of the many species of fish and birds I knew so thoroughly, thanks to the early onset of my love for animals. Soon after this I met Oskar Heinroth, the discoverer of my discovery, and early in the 1930's both of us learned through communication with the American ornithologist, Margret Morse Nice, that Charles Otis Whitman had come to essentially the same conclusions as Heinroth about ten years earlier. At the same time all this was happening, we met the most distinguished of Whitman's students, Wallace Craig.

Neither Whitman nor Heinroth ever expressed any views concerning the physiological nature of the homologous movement patterns they had discovered. My own knowledge of the physiology of the central nervous system came from lectures and textbooks in which the Sherringtonian reflex theory (1906) was regarded as the last word and the incontestable truth. The expression "reflex" evokes, linguistic-logically, the vision of a simple, linear causal relationship between the incoming stimulus and the response given to it by the organism. In this simplicity lies the seductive effect of the concept: It is just as easy to understand as it is to teach.

Under Karl Bühler's tuition I gained enough knowledge of the two prominent schools of American psychology to feel myself qualified to criticize them on two fundamental points. The first was that the infallible, preternatural "instinct" in which the purposive psychologists believed simply did not exist; too often had I seen innate behavior patterns taking their course in completely blind and senseless sequences. The second criticism was that the point of view of the behaviorists, that all animal behavior is learned, was totally false.

I had published several short articles, based on my own observations, about the problem of the innate and homologous in motor patterns when my friend, Gustav Kramer, imposed himself on the course of these events by influencing the biologist, Max Hartmann, to invite me to give a lecture to the Kaiser Wilhelm Society for the Advancement of Science (now the Max Planck Society). Kramer was carrying out his intention of providing a setting for a discussion between Erich von Holst and me. He was von Holst's friend as well as mine, and he was well aware that the phenomena which I was observing in the motor patterns of intact animals were very closely related to those processes which von Holst was investigating experimentally at the neurophysiologic level. Gustav Kramer believed that the congruity between von Holst's research results and mine would be that much more startling and convincing the longer we

worked completely independently of one another; that is why he per-
petuated this remarkable feat of extended reticence.

So then, in 1935, I gave my lecture at Harnack House in Berlin. Its
theme was based on my article, "The Concept of Instinct Then and
Now." (1932) There I made it clear that any animal is perfectly capable,
through goal oriented and variable behavior, of striving toward a purpose, but that this purpose may not, as the purposive psychologists supposed, be equated with the achievement of the teleonomic function of
behavior. The purpose toward which the animal, as subject, is striving,
is simply a run-through or discharge of that kind of innate behavior
which Wallace Craig designated as "consummatory action" (1918) and
which we now call the drive-reducing consummatory act. Up to this
point what I said then is more or less what I believe today.

But what I had to say about the physiological nature of fixed action
patterns was influenced by doctrinaire bias. Led by MacDougall, the purposive psychologists had continued their battle against the reflex theory
of the behaviorists and, quite rightly, had emphasized the *spontaneity* of
animal behavior. "The healthy animal is up and doing," MacDougall had
written. I was already thoroughly familiar with the writings of Wallace
Craig and, through my own research, I was well acquainted with the
phenomena of appetitive behavior and of threshold lowering for releasing stimuli—and I should have borne in mind a particular sentence of a
letter Craig had sent shortly before, in which he had argued against the
reflex concept: "It is obviously nonsense to speak of a re-action to a stimulus not yet received."

At that juncture mere common sense ought to have prompted me to
put the following question: Innate motor patterns have, apparently,
nothing to do with higher intellectual capacities; they are governed by
central nervous processes which occur quite independently of external
stimuli and they tend to be repeated rhythmically. Do we know of any
other physiological processes which function in a similar way? The
obvious answer would have been: Such motor patterns are very well
known, particularly those of the vertebrate heart for which stimulus producing organs are anatomically known and the physiology of which has
been thoroughly studied.

I lacked the independence of mind and the self-assurance that would
have been necessary to ask this question. My valid aversion toward the
preternatural and inexplicable factors which the vitalists had summoned
to interpret spontaneous behavior was so deep that I lapsed into the
opposite error; I assumed that it would be a concession to the vitalistic
purposive psychologists if I were to deviate from the conventional
mechanistic concept of reflexes, and this concession I did not wish to
make. During the course of that lecture I did cover completely, and with
especial emphasis, all those characteristics and capacities of fixed action

patterns which could *not* be accounted for by means of the chain reaction theory, yet, in my summary at the end, I still concluded that fixed action patterns depended on the linkage of unconditioned reflexes even if the cited phenomena of appetitive behavior, threshold lowering, and vacuum activity (I will return to this on page 127) would require a supplementary hypothesis for clarification.

Sitting next to my wife in the last row of the auditorium was a young man who followed the lecture intently and who, during the exposition on spontaneity, kept muttering, *"Menschenskind!* That's right, that's right!" However, when I came to the concluding remarks described above, he covered his head and groaned, "Idiot." This man was Erich von Holst. After the lecture we were introduced to one another in the Harnack House restaurant and there it took him all of ten minutes to convince me forever that the reflex theory was indeed idiotic.

The moment one assumed that the processes of endogenous production and central nervous coordination of impulses, discovered by von Holst, and not some linkage of reflexes, constitute the physiological bases of behavior patterns, all the phenomena that could not be fitted into the reflex theory, such as threshold lowering and vacuum activities, not only obtained an obvious explanation but became effects to be postulated on the basis of the new theory.

A consequence of this new physiological theory of the fixed motor pattern was the necessity to analyze further that particular behavioral system which Heinroth and I had called the *arteigene Triebhandlung* (literally, species–characteristic drive–action) and which we had regarded as an elementary unit of behavior. Obviously, the mechanism which selectively responded to a certain stimulus situation must be physiologically different from the fixed motor pattern released. As long as the whole system was regarded as a chain of reflexes, there was no reason for conceptually separating, from the rest of the chain, the first link that set it going. But once one had recognized that the movement patterns resulted from impulses endogenously produced and centrally coordinated and that, as long as they were not needed, they had to be held in check by some superordinated factor, the physiological apparatus which triggered their release emerged as a mechanism sui generis. These mechanisms that responded selectively to stimuli, in a certain sense served as "filters" of afference, were clearly fundamentally different from those which produced impulses and from the central coordination that was independent of all afference.

This dismantling of the concept of the *arteigene Triebhandlung* into its component parts signified a substantial step in the development of ethology. The step was taken in Leyden at a congress called together by Prof. van der Klaauw. During discussions that lasted through the nights, Niko Tinbergen and I conceived the concept of the *innate releasing mechanism* (IRM), although it is no longer possible to determine by which one of us it was born. Its further elaboration and refinement, and the exploration of its physiological characteristics, especially its functional limitations, are all due to Niko Tinbergen's experiments.

Concurrent with the conceptualization of the IRM, the concept of the fixed action pattern or instinctive motor pattern was also narrowed and made more precise, and in exactly the way Charlotte Kogon had proposed as early as 1941 in her book, *The Instinctive as a Philosophical Problem*, a book which regrettably remained unknown to me until just recently. Subsequently, and up to the present, the concepts of IRM and of the fixed motor pattern have proved their worth; their utility in the most diverse kinds of flow diagrams make it probable that they are, in fact, functionally if not also physiologically identical mechanisms. For the visualization and presentation of hierarchically organized instincts (Tinbergen, Baerends, Leyhausen) they have been especially useful.

During the years that followed ethology developed quickly, both in the results achieved and in the increasing number of researchers. A large store of data was laboriously assembled; many unique discoveries were made. If one chooses to criticize this period of felicitous research, it can be reproached for one-sidedness, even for a certain failure to think in terms of systems. This was inherent in an orientation that almost completely ignored *learning processes*; above all, the relationships and interrelationships that existed between the newly discovered inborn behavior mechanisms and the various forms of learning were barely touched. My modest contribution, which comprised a formulation of the "instinct-learning intercalation" concept, got no further than formulation; besides, the example on which the conceptualization—correct in itself—was based, was false. (See page 60.)

In 1953 a critical study appeared which had a behaviorist point of view but which did not come from a behaviorist. In "A Critique of Konrad Lorenz's Theory of Instinctive Behavior" Daniel S. Lehrmann dismissed, on principle, the existence of innate movement patterns and, in so doing, supported his argument substantially by using a thesis of D. O. Hebb (1940) who had maintained that innate behavior is defined only through the exclusion of what is learned and, thus, as a concept was "nonvalid," that is, unusable. Drawing on the findings of Z. Y. Kuo (1932), Lehrmann also asserted that one could never know whether or not particular behavior patterns had been learned within the egg or *in utero*. Kuo had already recommended abandoning the conceptual separation of the innate and the acquired. All behavior, in his opinion, consisted of reactions to stimuli and these reflected the interaction between the organism and its environment. The theory of a pre-extant relationship between the organism and the conditions of its environment is no less questionable, for Kuo, than the assumption of innate ideas.

My answer to Lehrmann's critique was short and forceful but, at first, missed the most essential mark. The assertion that the innate in comparative studies of behavior is defined only through the exclusion of learning processes is entirely false: like morphological traits, innate behavior patterns are recognizable through the same systematic distribution of attributes; the concepts of innate and acquired are as well defined as genotype and phenotype. The reply to the theory that the bird within the egg or the mammal embryo within the uterus could there have learned behavior patterns which then "fit" its intended environment was formulated by my wife and with a single phrase: "Indoor ski course." I myself wrote at the time that Lehrmann, in order to get around the concept of innate behavior patterns, was actually postulating the existence of an innate schoolmarm.

My formulation of the concept of the "innate schoolmarm" was clearly intended as a reductio ad absurdum. What neither I nor my critics saw was that in just this teaching mechanism the real problem was lurking. It took me nearly ten years to think through to where, actually, the error of the criticism and the counter-criticism was located. It was so very difficult to find because the error had been committed in exactly the same way by both the extreme behaviorists and by the older ethologists. It was, as a matter of fact, incorrect to formulate the concepts of the innate and the acquired as disjunctive opposites; however, the mutuality and intersection of their conceptual contents were not to be found, as the "instinct opponents" supposed, in everything apparently innate being, really, learned, but the very reverse, in that everything learned must have as its foundation a phylogenetically provided program if, as they actually are, appropriate species-preserving behavior patterns were to be produced. Not only Oskar Heinroth and I, too, but other older ethologists as well, had never given much concentrated thought to those phenomena which we quite summarily identified as learned or as determined through insight and then simply shoved them to the side. We regarded them—if one wishes to describe our research methods somewhat uncharitably— as the ragbag for everything that lay outside our analytical interests.

So it happened that neither one of the older ethologists nor one of the "instinct opponents" posed the pertinent question about how it was possible that, whenever the organism modified its behavior through learning processes, the *right* process was learned, in other words, an adaptive improvement of its behavioral mechanisms was achieved. This omission seemed particularly crass on the part of Z. Y. Kuo (1932) who had so expressly disassociated himself from every predetermined connection between organism and environment but who, at the same time, regarded it as axiomatic that all learning processes induced meaningful species-preserving modifications. As far as my knowledge goes, P. K. Anokhin (1961) was first among the theorists of learning to grasp the conditioned reflex as a *feedback circuit* in which it was not only the stimulus configuration arriving from the outside, but more especially the *return notifica-*

tion reporting on the completion and the consequences of the conditioned behavior that provided an audit of its adaptiveness.

As in many other cases of erroneous reasoning, the behaviorists' exclusion of questions concerning the adaptive value of learned behavior may be traced to their emphatic antagonism to the school of purposive psychology. The latter's uninhibited commitment to behavior's extranatural purpose created in the behaviorists such antipathy to all concepts of purpose that, along with purposive teleology, they also resolutely refused to consider any species-preserving purposefulness, including teleonomy as defined by C. Pittendrigh (1958). This attitude, unfortunately, made them blind to all those things that could be understood only through a comprehension of evolutionary processes.

The innate schoolmarm, which tells the organism whether its behavior is useful for or detrimental to species continuation and, in the first instance reinforces and in the second extinguishes that behavior, must be located in a feedback apparatus that reports success or failure to the mechanisms of the first phases of antecedent behavior. This realization came to me only slowly and independently of P. K. Anokhin. I published my theories on this subject also in 1961 in my monograph, *Phylogenetische Anpassung und adaptive Modifikation des Verhaltens,* which I later extended and enlarged for a book in English, *Evolution and Modification of Behavior.* As I emphasized in that publication, whenever a modification of an organ, as well as of a behavior pattern, proves to be adaptive to a particular environmental circumstance, this also proves incontrovertibly that *information about this circumstance* must have been "fed into" the organism. There are only two ways this can happen. The first is in the course of phylogenesis through mutation and/or new combinations of genetic factors and through natural selection. The second is through individual acquisition of information by the organism in the course of its ontogeny. "Innate" and "learned" are not each defined through an exclusion of the other but through the *way of entrance taken by the pertinent information* that is a prerequisite for every adaptive change.

The bipartition, the "dichotomy" of behavior into the innate and the learned is misleading in two ways, but not in the sense maintained in the behaviorist argument. Neither through observation nor through experimentation has it been found to be even in the least probable, still less a logical necessity, that every phylogenetically programmed behavior mechanism must be adaptively modifiable through learning. Quite the contrary, it is as much a fact of experience as it is logical to postulate that certain behavior elements, and exactly those that serve as the built-in "schoolmarm" and conduct the learning processes along the correct route, are *never* modifiable through learning.

But, on the other hand, every "learned behavior" does contain phylogenetically acquired information to the extent that the basis of the teaching function of every "schoolmarm" is a physiological apparatus that evolved under the pressure of selection. Whoever denies this must assume a prestabilized harmony between the environment and the organism to explain the fact that learning—apart from some instructive failures—always reinforces teleonomic behavior and extinguishes unsuitable behavior. Whoever makes himself blind to the facts of evolution arrives inevitably at this assumption of a prestabilized harmony, as have the cited behaviorists and that great vitalist, Jakob von Uexküll.

The search for the source of information which underlies both innate and acquired adaptation has, since those earlier years, yielded significant results. I will mention only the research done by Jürgen Nicolai (1970) with whydah birds (Viduinae) in which the information can be "coded" in such an intricate way: essential parts of the adult bird's song have been learned by monitoring the begging tones and other tonal expressions of whichever species of host bird the whydah happened to be hatched and reared.

Inquiry into the phylogenetic programming of the acquiring processes has proved to be important in many respects. Like imprinting, some acquiring processes are impressionable only during specific sensitive periods of ontogeny; a failure to perceive and meet their needs during those crucial periods in animals and humans can result in irremediable damage. Within cultural contexts the distinction between the innate and the acquired is also significant. Man, too, and his behavior are not unlimitedly modifiable through learning and, thus, many inborn programs constitute human rights.

As early as 1916, Oskar Heinroth wrote in the conclusion of his classic paper on waterfowl:

> I have, in this paper, drawn attention to the behavior used in social intercourse and this, especially in birds living in social communities, turns out to be quite amazingly similar to that of human beings, particularly in species in which the family—father, mother and children—remain together living in a close union as long as, for instance, geese do. The taxon of Suropsidae [the branch formed by reptiles and birds; see Figure 6, page 75] has here evolved emotions, habits and motivations very similar to those which we are wont to regard, in ourselves, as morally commendable as well as controlled by reason. The study of the ethology of higher animals (still a regrettably neglected field) will force us more and more to acknowledge that our behavior towards our families and towards strangers, in our courtship and the like, represents purely innate and much more primitive processes than we commonly tend to assume.

This early admonishment notwithstanding, ethology was curiously tardy in approaching Man as a subject.

In the investigation of humans it is not easy to fulfill the primary task of ethology, which is the analytical distinction of fixed motor patterns.

No less a man than Charles Darwin in his monograph, *The Expression of Emotion in Man and Animals* (1872), pointed out the homology of some human and animal motor patterns. The homology was convincing, but solid proof still remained necessary.

Irenäus Eibl-Eibesfeldt (1973) was the first to afford this proof. He chose the same movements which Darwin had studied—those expressing emotions. For obvious reasons, the experiments involving social isolation that are generally used to prove a motor pattern to be independent of learning could not be used with humans, so Eibl fell back on the study of those unfortunates with whom an illness had already initiated this experiment in an equally cruel and effective manner: he studied children born deaf and blind. As he was able to demonstrate by means of film analyses, these children possessed a practically unchanged repertoire of facial expressions although, living in permanent and absolute darkness and silence, they had never seen or heard these expressed by any fellow human.

As a second route of approach, Eibl-Eibesfeldt (1967, 1968) used the cross-cultural method to study the expression of emotions in humans. He observed and filmed representatives of as many cultures as he could, in standardized situations such as greeting or taking leave, quarreling, experiencing grief and enjoyment, courting, and so on. The essential patterns of expressing emotions proved to be identical in all the cultures he was able to study, even when the patterns were subjected to minute analysis by means of slow motion films. What varied was only the control exerted by tradition: this affected a purely quantitative differentiation of expression.

The most important result of Eibl-Eibesfeldt's extensive and patient research can be stated in a single sentence. The motor patterns shown undiminished by deaf-and-blind children are identical to those that, through cross-cultural investigation, have been shown to be inaccessible to cultural change. In view of these incontrovertible results, it is a true scientific scandal when many authors still maintain that all human expression is culturally determined.

A strong support for human ethology has come from the unexpected area of linguistic studies; Noam Chomsky and his school have demonstrated that the structure of logical thought—which is identical to that of syntactic language—is anchored in a genetic program. The child does not learn to talk; the child learns only the vocabulary of the particular language of the cultural tradition into which it happens to be born.

A surprising and important extension of ethological research was the application of the comparative method to the phenomena of human culture. In his 1970 book, *Kultur und Verhaltensforschung*, Otto Koenig demonstrated that historically induced, traditional similarities on the one hand, and, on the other hand, resemblances caused by parallel adaptation—in other words, the reciprocal action between homology and analogy—are interacting in the development of human cultures in much the same manner as in the evolution of species. For an understanding of cultural history, the analysis of homology and analogy is obviously of the greatest importance.

As a later development of ethology, I should like to mention the consequences of my own sallies into the field of the theory of knowledge. When a stroke of chance shifted me onto the chair of Immanuel Kant in Königsberg, I was forced to come to terms with Kantian epistemology. To anyone familiar with the facts of evolution, the question concerning what Kant himself would have thought of the a priori must obtrude itself. That is, if he had known about evolution, what would he have thought about everything that is given us without previous experience, and must, indeed, be given to us in order to make experience possible at all? From the viewpoint of the history of science, it is by no means astonishing that at least three people not only asked this very question at the same time, but also simultaneously and independently of one another found the same answer: Sir Karl Popper, Donald Campbell, and I myself.

In a textbook on basic ethology, I need not necessarily be concerned about theory of knowledge, but I think it advisable to attach to the English version of this book an appendix containing a few words about the nature of man and about the nature of man's cognitive functions as they appeared to me on the basis of my critique of Kantian epistemology. This critique seemed controversial during the long-gone days of my professorship at Königsberg University. Since ethology has—and especially I myself have—so very often been accused of underestimating the differences between man and all other living creatures, I feel justified in mentioning, as one of the latest steps in the development of our branch of science, the full recognition of just how different man is from all other animals. Therefore, a short concluding chapter dealing with the uniqueness of man will be appended to the last part of the English version of this book.

Part One
Methodology

Chapter I
Thinking in Biological Terms

1. The Differences Between the Goals of Physical and Biological Research

In physics the search is for the most general laws governing all matter and all energy. In biology the attempt is to understand living systems as they are. Since the time of Galileo, physics has proceeded by using the method of the *generalizing reduction*. A physicist always considers the individual system he happens to be examining at the moment—it could be a planetary system, a pendulum or a falling stone—as a special case within a *superordinated* class of systems. In the examples cited, this is a system comprising mass within a gravitational field. Then the physicist proceeds to find the lawfulnesses prevailing in one of the special systems, such as the Keplerian laws and the laws governing pendulums, and tries to relate these to the more general laws of the superordinated class of systems; in our example, to the Newtonian laws. For this purpose he must, naturally, investigate the structures of the special systems. Among other things, he must consider the mechanics of the pendulum— the axis, the length of the pendulum rod, the weight of the pendulum. But, for the physicist, understanding the structures and functions of special systems is only a means, only an interim goal on the way toward an abstraction of more general laws. As soon as this abstraction is achieved, the attributes of the special systems are no longer of any interest at all. The individual characteristics of the solar system through which Newton discovered the laws of gravitation are completely irrelevant to the validity of those laws. He would have arrived at an abstraction of the same laws had he contemplated a completely different solar system, a system of celestial bodies having different dimensions, intervals, and revolutions.

Without exception, the process of the generalizing reduction is intended to show how the *structure* of the special system determines the form in which the more general laws take effect in the system in question. The physicist must show, in the case of a pendulum, how the falling weight, fixed to a rod of constant length revolving upon an axis, is forced into an orbit and, after reaching the lowest point, must move upward again within the same orbit; that the frequency of oscillation is determined by the length of the pendulum rod and the weight of the pendulum; and so on.

On the basis of their knowledge of general physical laws, theoretical physicists can also, in principle, *deduce* which special lawfulnesses prevail in a particular mechanism, for instance in a pendulum. However, in the history of physics just as in the history of science as a whole, it was more often than not a case of the investigator stumbling upon a *real* pendulum before he began to think about its lawfulnesses. Because of this, as might be expected, he was also faced with conditions that did not fit neatly into his attempts at abstraction. The rod of a real pendulum is neither weightless nor free of inertia; the axial part is not free of friction. Yet all these very real facts are for the physicist, at least initially, only *obstructions* which he certainly must take into consideration and, in some cases, even measure, but which do not enter into the formulation of the law that is finally abstracted. The system a physicist examines during his search for general laws holds, in itself, no interest for him, and even less interesting is the system's structure. As already stated, understanding a system's structure is essentially only an interim goal along his research route. He moves, quite literally, by and beyond this as he progresses downward and farther downward, to more general and still more general laws, down to the conservation principles of physical law.

Investigators of living systems employ the same method, but with certain restrictions to its applicability—a theme I will return to later. But in their pursuit of knowledge the goal is not that of the physicist: the biologist desires to learn to understand the living system, even if it is only a partial system, in itself and for its own sake. All living systems interest him equally regardless of their levels of integration, their simplicity or their complexity. Just as in the analysis performed by the physicist, the biologist also proceeds from the "top" toward the "bottom," from the more particular to the more general. We biologists are also convinced that one single set of more general and more special laws, in itself devoid of contradiction, is ruling the universe. Of these laws the more specialized ones can, in principle, be reduced to the more general ones provided one knows the structure of the matter in which they prevail as well as the historical genesis of these structures.

That this second requirement very often fixes limitations for our attempts at reduction is something we will discuss further on. This not-withstanding, our endeavors to understand living matter would be meaningless if we did not proceed from one basic assumption: Were we ever to achieve the utopian goal of completely understanding all life processes, including those transpiring within our own brain—as far as they are accessible to objective physiological research—we should be able to explain them in terms of the most general laws of physics, provided, of course, that we also possess complete insight into the colossally complex organic structures that prescribe the various and unique forms in which these laws take effect. As investigators of behavior, we hope in the end to trace the phenomena which we study back to physical and chemical processes such as those that take place at the synapses, among the electrically charged cell membranes, and in the conduction of excitation. We, too, are "reductionists," although we forget neither that organic life has a history nor that the body-mind problem is insolvable.

Biologists would be interested in the structures of living things, and for their own sakes, even if physiology were not so inextricably intermeshed with pathology. Whoever in day to day work must constantly cope with living systems, whether a farmer, a zoo director, a physiologist or a physician, cannot help but be involved with *disturbances* in the functions of living systems. One repeatedly comes up against the indissoluble connection between physiology and pathology for, in order to be able to correct a malfunction, one first must understand the normal function and, inversely, it is almost always a malfunction which leads to an understanding of the normal function. The chances of success are negligible if a therapeutic intervention is not guided by insight into the normal function of the system and into the nature of the disturbance. This is just as true when the carburetor of an automobile is clogged as when it is a case of human illness.

2. The Limits of Reduction

In his significant paper on the role of theory in science, "Scientific Reduction and the Essential Incompleteness of All Science," (1974) Karl Popper discusses the successful and unsuccessful attempts at reduction undertaken within various branches of science, and he demonstrates that even the most successful of these to date, the reduction of chemistry to atomic physical processes, has a remainder, a residue that is impervious to further reduction. Popper writes:

> In the course of this discussion, I will defend three theses. First I will suggest that scientists have to be reductionists in the sense that nothing is as great a success in science as a successful reduction (such as Newton's reduction—or rather explanation—of Kepler's and Galileo's laws to his theory of grav-

ity). A successful reduction is, perhaps, the most successful form conceivable of all scientific explanations, since it achieves what Meyerson (1908, 1930) stressed: an identification of the unknown with the known. Let me mention however that by contrast with a reduction, an explanation with the help of a new theory explains the known—the known problem—by something unknown: a new conjecture.

Secondly, I will suggest that scientists, whatever their philosophical attitude towards holism, *have* to welcome reductionism as a *method:* they have to be either naive or else more or less critical reductionists; indeed, somewhat desperate critical reductionists, I shall argue, because hardly any major reduction in science has ever been *completely* successful: there is almost always an unresolved residue left by even the most successful attempts at reduction.

Thirdly, I shall contend that there do not seem to be any good arguments in favour of *philosophical* reductionism, while, on the contrary, there are good arguments against essentialism, with which philosophical reductionism seems to be closely allied. But I shall also suggest that we should, nevertheless, on methodological grounds, continue to attempt reductions. The reason is that we can learn an immense amount even from unsuccessful or incomplete attempts at reduction, and that problems left open in this way belong to the most valuable intellectual possessions of science: I suggest that a greater emphasis upon what are often regarded as our scientific failures (or, in other words, upon the great open problems of science) can do us a lot of good.

Then Popper cites a series of examples which illustrate how becoming bogged down during attempts at reduction has led to the discovery of previously unrecognized problems. According to Popper, this was already evident in mathematics and the attempt at "arithmetization;" that is, the reduction of geometry and the irrational numbers to rational sums did not lead to complete success. Popper states:

> But the number of unexpected problems and the amount of unexpected knowledge brought about by this failure are overwhelming. This, I shall contend, may be generalized: even where we do not succeed as reductionists, the number of interesting and unexpected results we may acquire on the way to our failure can be of the greatest value.

Another example of the same principle and especially important for our purposes is afforded by the attempt to reduce chemistry to quantum physics. Even if one chose to assume that it could be possible to reduce the nature of the chemical bond to principles of quantum physics—something which has not yet been achieved—and even if, for the sake of argument, one chose to assume that one had in hand thoroughly satisfactory theories of nuclear forces, of the periodic system of elements and their isotopes, etc., the attempt to reduce chemical processes to quantum mechanics would still be stopped by a barrier, by an idea fundamentally foreign to the way a physicist thinks and to the body of physical theory: the historical concept of becoming, of genesis. Bohr's new theory of the periodic system of elements assumes that the heavier nuclei have been formed out of lighter ones, in other words, they came into being through a prior *historical* process in which, in thinly scattered and exceedingly uncommon cases, hydrogen nuclei fused into heavier nuclei—something that can occur only under conditions which, apparently, are very rarely encountered in the cosmos. Physicists have strong indices in favor of the view that this really happened and still happens. Beginning with helium, all the heavier elements are the result of cosmological evolution. "Thus," says Popper, "from the point of view of method, our attempted reductions have led to tremendous successes, even though it can be said that the attempted reductions have, as such, usually failed."

3. Ontological Reductionism

The assumption on which all science is based, that everything existing came into being through combinations of material elements in the course of a great cosmic creation and, even to this day, is still governed by those same laws which prevail in these elements, can easily lead to a philosophical error that is dangerous because it tends to discredit all natural science in the eyes of sensible, thinking people. This error arises, as do so many others, through the neglect of the *structures* within which the omnipresent laws of physics operate in the form of highly complex special laws. These, however, have every right to be designated as natural laws and as having the same dignity as the first law of physics or the laws of conservation.

The consequence of this error is the expression, everything that is composed of matter is "nothing else but" this matter. Although this "nothing else but" has been shown to be erroneous at even the most basal physical levels, great scientific innovators have continued to cling to it with remarkable tenacity. Popper (1974) presents the example of Eddington who, for a long time, continued to believe that with the advent of quantum mechanics the electromagnetic theory of matter had been finally settled and that all matter consisted of electrons and protons—at a time when the meson had already been discovered.

Ontological reductionism becomes really dangerous when applied to the subject of living organisms. If, for example, we say: "All life processes are chemical and physical processes," anyone accustomed to thinking in scientific terms would not question the correctness of the statement. But if we say: "All life processes are *essentially only* chemical and physical processes," every biologist would protest, since it is with regard to just this, to what they essentially are, that life processes are different from all others: they are not just chemical–physical processes. The failure of ontological reduction becomes even more conspicuous when we compare two other statements: "Humans are beings of the class of mammals and the order of primates," and "Human beings are essentially nothing else but mammals of the order of primates."

The "nothing else but" of ontological reductionism, for which Julian Huxley coined the term "nothingelsebuttery,"* aptly describes a blindness to two most essential realities: first, to the complexity of organic structures and the various levels of their integration, and second, to those sensibilities of value which every normal human being extends toward the lower and higher achievements of organic genesis.

During evolution, new systemic properties often arise through the integration of subsystems which, up to that moment, had been functioning independently of one another. A simple electrical model (Figure 1) taken from a book written by Bernhard Hassenstein (1966) can illustrate how, through such an integration, completely new systemic properties can be generated instantaneously, properties which did not exist before and, most important, also *gave no prior indication* of existence. Herein lies the truth of the mystical-sounding but nonetheless completely accurate statement made by Gestalt psychologists: "The whole is more than the sum of its parts." Through cybernetics and system theory the sudden emergence of new systemic characteristics and functions has been accounted for by means of a purely physical approach and those who have done the research and written the descriptions have thus been freed from any suspicion of a vitalistic belief in the miraculous.

Philosophers not familiar with this characteristic process of evolution tend to believe that all evolutionary changes are accomplished in slow, gradual transitions. As a result of this belief there are frequent ontological disputes about whether, for the organism in question, the difference between two evolutionary stages is one of degree or one of *essence*. Understandably, this dispute rages most vehemently about that evolutionary stage where the step from animal to human being was taken. Mortimer J. Adler has dedicated an entire book, *The Difference of Man and the Difference It Makes* (1967), to a discussion of this question. In reality, almost every larger evolutionary step signifies the emergence of a differentiation of essence since it consists in the appearance of something that had never existed before. This is also true, in principle, even for the differentiation in Hassenstein's inorganic systems which were brought in as illustration.

---

* I was introduced to this term by my friend, Donald Mackay, but my much older friend, Sir Julian Huxley, was able to demonstrate a priority for this beautiful expression.

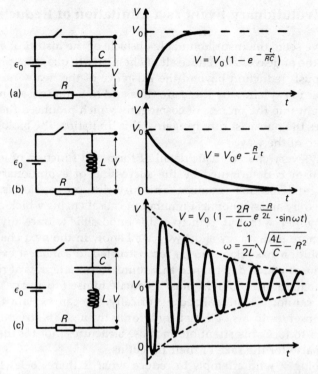

Figure 1. Three electric circuits, among them an oscillating circuit (c), illustrate the concept of "systemic property." A current is passed between the poles of a battery with electromotive strength ϵ_o and with the potential tension or terminal voltage V_o. The resistance of the circuit, in ohms, is concentrated in R. Circuit (a) has a condenser with capacity C; circuit (b) has a coil with inductance L; circuit (c) has both condenser and coil together. The voltage V can be measured at the two terminals. The diagrams at the right represent the changes in voltage after the circuit is closed. In circuit (a) the condenser gradually charges through the resistance until voltage V_o is reached. In circuit (b) the current, initially impeded by the self-induction of the coil, increases until it reaches the strength laid down by Ohm's law; the voltage V is then theoretically zero because the total resistance is concentrated in R. In circuit (c), closing the circuit causes diminishing oscillations. It is apparent that the systemic properties of (c) are not the result of superimposing the properties characteristic of (a) and (b) although (c) can be thought of as having arisen through a combination of (a) and (b). The diagram is valid, for example, for the following values: $C = 0.7 \times 10^{-9}$ F; $L = 2 \times 10^{-3}$ Hy; $R = 10^3$ ω; $\lambda = 1.2 \times 10^{-6}$ sec. This last value also defines the time axis, which is the same for all three curves. Calculations by E. U. von Weizsäcker. (Hassenstein, B.: *Kybernetik und biologische Forschung*. Handb. der Biologie I. Frankfurt: Athenaion, 1966.)

4. The Evolutionary Event as a Limitation of Reduction

As we have seen, the insurmountable obstacle of the historical event has impeded the endeavors to reduce all of chemistry to quantum physics. In order to push reduction beyond the existence of the heavy nuclei, that is, in order to explain why these are thus and not otherwise, one would need insight into the process of cosmogeny which produced them. Only rarely does the physicist run up against this limitation; the biologist does it each step of the way.

Literally every characteristic detail of form and function of every living organism is determined by the succession of evolutionary events which engendered that organism. This historical progression is, in turn, determined by an astronomical number of causal chains which converge into its channel so that, in principle, it is impossible to trace any of them back for more than a very short way. As I show in the next chapter, the route evolution has taken can be reconstructed to a modest extent, but not the causes which determined that route. In his attempts at reduction and explanation, the biologist must reconcile himself to a very large residue that cannot be rationalized historically. He can explain the functions he observes in his object of study only through its structures. This forces him to focus his attention on those structures, not for themselves alone but also for the sake of their functions.

The biologist who attempts to reduce what is there to lawfulnesses already known, or to explain what exists through new hypotheses, is confronted with two tasks which, although they overlap and merge, can still be clearly differentiated. The first task is an analysis of the form and function of the living system *as it is at this moment* in evolutionary time; the second task is to make understandable how this system *got to be* that way and no other. The duality of this problem can best be illustrated by using a man-made machine as an example. If a combat airplane built by the Russians were to fall into the hands of the Japanese, they would take it apart, they would analyze it in a literal sense, and most likely this analysis would succeed to such an extent (still utopian for living systems) that they would be capable of complete resynthesis, that is, they would be capable of constructing a replica of the airplane. But they would also certainly find quite a few details of construction that were ingeniously thought out and which would cause them to wonder how in all the world the designer had hit upon this original solution. The prerequisite for finding an answer to the question why the foreign designer had devised a particular part in such a way and not in another would be, to begin with, not only an immense amount of information about the history of Russian aircraft construction, but, over and above this, also about the thought processes, the brain and nerve physiology of the designer, and so on and so forth back into the entire phylogeny of *Homo sapiens.*

That the two tasks can also be undertaken separately for the examination of a living system is confirmed by the fact that analysis of living systems as they are at the moment was considerably far advanced before questions concerned with how they had gotten that way were ever asked. Harvey had clearly comprehended the function of the circulatory system and had consequentially postulated the existence of capillaries, which one could not even see at the time. An entire series of discoveries, made independently of any historical consideration of organic genesis, is a part of the past of the science of medicine.

For a long time, long before the main causes of all adaptation (genetic change and natural selection) had been discovered, those who worked with living systems had been aware that their constructions were constituted, in general and in more special and improbable ways, to sustain the life of the individual, its progeny, and, consequently, its species. Those who believed in a singular act of creation explained this species-preserving purposefulness either through the wisdom of the creator or, as Jakob von Uexküll (1909), who rejected evolutionary ideas, through a prestabilized harmony between the organism and its environment. Those who can be content with these explanations are spared the asking of many difficult questions but, it must be remembered, at the price of having to close their eyes to certain phenomena—and these are the many characteristics extant in the construction of living organisms that are inexpedient for survival.

5. The Question "What For?"

At this point, the historical barrier of reduction forces the researcher to ask a question with which, up to this point in his attempts at reduction and explanation, he has not been confronted: he is forced to ask about purpose. Processes which are determined by an end or a goal exist in the cosmos exclusively in the realm of organisms. According to Nicolai Hartmann (1966), a goal-directed action can only be understood on the basis of insight into the interaction between three processes: First, a goal must be set and in this setting something that will happen in the future must be anticipated by "skipping" spaces in time. Second, the choice of means, dictated by the set goal, must be made. Third, the realization of the set goal, through the causal sequential unfolding of the chosen means, is achieved. These three acts form a functional unit and are performed at various levels of integration within the realm of the organic (Figure 2).

Nicolai Hartmann believed that the actor and the goal setter could never be anything but a consciousness for, as he said, " . . . only a consciousness has maneuverability within conceptual time, can leap beyond sequential time, can predetermine, anticipate, choose means, and retro-

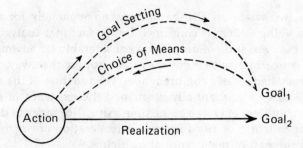

Figure 2. Hartmann's conceptualization of the processes underlying goal-directed action. (Hartmann, N.: *Teleologisches Denken*. Berlin: Walter de Gruyter, 1964.)

spectively go back in thought over the skipped spaces through to the first one at the beginning." Since Hartmann wrote this statement, research into the biochemistry of morphogenesis and also into that of appetitive behavior in animals (Two/I/10) has revealed processes in which the three acts required by Hartmann are performed in distinct interaction and yet in sequences that are certainly not dependent on or associated with consciousness.

If the preexistent "blueprint" in the genome anticipates the construction of a new organism as a goal, and if, subsequently, this goal is attained through a quite variable and adaptive choice of those means proffered by the milieu and within a strictly causal sequence of developmental steps, this then conforms to the combined functions of the three acts postulated by Hartmann. The same is true for the admittedly somewhat more complicated processes of appetitive behavior through which an animal achieves a goal meaningful for species preservation, which are also programmed in the genome. Although these processes of embryogenesis and those of behavior are certainly not governed by an anticipatory individual consciousness, but are enacted at a very much lower level of organic occurrence, they must still be regarded as completely purpose-oriented or "determined by their ends or goals."

The processes of phylogeny, which generate the "blueprints" under dicussion, accomplish truly marvelous things, yet they lack completely the infallibility of an all-knowing, purpose-setting creator as well as the constancy of a prestabilized harmony. All along the way, the comparative phylogeneticist meets "errors" of evolution, faulty constructions of such shortsightedness that one would not credit them to any human engineer. Gustav Kramer cited many examples of this phenomenon in his publication on the inexpedient in nature (1949). Just one of these examples will suffice here. During the transition from aquatic life to terrestrial life the swim bladder of the fish became an organ for breathing. In the circulatory system of fish, and already evident even among the jawless cyclostomes (Cyclostomata), the heart and gills are coupled in tandem, that is, all the blood pumped from the heart must, of necessity, pass through the gills, and from there the richly oxygenated blood is circulated throughout the body. Because the swim bladder is an organ serviced within the body's system, and has remained so even after becoming an organ of respiration, the blood emerging from it flows directly back into the heart. Hence the heart is the recipient of oxygen-poor blood from the body and oxygen-rich blood from the lungs and a mixture of these is what is continually being recirculated. Although from a technical point of view this is a most unsatisfactory solution, it has been maintained through many geologic eras and up to this day by all amphibians and almost all reptiles. It may be because of this kind of construction of the vascular system that none of the animals just mentioned is as capable of sustained muscular exertions as are many sharks (Selachii) and bony fishes (Teleostei), as well as all birds and mammals.

The fact that individual development, the ontogeny of every living creature, represents a genuine goal-directed process, the realization of a preexistent plan, must not lead to the altogether erroneous conclusion that the same is true for evolution. This error, unfortunately, is suggested by the very words "development" and "evolution."

Evolution is emphatically not purpose-oriented in that it is absolutely unable to foresee what might be expedient in the future. Evolution is incapable of accepting even the smallest disadvantage for the sake of a future advantage. In other words, evolution can exploit only those factors which tender an immediate "selective advantage," somewhat in the same manner that even the most farsighted and benevolent politician is confined to the exploitation of those issues and measures which are capable of providing him with an immediate "electoral advantage."

Thanks to some very old discoveries made by Charles Darwin, we know which processes of mutation and natural selection provided organisms with sufficient purposefulness (in the sense of species preservation) and, thanks to some new knowledge gained through molecular genetics, we now know fairly precisely how the information underlying all adaptation is coded in the "blueprint" of the genome. Manfred Eigen has convincingly demonsrated that selection, the natural choice of the most suitable, is operative even at the molecular level and that it played a decisive role in the origin of life. But the stuff on which selection gets to work is always only the purely happenstance alteration or new combination of heritable characteristics. It is technically correct to say that evolution proceeds only according to the principles of blind chance and through the elimination of what is incapable of sustained existence, and yet this way of expressing it is misleading. The fact, indisputable in itself, that the few billion years of existence reckoned for our planet by radiation researchers should have, in this way and by these means, sufficed for the evolvement of man from pre-life forms similar to the most simple blue-green algae (Cyanophyta), seems incredible to those not conversant with all that is involved. The wildness of chance is, in these circumstances, "tamed"—as Manfred Eigen (1975) expresses it—by the benefit it brings on very rare occasions. The likelihood of a mutation which improves the organism's chances of survival is extremely small; in fact, the probability is assessed by great geneticists as amounting to 10^{-8}. The improbability of such a happy event is compensated by the correspondingly great increase of the probability of survival that is enjoyed by the "lucky winner."

If the genetic equipment of an individual increases his chances of survival relative to those of his conspecifics, this is then so only for that unique constellation of environmental factors with which this creature must actually contend. For a different kind of environment, the newly acquired genetic equipment could very well be inexpedient. If, in the course of time, the environment of an animal species changes (climatic changes, for example, or new conditions concerning food sources, or an increase in the number of predators), then the average genetic equipment transmitted by individuals of the species is usually no longer optimally adapted. Selection, consequently, supports some of the genetic variations available in stock and suppresses others, so that after a corresponding period of time, a new set of genetic equipment better adapted to the incursive conditions is achieved. One can describe this process with the help of communication concepts and by means of the following formulation: Through the process of selection, new data concerning the conditions of the external environment reach the genome and are henceforth stored there as "instructions" (Eigen 1975). With regard to this acquisition of environmental information, the process of evolution resembles the cognitive process of the acquisition of knowledge. This knowledge, however, like invested capital, pays such high "dividends" that it compensates for the rareness of advantageous genetic change.

To quote Eigen once again: "Life is a game in which nothing is stipulated but the rules." The family tree of all living things is a typical example of what game theorists call a "tree of decisions." Eigen chose an aerial photograph of the Colorado River delta (Figure 3) as an actual example representing such a tree: billions of unknowable causal influences determine which course every single rivulet and channel has taken.

If one knows a little bit about the rules of the game being followed in the growth of the family tree of life, one is no longer astonished to find in the structures of living organisms not only the constructive solutions suggesting genius but also those that could be appreciably improved by any human engineer. No plumber, for example, would lay the pipes and tubes for the blood vessel system of a lizard so impractically as evolution has done it. The principles of mutation and selection make it understandable that in the realm of the organic we meet not only characteristics of

Figure 3. The Colorado River delta at the Gulf of California. (Eigen, M., Winkler, R.: *Das Spiel*. München: Piper, 1975. Courtesy of the Aero Service Corporation, Philadelphia, Pennsylvania, U.S.A.)

structure and function which are practical but also those which are not so impractical that they lead to the elimination of the bearers.

One other important characteristic of all living organisms, readily understandable through some knowledge of the ground rules of the evolutionary game, is the extreme "conservatism" of their structures. But through a change in an organism's way of life, especially when adaptations are required to a new environmental niche, old structural features can become meaningless. As long as their presence does not directly threaten the continued existence of the species in question, they can be lugged along almost indefinitely, and this happens if their retention does not result in a loss of too many individuals of the species. Before the development of modern surgery, for example, thousands of humans perished every year from peritonitis because an organ which had become funtionless, the vermiform appendix, a narrow blind tube extending from the caecum, tended to become inflamed.

In many cases, structures which have become functionless are converted to serve other useful functions, simply because they are there. From a gill cleft, the spiracle (Spiraculum) of sharks and primitive fishes, comes the ear of higher vertebrates; from the first gill arch, the hyoid bone with its two pairs of branches; and so on.

Thus the over-all construction of an organism is never comparable to a human edifice that has been designed in a unique process of planning by farsighted architects and engineers. An organism's structure is much more like the do-it-yourself house of a homesteader who first puts together a simple log cabin as protection against the wind and rain and then, as the extent of his holdings and the number of people in his family increases, periodically enlarges his dwelling. The original cabin is not torn down; instead, it is used as a storeroom, and almost every room of the expanding house will, in the course of the structure's development, be used for some purpose other than that for which it was originally intended. The older parts of the house, recognizable for what they are, are retained because the evolving structure could never be entirely dismantled and newly planned; this is not possible because every part has been continuously occupied and intensively used.

In an analogous way, characteristic structural details that are retentions of "yesterday's adaptations" can be found in every organism. Their existence is a stroke of really good luck for the researcher who wants not only to learn the game rules of evolution but who also wants to know the path along which evolution actually has proceeded.

All of the preceding paragraphs have been written with the intention of explaining to those who are not biologists what is meant when a biologist asks the question, foreign to physicists, "What for?" If we ask "What does a cat have sharply pointed, curved and retractile claws for?" and answer straightaway "To catch mice," this question and answer do not signify in any way an acknowledgment of an inherent purposive orientation of the universe and of organic evolution. It is, rather, an abridgment of the question, "Which is the particular function whose survival value has bred cats (Felidae) with this form of claw?" Colin Pittendrigh (1958) has designated this way of regarding species-preserving purposefulness as *teleonomy* in order to draw as sharp a distinction between it and a mystical *teleology* as exists today between astronomy and astrology.

In the structural plan of an animal—more than in that of a plant—hardly any characteristic exists that is not in some way influenced by selection and is, in this sense, thus, teleonomic. If I were to search for examples of purely happenstance characteristics and characteristic diversifications, it would be difficult to cite any occurring among wild animals. Certainly it is teleonomically irrelevant if a barnyard chicken of no recognizable breed is white and another brown or mottled. Among wild animals, the African hunting dog *(Lycaon pictus L.)* is one of the few examples of a species whose individuals exhibit variable dappled patterns though in fairly uniform colors. But even here, in the highly variable color patterns of these wild animals, the question arises if this variability, as such, could not also be teleonomic and thereby the result of selection. It is certainly possible that, among these extraordinarily social predators, if individual animals are able to recognize one another even at great distances, this capability can have value for the preservation of the species. The balanced dimorphism of male ruffs *(Philomachus pugnax L.)* can, with assurance, be explained in this way.

When dealing with such superficial physical characteristics it is particularly difficult to find any which demonstrably have nothing to do with teleonomy. Within complex configurations of various characteristics there are probably none for which patient research could not currently accumulate factual confirmation that its explicit function was selected in just this way because of its species-preserving value. The more complex and generally more improbable such a combination of characteristics is, with that much more certainty can one conclude from these a relationship between function and selection, and that much more easily answer the question, "What for?"

In a paradoxical way, characteristics which apparently disturb a particular function generally important for survival are exactly those which provide us with the most certain answers to the question, "What for?" Citing only one example, the fish *Heniochus varius*, classified among the Chaetodontids, has two horns just above its eyes and above these, on its nape, another thick, rounded horn; between them there is a deep saddle-like indentation (Figure 4). These structural characteristics are obviously cumbersome, certainly not streamlined and, for slipping through narrow passages—an activity that belongs to the daily routine of this coral-reef

Figure 4. *Heniochus varius Cuvier.* The horns above the eyes and the hump on the upper back serve in ritual fighting; this fighting certainly developed from the damaging fighting of the related Chaetodontids who spear their rivals with the spines of the anterior dorsal fins.

fish, most disturbingly in the way. The argument that these disadvantages must somehow "pay off" through some kind of selective value is compelling. In fact, when I first got one of these fish, I predicted the function of this saddle that is bordered above and below by horns: The species would engage in ritual fighting during which opponents, when confronting one another, would lie aslant, both leaning either to the right or to the left so that the saddles fitted into one another, and then the combatants would shove against one another with all their strength. Our first "What for?" is, thus, satisfactorily answered with the reply, "For ritual fighting." What ritual fighting should have a selection premium for in a species of fish that normally swims around in large schools is another question, and the answer to this question I hope to reach through further observation. The prediction is that it is bred by intraspecific selection.

Adaptations like the ones just cited, those which serve exclusively for combat with conspecifics, are by no means always conducive to species preservation. The teleonomic query, "What for?" does, in fact, get a clear answer since the value for selection that the behavior or structure in question has developed for the genome of the individual is easy to demonstrate. But whether the connection in question is advantageous for the preservation of the species as a whole is not at all certain. Quite the contrary, "intraspecific competition" among rival conspecifics can easily lead to an escalation of extremes in forms and functions, extremes which are not conducive to the continuation of that species. Those specialized wing primaries of the Argus pheasant *(Argusianus argus)* enhancing the effect of some particular courting movements are no longer much good for flying. Yet the larger they are, the greater are the chances for the cock possessing them to foster numerous offspring—but, at the same time, the greater are his chances of being eaten by ground predators. As always, life's forms and their functions are a compromise between several kinds of selection pressure.

Understandably, the selection pressure exerted by one individual of a species on other individuals of the same species does not provide any information about which interactions with its environment are advantageous or disadvantageous for that species. When deer (Cervidae) "take a fancy to" a particular kind of ritual fighting whose outcome depends on the size of the antlers growing out of the foreheads of the males, and when, in addition to this—as Bubenik (1968) has shown for the red deer (*Cervus elaphus*)—females actively choose partners according to the size of these antlers, there is nothing to hinder the bulk of these osseous trees (which must, moreover, be grown anew each year) from increasing to the limits of what can be carried.

Among some mammals living in social groups, intraspecific selection impels the appearance of phenomena that one could regard almost as deformities; but these incorporate the same principle as that of the deer antler. Among some Asiatic monkeys (Semnopithecinae), each male commands a large harem of females. Each change of such a commander is accompanied by general infanticide within the harem. Because females deprived of their offspring come into estrus earlier than those allowed to rear their young, the new tyrant has a much greater opportunity for transmitting his genome. "The egoistical gene" has become the popular phrase to use when referring to this remarkable phenomenon. It is not at all easy to decide to what extent such "egoism" can be carried before it harms the entire species and, finally, the gene itself as well.

With this the difficult problem of kin selection is broached. It does not matter which example of pronounced "altruistic" behavior one chooses to use, be it food regurgitation among African hunting dogs (*Lycaon pictus L.*) or mutual defense of comrades among jackdaws (*Coloeus monedula*); when one asks oneself why a mutation excluding this altruistic behavior—an excluding mutation that must certainly occur from time to time and, when it does, must obviously be selectively advantageous for that individual—is not at once and prolifically further selected for, one finds no answer. Questions concerning those factors which prevent a massive emergence of social parasites among animal societies remain to be answered adequately. It is nothing short of astonishing that, among communal vertebrates, social parasitism is as good as unknown and infanticide, to date, known to occur only among a few species. Among higher and longer-lived Metazoa, at the level of entireties of cellular organisms, there is a highly complicated system of antibody formation that exists so that asocial elements can be eliminated whenever this becomes necessary. At the level of human culture, no single ethnic group is known which does not have comparable, complex systems of laws and tabus for the suppression of every kind of antisocial behavior. Among animal societies, which can be classified at a level of integration somewhere between human society and the bodily entirety of Metazoa, no mechanisms for the prevention of social parasitism are, as yet, known.

As can be seen, the teleonomic question, "What for?" often elicits responses that indicate goals that are rather narrow-minded and short-sighted; for species preservation, the results of intraspecific selection often are decidedly detrimental.

Answers are apparently not forthcoming to the teleonomic question where structures and even behavior patterns have changed their former functions. "Yesterday's adaptations" are to be found everywhere in morphology and in behavioral science. Structures which have become meaningless are seldom simply disassembled; instead, they are almost always put to use serving a function other than that for which they were initially intended: a gill aperture becomes an auditory canal; an organ which served for the collection of nutriment becomes an endocrine gland.

6. Teleological and Causal Views of Nature

Among the two great schools of the behavioral sciences, only those scientists identified with the school of purposive psychology—out-and-out teleologically and in no way teleonomically oriented, and represented by distinguished researchers such as William MacDougall (1923), Eduard C. Tolman (1932) and others—concentrated their entire research interest on the question, "What for?" In other words, they proceeded as if every question would be answered and all problems would be solved by determining the goal of any animal behavior. If one has understood that flying southward in autumn serves birds of passage as a species-preserving end or goal, then, in the opinion of the teleologically oriented animal psychologist, Bierens de Haan (1940), all the problems of bird migration are solved in a "satisfactory and elegant" way. An enormous amount of one-sided thinking is required in order to be able to regard only the question of ends and goals as fundamental and to neglect completely questions of cause.

There are cases in which the function of a particular morphological structure becomes apparent even after superficial observation. One thinks, in this context, of the patterns of vivid color that play a role for so many releasing mechanisms. The white collar of the drake mallard has been shown to act as a signal during courtship. What constitutes this collar is a differential color distribution among the neck feathers involved. These look as if the white had been applied with a paint brush over the already completely formed and finished feathers. At the top of the collar, near the head, the white begins as a border along the lower edges of the green feathers. Farther down and back, the white border gradually becomes broader until the feathers are completely white from the base to the tip. At the bottom or back of the white collar, the brown color of the lower neck feathers begins to appear; the otherwise white feathers have borders of brown and these borders broaden until the feathers are completely brown. It is very easy to recognize that the white collar which separates the green of the head from the brown of the lower neck is "intended" to appear sharply delineated. In contrast to this easy recognition, a reduction of this "artistic" structure to its physiological and genetic causes is very difficult to achieve. One must realize how complex the morphogenetic processes producing such a structure must be, and then, even more difficult, one must try to imagine what the phylogenetic processes may be that lead to the blueprint of this morphogenesis. "Cases such as these," Otto Koehler (1933) has said, "which at first afford an understanding only of goal-directedness, can easily *seduce* [emphasis mine] the research worker into making hasty Lamarckian interpretations; these cases are actually there to be regarded as challenges for causal analysis."

Understandably, these "challenges" do not exist for the biologists and behavioral scientists who think in vitalistic and teleological terms. For them the acceptance of extranatural factors makes it possible, with no ado at all, to answer every "What for?" question with a spurious "Because." The most unfortunate consequence of this methodological and conceptual attitude was its effect on the opposing school: the purposivists' misuse of goals and ends for what pretended to be an explanation aroused in the behaviorists an emotional opposition to all considerations of purpose, so that they developed a "blind spot" for the concept of species-preserving purposefulness as well. It is now part of history that those of the behaviorist school of psychology, motivated by their antagonism to teleological purposive psychology, dismissed all considerations of species-preserving teleonomy—a classic example of how, because of antagonism among members of two schools of thought, a rejection of knowledge can be occasioned.

When engaged in research on a complex living system, it is obvious that questions concerning ends and goals as well as questions concerning causality must be asked simultaneously. I would like to illustrate this by means of a parable about a man and a man-made system. The man is traveling overland in his automobile; the purpose of his journey is a lecture which he is scheduled to deliver in a distant city. The man is underway "for lecturing"; his automobile, a means serving the same end, is there "for traveling." The man takes delight in contemplating this wonderfully graduated and integrated complex entirety of interacting ends and goals. Perhaps, at just this moment, he is admiring the phrase, *"vitale Phantasie,"* which F. J. J. Buytendijk (1940) used to describe and explain the purposefulness of body structure and behavior, something which the automobile manufacturer has apparently confirmed in the design and planning of this purposeful vehicle. Then something happens that happens often; the automobile motor coughs, splutters, and stops. All at once the driver is most impressively presented with the fact that the goal of his journey is not what makes the automobile move. As I choose to express it, goal-directedness does not "exert pull" in the direction desired. Now it would behoove the man in the automobile to forget, for the time being, the aim of his journey and to devote his attention to the causality of the normal function of the motor as well as its momentary malfunction. On the success of his causal investigations will depend the possibility of further pursuing the goal of his journey.

The "goal-directedness" of every systemic whole is not one mite less dependent on the causality of its organs than is the goal-directedness of the traveling lecturer in our parable on the functioning of his automobile motor. With regard to organic systems, the regulating function of causal research has an incomparably more difficult task to perform, not only because these systems are much more intricately structured than the most complicated machine, but also because, in contrast to machines, they have not been put together by men and we have only very incomplete insight into their origin and the history of their formation. Thus the physician who attempts to repair a malfunctioning organic system has that much more difficult a task than the automobile mechanic. But the success of what he does to regulate the functioning of a whole system will also depend, basically, on his investigation of causality and will be influenced just as little by the amount of "urgency" that exists for reaching the now problematic goal.

Questions about how the malfunctioning systemic whole originally came into being are fundamentally of no real importance in the relationship referred to here between its goal-directedness and the mode and manner of its causal comprehensibility. If an engineer constructed the purposeful system, if a God created it, or if it came into being by means of a natural evolution in which, besides mutation and selection, many other processes could also have played a role—all these "ifs" are quite irrelevant to the capacity of human comprehension of causality, to an insight that can master such a system and, when the proper functioning of the system is endangered, can actually restore it.

The ultimate significance of human research into causality is to be found in the fact that *this research gives us,* as the most important regulating factor, *the means to control natural processes.* Whether these processes are external and inorganic, such as lightning and storms, or internal and organic, such as diseases of the body or "purely psychic" symptoms of decline in the social patterns of human behavior is, moreover, of no consequence. Never is the pursuit of an actively predetermined goal possible without causal comprehension. On the other hand, causal analysis would have no function if questing humanity did not pursue goals.

The endeavor "to search, as far as it is possible for us, among the world's causalities and to trace the chain they form as far as they are linked to one another" (Kant) is not "materialistic" in some moralistic sense, as some teleologists choose to describe it, but signifies a potential for the most intensive active service to the ultimate aims of all organic processes in that we, where success is achieved, are endowed with the power to intervene, helpfully regulating, where values are endangered, while the purely teleological observers can only lay their hands in their laps, deedless, mourning the disintegration of the whole.

Chapter II
The Methodology of Biology and Particularly of Ethology

1. The Concept of a System or an Entirety

The goal of biologists is, as I have said, to make an organic system understandable as a *whole*. This does not mean that the biologist regards the entirety of a system as some kind of miracle. It is necessary to make this clear at the very beginning since there are some atomistic theoreticians who regard it as a confession of vitalism if one merely utters the words "whole" or "entirety." The biologist does not believe in "whole-producing factors" that are neither in need of nor accessible to an explanation, but he remains aware that the systemic character of the organism excludes the utilization of some of the less sophisticated research methods. Above all, with regard to an organic system, one cannot track simple and unidirectional linkages between causes and effects. In his 1933 monograph, "Die Ganzheitsbetrachtung in der modernen Biologie," Otto Koehler developed in detail the methods which are necessary in order to analyze a systemic entirety. In this publication he grants the Gestalt psychologists the credit they deserve for having perceived the nature of organic entireties, although he justifiably criticizes them where necessary in a way that can be summarized as follows: Every gestalt is an entirety, but not every entirety is a gestalt; in other words, the concept of gestalt must be reserved primarily for the processes of perception. Koehler also appropriately emphasized the fact that impassioned champions of the principles of entirety, such as B. H. Driesch (1928), alienated many researchers from the theory of entireties because they "dressed it in the vestments of vitalism." This I can readily verify; as a young natural scientist I, too, was convinced that only atomistic component analyses could claim to fulfill the requirements characteristic of an exact science.

Otto Koehler (1933), together with Ludwig von Bertalanffy (1951), rendered a great service by showing that an organic system requires a special analytic methodology of its own, even if one were to undertake an analysis that was intended to be purely physical. There is, said Koehler (1933), no "vital force," and no "whole-producing factor"; there are, "instead, harmonious systems of amboceptor [that is, operative in both directions] causal chains, entangled and integrated, whose harmonious interactions are just what constitutes the configurational entirety."

This does not imply, by any means, that an entirety is fundamentally inacessible through causal analysis. Koehler (1933) said:

Everyone who does research—and all of our research is primarily analysis—is consciously 'simplistic', and must be so in order to maintain his own momentum. To this extent it is understandable if just those particularly successful men who make discoveries—Loeb was one of them—approach a set task with grotesquely simplified initial conceptualizations. Their professional success appears to have justified them; and yet, after the work was completed, their continued rigid adherence to the intolerable simplism of the working hypothesis had its effect by bringing discredit, in part completely undeserved, that has endured to this day. Anyone who, before beginning a project, delineates all the difficulties that face him, will perhaps never hazard a beginning. But once success is there, it will then be examined from a more distant vantage point and be incorporated within broader contexts; then the retention of a simplism that was initially a virtue turns itself into a vice.

A moderately critical simplism is permissible particularly when, as will be discussed in One/II/10, the research concerns a "component that is relatively independent of an entirety."

In another passage Koehler says:

An aim of the foregoing presentation was to point out examples of the kind of damage that can accrue for us, as biologists, in our own discipline, if we persist in outmoded, piecemeal thinking and forget the whole; an additional aim was to renew our conscious recognition of how extensive, to date, the group of biologists already is who sense acutely the necessity to convert from a purely static view to a consideration of dynamic processes and to become aware of the *systematic character of all living things* [emphasis mine]. If some authors preface their confessions of faith in entireties with an apology, this is because of a clear recognition that talking about wholes is not enough; what really counts is the day to day work which is guided by continual cogitation that envelops, with the same energy, the particular and the most particular aspects of the questions just now being considered, as well as their order of proper integration within a question complex at a higher level of abstraction.

H. J. Jordan (1929) in his general work on the comparative physiology of animals, formulated the same principle using the words, "much analysis, modest synthesis, and as objective, life as a whole."

2. The Sequence of Cognitive Steps Dictated by the Character of Systems

The definition of an organic entirety given by Otto Koehler states clearly enough that, in organic systems, there is no such thing as a unidirectional linkage between cause and effect, apart from certain exceptions that will be taken up later. Thus one is guilty of a fundamental methodological error if one isolates a causal relationship experimentally, or even conceptually, and explores this in one direction only. Yet it stands to reason, as Koehler says in the lines quoted above, that this is repeatedly necessary; in a physiological experiment it is not possible to proceed in any other way than to set up some cause and to study its effect. But while doing this, one must remain aware that one has contrived to produce an artifact.

All sorts of approaches and all methods are permitted; only the *sequence* of their utilization is dictated by the recognition that an organism is a system in which everything is interrelated and interacts with everything else. The following example of a man-made technical system can serve to illustrate just how obligatory is the sequence of cognitive steps under discussion: Let us assume that a resident of Mars has landed on earth and, as the first object for investigation, has found an automobile. His comprehension of this fabrication will most certainly make no progress before he has answered the teleonomic question, that is, before he has found out that this thing is an "organ" of locomotion for *Homo sapiens*. A biologist in unfamiliar territory who comes upon a creature that is completely new to him will also, most certainly, first seek to understand the species-preserving "what for" of its various organs and, therewith, the ecological relationships between the organism and its environment. In other words, he will begin his investigation using as broad a frame of reference as possible.

After he has become fairly well oriented to the teleonomy of the most general ecological relationships, the researcher will turn his attention to an *inventory of the parts* and attempt to understand the interrelationship of each of them to all the others and the way they affect one another reciprocally and, thereby, the entirety. One cannot master set research tasks if one makes a single part the focus of interest. One must, rather, continuously dart from one part to another—in a way that appears extremely flighty and unscientific to some thinkers who place value on strictly logical sequences—and one's knowledge of each of the parts must advance at the same pace.

It is in the nature of our language and our logical thinking that we can give and receive information only in linear temporal successions. Goethe, who discerned this, said: "Doch red' ich in die Lüfte, denn das Wort bemüht sich nur umsonst, Gestalten schöpf'risch aufzubau'n." ("But I only talk into the air, for the word struggles in vain to construct forms creatively.") In teaching, the assimilation of information has to struggle with the same difficulties as in research. For this reason a didactic example can illustrate both, and again I choose one that is mechanical in order to elude the suspicion of endowing biological entirety with mystical properties.

Imagine that you have to explain to someone who knows nothing about the thing, the functional operation of a complex machine, for example, an ordinary auto motor, the Ottomotor. In such a case one usually begins with a description of the structures and functions of the crankshaft and the piston, if only because these can be depicted through the use of graphic gestures. Then one explains how the descending piston sucks a "mixture" from the "carburetor," using this terminology all the while, although the listener has no clue to and cannot yet imagine what these words mean nor what these things might be. One hopes that, during this explanatory process, the listener is forming for himself a kind of conceptual diagram in which he holds open some empty spaces for "carburetor" and "mixture," spaces that will be filled in later as the concepts take on a firmer form. In principle, this is the same as the designing of a so-called flowchart that, with its so-called "black boxes," anticipates functions of a mechanism which remain, for the time being, unexplained.

The provisional sketching of the entire system is indispensable because the learner-listener, exactly as the researcher, can understand the single part, the "subsystem," only when he has also understood all the other parts. From what source, for example, the piston gets the energy that enables it to develop a capacity for suction can first be comprehended by the learner after he has understood the functions of all the other parts which provide the flywheel with kinetic energy; he must know why and to what end the camshaft runs half so fast as the crankshaft and how it opens the intake valve on the intake stroke and holds the exhaust valve shut, how it closes both valves on the compression and explosion strokes and opens only the exhaust valve on the exhaust stroke; he must understand how it is that the mixture is ignited at the right moment of the compression stroke, and so forth and so on. Systemic function can be defined quite simply in that its partial functions can be understood all together and synchronously or not at all.

Before at least an approximation of this synchronous understanding is achieved, it is senseless to turn one's attention to a more meticulous analysis of a partial function. Measurements are also meaningless before one's knowledge has arrived at this stage. Quantification can contribute nothing to reaching it, no matter how important this becomes later for verification and for the confirmation of what other cognitive capacities brought to light.

Rupprecht Matthaei (1929), in his book *Das Gestaltproblem*, has compared the approach of the researcher endeavoring to analyze an entirety with that of a painter:

> A cursory slapdash sketch of the whole is gradually filled in and elaborated, whereby the painter develops, as far as this is possible, all parts of the picture simultaneously; at every stage through which it is brought, the canvas looks as if it were finished—until the painting finally appears in its wholly visible self-evident completeness.

Then Matthaei adds the following remarkable sentence:

> Perhaps, at the end, one will say that such a step-by-step progression must certainly have been preceded by a kind of analysis; then, though, it would have been one that had been guided by gestalt insight!

This progression in a direction from the entirety of the system to its parts is, in biology, *obligatory*.

Naturally a researcher is free to make any part of an organic entirety the object of his investigation; it is equally legitimate and equally accurate to examine the whole organic system within the context of its environmental niche, as the ecologist does, or to concentrate interest on molecular processes, as the biogeneticist does. But an insight into the network of the system must always be present so that the specialized researcher can be oriented with respect to where, in the total organic structure, the subsystem he is studying has its place. Only the sequence of the research steps is prescribed.

3. The Cognitive Capacity of Perception

Wolfgang Metzger (1953) once said: "There are people who, through theoretical considerations of cognition, have incurably crippled the utilization of their senses for the purpose of natural scientific understanding," and meant, by this, to describe particular philosophers. Paradoxically, however, this sentence also applies to many others, among them extremely acute natural scientists who believe that they proceed especially "objectively" and "exactly" in that they exclude, as far as possible, their own perceptions from their research methodology. The epistemological inconsistency of this approach is identifiable in that perception is granted scientific legitimacy when it serves enumeration or the reading of a calibrated instrument, but is disallowed when it serves the direct observation of a natural process.

Absolutely all of our knowledge about the reality surrounding us is based on the reporting done by a wonderful and already well researched sensorial and neural apparatus that forms perceptions from data supplied by the sense organs. Without this apparatus, but above all without the objectifying capacity of its constancy mechanisms, to which gestalt perception also belongs, we would know nothing about the existence of those natural units which we call objects—living beings, places, things. The messages of this apparatus, which every normal person takes on trust as "true," are based on processes which, although completely inaccessible to introspection and rational control, are, nevertheless, through their functions, analogous to such rational operations as the reaching of conclusions and the making of computations. This, as is known, led Helmholtz (1887) to equate these two kinds of processes. Egon Brunswick (1957), one of the most successful researchers in the field of perception, designated what Helmholtz called unconscious conclusions as *ratiomorphic* functions and therewith expressed not only the strictly functional analogy but also the physiological differentiation of these two kinds of cognitive processes.

The complexity of the operations accomplished by ratiomorphic functions is well-nigh unlimited, even among creatures whose rational capacities are limited to the simplest thought processes. Try to imagine, for example, the level of complications that the stereometric and mathematical "computations" must attain so that an irregularly shaped object which revolves before one's eyes can appear to have a form that remains constant, that is, so that all the innumerable changes which its retinal image undergoes in the process of turning, can be interpreted as movements of the solid object in space and not as changes in its form. Yet the perception of every higher vertebrate performs this function.

Over and above the complexity of its functions, the most striking attribute of gestalt perception is its specific weakness—the ease with which it can be misled to fallacious "conclusions" by a deceptive set of data. The manifold optical illusions grant us insight into the "conduit of computation" through which the mechanism of perception comes up with a finding that, in as far as its "conclusions" have been based on false premises, is as demonstrably false as it is incorrigible through rational reflections. The so-called simultaneous contrast (see below) can serve as an example of such a false report.

The teleonomic function of our color perception is to make objects recognizable by their inherent reflectional qualities. As Karl von Frisch (1960) has demonstrated, the bee has evolved a completely analogous apparatus. Bees, like humans, are not interested in ascertaining the exact wavelengths of light. What they must be able to do is recognize a biologically relevant object by means of its reflectional qualities. These are the qualities that we say, simply, are "its" color. This recognition function is performed by an apparatus which separates, quite arbitrarily, the continuum of wavelengths into a discontinuum of the so-called spectral colors, for no other reason than to shunt their signals in such a way that the colors stand out in pairs, as so-called complementary colors, and through these particular combined relationships, convey the color white—which has been "invented" expressly for this purpose. The color "white" is a qualitatively consistent form of experience which does not correspond at all to anything simple in extra-subjective reality. Since no paired correspondent, in the form of actual wavelengths, exists for the middle of the spectrum, there to be used for compensative cancellation, that is, for the formation of "white," a complimentary color that we call purple has been "invented" in the same way as white, whereby the band of colors is completed and closed to form a color ring.

The species-preserving function of this entire apparatus lies exclusively in its capacity to compensate for incidental variations in the color of the lighting and, by doing this, to abstract as constants the inherent reflective qualities of objects. This happens in the following way: the impingement of light of a particular wavelength on a part of the retina induces the entire remaining area of the retina not only to increase its readiness to receive the complementary color but also actively to create that color. Erich von Holst (1969, 1970) demonstrated this experimentally by allowing a portion of the field of vision to perceive a spectral color, blue for example, but then beamed to the other remaining part of the field a "white" which did not comprise the wavelengths of the complementary color, yellow, but was generated through a combination of red and green. Nevertheless, the subject in the experiment saw the region bordering the blue area as yellow and not as white.

If in a given illumination a particular wavelength predominates, this will be compensated for completely by the mechanism just described, and that is why we always perceive a piece of "white" paper as white, although it may be viewed in the yellow of an electric light, in the reddish light of a sunset, or in the bluish light of a foggy day. But this compensating apparatus can also easily be "taken for a ride" if the prevalence of a color in the field of vision is not contingent on the lighting, but is dominant simply because a majority of the objects being seen reflect the color in question more readily than others. In such a case, we see all the other objects that do not do this as manifestly reflecting the complementary color. This phenomenon is called the simultaneous contrast.

This phenomenon can also be made understandable through a translation of the ratiomorphic processes into rational ones. The mechanism of color constancy proceeds from an established premise which "assumes" that the objects simultaneously present in the field of vision reflect, on average, all spectral colors uniformly. The apparatus does not "reckon" with the hardly probable possibility that, for some reason, the field of vision might be filled with nothing but objects which "are red," that is, with objects reflecting much more red than other colors, and thus "concludes," consequentially but incorrectly, that if red dominates the field of vision, this must be due to the lighting. But in red lighting, everything that reflects a "colorless" light must logically reflect green more intensely, or else they would at least have to appear lightly tinged with pink. And for the same reason, one would also see everything gray tinged in "contrasting" green.

As this example (intentionally chosen as the simplest possible) shows, perception is in a position to process a vast amount of incoming data and to draw from these a completely consistent conclusion. *Only this conclusion is communicated to the consciousness!* Perception, thus, is comparable to a computer. Erich von Holst has shown that almost all of the so-called "optical illusions" are based on the same principle as the simultaneous contrast: the premises from which the ratiomorphic operation proceeds are counterfeited by means of an extraordinarily improbable stimulus configuration and in such a way that the "computation," in itself logical, leads to an erroneous conclusion.

Perception invariably evaluates relationships, configurations, but never absolute data. Even the most unmusical person can recognize a fifth or a third unmistakably, but a statement about the absolute pitch would be beyond him. It is immensely characteristic of perception that it is independent of absolute data. We recognize a melody again and without difficulty whether it is played in the bass clef or in the treble clef. Christian von Ehrenfels (1890), one of the pioneers of Gestalt psychology, incorporated this *capacity for transposition* as an essential criterion of gestalt perception.

If a comprehension of modern computers can convey more than a mere conceptual model for any portion of the physiology of the central nervous system, then it is in the region of that mechanism which, from the multifariousness of the sense data, extracts the biologically relevant, teleonomic perceptions. Far from making the impression of being, in principle, inaccessible to research and conducive to misleading mystical–vitalistic interpretations, its function—and still more its extremely instructive malfunctions—bear so clearly the character of the mechanical or, better said, the physical that, more than any of the other complex phenomena of life, it fortifies our research optimism.

In spite of this, many modern researchers, and especially those who claim a monopoly for quantification as the only legitimate cognitive function, do not accept perception as a source of knowledge. In part this is because the messages of gestalt perception, obviously originating somewhere other than through the results of the rational and, for that reason regarded as "intuition," "inspiration," "revelation," and such like, are suspect to the scientist. To this must also be added the circumstance that those people who are extraordinarily gifted for the perception of complex configurations usually lack the keenness for analytical thinking. Only a few of the very great geniuses, but not all of them, had both.

Goethe himself considered the revelation of perception the only substantial source of knowledge: "Geheimnisvoll am lichten Tag, Lässt sich Natur des Schleiers nicht berauben, Und was sie deinem Geist nicht offenbaren mag, Das zwingst du ihr nicht ab mit Hebeln und mit Schrauben." ("Nature does not allow herself to be robbed of her veil of mystery in the bright light of day, and what she chooses not to disclose to your mind you cannot force from her with levers and jackscrews.") The obvious fact that gestalt perception and rational thinking both belong in like manner to the cognitive apparatus of humans and are capable of functioning fully only together, is as difficult for some people to comprehend as is the complementarity of the goal-directed, that is to say the teleonomic, and the causal considerations of a living system.

Gestalt perception is the function of a computing apparatus which, in complexity and capacity, surpasses by far every man-made machine. Its great strength is to be found in the simply prodigious amount of isolated data it takes in, the innumerable interrelationships it registers among them, and its ability to abstract from these relationships the inherent lawfulnesses. In this it surpasses even the most recently marketed computers which are able to extract, from a superposition of a great many curves, the single lawfulness prevailing in all of them.

The second, and perhaps even more intrinsic capacity through which perception surpasses all computers, is to be found in its ability to discover *unforeseen* lawfulnesses. Rational research and, more obviously, all computers can answer only those questions which have already been clearly formulated by means of human reasoning; at least the supposition that a lawfulness exists is always necessary before it is possible to provide an experimental or a quantifying verification. But even to those researchers who would prefer not to have it so, it is their own gestalt perceptions that will have intimated that supposition.

The third great strength of gestalt perception, and what really makes it rightly the basis of all knowledge about complex systems, is to be found in its extraordinarily protracted *retentive memory*. The fact which Goethe so clearly recognized, that the linear succession of words is incapable of depicting, comprehensibly, complex systemic wholes, is based quite simply on the realization that our rational recall has long forgotten the facts ingested at the beginning of an explanation as it continues to receive subsequent information about the same system. Most important, it never succeeds in grasping the relationships, going in all directions, that exist among the isolated data. One has only to read, for example, the description in an ornithological textbook of a cryptically speckled bird, somewhat similar to a skylark, and one will discover that one cannot make a mental "picture" from the descriptive phrases because one has long forgotten what was written about the brown speckling by the time one is reading the delineation of an adjacent region of the bird's body. That this difficulty is actually one of memory and that, in principle, it is

perfectly possible to construct a gestalt from a temporal sequence of isolated data, is confirmed by television, a medium through which the
transmission of facts follows so rapidly that the afterimage on the retina
takes over those tasks on which, through the vocal transmission, our verbal recall has long since foundered.

It borders on the miraculous the way in which gestalt perception can
abstract configurations of distinctive features from a chaotic background
of accidental stimulus data, and then retain these over the years. An
example of this, described here, is one that will be familiar to every older
physician. Several years ago, let us say, a certain complex of symptoms
was observed a few times, or it could have been but once, without your
having realized at the time that a particular gestalt quality had been perceived. But, seeing the same complex of symptoms again much later, it
can happen that, in a flash, from the depth of the unconscious, the gestalt
perception with the indubitably correct message is there: "You have seen
this exact same pattern of pathology once before."

Perception's most important characteristic for science in general, but
especially for comparative studies of behavior, is its capacity for storing
configurations of data almost indefinitely. And all those functions of
information collection from a disordered "background," a background
that is made up of what is to be collected as well as a lot of insignificant
data, require a repetition of the extraction process. The louder the
"noise" is on the band tuned for receiving, that much more often must
the message be sent. "Redundancy of information compensates for the
noisiness of channel" is the single sentence my friend, Edward Grey
Walter, chose to summarize a lecture I once gave on the necessity of
repeated observations.

One day, after a long period of unconscious data accumulation, the
gestalt that has been sought is there, often coming completely unexpect-
edly and like a revelation, but full of the power to convince. The enormous fund of facts that the perceptual mechanism must amass before it
is brought to a position to be able to convey such a result plays, in the
function of ratiomorphic abstraction, a role which is analogous to that of
collecting the basis in inductive research. And getting it to that stage of
completion and production, perception takes just as long a time, if not
longer, than rational induction. This explains why the discoveries made
by a great biologist who continues to use the same research object are
sometimes separated from one another by decades. Karl von Frisch published his first findings on bees in 1913; in 1920 he wrote for the first
time about their ability to communicate by means of dances; in 1940 he
discovered the mechanism for orientation which responds to the position of the sun and which has, as a prerequisite, an "internal chronometer" and also the directional instructions for returning to the hive,
which employ a transposition of the sun's location and which, in these
dances, are communicated by means of symbolizing the direction of the

sun through the perpendicular. In 1949 he discovered the amazing "computing apparatus" that is capable of calculating the position of the sun by using the plane of polarization of the light coming from a clear sky.

No matter how much truly diligent experimentation and conscientious verification also went into every one of the magnificent discoveries made by this great naturalist, it is certainly no accident that a major portion of each of them was made when Karl von Frisch was on holiday and while he was observing the bees of his own hives near his summerhouse. For one of the very pleasing peculiarities of gestalt perception is this, that it collects and stores information most zestfully just when the perceiver, immersed in the beauty of what is he observing, presumes he is pursuing nothing but the deepest spiritual repose.

4. So-Called Amateurism

It is apparent from the described qualities of gestalt that a tremendous amount of data must be fed into its computing apparatus if it is to fulfill its essential function. The amount of such data needed increases in proportion to the complexity of the lawfulness being sought and also in proportion to that part of the total incoming data that is accidental and irrelevant. Among the most complex lawfulnesses we actually know are those which control those capacities of the sensory organs and the nervous systems of higher animals, whose function is their behavior. Many of the behavior patterns which the researcher absolutely must be able to recognize—if his investigation of the total behavior of an animal species is to have any success—are the exceedingly complex temporal configurations (Erich von Holst speaks of "impulse melodies") and are, in most cases, overlaid by still other kinds of movements which are apt to conceal their gestalt. One has to have seen these sequences again and again before their gestalt, through a sudden act of recognition, emerges from the background of the accidental and presents itself, as an unmistakable unity, to the consciousness of the investigator.

This sudden emergence, one would like to say "eruption" of the gestalt is, for the observer, a qualitatively unmistakable experience which is always accompanied by a kind of astonishment that something so obvious had not been seen much earlier. Here is an example of this experience. At the beginning of the nineteen-forties, when studying courtship movements of the Anatidae, I suddenly noticed a movement pattern performed by a garganey drake (*Querquedula querquedula*) that consisted of the bird lifting back its wing at the shoulder joint, stretching its bill toward the wing and then running its bill on the inner side, along the secondary quills, like a small boy with an outstretched stick moving along the slats of a lath fence, producing a very audible, comparable sound. When I perceived this behavior pattern (certainly innately coordinated) in the garganey duck, I had a vague inkling that I had already seen the same thing in some other species of duck, but I could not put my finger on which one. Then I believed it to be the Madagascar duck (*Anas melleri*) because that was the next species in which I discovered this movement. Soon after this I was forced to confirm that the drakes of all the surface-feeding duck species to which I had access at the time exhibited the same movement pattern.

As will be shown in a subsequent section, the instinctive movements or fixed action patterns, as relatively entirety-independent components, constitute a framework, in a certain sense, of the behavior patterns of an animal species. Taking an inventory of the parts or subsystems integrated into an entirety (already brought up and discussed in One/II/3) is the first and indispensable step in the analysis of a complex organic system. Gestalt perception is the only cognitive capacity we possess by means of which we can take this step.

A simply prodigious amount of time, spent in presuppositionless observation, is necessary in order to collect and store the factual material which the great computing apparatus needs in order to be able to lift the gestalt from its background. Even a Tibetan priest schooled in the practice of patience would not be able to remain stationary in front of an aquarium or adjacent to a duck pond or even in a blind constructed for observations in the open as long as is necessary to accumulate the data base for the perceiving apparatus. Such sustained endeavours can be accomplished only by those men whose gaze, through a wholly irrational delight in the beauty of the object, stays riveted to it. Here the great scientific value of so-called amateurism becomes manifest: the great pioneers of ethology, Charles Otis Whitman and Oskar Heinroth, were "lovers" of the objects of their studies, and it is no accident that so many of the fundamental discoveries in ethology were made within the zoological class of birds. It is one of the greatest fallacies to think that the expression *scientia amabilis* has a derogatory connotation concerning the branch of knowledge being referred to.

5. Observing Animals in the Wild and in Captivity

The love of animals, which constitutes a prerequisite for sufficiently sustained observation, can be traced to two motivational sources in man — to that of the hunter and to that of the herder. Among a great many successful ethologists, the choice of the object of their studies and their methodologies are determined to a great extent by the joy of stalking and lying in wait for animals, in short, by the pleasure of "outwitting" them. Studying a captive animal is hardly any fun at all to them and, in fact this seems to some of them to be "unsportsmanly." They easily rationalize this purely emotional antipathy through the use of the argument that, with captive animals, one can never know for certain how much of their behavior has been altered by the abnormal conditions of their confinement. And in point of fact, in order to eliminate this source of error, repeated observations of animals in a natural habitat are absolutely necessary. But the primary advantage of observations made in a natural setting is that they can comprehend directly the ecological integration of the animal species being studied.

The "hunter type" of behavior researcher, embodied in my friend, Nikolaas Tinbergen, is the opposite of the "herder type" who wants to own animals and, above all, to breed them and increase their number. Herders stalk animals only in order to capture them and, subsequently, to keep them. C. O. Whitman and Oskar Heinroth were such animal keepers; I, myself, am also one. The single great disadvantage associated with observing the behavior of captive animals has been stated above. Yet, at the same time, there are many advantages which compensate for this.

The most important of these advantages is the opportunity provided the researcher who keeps animals to observe the behavior of several species simultaneously and in juxtaposition. This advantage is even further enhanced by the tendency amateurs often have of limiting themselves to particular classes of animals; in many cases they begin with a small group, a genus, or a family, and then only gradually do they expand their interests to include larger taxonomic categories. My first object of study was the mallard; then my interest slowly extended to embrace the entire group of Anatidae. Heinroth and Whitman were also lovers of animal groups: from early youth onward Whitman kept and studied pigeons; Heinroth kept and studied Anatidae. Discovering the homology of those innate sequences of coordinated movements which we call fixed motor patterns, which proved to be basic for all comparative studies of behavior, could have been achieved by no one except a lover of animals, and particularly a group of animals—in other words, by a so-called amateur.

Another great advantage for observing animals in captivity is to be found, paradoxically, among just those disturbances of behavior which are brought about by the unnatural conditions of the environment. If, for example, a researcher is able to observe the way in which a wolf in the wild carries the remains of a kill to a covert place, digs a hole in the earth there, pushes the piece of plunder in with his nose, shovels the excavated earth back—still using his nose—and then levels the site through shoves with the nose, the teleonomic question concerning this behavior sequence is easy to answer, but the question concerning the causal origin of this behavior pattern remains completely unanswered. If, in contrast to this, the observer of captive animals sees the way in which a young wolf or dog carries a bone to behind the dining room drapes, lays it down there, scrapes violently for a while next to the bone, pushes the bone with his nose to the place where all the scraping was done and then, again with his nose and now squeaking along the surface of the parquetry flooring, shoves the nonexistent earth back into the hole that has not been dug and goes away satisfied, the observer knows quite a lot about the phylogenetic program of the behavior pattern. If he then sees (what every dog owner has experienced) that the pup, after he has once gone through the described behavior sequence out in the open, never again makes the futile attempt to bury a piece of booty on a solid surface, then it will be clear to him that the presence of certain associated stimulus configurations function as a reward to "condition" the behavior to the normal situation and that, conversely, their absence works to weaken, that is, "extinguish" it. In this way the observation of performance failures caused by captivity often produces an unexpected amount of information about the nature and the composition of the sequences of behavior observed.

Disturbances of behavior that are pathological are a second source of knowledge. Just as pathology in general is one of the most important sources of physiological knowledge, and just as the pathological deficiency of a particular function makes the researcher aware of a particular mechanism, just so does the student of behavior very often learn something of the greatest importance from pathological disturbances of behavior.

One of the most prevalent of these disturbances among captive animals is the diminution of the intensity with which certain instinctive movements, and the complex behavior patterns they combine to form, are carried out. A typical example of this is the construction of nests by caged birds. How often nest-building activities are begun in the aviaries of amateurs and in zoos, and by such a great variety of birds, and then how seldom it is that a nest characteristic of the species is ever completed.

This pathological disturbance of a phylogenetically programmed behavior pattern is very similar to the normal incompleteness which we observe in the ontogenesis of young animals. In 1932 I wrote the following:

Among the young [I am writing here about young birds], drives intended to be directed toward a particular object at first develop without this object being present, and then only secondarily are they conditioned to an appropriate object. Among animals having a high level of intelligence and within whose chains of instinctive behavior sequences many such links are intercalated, that is, links which are modifiable through personal experience, the actual purpose of a course of action which does not achieve its real goal might be that of preparatory practice for the young animals and is thus of biological significance.

The behavior sequences which remain uncompleted because of a lack of intensity frequently stop just short of fulfilling their species-preserving function. This fact was what first convinced me that the animal had no idea about the teleonomy of its own behavior and that the purposive psychologists were quite wrong in supposing that the survival value of any action was to be equated with the goal at which the animal,' as a subject, was striving. I also wrote in the monograph mentioned above that an instinctual programming of behavior must be postulated whenever "there is an obvious incongruity between the normal intelligence capacities generally observed in the animal concerned and those which would have to be present for the completion of the given behavior pattern," and secondly, whenever "imperfections appear in a behavioral sequence which distinctly indicate that the animal itself is not conscious of the purpose of the behavior pattern concerned."

Because the intensity of so much instinctive behavior is directly dependent on the physical condition of the animal, extreme caution becomes particularly necessary if, from the absence of a particular behavior pattern in a captive animal, a conclusion were to be reached concerning its presence or absence in the species as a whole. Concluding that a particular behavior pattern is not present among a certain animal species is, in principle, inadmissible when this is based only on observations of caged animals. When Gustav Kramer (1950) demonstrated the extreme aggressiveness of *Lacerta melisselensis*, a lizard of the Muralis group, his findings were questioned by some herpetologists who, for years, had kept and even bred the same species in terraria; none of them had ever witnessed any serious fighting. Under normal terrarium conditions, under which the animals stay alive for years, one can keep several males of this species together with no trouble, but in their natural habitat this species belongs to those few animals among which an immediate and fatal outcome is observed in battles between rivals. Kramer demonstrated that the decrease of aggressiveness among captive animals is caused by climatic conditions; these animals need cool air for breathing while the blood heat necessary for normal behavior must be supplied by radiation. Statements concerning the non-existence of a particular behavior among captive animals carry no weight at all.

On the other hand, the positive observation of a fairly complex behavior pattern in a captive animal justifies a confident assertion that the behavior in question is characteristic of the species. In other words, the influences of captivity can lead, essentially, only to the *disappearance* of behavior patterns, but can never *give rise to* a complex and, above all, an obviously teleonomic behavior. When, at an ethology congress in Den Haag, Janet Kear-Matthews reported on her successful breeding and rearing of the Magpie goose (*Anseranas semipalmatus*) and how this bird was the only one among all the Anatidae to consistently feed its young and how the young had a repertory of appropriate begging movements, a well-known Australian field observer maintained, during the discussion, that the behavior of *Anseranas* that Kear-Matthews had observed and had shown in a film was an artifact induced through circumstances of captivity. He based his statement on the fact that he had never seen anything like this during his observations in the field. This way of reasoning bears witness to the most profound ethological ignorance.

6. Observing Tame Animals Not Kept Captive

A possible compromise between observations in the field and keeping animals caged can be achieved with some highly organized vertebrates if one rears young animals of a social species within a suitable biotope and then observes these tame individuals as they move about unhindered. The advantages of this research method are obvious. Some limitations are set by the characteristics of what is termed imprinting; these play an important role, particularly among birds. Among ravens, parrots, herons, and others, it is difficult to rear the birds so that their filial instinctive patterns and their social attachments do, actually, become fixated on humans, but not those behavior patterns associated with sexuality and fighting among rivals. An adult great yellow-crested cockatoo (*Cacatue galerita*) or a male raven can frustrate all further observations if he begins to treat the person who has reared him as a rival. Geese (*Anserini*) of the most diverse species are so well suited for the research method being discussed here because the behavior patterns directed toward the parent and toward the social companion can easily and enduringly become fixated on the human caretaker, but a sexual imprinting of these birds to humans is next to impossible.

If, for the purposes of observation, one attempts to establish a population of non-captive animals or tries to incorporate within a natural population an individual reared tame, one sometimes comes up against an unexpected difficulty, especially among the most highly developed mammals. Even if settled with success within a living space that corresponds extensively to the natural habitat, animals reared by humans form a type of society that is not typical of their species. Attempts made by Americans to settle in spacious enclosures those chimpanzees who, as test animals, had earned the right to retirement, miscarried completely. And Katharina Heinroth (1959) has reported graphically on her futile attempts to integrate a hand-reared young female baboon (*Papio sphinx*) into a troop of animals of the same species that lived on the large cliffs for apes at the Berlin Zoo. Again and again the young female reared by Dr. Heinroth stirred up the greatest indignation among her conspecifics through behavior that was not "socially acceptable." As Dr. Heinroth expressed it, "She made social gaffes." The discrepancies are significant because they permit the conclusion that traditional social norms are operative.

Among hand-reared wild boar (*Sus scrofa*), the difficulty just described does not arise. Apparently the entire behavior inventory they need for social interaction is firmly set genetically and does not have to be supplemented by social tradition. This problem of social tradition can be properly studied only through comparisons between a natural population of animals and another free-ranging population reared by man.

In the observation of highly organized creatures, the methodological ideal is achieved when it has become possible to accustom free-ranging wild animals to the observer to such an extent that their behavior is not influenced by his presence and he can, in fact, conduct experiments with them within a natural environmental setting. This research methodology is of particular importance when investigations are undertaken with primates—because their social tradition plays such a prominent role, so prominent that tame animals which have been kept captive and then set free cannot be expected to exhibit social behavior characteristic of their species. That is why the observations of chimpanzees made by Jane Goodall (1971) received the recognition they deserved. The observations of baboons made by Washburn and de Vore (1961) and especially the studies done by Hans Kummer (1957, 1968, 1971, 1975) show, through their results, how very much this extremely time-consuming and sacrifice-exacting method pays off.

7. Knowing Animals: A Methodological Sine Qua Non

When Erich von Holst (1969/70) was conducting his classic experiments involving the electrical stimulation of the hypothalamus of chickens, he emphasized repeatedly that such an investigation could not forego, as a basis, the most exact knowledge of the entire behavior inventory of the species being studied. For this reason, he persuaded Erich Baeumer (1955) to join him as a co-worker. Baeumer, by profession a country doctor, had through his love for these animals accumulated a profound knowledge of the behavior of all the breeds—an indispensable resource for von Holst's experiments—and could provide an exact diagnosis of a particular behavior pattern even when presented only with its most minimal indication or with just a pattern fragment. In his time and for the same reason, W. R. Hess (1954) needed Paul Leyhausen to join him for the evaluation and interpretation of films made of the hypothalamus stimulation experiments done with cats. Leyhausen had the entire behavior inventory of cats "at his fingertips," an inventory that is much more complex than that of the domesticated chicken. It is my opinion that, without this prerequisite knowledge, hypothalamus stimulation experiments are meaningless.

I would like to propose the speculation that this prerequisite pertains to all investigations of animal behavior. Even if one consciously limits the research interest to a very small subsystem of an entirety, it seems to me that knowledge of the total behavior inventory of the studied animal species is absolutely indispensable. Without this knowledge the researcher cannot possibly know what answers the system is giving through its responses to his own operations, whatever these might be.

If only in order to know whether an observed behavior pattern corresponds to the proper behavior of the species in its natural setting, or if the behavior is pathological, the researcher must know his animal species very thoroughly. A great number of errors can be attributed to the circumstance that a pathological loss of intensity or the complete lack of certain centrally coordinated movements were regarded as "normal." For use as a research model and as one part of the knowledge of animals must also be included a certain measure of what, among older physicians, is called the "clinical eye." This is something that can be acquired only through extensive experience. I regret that a very large proportion of the younger researchers who consider themselves ethologists show a deplorable lack of knowledge of animals and particularly a lack of the "clinical eye."

8. The Non-Obtrusive Experiment

All that has been said in Section 2 of this chapter about the systemic character of the organism and the sequence of operations prescribed implies a series of important consequences of which the experimenter must be aware and to which he must conform.

It stands to reason that any encroachment by experimentation makes sense only after the system has been analyzed far enough to give some notion of the subsystems comprising it and the way in which they interact. These provisional notions must possess a sufficient probability of being correct in order to make their testing worthwhile. Hazarding just any action, "just to see what will happen," has but minimal prospects for any acquisition of knowledge.

At any rate, the experimenter must limit his encroachments to measures that are sure not to upset the equilibrium of the entire system. The smaller his experimental interference, the more certain he can be that the response shown by the whole organism is indeed caused by the experimental influence.

Experiments fulfilling all the above postulates have been termed, by Eckhard Hess (1973), "unobtrusive" experiments.

If experimental questions are put too early, this can easily lead to an underestimation of the complexity of the system being examined. Consideration of the system as an entirety and questions concerning the teleonomy of its individual parts are mandatory. However, they may not be elevated to a goal in themselves. During the preparatory work, the goal of the research must be kept in mind and this goal is always the causal analysis of the entire system. The necessary cooperation of gestalt perception comprehending the entirety, on the one hand, and the analysis and the experimentation, on the other, has been depicted by Otto Koehler (1933) in a beautiful comparison.

If our ignorance of the essence of life can be likened to a large mountain, then the individual branches of biology and their auxiliary sciences are tunnels that penetrate into its interior from the most varied points of departure, extending in various directions, some into the depths, others nearer the surface. Researchers working with the methods of natural science are the tunnel crew; one crew scrapes the wall, another blasts away at the tunnel's end, a third removes the rubble. But when a great event occurs, such as Boveri's and Sutton's hypothesis that the processes in the chromosomes and those of heredity can be bracketed to one explanation, so that from both sides predictions not only become possible but are actually fulfilled, then this intellectual achievement is comparable to the final blow of the pickax that breaks through the remnant of wall separating two tunnels meeting within the mountain's interior.

As a contrast to an undertaking of the tunnel work that has been described here, what most readily comes to mind is a walk along the trails on the surface of the mountain. After their week of daily work, the men will certainly be granted an unlimited panoramic view on Sunday. Eyes that have become accustomed to the dark can delight in the brightness of the day; and besides the respite that is afforded as a result of the week's work, direct benefits can also accrue from such circuit tours if they serve to confirm the direction of the tunnels, to observe the progress made by a neighbor and, together with him, to plan future tunneling. Such circuits of the surface become of questionable value only when they are repeated too often and become an end in themselves, or when they lead to a disregard of the efforts being made by the men in the mountain's interior. No number of treading hikers will ever trample the mountain down; it would appear much more likely that the mountain could collapse if new tunnels continue to be bored through it and stronger and still stronger detonations are ignited. But this eventuality is part of the far distant future, for the mountain is immense.

Every researcher has every right to choose where, within a system, he or she wants to bore in depth—as long as the researcher knows where that place is located with reference to the entire system. It is just as legitimate to begin research at the highest level of integration of the organic system, that is, at the level of its interaction with the immediate environment, at the ecological level, as it is to choose a small subsystem to be the object of study—provided the prerequisite specified above is fulfilled. The only strategy that is dictated to us by the very nature of the system is, as has already been specified, the sequence in which the survey of the entirety and the analytical experiment are initiated: the latter must follow the former.

What must constantly be kept in mind are the various side effects on the entire system and, therewith, the repercussions on the investigated subsystem any experimental encroachment might have. This problem is that much easier to solve the more the examined part or subsystem bears the characteristic of a relatively independent component of the entirety (One/II/10). In addition to this, one must always take into consideration that an experimentally established conditional change can have a similar and predictable effect a second time only if the entire system finds itself at the time of both influences in exactly the same condition. H. J. Jordan (1929) has made this imaginably concrete by means of a very neat mechanical example. If, within a large railroad yard, switch X is moved from its connection with a sidetrack so that the main track is thrown open, express train Y will collide with freight train Z. The reproducibility of this successful maneuver depends, understandably, upon all the switches in the system being set as they were in the first experiment and, moreover, that the trains Y and Z are in the exact same places at the moment of the shunting, moving in the same directions as before and at the same speeds. Transferring switch X from the siding at any other than the prior time would result in a completely different development.

If the system being examined is a relatively small subsystemic part of the organic entirety, it is in some cases possible to achieve by artificial means the sameness of prevailing circumstances which, in Jordan's illustration, is represented by the necessity of prior sameness for all the switch settings and train movements. In physiology this method is generally applied and is tolerably successful. But the system of sensory and nervous functions underlying the behavior of higher animals is quite the most complex system that we know. It is naive to imagine that one can create, for an intact organism, a repetition of completely identical circumstances and processes by simply confining it to "constant and strictly controlled laboratory conditions."

As will be discussed in Two/III/2 and 3, concerned with readiness-increasing and releasing stimuli, a higher animal requires a vast number of continuously effective, often quite complicated stimulus impingements in order to be able to maintain its good health and not show signs of pathologic behavior. The "controlled laboratory conditions" inevitably cancel out an unpredictable number of stimuli situations indespensable to the animal, at the same time producing an equally unpredictable number of chaotic, abnormal stimuli. In her classic work on the spontaneity of aggressive behavior in the coral-reef fish, *Microspathodon chrysurus* (Pomacentridae), Ann Rasa (1971) showed experimentally how, even for such a "low" vertebrate, a monotonously maintained environment predictably produces a pathological waning of over-all excitability.

Anyone who has kept higher animals knows all too well how difficult it is to avoid the consequences of the monotony of conditions under which the captive animal has to live. Even among free-flying greylags it has been demonstrated that a measurable reduction of general excitability is brought about if the birds live constantly on one and the same pond or small lake. Compared to the wild geese presently living (one could hardly say "kept captive") at Grünau in the Alm valley, which fly a distance of 16 km daily from where they sleep to where they they feed and back again, and which nest at still other locations, our Seewiesen geese now appear to have been somewhat sleepy. At Seewiesen, rival ganders almost never demonstrated the aerial combat behavior that, in early spring, is a daily occurrence at Grünau.

In view of the unpredictable alterations in the behavior of higher animals that are caused by even the mildest forms of semi-captivity, all attempts to achieve uniformity of response to specific stimulation by "controlling" environmental conditions would appear to be hopeless. Recognizing this, some research workers, and particularly those who are profoundly conscious of the systemic character of their study object, have become completely averse to experimentation generally.

If one looks through the most modern literature concerned with behavior research, one could almost get the impression that the attributes "system conscious" and "experimental" contradict one another and can hardly ever be applied simultaneously to the same investigation. Altogether too many experiment oriented behavior researchers working exclusively in laboratories—as a majority of American psychologists do—are experimentally highly gifted but are often also afflicted with a complete lack of biological and ecological sense while, at the same time, some behavior researchers who are well able to think in biological and ecological terms, dedicate themselves only to observations in the field and choose not to know very much about experiments, particularly those experiments carried out under laboratory conditions.

In view of this deplorable state of affairs, all modern students of behavior might take to heart the following statement written by the botanist, Fritz Knoll in 1926:

In order to make an experiment with animals useful to floral ecology, the experimenter must first acquire a thorough knowledge about the general way of life of the animal that is to be studied. This can be accomplished only through prolonged periods of close observation in the natural environment of flora and fauna associated with it. Only after such preparation should one proceed to designing and making an experiment. Initially it is advisable to carry out the planned experiment within the natural habitat of the studied flowers and insects. Certain experiments for which the original environment is not suitable will be carried out in the open, in situations more appropriate to the experiment's purpose. Finally, for such experiments which should be made under very specially adapted circumstances, one will have recourse to the laboratory. Appropriate laboratory experiments arranged with all necessary caution often permit us to ascertain the very last nuances about a phenomenon which, in the too complex natural environment, have eluded a clear analysis.

These sentences are by no means valid only for those behavior patterns through which the insects interrelate with the blossoms that they visit. They are unconditionally valid for the study of behavior as such. There is no such thing as a behavior, just as there is no such thing as an animal life form, that can be understood in *any other way* except within the context of the ecology of the species. The sentences quoted above are even valid, in fact, for pathologic behavior because, as is well known, the pathologic can be defined only by having recourse to ecological concepts.

The strategy of the experiment so clearly outlined by Fritz Knoll corresponds exactly to what Eckhard Hess termed the "unobtrusive experiment," a designation which I, in the German-language edition of this book, called the "non-disruptive" experiment. What is essential and what also emerges from Knoll's writings is this: experimental impingements on the natural conditions of an animal's existence should change those conditions as little as possible. The smaller the impingement, the greater is the probability that it will take effect on only a single part of the systemic whole and, therewith, the observed effect will actually be caused in a relatively direct way by the experimental impingement. The grand master of the unobtrusive experiment is Nikolaas Tinbergen, whose books and articles, particularly for the sake of his methodology, should be studied thoroughly by every budding ethologist. His article on the grayling moth *(Eumenis semele L.)* (1943) proves that the entirety oriented experiment can also, ultimately, lead to quantifiable verification.

9. The Deprivation Experiment

That experiment involving the withholding of specific experience plays a decisive role in the unfortunate and heavily belabored discussion of the question concerning whether innate, that is, phylogenetically programmed behavioral elements can be differentiated from acquired behavior elements. This experiment can fulfill its intended task only if the experimenter has learned to think in biological terms and only if he follows the methodological rules put forward in this chapter.

The kinds of blatant blunders that are committed against the demands of the unobtrusive experiment can be illustrated by means of an example. Young chimpanzees were reared in complete darkness and when, finally, they were brought into the light and did not possess the capacity of image vision, it was concluded that the capacity of point discrimination and, therewith, seeing images must be "learned". Although visual experience is necessary to *maintain* the mechanisms of innately specified visual processing of sensory data, and in perfecting the calibration of binocular depth vision, it is misleading to state that point discrimination must be learned.

What, if anything, can be concluded from a deprivation experiment?

Cogent conclusions can be drawn only if, in spite of the withholding of very specific information, the experimental animal still unmistakably possesses just this information. The premises for this reasoning are simple: adapted behavior always presupposes that information about the circumstances of the environment, to which the adaptation relates, has got into the organism. There are only two ways this can happen: either during phylogeny, during which *the species* interacted with just these environmental givens, or the *individual* in the course of its life had occasion to experience that which provided the information. Phylogenetic adaptation and individual adaptive modification of behavior are the only two possible ways extant for the acquisition and storage of information. What the deprivation experiment can do, in favorable instances, is give us an answer to the question: From which of these two possible sources has the information for behavioral adaptation come? If it is possible to exclude with certainty one of these sources, then we know that the other has supplied the information. For the reasons already given, it is easier to exclude with certainty individually acquired information than it is to exclude information acquired phylogenetically.

If we rear a male stickleback (*Gasterosteus aculeatus*) isolated from its conspecifics from the egg stage onward and when, during the following spring, it turns out that the fish, in a selective and specific way, responds to a display of "red-below" with the movement patterns of rival fighting, or if a young dog which has never before dug up earth and, without any previous experience, performs each of the bone-burying movements in the correct sequence (as was described in Section II/5), we know with certainty that the adaptive information for these teleonomic behavior patterns is contained in the genome. Remarkably, this certainty is contested by some groups of scientists. It is said again and again that the organism could have acquired information through learning while still in the egg or in the uterus. One must then ask: But from where? As has already been said in the introduction to this book, the assumption made by Kuo (1932) and other behaviorists, that the mechanisms of learning "know" without any previous experience what is and what is not useful for the organism, contains the covert postulation of a prestabilized harmony to which the great vitalist, Jakob von Uexküll (1921), overtly testifies. If one does not believe in miracles—and a prestabilized harmony would be one such—it remains simply incomprehensible where, for example, within the aquarium in which the young stickleback was reared—among all the diversity of its animal and plant world—the information should be contained that the rival to be attacked is red on the ventral side.

But this certainty exists only for those cases in which, despite the withholding of experience, the information appears undiminished. Stating the reverse, that is, to say after conducting the experiment that the missing information must be learned, has far less certainty. If, supposing, our stickleback had not produced the specific reaction to the wedding suit of a rival, we would in no way be in a position to state with certainty that this reaction had to be learned individually. For, in such cases, there is always another possible explanation. This is that, through the measures which were necessary in order to withhold from our experimental animal certain specific information, at the same time and without intending to, some other "components" essential to the realization of the behavior fixed in the genome were also withheld. Moreover, there is yet another possibility. When arranging the experiment cited in our example and when first introducing the rival fish to our experimental stickleback, some unspecified stimulus combination necessary to the release of the behavior being studied might have been missing. Male sticklebacks as well as a host of other territorial animals fight only in an area they have thoroughly explored and which they regard as their very own. If they are put into an unknown environment and together with that object which is expected to release in them rival fighting, they will most certainly not react as anticipated.

A second example of the kinds of mistakes that can be made when using deprivation is afforded by the experiments conducted by Riess (1954). He reared rats in such a way that they were never given an opportunity to lift or to carry any sort of solid object. When he then, under strictly controlled and standardized experimental conditions, placed them in enclosures supplied with nest materials, the rats built no nests. From this he concluded that nest building is impossible for rats if the handling of solid objects has not been learned beforehand. What he overlooked was that the time span allowed to the experimental animal was much too short. In absolutely new surroundings, such as the test situation was for the rat, the animal will spend a very long time in exploring the new container, mainly trying to get out. It will not even begin to build a nest before it has thoroughly familiarized itself with the new container. No rat, with or without the normal experience of managing solid objects, would have begun to build a nest within the time that was experimentally allotted. Before Eibl-Eibesfeldt (1958) initiated his own experiments with rats which were to prove Riess's conclusions wrong (as will be explained later), I had the greatest difficulty convincing Eibl that it was necessary to repeat the Riess experiments and, as a particular step, inducing him to place an old and experienced rat in the same test situation that had been used by Riess. Eibl regarded all of these repetitious research steps as ridiculous because, through his excellent knowledge of animals, he knew with certainty that a rat placed in a strange environment will not build for a long time. But this was something that Riess did not know.

Very often innate information also fails to appear if the experimental animal is not in first-class physical condition and is not capable, therefore, of achieving the necessary degree of general arousal. An example of an error which I committed more than forty years ago is relevant in this context and can serve as an illustration. I reared young red-backed shrikes *(Lanius collurio L.)* and observed the ontogeny of the interesting behavior pattern by means of which these birds impale captured prey on thorns for safekeeping and storage. My birds did perform normally the motor pattern of wiping captured prey along twigs and pressing down when, during this process, resistance was encountered, but they showed no propensity whatsoever for orienting this motor pattern to thorns on which the captured prey could be firmly impaled. This orientation they learned later when a run-off of the complete sequence of movements was successful, quite accidentally, several times. Nothing was easier to assume (at least then) that just these successes, that is, the reporting back of the successes—the desired result having been achieved—involved a conditioning effect, and that recognition of the thorn is, in this way, learned. At that time I spoke about an instinct–learning intercalation and I was as yet completely unaware that everything that is conditioned by reinforcement is learned in this way and that everything that is learned is based on a phylogenetically evolved program.

Later experiments which U. von St. Paul and I initiated showed that the innate "recognition" of the thorn by red-backed shrikes *(Lanius collurio L.)*, as well as by greater shrikes *(Lanius excubitor L.)*, is completely innate. Young birds of these species, with no experience whatsoever, approached all objects resembling thorns—such as nails driven through a perch—at once, nibbled at them exploratively and then turned their attention immediately toward an object, even some substitute object (a piece of paper, the dried wing of a butterfly) in order to be able to impale this directly in a workmanlike manner and in accordance with all the rules of the art. Reversed, that is, when presented with a juicy and ideal object for impalement, such as a newly hatched chick, or just the piece of one, the appetence for a thorn was activated at once. St. Paul and I then tried to rear red-backed shrikes as badly, as negligently and inadequately as I had apparently reared them forty years before. But this miscarried completely; U. von St. Paul takes such good care of birds that she was simply incapable of bringing herself to rear them as badly as would have been necessary to cause the previous behavior deficiency.

The fact that the presence but not the absence of phyletic information can be conclusively affirmed by means of the deprivation experiment led some of those of the behaviorist opposition to the erroneous belief that ethologists desired to disavow the existence of learning processes; these opponents labeled the above, absolutely irrefutable facts a "highly protective theory," as if, on the basis of these findings, we ethologists would deny that learning can be ascertained.

There are cases in which reciprocal reasoning processes permit, to a certain extent, the exclusion of the presence of innate information without having to conduct special experiments for confirmation of this, and allow the assertion that the teleonomy of a particular behavior pattern has been achieved through individually acquired information. This is possible when, for example, an organism masters in an unmistakably teleonomic way an environmental situation that its species demonstrably could never before have come up against.

Curt Richter told me that he once experimented (1942–43) with various animals, among them three-toed sloths (Bradypodidae), in a way that involved a selection of foodstuffs by the test animals. In their natural environment sloths eat tree leaves almost exclusively and, like many leaf-eaters, are not easy to please or satisfy with substitute foods when kept in captivity. By offering his captive animals just about every kind of fresh vegetable matter available on the open market and by letting them choose from this what they wanted to eat, he was able, subsequently, to feed each of them most successfully on the "menu" it had itself selected (personal communication, 1955). With rats he set up and conducted the following significant experiment. He presented them with the most varied foodstuffs broken down, as far as possible, into their chemical components—protein, for example, in the form of its constituent amino acids. Each component was presented in a particular dish to an amount that had been previously weighed, and what was eaten was measured. The rats took from each of the dishes just that amount necessary to constitute a well-balanced diet. The amounts of the individual amino acids the rats consumed corresponded to the proportional amounts that would be necessary for the synthesis of protein.

Because no animal since the appearance of life on earth can have been in a position to put protein together from amino acids, it is impossible for rats to have any inborn information about this, or about which proportions of those components of their food belong together so as to comprise a healthy diet. This knowledge, thus, must have been acquired during an individual animal's life and the way this happens was discovered by John Garcia (1967) and his colleagues. It was impossible for them to get a rat to leave off eating a particular foodstuff by infliction of pain, by electric shock, by forced swimming in cold water, or by the effects of other quite gruesome punishments; an association between these stimuli and the eating of a particular foodstuff was absolutely impossible to establish. If, on the other hand, the punishment stimulus used was a small dose of x-rays or the injection of a small amount of apomorphine, the effect of both being intestinal nausea, the rats at once related this disagreeable experience to that foodstuff which they had last eaten, following exactly Wilhelm Wundt's old law of successivity and contiguity. In only one single set of circumstances did their reaction not follow this law: when the rats were given a new foodstuff along with an extensive sequence of dishes, all of which were known to the animals, they related the subsequent nausea to the new food, even when this was by no means the last one to be eaten. The wonderful teleonomy of this innate disposition for learning is striking. As this example shows us, even when we know with certainty that the teleonomy of a behavior is based on learning, we can understand this process of learning only after we comprehend the phylogenetically evolved system into which the process has been incorporated.

With the exception of rare cases of this kind, it is more difficult to prove the assertion that the teleonomy of a behavior is based on learning and not on innate information than it is to prove the opposite. For all that, a researcher who knows his animals thoroughly and who possesses the indispensable "clinical eye" for their states of health can almost always determine, with quite reliable certainty, whether the absence of a particular behavior is the result of a lack of learning opportunities or the result of a lack of sufficient "condition" or "tone" on the part of the experimental animal.

The only procedure that justifies concluding a lack of learning opportunities consists of first excluding those opportunities and then eliminating the disturbances thus caused, through a deferred presentation of the learning opportunity. When Eibl-Eibesfeldt studied the nest-building behavior of inexperienced female rats (1958), he reared them in receptacles containing no objects with which they could perform the "carrying-to-nest" motor patterns. Even the food they were given was reduced to tiny particles. Yet the first group of experimental animals had to be let go because they treated their own tails as nest-building material. They went out from where they had slept, in search, and "found" their tails. They carried these to the place they had chosen for a nest site and carefully laid them down there. A second group of experimental animals was reared after their tails had been amputated while they were still in the nest, and when they were not yet sexually mature they were given shredded blotting paper as nest material. The reaction of the experimental animals differed from that of the normal, control animals only in its intensity; the experimental animals virtually flung themselves at the nest material and began to build with abnormal intensity, that is, they behaved in exactly the same way a normal rat would behave after having been deprived of nest materials for a comparable length of time; there was clearly a "damming up" of motor patterns which, until then, had been denied expression. The single behavior patterns—the searching, the picking up, the carrying back and the laying down of the nest material, as well as the scraping movements by which a circular nest wall is built, and the motor patterns of smoothing down the inside surface— were not different from those of the normal animals, not even when the behaviors recorded on slow-motion films were compared.

The sequence in which the cited motor patterns were carried out was the only way in which the behavior of the inexperienced rats actually differed from that of normal controls. A normal rat never makes the scraping movements for piling up the nest wall before enough material for this is at hand, and even less does a normal rat execute the "upholsterer movements" with its forefeet, by which the inside surface of the nest is patted smooth, before the nest has an inside surface. The experimental animals often exhibited the movements for piling up the nest wall and for upholstering after only one or two shreds of paper had been brought in and, left lying flat on the floor, were not even touched as these motor patterns were performed. One got the impression that the high intensity of the nest-building activity was partially at fault for the topsy-turvy and disordered way in which the movements tumbled out; but gradually, after they had been provided with nest material for a longer period, the obligatory sequence of the single movements righted itself among the experimental animals until each became ordered in the completely normal way.

Through this non-disruptive experiment undertaken by Eibl-Eibesfeldt, an experiment demanding extensive knowledge of animals, we learn a great deal that is by no means confined to questions concerning the innate, but which is much more relevant to an understanding of the processes of learning itself. That after a short time the rats stopped performing in the air those movements meant for piling up the nest wall and for upholstering can be due only to a conditioning process during which the *reafference*, that is, the feedback from stimuli which are self-produced through execution of the motor pattern, has a positive conditioning or an avoidance conditioning effect. Apparently it is "rewarding" for a rat, when piling up the nest wall and when upholstering the inside of the nest, to receive the teleonomically adequate stimulus combination and, very probably, it is not at all satisfying if, when executing these movements, the phylogenetically programmed "expectation" of extero- and proprioceptor stimulus configurations remains unfulfilled.

No generalizing prediction is possible concerning where the learning processes of such systems of behavior patterns are located, nor in what way, organizing and adjusting, they are programmed to interact with the material of innate movement and reaction patterns. In the bone-burying behavior of a young dog, for example, the sequence of actions is apparently phylogenetically prescribed; what effects positive conditioning are, apparently, the reafferences received through digging in earth and, perhaps also, in a later phase of the learning process, the recovery of the buried booty.

We can formulate five rules that, in the conduct of experiments involving the withholding of experience, must be strictly followed.

1. What the experiment can tell us is only that a particular element of behavior does not need to be learned.
2. The experimenter must possess extensive and exact knowledge of the action system of the animal species being tested in order to be able to recognize incomplete fragments of behavior patterns which, through the exclusion of learning processes, have been deprived of their normal interconnections with other elements of behavior. Only by means

of such knowledge can the role of the learning process be ascertained and its ontogeny studied.

3. The experimenter must know precisely that stimulus situation which, in a normal animal, releases the behavior pattern being studied, otherwise he may mistake behavior deficiencies that are caused by a momentary absence of stimuli for the consequences of the preceding withholding of experience (Riess 1954).

4. The experimenter must have an extensive amount of experience with the bearing, carriage, posture, and comportment of healthy specimens of the species investigated, and must have a good "clinical eye" for the pathological consequences of an inadequate condition or a faulty constitution, especially for the pathological loss of intensity in particular motor patterns.

5. When experimenting with an animal reared under conditions involving the withholding of experience, one must always begin first with the simplest stimulus situation possible because the learning processes of an animal reared under conditions of withheld experience often take place with such lightning-like speed at the first presentation of any object that afterwards one does not know which of the proffered attributes was responsible for the innate response.

10. The Relatively Entirety-Independent Component

Fortunately for our analytical endeavors, the Koehlerian definition of the entirety as a system of universal interrelationships does not correspond completely to some systems and some system parts. There are, so to speak, pieces in the fabric of every organism that are comparatively rigid and unalterable inclusions in the causal network of the rest of the system. Because of this, and as an example, the finished feather of a bird is no longer influenced by the causal network of the entirety; it is a "dead" element in the atomistic sense. In a restricted sense the same is also true for many skeletal elements, at least in their completed condition. Neither in form nor in function are these parts of the whole substantially influenced by the entirety but, on their part, they influence the form and function of the entire system in a vital and decisive way. They thus stand in a *unidirectional* causal relationship to the entirety. We call them the *relatively entirety-independent components*.

An incorporation of the modifying word "relative" in the definition of such components is necessary because such components exist in almost every imaginable transitional form. There are those which are absolutely independent and stand in a purely one-sided causal relationship to the system, and there are those which, during their ontogeny, are plastic and pliable and subject to the influence of the entirety—as are the bones of a vertebrate. Examples of the borderline case, of a truly and absolutely entirety-independent component, are difficult to find; even the famous half ascidian that, as is known, develops from one half of the ovum split during its two-cell stage, is still covered with epidermis on that side from which the other half is missing, something that would not be so normally.

The discovery of a relatively entirety-independent component presents, within the immeasurably complex framework of the organic system, a most welcome point of departure for causal analysis: such a component can, without committing too gross a methodological error, be isolated. In addition, for relatively independent components one can also predict that in the course of the analysis, if not exclusively then at least more often than not, they will appear as cause rather than as effect. For this reason, in research and in theory the rigid structure always represents the Archimedean point from which the investigation proceeds.

Every text on anatomy begins with a description of the skeleton and, in like manner, for research done on behavior, it was from a base of certain *not modifiable* capacities of the central nervous system that analyses and comparative studies of behavior were legitimately launched. The discovery of the reflex process crystallized into the established focal point for the development of the physiology of the central nervous system; the discovery of the conditioned reaction opened the way for the founding of the Pavlovian school of reflexology and for the development of behaviorism. Both of these, of course, succumbed to the error of explanatory monism. Finally, as was cited in the introduction and will, in a later section, be discussed with more thoroughness, the discovery of the fixed action pattern or instinctive movement by C. O. Whitman (1898) and O. Heinroth (1910) provided the Archimedian point on which the comparative study of behavior has been built.

The analytical possibilities which are thrown open through the discovery of a relatively entirety-independent component make it all too easy, sometimes, to forget that the methodology used when concentrating on an isolate is legitimate only for that component under consideration; the researcher must remain ready to return to the otherwise obligatory methodology of analysis along a broad front, that is, to considerations of the entire network of amboceptory causal relationships, once he has gone beyond the boundaries of the fixed element.

Chapter III
The Fallacies of Non-System-Oriented Methods

1. Atomism

The sequence of research steps that has just been discussed is prescribed for us by the complex interacting structural framework of all living systems. The more complex a living system is, that much more strictly must the sequence of research steps be followed. But when dealing with simpler systems, and particularly with inanimate objects, the sequence need not be so strict. Let us assume that the Martian whom we have already used as an example has the task of analyzing a clock with a pendulum. It is possible to imagine that after he has understood the teleonomy of the object and has gone on to observe more about the speed relationships of one to twelve between the clock's two hands, as well as the oscillations of the pendulum, he would be capable, independently, of reinventing the mechanism of the pendulum clock. Provided he knows the laws of the lever and of the pendulum, not all that much inventiveness is required; and if he has a fair amount of luck, our Martian will, in fact, hit upon the same mechanism that the earthly clock-maker brought into use.

That procedure followed for reconstructing a complex system on the basis of its observed performance and from known general lawfulnesses *without examining its structure* is described as *atomistic*.

As our example indicates, atomism is by no means doomed to failure in principle. It merely represents a research strategy which promises that much less success the more complicated is the system to be analyzed. An organic system together with its capacities is understandably much more difficult to invent than is a pendulum clock. Nevertheless, there exist several organic functions that have been invented by technicians prior to their having been comprehended by biologists. Thus, for example, it is somewhat humiliating for us, as biologists, that the immense importance of the self-regulating circulatory processes of homeostasis was first fully appreciated after such mechanisms had been devised by control technicians. Even in such cases where the complexity of the system seems to indicate that an independent construction of all of its structural and internal relationships is hopeless, the atomistic approach can achieve something of value through providing a conceptual model that allows us, at least to a certain extent, to estimate the number of single functions to postulate.

2. Explanatory Monism

While atomism as such does by no means always represent a research strategy which is false in principle, explanatory monism is always and under all circumstances a fallacy. Although explanatory monism and atomism are often found in combination, especially among researchers who think "technomorphically," they must still be thoroughly differentiated. While the atomistic researcher is not at all blind to the fact that in the system he is examining many very different subsystems can be involved, each of which responds to its own lawfulnesses, the explanatory monist arbitrarily clutches a single part of the entirety of a living system and, using a simple research methodology that is readily at hand for determining its lawfulnesses, tries to understand the overall systemic function through the lawfulnesses of this single, arbitrarily selected part, without bothering about the other structures which form equally important parts of the systemic whole. In order to illustrate the error of this way of doing research, I return again to the Martian and to the automobile. This creature would become guilty of explanatory monism if, after isolating a particular mechanical part—a bolt and the nut that belongs to it, for example—he then turned his back on the remainder of the system and attempted to resynthesize the entirety from these two easily isolated parts. There are highly reputed schools of psychology whose members obstinately persist in this methodological error by claiming that that mechanism which enables the higher animals to learn through experience is the only explanatory principle on the basis of which all animal and human behavior can be understood.

The noteworthy partial successes which are attained through this limited (and I use that word in its most literal sense) approach can be explained by the fact that just this kind of "learning apparatus" has evolved in analogous ways in quite varied organisms and is, at the same time, a good example of that kind of partial system which can be described and defined as a relatively entirety-independent component.

3. Operationalism and Explanatory Monism of the Behaviorist School

Nowadays a majority of civilized people do most of their day's work with objects that can be and have been made by man. Most people have virtually nothing whatever to do with living organisms and have forgotten how to deal with them. Worst of all, they have lost the respect that is due to all that humans are unable to make themselves. On the other hand, they have an exaggerated esteem that borders on veneration for their own technical products and for the sciences of physics and chemistry which contribute to their manufacture. This attitude with regard to the so-called exact sciences is indubitably inspired by the impressive gain of power which humanity has acquired through analytical science—notwithstanding the fact that this power has persistently proved to be the very opposite of beneficial.

Because these exact sciences (often grouped together and called "big science") are based on analytical mathematics, many people assess the "exactitude" and, with it, the value of every scientific result by that proportion which mathematical operations have contributed toward achieving it. In consequence, a surprising number of people, even including scientists, regard counting and measuring as the only legitimate sources of knowledge. Therefore they try to understand mathematically the whole universe and everything that is in it. In other words, they approach the universe as if humans did not possess any cognitive capacities beyond those of counting, measuring, and calculating.

It should be emphasized that the physicist himself is very far from thus limiting his own cognitive functions. No less a scientist than Werner Heisenberg (1969) has pointed out that the laws of logic and mathematics are not inherent to the extra-subjective universe surrounding us but, quite the contrary, are inherent in one particular cognitive function of man which, although it is by no means the only one, is a very great help to our understanding of nature. The universe, he has said, cannot calculate, but it allows itself to be calculated. Heisenberg has certainly not underrated the cognitive function of gestalt perception. He has called it "intuition," but he certainly recognizes its indispensability.

In atomic physics and in the study of those minute particles which, at the present state of our knowledge, defy division, the physicist enters regions where most cognitive functions fail, regions where even the categories and the forms of ideation that Immanuel Kant regarded as aprioristic and indispensable prove unable to help further scientific progress. The evident realities of space and time come to nothing and the physicist has to deal with phenomena that can neither be described nor visualized. They can, therefore, be defined only by means of the operations which produce them. Because these operations are the only way by which the scientist can acquire knowledge concerning these realities, and because they can be defined only by these operations, P. W. Bridgeman (1958) has called their conceptualization *operational*. Practically all of the concepts and the terminology used in atomic physics are of this kind.

The reason physicists use operational methods and conceptualizations is not because they regard them as particularly "exact" or "scientific"; they use them simply because they have no other methods and conceptualizations at their disposal for work in the field under discussion. If and when, in everyday life, the physicist has to deal with objects that can be approached by the usual mechanisms of cognition, he uses these and would not dream of resorting to operational methods. If we should ask a physicist to repair some electronic apparatus built by someone else, he would certainly take the machine apart and determine which elements had been used in putting it together and how they were wired. Like any normal human being, he would begin his research by investigating structure. He would not dream of inventing a special operation, nor would he stick to it as if it were the only salvation.

As has been explained, the more complex the organic system under investigation, the more indispensable is a description of structures, and, with this, the more multifarious are its subsystems' structures and their interactions. The most complex systems known to science are the central nervous systems of higher animals and man, and, in particular, the interactions between many such individual systems: in other words, the supra-individual system of a society. Paradoxically, in behavioral science, in psychology and, most amazingly, quite particularly in sociology there prevails a fashionable tendency to ape atomic physics. The word aping is used intentionally because it means imitating the behavior of others without understanding their motivations. The physicist using the method of the generalizing reduction discussed in One/I/1 investigates structures not for their own sake, but in order to abstract the laws prevailing in them and to reduce these laws to more general ones. Operational methods are resorted to only in those cases where there are no structures—when all other cognitive functions have failed. The physicist neither believes that structures are negligible nor that their investigation is dispensable. Least of all does the physicist despise the multiplicity of various cognitive functions.

All of these errors are committed by a great number of psychologists and sociologists. They obviously cherish the hope of finding a shortcut to an understanding of the most complicated organic systems by operational and statistical methods. In other words, they hope to circumvent the weary and demanding task of gaining any causal understanding of the physiological machinery whose function *is* animal and human behavior.

At present the most consistent representative of this school is B. F. Skinner (1938, 1971), whose "empty organism doctrine" has exerted a tremendous influence on American as well as on European psychologists. His operational method is confined to a study, by statistical means, of the contingencies of reinforcement, that is, of the changes wrought in animal and human behavior by means of reward and punishment, but chiefly by reward alone. No thought is given to what it is that is being changed during the course of this process. A great number of present-day scientists believe that this method of approach is not only scientifically legitimate but actually the sole legitimate method for approaching the problems of behavior.

If this belief has been partially sustained, it is because all of those creatures so studied have, independently of each other, evolved physiological mechanisms that react in the same way to the experimental operations chosen by behaviorists. As will be explained in Part Three of this book, all of the phyla of animals which have evolved a centralized nervous system have hit on the "invention" of feeding back to the mechanism initiating a behavior the consequences of its performance. In the case of biological success, this feedback results in reinforcement; in the case of failure, it has an extinguishing effect. The enormous teleonomic advantages of this kind of apparatus explain the fact that cephalopods (squids and octopuses) and arthropods (insects, crustacea, and spiders) all possess virtually identical capabilities for learning by success and failure.

The great scientific results attained by behaviorists are not due to the correctness of the empty-organism doctrine, but, paradoxically, to the very thing whose existence this doctrine denies, that is, to the highly specific analogous structures convergently evolved in practically all organisms possessing a centralized nervous system. Without the least knowledge of convergent adaptation, the behaviorist school had the very good luck to strike, in very different organisms, strictly analogous mechanisms and, in addition, to hit upon one which represents a "relatively system-independent element" in the sense explained in One/II/10. The process of learning by reinforcement can, therefore, be experimentally isolated without creating a dangerous source of error.

Learning by reinforcement plays a highly important role in the life of higher animals and humans, and for this reason the behaviorist school has achieved really great breakthroughs. It is necessary to emphasize this here because ethologists are unjustly accused of denying any merit that might be attributed to behaviorist research. What we reproach behaviorists for is certainly not what they do; they do what they do in the most excellent manner. Our criticism refers only to their belief that there is nothing else in behavior to investigate. Most behaviorists shy away from investigating anything that is not directly connected with learning by reinforcement. Their program excludes even the investigation of the many other kinds of learning processes. In Part Three of this book these very different mechanisms will be discussed.

What behaviorists exclude from the narrow circle of their interest is not only other learning processes, but simply everything that is not contained in the process of learning by reinforcement—and this neglected remainder is neither more nor less than the whole of the remaining organism! The physiological mechanism achieving learning by success is so similar in all of the various animals mentioned above, that not only the same method, but very often even the same apparatus is applicable. What remains uninvestigated is all that makes an octopus an octopus, a pigeon a pigeon, a rat a rat, or a man a man, and, most important of all, what makes a healthy man a healthy man, and an unhealthy man a patient.

When I. P. Pavlov was performing his classic experiments on the conditioned salivating reflex of dogs, he hog-tied his experimental animals in such a way that they had, within their behavioral repertory, no other choice than to salivate or not to salivate. This was completely legitimate as long as the experimenter remained conscious of the fact that he was investigating an artificially isolated part of a system, exactly as a physiologist does who performs experiments of excitation conduction within a bundle of neurites cut out of the sciatic nerve of a frog. When, on the other hand, behaviorists put experimental pigeons into an opaque box preventing perception of any information except that of when and how often the pigeon presses on a key, I cannot help feeling that they do not *want* to see the many other things undertaken by the animal, because they are afraid that what they see might undermine their belief in their own explanatory monism. The ideological reasons for this are, however, no subject for a textbook on ethology.

Chapter IV
The Comparative Method

The first four sections of this chapter are addressed to psychologists and other non-biologists who may not be familiar with the facts of evolution. Biologists, particularly zoologists and paleontologists, should not only skip the first four sections, but are kindly asked to do so. This presentation of the sources of our knowledge concerning evolution is extremely simplified and to an extent that, to the initiated, may seem impermissible. What is important for ethologists is contained in sections 5 through 14.

1. Reconstruction of Genealogies

When we speak of "comparative" anatomy or "comparative" ethology, the adjective has a very special connotation. It does not mean simply a comparison of the similarities and differences that exist, among different species of animals, between the bodily forms or the behaviors—as was misleadingly assumed by the scientists who appropriated the word for use in the title of the *Journal of Comparative Psychology*. Comparative science is the attempt to reconstruct, from the distribution of similarities and dissimilarities among living creatures, the paths along which their evolution has proceeded. It is necessary to discuss this method here in some detail because we are indebted to it for the basic discovery that gave rise to the science of ethology. Ethological research started from the fact that there are certain sequences of movements which are as reliable as characteristics of species, genera, and higher taxonomic units as are any of the morphological characteristics used in comparative anatomy. The concept of *homology* is equally applicable to them.

This fact alone settles a dispute which, for purely ideological reasons, is still going on: the age-old nature–nurture controversy. The same factual basis which makes evolution a certainty proves that the form of homologizeable motor patterns is programmed in the genes exactly as morphological characteristics are. It is necessary to state and restate this banal fact because, amazingly, some authors still maintain that the two concepts of the phylogenetically programmed and of the acquired portions of animal and human behavior are not only dispensable, but that they are actually false. These two concepts are no more false, nor are they any more dispensable to ethological research than are the concepts of the genotype and the phenotype to genetics, population dynamics, or sociobiology.

Whence do we obtain the knowledge that all living creatures were not, as the noun etymologically implies, created in their present forms but have obtained these through the long-lasting process which we call evolution? If one puts this question to erudite non-biologists, their answers are very frequently that we owe our knowledge of evolution to the study of fossils which, enclosed in successive layers of the earth's crust, furnish documentary evidence of the different stages through which the development of life has passed on our planet. They do indeed furnish proof, but they are not the unique, nor even the most important source of our knowledge. Even without them the main facts of life's history upon earth could be proved without reasonable doubt.

The German mind is very orderly and it is probably due to the influence of German idealism that, toward the end of the seventeenth and at the beginning of the eighteenth century, very sophisticated attempts were made to bring some sort of order into the apparently chaotic multiplicity of life forms. One example to such attempts is the "natural system" invented by Johann Jakob Kaup (1854) who tried to represent the relationships of living bird species in a diagram consisting of pentagons and pentagrams. He explained the choice of this particular figure by saying that the "sacredness" of the number five was derived from the number of our senses. As shown in Figure 5, some of the angles of the pentagrams had to remain empty; Kaup explained this by assuming that the groups of birds necessary to fill these gaps were living, still undiscovered, in some remote countries. That was in 1854.

It is remarkable that abstruse theories such as this one could be seriously proposed more than three-quarters of a century after the German zoologist, Simon Peter Pallas, had written:

Among all other diagrammatical representations of the system of living bodies, it would probably be best to visualize the system as a tree which, right at its root, divides to form a trunk consisting of the most primitive animals and plants, thus forming an animal and a vegetable branch, although both occasionally tend to come very close to one another. The first branch, orig-

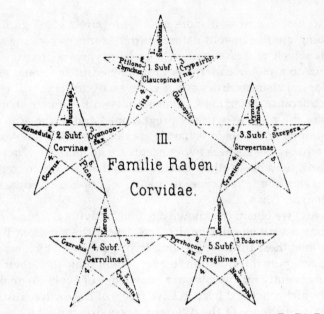

Figure 5. Johann Jakob Kaup's pentagram, 1854. (Stresemann, E.: *Die Entwicklung der Ornithologie.*)

inating with the shell-less animals and rising up to the fishes, after having given off a great side-branch leading to the insects, would then lead on to the amphibia. And in the same manner, this branch would have to carry the four-legged animals at the height of the tree's top, and it would have given forth, just below that, an almost equally large branch for the brids.

This quotation, translated here from the original German, was taken from Erwin Stresemann's important book, *Die Entwicklung der Ornithologie* (1951). Stresemann comments on this passage: "With these few sentences, young Pallas has expressed a dawning idea of the real relationship between living organisms. He was the first to choose the image of a tree to express this relationship."

2. Criteria of Taxa

The image of the tree which Pallas saw with the vision of genius can be constructed in a manner that is as simple as it is free from hypothesis. I choose for its construction the taxon of the chordate animals (Chordata) because the vertebrates which form its most important branch are well known to most readers.

We represent the innumerable kinds of animal life forms by vertical lines and connect them by horizontal stripes which represent characteristics common to the animals thus enclosed (Figure 6). I restrict myself to a small number of characteristics and try to choose those which are either

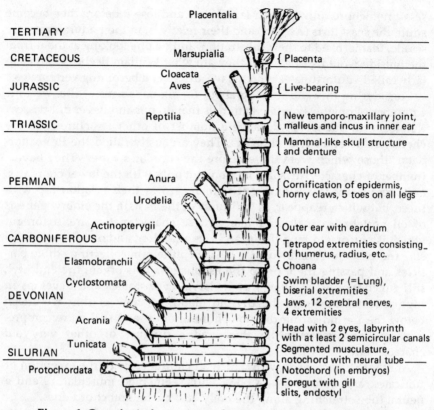

Figure 6. Genealogical tree. An explanation is contained in the text.

easy to describe or are so well known that description is unnecessary. The construction I am going to undertake becomes most convincing when it is executed as a three-dimensional model for which stiff wires are used for the animal life forms and tape is used for the characteristics tying some of them together. To each of the tapes a label is attached indicating the morphological characteristic it represents. These bindings are applied to arrange the great number of forms of chordates in a certain order; this is determined by the number of animal forms each characteristic embraces. The only way in which I might be accused of smuggling a hypothesis into my construction (after having promised that it would contain none) is this: I am arranging the characteristics most generally shared at the lowest level. Otherwise the construction of the tree, which so marvelously fits Pallas's vision, would be growing upside down, as do some corals from the roof of a marine cave. However, it still would be a tree.

So we begin to tie together the whole bundle of Chordata forms, with the characteristic that is common to all of them, the chorda dorsalis or notochord, which is the primitive precursor of the backbone. Even at this early stage we encounter a difficulty: there are some animals which possess a notochord only in their larval state and lose it before they become adult; the seasquirts (Ascidia) and their relatives, in their adult forms, are sessile, that is, fixed to their substratum, and no one looking at them from the outside would suspect that they are what William Beebe (1938) jocularly called "unfortunates which have just missed becoming vertebrates."

Considering this and looking about for similar forms of life, we find a number of obviously related animals that do not and never did possess a notochord, but which do have a number of other structures that are characteristic of all true chordata. They are justly called the Protochordata, "those which were there before the chordates were." They have a number of characteristics in common, not only with the lower chordates, and, because of this, significant with regard to their relationship with these, but which reappear, as indicators of the past, in the embryogenesis of all vertebrates including man. These characteristics are: a foregut which is perforated by gill slits and acts as a filter, and on whose ventral side there is a furrow lined with ciliary epithelium collecting edible particles and passing them on to the esophagus. This organ, the endostyl, still functions in the same way in larval cyclostomes and develops in higher vertebrates into the thyroid gland. In view of this, we attach below the tie indicating the notochord another and still more comprehensive band representing this—and a number of other very old characteristics.

Another characteristic with which all chordates, with the exception of tunicates, are endowed, is a body with segmented musculature and a neural tube stretching along the body, just as the notochord does.

Searching for further old and widespread properties, it strikes us that vertebrates have a head with two eyes and other sensory organs, such as an inner ear with semicircular canals serving equilibration. And to the surprise of some non-zoologists, we must here point to a curious animal which possesses a front and a rear end, as well as many fish-like characteristics, but has no head. This creature, "fishy" in every sense of the word, is Amphioxus, belonging to the sub-phylum Acrania—the headless. Their notochord runs forward right into the tip, and their neural tube ends at the front end without any sort of brain-like structure. So we must allow the acrania to diverge from the remaining trunk of the vertebrate phylum before binding our big bundle of animals together with a new band that indicates a head with two eyes and a labyrinth with (at least two) semicircular canals—and other important organs such as a brain.

It seems self-evident to most people that an animal with a head, a mouth, and two eyes should also possess an upper and a lower jaw, two pairs of limbs, and other well-known organs, such as two nostrils. Before inserting the symbolic connecting band representing these characteristics, we must consider a small but important group which does not possess them: the "round-mouths," or Cyclostomata. They do indeed have a head with two perfectly vertebrate-like eyes, but they completely lack limbs. They have fish-like gill slits and a large circular mouth with teeth all around it, but no jaws. Unlike all other vertebrates, they have only two semicircular canals in their labyrinth and only ten cranial nerves instead of twelve. A very significant ancestral characteristic merits mentioning: the foregut in the *larva* of some cyclostomes is constructed exactly as that of many protochordates and tunicates, and performs the same function of filtering the nutrients that are caught and conveyed to the esophagus by way of the endostyle which, in the later ontogeny of this species, is metamorphosed into a gland with internal secretion, the thyroid gland, which we still possess.

All the remaining vertebrates, the gnathostomes or jawed-mouths, are united into a well-defined group by having upper and lower jaws, two pairs of limbs, twelve cranial nerves, and other characteristics in common. This group includes all those vertebrates that are familiar to everyone.

A superficial glance at this group would seem to reveal a division into two main branches, the fishes and the four-legged animals—the latter, of course, including birds. However, our method of bracketing life forms according to common characteristics shows a dichotomy in quite another place. Older taxonomists assumed that a differentiation of true osseus tissue was the more modern acquisition, while a cartilaginous skeleton represented the primary state. For this reason we were taught at school that the sharks (Elasmobranchii) were the ancestors of all other vertebrates. This was an error. According to more recent discoveries (Jarvik 1968), for example, the very oldest gnathostomes known to science possessed true bones and very probably are the ancestors of higher vertebrates, while the sharks and rays represent an independent side branch.

The remaining taxon, that of the bony fish (Osteichthyes), is characterized by one important organ: the swim bladder which appears either in the guise of a hydrostatic or in that of a respiratory organ. Very probably the respiratory function was the original one and this would argue for the taxon having orginated in fresh water that was not too rich in oxygen. Fin rays are also common to all these fishes, although the base of the fin is shaped in various ways; the biserial form, as shown in Figure 7, was probably the precursor of the fin of most of the fish living now. In order to keep the diagram of Figure 6 as simple as possible, we can tie all Osteichthyes together as one branch containing three classes: first, the crossopterygians—today represented only by the famous coelacanth latimeria; second, the lungfishes (Dipneusti); and third, the teleosts, which designates all the other fishes.

Among the creatures which, externally, must have looked very much like the crossopterygians or, for that matter, like the Australian lungfish (*Neoceratodus*), a very particular characteristic is to be found: the inner nostril, or choana. This characteristic ties together these old fishes (Rhipidistians) with all recent four-footed land animals. Some members of this group, besides having choanae (nostrils opening into the mouth cavity), also possess an arrangement of skeletal elements in their biserial limbs

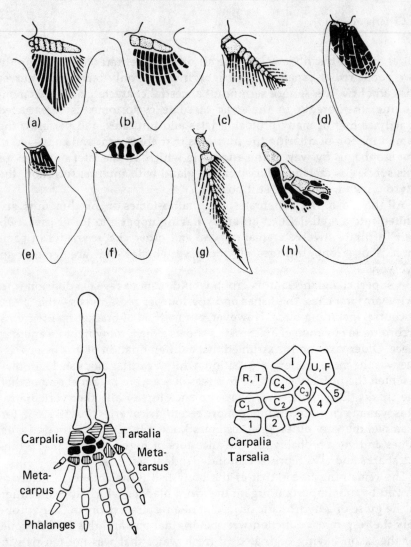

Figure 7. *Above:* Pectoral fins of various fishes. (*a*) Cladoselachii, primitive shark with parallel arrangement of radials; (*b*) Isurus, highly developed shark with small fin base; the basalia (dotted) are merged into three large cartilage elements: Pro-, Meso-, and Metapterygium; (*c*) Xenacanthus, paleozoic shark, with basalia forming an axis of the fin; (*d*) Cornubiscus (Actinopterygii, Palaeoniscoidea); (*e*) Amia (holostei), the radials are arranged parallel; (*f*) Serranus (teleostei) with reduced fin skeleton; (*g*) Neoceratodus (lungfishes), biserial archipterygium; (*h*) Eusthenopteron, fossil crossopterygii, arrangement of the fin skeletal part already resembles that of the tetrapoda. *Below:* Tetrapod extremity showing the carpus (wrist) or the tarsus (ankle). Labels at the left pertain to fore extremities, those at the right to hind extremities. *Carpus:* R Radiale, U Ulnare, the proximal wrist bones; T Tibiale, F Fibulare, the proximal ankle bones; I Intermedium; C_1–C_4 Centralia; 1–5 Carpalia (hand) or Tarsalia (foot). (Remane, Storch, Welsch: *Kurzes Lehrbuch der Zoologie.*)

that is undoubtedly a foreshadowing of the organization of tetrapod limbs. In our diagram, concerned exclusively with phyletic descent, it is unavoidable that seemingly non-homogeneous taxa, such as the choanatae which comprise fish-like forms as well as primates, are also presented. The rhipidistia are not represented in the diagram; they ought to be situated between the ray-finned fish (Actinopterygii) and the newts (Urodela).

All the remaining vertebrates are plainly characterized by the possession of four legs, with an obviously homologous skeleton, consisting of humerus, radius, ulna, carpus, metacarpus, and phalanges in the forelegs and corresponding bones in the hind legs. Among the animals with limbs of this kind we are again forced to mark a dichotomy because some of these creatures have ears with eardrums and other subservient auditory organs, while some do not. Among the amphibians, only the frogs have ears; ears are lacking in salamanders (Urodela). These animals comprise a rather mysterious group because one cannot be quite sure whether they have lost their auditory organs or whether these were "invented" after a division of the two amphibian branches.

However that may be, all other tetrapods (four-footed animals) do possess ears with eardrums and inner ears constructed much like our own. In respect to inner ear construction, a frog and a man are more similar to one another than a frog is similar to a salamander, their other similarities notwithstanding.

A much stronger cornification of the epidermis characterizes all the rest of the tetrapods; a concomitant characteristic is the claw which is also formed of horny substance. The horny skin makes these animals more independent of water; they are all distinctly terrestrial. As a result of this the eggs must also be made more independent of moisture: all the life forms united by the characteristic of skin cornification and by the possession of horny claws either lay large eggs with yolks and albumens, or they bear live young. In either case the embryo develops a very special organ serving respiration as well as nutrition, the so-called amnion, which grows out of the urinary bladder. For this reason the entire group is called the amniota and it comprises reptiles, mammals, and birds.

The remainder of our genealogical tree is well known, but complicated, and for our purposes can be presented here only in a simplified and, as a consequence, somewhat inexact manner. A mysterious transformation of the maxillary joint is characteristic of some reptiles and of all mammals. The bones originally forming the joint of the jaw, that is, the articular bone and the quadrate bone, are disengaged from the mandible and change their function into that of auditory organs: they are turned into the hammer (malleus) and the anvil (incus) in the inner ear, while an altogether new temporo-maxillary joint is developed. This new invention is common to some extinct reptiles and to all mammals.

Leaving out of consideration the further branching off of reptiles and birds, we turn to the mammals. All of them possess the auditory ossicles derived from what originally were the bones of the maxillary articulation already mentioned; all have hair with sebaceous glands from which mammary glands have evolved. Most of them give birth to live young, but some of them lay eggs. Those which lay eggs do not suckle their young because they have no teats, but they do nurse their babies after hatching them by means of incubation: the young feed from flat skin areas excreting milk. These animals, of which the Australian platypus (*Ornithorhynchus*) is the best known, have a cloaca, that is, a common opening through which urine, genital products, and faeces are discharged, exactly as reptiles and birds have. Deceptively, these "cloacata" also have a bill and no teeth, which made naive taxonomists regard them as a "missing link" between mammals and birds.

All other mammals bear live young, but are divided into two sharply distinct groups on the basis of the stage of development at which these young are delivered and by the way the embryos are nourished. A vast majority of surviving mammalian forms belong to the group of Placentalia (or Eutheria). The embryo develops a special alimentary organ, the placenta, which permits it to absorb nutrients from the mother's body. This makes it possible to postpone the date of birth considerably and thus to produce more completely developed offspring. The comparatively small group of non-placentalian mammals, the marsupials, have to deliver their young at a much less developed stage and at a much smaller size. The neonate of the largest marsupial, the great red kangaroo (*Macropus rufus*), is the size of a bean; that of the blue whale (*Sibbaldus musculus*) is six meters long. Everyone knows the size of a young calf or deer at birth. The neonate marsupial, which looks very much like a placentalian embryo, enters the pouch (marsupium) of its mother and finds the teat, whereupon the epithelium of its lips fuses with that of the teat so as to form a hermetic connection through which milk is pumped into the baby's intestinal tract. In a manner of speaking, the babies attach themselves to a secondary umbilical cord.

Dispensing with a more detailed description of the rather well-known part of the genealogical tree comprising mammals and birds, we can proceed to the question concerning what conclusions can be drawn from the fact that the immense multiplicity of living creatures, by a method devoid of any preconceived hypothesis, can be arranged to form a diagram which automatically and without any constraint assumes the form of a tree. This diagram could be extended and vastly enriched by adding an immense number of further characteristics that would, by fitting in without difficulties or contradictions, bring the probability of the conclusions to be drawn near certainty. Even without the additional testimony of fossils, it can only be regarded as an historical fact that evolution has taken place. Historians would consider it an affront if somebody were to demand of them further proof supporting their "theory" that Caesar or Charlemagne had existed. Evolution is better documented than that!

3. The Hypothesis of Growth

Wherever in nature we encounter the form of a tree, we automatically assume that it has grown. A plant, a colony of corals, a tree, the antlers of a deer, all have started their existence as a single sprout which, growing longer, has divided into a number of branches. Even the ice crystals ornamenting our window panes in cold weather have done so. From the facts which have been mentioned and from an immense number of facts not mentioned, we deduce a hypothesis explaining their relationship: we assume that the characteristics which are common to a certain number of living forms are those which their common ancestor possessed. We say that these characteristics are *homologous*.

The particular form of our genealogical tree of chordates is explained by the assumption that all of them are descended from creatures possessing the characteristics identified with the lowest crossband in our diagram. The term "descended," by the way, is quite misleading; "ascending" would be, on the whole, much better. Furthermore, we assume that if only a small number of forms possess a certain characteristic, then this represents a new accomplishment in evolution, a new "invention" achieved by the method of random genetic change and natural selection. It is the coming-into-existence of something new that is symbolized by the growth of the tree in our diagram. This assumption is only reliable when the new characteristic is not brought about by mere simplification, let alone by the disintegration of a structure which already existed. In fact the "newness" must be documented by reliable evidence proving that this particular characteristic has originated by complication and differentiation and as a systemic property of the organisms that did not exist previously. This proof can indeed be proffered and found to be beyond any reasonable doubt whenever structures that are characteristic of only a special branch of the genealogical tree can be traced back to other structures that were simpler and were found in a greater number of forms at a lower level. Examples of such structures are the tetrapod limb evolving from the rhipidistian fin (Figure 7h) and the bird's feather evolving from the reptile's scale.

Considering all that has been said in this and in the preceding section, the growth of the genealogical tree—evolution—would be a near certainty on the basis of comparison alone, even without the additional testimony of fossils.

4. Documentation Through Fossils

If our interpretation of the distribution of older and of more recent characteristics is correct, the more widely distributed characteristics should appear first, in the lower, that is, in the older strata of our planet's crust.

The more special characteristics should make their appearance in the same sequence of geologic levels as they do in the levels of our tree diagram which, constructed on a basis of comparison, has automatically made them appear—and indeed they do!

There is no fossil documentation recording the evolution of protochordates. Because none of these animals possesses any skeletal elements hard enough for fossilization, this is to be expected. During the Silurian a considerable number of fossil fish appear, all of which belong to the cyclostomes, as very thorough investigations by Stensiö (1927) have revealed. The forms of these fishes' bodies are not always like those of lampreys or other modern cyclostomes, all of which have evolved, in adaptation to their special ecological niches, an elongated, eel-like shape. The old cyclostomes varied in form; some were spindle-shaped and probably led a free-swimming life; others, like the cephalaspids, were dorsoventrally flattened and heavily armoured with osseous plates and certainly living on the bottom of the sea. None possessed limbs or jaws. Very probably some or most of them lived by filtering nutrients from the water by means of the foregut, as the protochordates as well as the larvae of some extant cyclostomes do.

Gnathostomes, that is, fish posssessing jaws (palatoquadrate and mandible), arise during the Silurian, but unambiguously recognizable fossils are not found before the Devonian. Sharks and ray-finned fish appear approximately at the same level. According to Nelson, the Acanthodii are to be regarded as the most primitive gnathostomes, but opinions differ as to whether they are more closely related to the sharks (Elasmobranchii) or to the bony fish (Actinopterygii). The first fossil fish clearly belonging to this group show an unmistakable similarity to certain lungfishes (Ceratodiformes) as well as to the lobe-finned fishes (Crossopterygii) to which the famous coelocanth *Latimeria* also belongs. As early as the lower Devonian, the branches of sharks and ray-finned fishes (Actinopterygii) are clearly divided and, almost at the same time, the choanae are "invented" by the Rhipidistia. Among the Rhipidistia, *Osteolepis* hints at the origin of tetrapods through the form of its teeth, which are similar to those of amphibia, while the closely allied *Eusthenopteron* possess the limb skeleton shown in Figure 7h. Decisive steps of evolution often follow very quickly, one after another—which means within only a few million years.

One structural property of our hypothesis-free diagram will strike the attentive reader: few of the divisions result in two branches of equal thickness, that is, of an equal number of living representatives. The "invention" of jaws and limbs separates the very few still-living cyclostomes from all other vertebrates, that of the amnion gives origin to the host of reptiles, birds, and mammals, leaving behind the comparatively tiny group of amphibia. The only dichotomy which divides two approximately equivalent branches is the one between the fishes and the terrestrial tetrapods. The reason for this phenomenon is rather obvious: these two branches do not compete; the conquest of dry land by the tetrapods did not impair the chances for survival of the aquatic vertebrates.

In a majority of cases, however, the coming-into-existence of an unprecedented new physical organization, like that of the palatoquadrate with jaws, or of limbs, brought such overwhelming advantages to those which possessed them that those which did not succumbed to their competition. The obsolete forms occasionally became extinct; occasionally they succeeded in eking out modest existences in far-fetched ecological niches where they were exempt from competition with the more modern organisms. Lampreys and other surviving cyclostomes are an example of this success. They survive in the struggle for existence with the gnathostomes in a way analogous to that of sailing ships which still exist in coastal waters and for local trade, weakly competing with diesel engine motorboats.

An organ which has had an interesting evolutionary history is the swim bladder. The close similarity between the oldest actinopterygian (ray-finned) fishes such as *Cheirolepis* and contemporary crossopterygian (lobe-finned) fishes as well as lung fishes (Dipnoi) makes it probable that all these forms originated in fresh water that was not too rich in oxygen and which made an accessory respiratory organ desirable. Also the palaeoniscids, typical ray-finned fish of the periods following the Devonian, lived in fresh water. It is safe to assume that the swim bladder evolved first under the selection pressure of breathing and only later developed the function of a hydrostatic organ.

While the sharks (Elasmobranchii) have always been marine animals, the Actinopterygii conquered a place in the sea in spite of the elasmobranch's competition. They succeeded in doing so because the swim bladder permitted them to evolve a much more solid skeleton; without the help of the hydrostatic organ, such a skeleton would have increased their specific weight by too much. Also, they can twist their bodies to perform the undulating swimming movements common to chordates from the amphioxus upwards, with a much shorter "wave-length" than sharks can. This implies a tremendous increase in their propelling force. It is easily possible for a strong man to grasp and hold a shark the size of an adult arm, but just try this with a grouper (serranid) of the same size. The maximum speed attainable by a fish is, of course, directly proportional to the strength of its propulsion. It is easy to understand why the bony fish, on their return to the sea, found it easy to compete with sharks.

As early as during the late Devonian the vertebrates conquered "dry land," although they were certainly confined, at first, to rather moist areas. From this period we possess fossil documentation of bizarre forms intermediate between crossopterygians and amphibians, such as *Ichthyostega* which possessed typical tetrapod limbs but, at the same time, had a tail with a fish's caudal fin. The rhipidistian *Osteolepis* had true nostrils and choanae, as well as folded enamel layers on its teeth and a number of structural characters of the labyrinthodonts, amphibians which also make their first appearance during the Permian period.

During the Carboniferous, the epoch preceding the Permian, the division between amphibians and reptiles was accomplished. This division is not at first as sharply defined as it is between the living representatives of these two classes because the characteristics which came to distinguish them are not discernible in fossils and because they are not unequivocally distributed among the two classes. In the upper Carboniferous formations and in the lower Permian, a group of stegocephalians has been preserved which, in the structure of their skulls, closely resemble the first true reptiles—the cotylosaurians—but which, as juveniles, possessed a structure of the occipital region of the head clearly indicating that they were breathing through external gills—as many amphibians do during the larval stage. Nevertheless there is little doubt that the great innovations which made the Tetrapoda really independent of water and which were accomplished at the transition from the Carboniferous to the Permian, the cornification of the epidermis and the large egg having a water-impermeable shell and containing a large yolk and an embryo with an amnion, all represent "innovations" made during that eventful period.

Fossil documents show that the division of the reptiles into the two important branches, one leading to the birds and the other to the mammals, took place at a very early time, at the level of the cotylosaurians, which represent the most primitive of all true reptiles. The further evolution of the branch leading to reptiles and birds is complicated and concerns many extinct forms not familiar to non-zoologists, and will not be discussed further here. The group of pelycosaurians, originating in the upper Carboniferous and ending in the upper Triassic, evolved a gradually increasing number of characteristics foreshadowing mammals. In the Permian they gave rise to the therapsids, which resembled mammals very closely indeed with regard to the structure of the skull and particularly to that of the jaw articulation. They are found, in some 300 species, up to the lower Triassic.

The first remnants of true mammals are found in the upper Triassic. These remnants consist mainly of jaw bones and teeth which, because of their solidity, are the skeleton elements most likely to become fossilized. They clearly belong to mammals, yet they belong with equal unambiguity to neither the marsupials nor to the placentalians but very probably to common ancestors of both. It is certainly significant that these remnants of the earliest mammals are found in the same strata as those of the most mammal-like reptiles: in the upper Triassic of the Cape of Africa.

From this time onwards the mammals continued to lead an inconspicuous existence as small insectivores and externally shrew-like animals. They outlived the dinosaurians whose heyday lasted throughout the Jurassic and the Cretaceous. At the dawn of the Tertiary period the mammals suddenly proliferated and became the most successful group of terrestrial animals. Very probably this development was closely connected with the conquest of dry land by the flowering (phanerogamous) plants. The phanerogam's seed, enclosing a large store of nutrients and a comparatively large embryo, is curiously analogous to the amniote's egg. The rich source of food offered by the leaves and seeds of flowering plants offered innumerable opportunities for divergent adaptation.

Even the extremely limited selection of fossil documents referred to here should suffice to convince anybody that the "theory" of evolution is no longer a theory at all but plain history, and a history that is better documented than is any part of our own human history, either by means of the written word or through the testimony of old cultural relics. Never once has a fossil been found to indicate the existence of any animal at a lower level in the genealogical stratification than that in which its characteristics, according to the inferences to be drawn from our genealogical diagram, are expected to appear. And as will be remembered, the diagram was constructed without any hypothesis and on the exclusive base of a systematic evaluation of characteristics. In Figure 6, the horizontal lines corresponding to geological periods can be drawn in without ever leading to a contradiction between the deductions of comparative morphology and the findings of stratigraphical paleontology.

5. Homology and Its Criteria

For the purpose of comparative ethology, a very simple definition of homology is sufficient. This definition has already been stated in the Introductory History on page 3: Characters of two or more species are homologous when they owe their similarity to the common descent from ancestors possessing them. Adolf Remane (1952, 1959) has added a number of additional criteria serving to ascertain the homology of comparable organs in different species. As these have been conceived for the purpose of determining the homology of morphological structures, not all of them are applicable in the comparative study of behavior.

The first and, virtually, still the most important among Remane's criteria of homology is that of "special quality" (*spezielle Qualität*). This means that the homology of two structures is that much more certain the greater are the number of coinciding details both of them possess, the more complicated these details are, and the more precise their agreement. What has been said in One/II/3 about the cognitive functions of perception should explain that this criterion of special quality is not only accessible to direct observation but that, also, our gestalt perception is the main source of the knowledge on which assertions concerning the "special quality" of structures are based. Our direct perception is able to subsume, within one unmistakable quality, a greater number of details than any rational computation can. For this very simple reason any attempt at a "numerical taxonomy" is doomed to complete failure— which it well deserves because of the ridiculous epistemological error on which it is based. For reasons that are easily understood, the criterion of "special quality" plays an important role in the comparative study of behavior.

The second of Remane's criteria of homology is that of the position of a structural element in relation to the adjacent ones surrounding it. A bone in the skull of a vertebrate, for instance, can have become very small by a process of reduction and still remain recognizable through its relation to surrounding bones. With regard to behavior patterns, between which only a temporal relationship is possible, the criterion of position must be used with some caution. As the comparative study of courtship movements in dabbling ducks has shown, the same motor patterns can appear in different sequences or couplings in different species. The criterion of position would here be misleading. There are other instances, however, in which it is significant. The taxonomic dignity of criteria has to be assessed in much the same way as that of single characteristics, as shall be discussed in Section III/10.

The third of Remane's criteria of homology comprises the existence of transitional forms between two characteristics whose homology is to be ascertained. The fin skeleton of Eusthenopteron (Figure 7h) may serve as an example of a transitional form between the biserial fin skeleton of a crossopterygian (Figure 7g) and that of the tetrapod limb (Figure 9). As Wolfgang Wickler (1970) has emphasized, an assertion made on the basis of this criterion can, in some instances, be deduced from the correct use of the first two criteria of Remane. On the other hand, there are cases in which the existence of transitions can justify the assertion of homology even when the first two criteria are not applicable. A detailed series of transitions can prove the homology of characteristics which are neither qualitatively similar to one another nor positioned in a similar way. The criterion of transition is the more valuable the more certain the close relationship of the species concerned can be deduced from still other criteria. The homology of certain courtship patterns of Anatini, which are often qualitatively changed beyond recognition by the process of ritualization and which furthermore are in no way characterized by position, can still be ascertained with tolerable assurance exclusively on the basis of transitional forms.

6. The Number of Characteristics as a Criterion of Homology

Remane's criterion of "special quality" can be regarded from a quantitative point of view. The number of details, and the degree to which the coinciding characteristics of two living species are complicated, do not, after all, mean anything but the greater probability that both are indeed closely related to one another. Thus expressed, the criterion can, in a manner of speaking, be inverted. It is perfectly legitimate and correct to say: when two or more forms of life are found to agree in a very great number of characteristics and to be different from each other in but very few, it is safe to assume that the majority of characteristics are homologous and the few others are not. If, conversely, some creatures are similar to each other through only a very few characteristics, while each of them is tied to another group by a great number of characteristics, it is equally safe to assume that these few coinciding characteristics owe their existence to what is called convergent evolution—which will be discussed in the next section.

In the diagram of Figure 6, a loop is drawn around sharks, fish, amphibia, reptiles, birds, and mammals and is marked "four-limbed." It may have struck the attentive reader that some of the creatures thus entwined have *no* limbs. Moray eels among fish, gymnophionids among amphibia, slow-worms (Anguidae) among reptiles and, finally, snakes lack any kind of limb. By what right, if by any, do we assume that the limblessness of all these creatures is not a primary characteristic as it is in cyclostomes? Why do we classify each of them with another group of creatures that does have four limbs?

Our assertions are based on a very simple consideration of probabilities. If the lack of limbs in the four groups mentioned above were a primary feature, we should have to assume that a separate line of descent leads from the cyclostomes to each of these legless groups of animals. This is extremely unlikely because the moray is proved by innumerable other characteristics to be a bony fish, the slow-worm a lizard, and so on. The alternative explanation would be that all those many characteristics, which each of these legless creatures has in common with vertebrates other than cyclostomes, owe their agreement to convergent evolution— which is of an overwhelming improbability.

The more characteristics that are known, the greater the reliability of this computation. With fossils, for which only skeletal characteristics are available, the paucity of these can lead to errors when relating particular fossils to certain groups. A well-known paleontologist, Schindewolf (1936), related the Jurassic ichthyosaurians to whales, in particular to dolphins, although the former show through as many characteristics that they are reptiles as the cetaceans possess to prove that they are mammals. The external similarity between the two marine tetrapods rests on a very limited number of convergent characteristics, such as the streamlined form of the body, the fin-like limbs, the bill-like snout armed with small and uniform teeth, and others.

7. Convergent Adaptation

To be certain of homologies is all the more important because there is another way by which similarities can arise; these similarities could be mistaken for homologies and this would lead to erroneous conclusions concerning phyletic descent. This second way, which has already been hinted at, is convergent evolution: two or more groups of animals can, independently of one another, hit on the same way to cope with a certain environmental problem. Hawks (Falconidae), swifts (Cypselidae), swallows (Hirundini) and other birds have evolved falcate wings and a streamlined body in order to pass easily through the air, while sharks (Elasmobranchii), innumerable bony fishes of different orders (Teleostei), ichthyosaurians (Reptiles), whales (Cetacea), and dolphins (Mammalia) have found the same adaptation for swift movement in the heavier medium of water. Another classic example of morphological adaptation to a certain type of movement is represented by some large moths (Saturnidae), on one hand, and hummingbirds (Trochilidae) on the other; both have specialized in sucking nectar from flowers while hovering in the air in front of them. While doing this, these two extremely different kinds of creature look surprisingly similar and, on even closer examination, so do the proportions of their bodies and wings.

In some cases convergent adaptation can lead to results which are so excessively similar that, without a very close examination, one could be tempted to apply Remane's first criterion of special quality and take for homologies these results of convergent adaptation. Figure 8 shows longitudinal sections made through the eyes of a vertebrate and a cephalopod, a group which belongs to the mollusks, that is, to the same phylum as snails (Gastropoda) and clams (Bivalvae). The caption suffices to indicate the extreme similarity concerning even minute details. Nonetheless this similarity is the result of convergency, as can be shown by means of other criteria—by comparing embryogenesis, to name but one of them.

Wherever such a similarity of characteristics is found which definitely can not be explained by common ancestry, convergent adaptation to a common function can be assumed with an overwhelming degree of certainty. The probability of two forms of life evolving, by sheer coincidence, a certain number of identical characteristics, can be calculated. It is equal to $\frac{1}{2^{n-1}}$, n being the number of similar or identical characteristics.

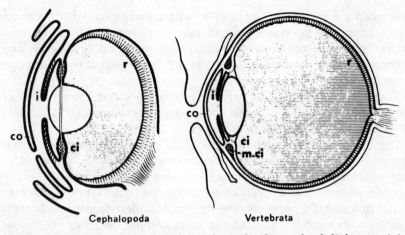

Figure 8. Detailed analogy in two independently evolved light-perceiving organs. *Left,* the eye of an octopus; *right,* the eye of a man; *co,* cornea; *ci,* corpus ciliare; *m.ci,* musculus ciliaria; *i,* iris; *r,* retina. (Lorenz: "Analogy as a Source of Knowledge.")

The probability of ten characteristics being present by pure chance in two unrelated forms of life is therefore 1:512.

Characteristics and organs which, in different forms of life, owe their similarity to the processes of convergent evolution are called *analogous.* The study of analogies is of particular importance to the investigation of social behavior in animals and man.

Exclusion of homology is a prerequisite for ascertaining analogies. On the other hand, the assumption of homology is the more certain, the more different is the function of the organs in which it is found. If we find the same skeletal elements in the forelimb of tetrapods, although it performs a very different function for each of them, their homology needs no further confirmation.

8. Analogy as a Source of Knowledge

Ethologists are often accused of drawing false analogies between animal and human behavior. However, no such thing as a false analogy exists: an analogy can be more or less detailed and hence more or less informative. Searching assiduously for a "false" analogy, I found a couple of technological examples within my own experience. I once mistook a ship mill for a stern-wheeler. A vessel was anchored on the banks of the Danube near Budapest. It had a little smoking funnel and at its stern an enormous, slowly turning paddle wheel. On another occasion, I mistook a small electric power plant, consisting of a two-stroke engine and a dynamo, for a compressor. The only biological example that I could find concerned a luminescent organ of a pelagic gastropod, which was mistaken for an eye because it had an epidermal lens and, behind this, a high cylindrical epithelium connected with the brain by a nerve. Even in these examples the analogy was false only with respect to the direction in which energy was transmitted.

There is, in my opinion, only one possibility for an error that might conceivably be described as the "drawing of a false analogy" and that is mistaking a homology for an analogy.

This fact becomes important in the study of behavior. Not being vitalists, we hold that any regularly observable pattern of behavior which, with equal regularity, achieves survival value is the function of a sensory and nervous mechanism evolved by the species in the service of that particular function. Of necessity, the structures underlying such a function must be very complicated, and the more complicated they are the less likely it is, as we already know, that two unrelated forms of life should, by sheer coincidence, have happened to evolve behavior patterns which resemble each other in a great many independent characteristics.

A striking example of two complicated sets of behavior patterns evolving independently in unrelated species, yet in such a manner as to produce a great number of indisputable analogies, is furnished by the behavior of human beings and of geese when they fall in love and when they are jealous. Time and again I have been accused of uncritical anthropomorphism when describing, in some detail, this behavior of birds and people. Psychologists have protested that it is misleading to use terms such as falling in love, marrying, or being jealous when speaking of animals. I shall proceed to justify the use of these purely functional concepts. In order to assess correctly the vast improbability of two complicated behavior patterns in two unrelated species being similar to each other in so many independent points, one must envisage the complication of the underlying physiological organization. Consider the minimum degree of complication which even a man-made electronic model would have to possess in order to simulate, in the simplest possible manner, the behavior patterns here under discussion. Imagine an apparatus, A, which is in communication with another apparatus, B, and which keeps checking continuously whether or not apparatus B communicates with a third apparatus, C, and which, furthermore, on finding that this is indeed the case, does its utmost to interrupt this communication. If one tries to build models simulating these activities, for example, in the manner in which Grey-Walter's famous electronic tortoises are built, one soon realizes that the minimum complication of such a system far surpasses that of a mere eye.

The conclusion to be drawn from this reasoning is as simple as it is important. Since we know that the behavior patterns of geese and men cannot possibly be homologous—the last common ancestors of birds and mammals were extremely primitive reptiles with minute brains and certainly incapable of any complicated social behavior—and since we know that the improbability of coincidental similarity can only be expressed in astronomical numbers, we know for certain that it was more or less identical survival value which caused jealousy behavior to evolve in birds as well as in man.

This, however, is all that the analogy is able to tell us. It does not tell us wherein this survival value lies—although we can hope to ascertain this through observations of and experiments with geese. It does not tell us anything about the physiological mechanisms bringing about jealousy behavior in the two species; they may well be quite different in each case. Streamlining is achieved in the shark through the shape of the musculature, in the dolphin by means of a thick layer of blubber, and in the torpedo with welded steel plates. By the same token, jealousy may be—and probably is—caused by an inherited and genetically fixed program in geese, while it might be determined by cultural tradition in humans—though I do not think it is, at least not entirely.

Limited though the knowledge derived from this kind of analogy may be, its importance is considerable. In the complicated interactions of human social behavior, there is much that does not have any survival value and never did have any. So it is of some significance to know that a certain recognizable pattern of behavior does, or at least once did, possess a survival value for the species; in other words, that it is not pathological. Our chances of discovering wherein the survival value of the behavior pattern lies are vastly increased by finding the pattern in an animal with which we can experiment.

When we speak of falling in love, of friendship, of personal enmity or of jealousy in these or in other animals, we are not guilty of anthropomorphism. These terms refer to functionally determined concepts, just as do the terms legs, wings, eyes, and the names used for other bodily structures that have evolved independently in different phyla of animals. No one uses quotation marks when speaking or writing about the eyes or the legs of an insect or a crab, nor do we when discussing analogous behavior patterns.

However, when using these different kinds of terms, we must be very clear as to whether the word we use at a given moment refers to a concept based on functional analogy or to one based on homology. The word "leg" or "wing" may have the connotation of the first kind of concept in one case and of the second in another. Also, there is the third possibility of a word connoting the concept of physiological, causal identity. *These three kinds of conceptualization may coincide or they may not. To make a clear distinction between them is particularly important when one is speaking of behavior.*

A homologous behavior pattern can retain its ancestral form and function in two descendants, and yet become physiologically different. In mammals motor patterns of locomotion that are demonstrably caused primarily by endogenous impulse production and central nervous coordination (von Holst 1969–70) can come under the control of higher loci. What has been, primarily, a step taken with the foreleg may become a voluntary movement. Jakob von Uexküll showed that in adult scyphomedusae the contraction of the umbrella was dependent on a "reflex" being released within the marginal bodies whenever the expanding umbrella suddenly reached the limit of its elasticity. As he said in his poetic manner: "It hears nothing but the tolling of its own bell." More recently, the marginal bodies have been shown to possess an autonomous generation of activity. Reflexes, however, do not seem to have been completely eliminated; I myself once removed all but two opposite marginal bodies in a large *Scyphostoma pulmo*. Its umbrella continued to pulsate although a certain "lagging behind" could be noticed in those parts of the umbrella located farthest from the remaining marginal bodies. When I put both hands on the umbrella just outside the marginal bodies and allowed it to expand very slowly, the pulsation stopped. Pulsation could be started again by means of a slight tap from the outside. At that time (more than fifty years ago) I had no idea about endogenous impulse production and so I did not wait for the umbrella's pulsation to begin again spontaneously. The specimen in question had been washed ashore and its lack of spontaneity may have been the result of its being at the point of dying. In *Scyphostoma* a stable position in the water is maintained by the different specific weights of the umbrella and the remainder of the body. The functions of the marginal bodies are not necessary for the maintenance of equilibrium. In Hydromedusae this is different; when the small medusae of Stauridium (Cladonema) swim at all, they start as unpredictably as a housefly taking off, and they then move upward with an irregular zigzag motion, obviously overcompensating, with each contraction, for the deviation from the vertical incurred during the preceding contraction. In Gonionemus and Craspidacusta the equilibrating movements are not noticeable.

A homologous motor pattern may retain its original physiological causation as well as its external forms, yet undergo an entire change of function. The motor pattern of "inciting" that is common to the females of most *Anatidae* is derived from a threatening movement and its primary function is to cause the male to attack the adversary indicated by the female's threat. In some species it has lost this function entirely; in the goldeneyes, for instance, it has become a pure courtship movement of the female.

Two non-homologous motor patterns of two related species may, by a change of function, be pressed into the service of the same survival value. The preflight movement of ducks, an upward thrust of head and neck, is derived from an intention movement of flying, while the corresponding signal of geese is derived from a displacement shaking of the head. When we speak of "preflight movements of Anatidae" we form a functional concept that embraces both.

These examples are sufficient to demonstrate the importance of keeping functional, phylogenetic and physiological conceptualizations clearly separate. Ethologists are not guilty of "reifications" or of illegitimate anticipations of physiological explanations when they form concepts that are only functionally defined—such as, for instance, the concept of the IRM, the innate releasing mechanism. They are, in fact, completely aware that this function may be performed mainly by the sensory organ itself, as has been demonstrated in the cricket by Regen (1924) and in the females of some mosquitoes, which respond exclusively to the sound frequencies produced by the males. In the eye of the frog, as Lettvin and his co-workers (1959) have demonstrated, a certain preliminary filtering of stimuli is performed by the retina which, however, actually is a part of the brain itself.

9. Homoiology

Besides homology and analogy, no other explanation can be found for the appearance of similar-to-identical characteristics in different forms of life. There are, however, mixtures of the two; there exist similarities which are caused by both. The wings of the flying saurian and a bat shown in Figure 9 are indubitably homologous with regard to their bony elements, while the flying membrane found in both has certainly been evolved convergently by reptiles and by mammals. Another example is furnished by the flippers of ichthyosaurians and whales: both possess homologous bones, but in both convergent adaptation to the same function has caused these bones to become shortened and flattened and, in the metacarpal bones as well as in those of the digits, has caused the middle part (diaphysis) to separate from the ends (epiphysis) so as to create three bones out of one (Figure 9, 3). All these analogies serve to broaden the flipper and to make it, as a whole, flexible. The results of such superpositions of convergent adaptations on pre-existing homologies are called homoiologies.

10. Systematics and the Need for Great Numbers of Characteristics

For obvious reasons, homoiologies are most abundant when two kinds of animals, closely related to one another in the first place, become even more similar to each other by convergent adaptation. The dual effect of homology and analogy can become very confusing and has often misled taxonomists into an erroneous grouping of non-related forms. A striking example of this is the genus *Aquila*, the "eagles" of older ornithology. All raptors exceeding a certain size were, at that time, subsumed under this genus. Size in these birds should be considered an adaptation to the

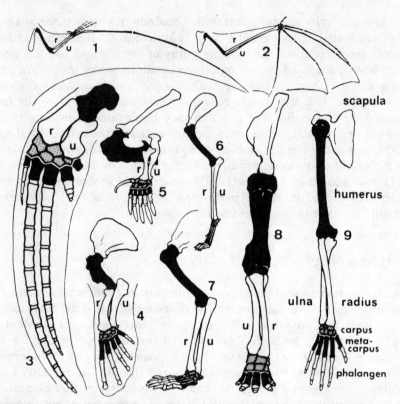

Figure 9. Anterior limbs of vertebrates. (1) Jurassic flying reptile; (2) bat; (3) whale; (4) sea lion; (5) mole; (6) dog; (7) bear; (8) elephant; and (9) man. The humerus and the metacarpal bones are tinged in black, the carpal bone in grey. (Lorenz: "Analogy as a Source of Knowledge.")

catching of comparatively large prey, and this explains why raptors of different genera, even of different families, have convergently evolved a number of conspicuous characteristics. All of them have a large, heavy head with a strong bill, large eyes shadowed by bony ridges—which simulate a savage frown, short legs with thick toes and large talons, a short tail, and broad wings—which have to do with the necessity of swift flight, of stooping, and of carrying away heavy loads. Even in the otherwise excellent *Tierenzyklopädie* of the *Urania Tierreich*, published in 1975, the "eagles" are treated as a phyletically coherent group, although they actually belong to four different families. The golden eagle *(Aquila chrysaetus)* and the imperial eagle *(Aquila heliaca)* originated from the buzzards *(Buteonini)*; the sea eagle *(Haliaetus albicilla)*, the bald eagle *(Haliaetus leococephalus)* and the Japanese giant sea eagle *(Haliaetus pelagicus)* belong to the family of the kites *(Milvini)*; while the booted eagle *(Hieraetus pennatus)*, Bonelli's eagle *(Hieraetus faciatus)*, and a number of huge tropical forms such as the harpy *(Thrasaetus harpyia)* are very probably descended from the goshawk family (Accipitrini). If one evaluates all of the less conspicuous details, of morphology as well as of behavior, the relationship of the several alleged eagles to these three groups can hardly be doubted. All the zoo people and all the falconers with whom I have spoken, who knew the groups in question by close and unprejudiced observation, regarded the grouping here proposed as obvious. Taxonomists, who work exclusively in museums, whom old Alfred Edmund Brehm despised so much he called them "Balgforscher" (skin scientists), tend to over-assess the importance of skeleton structures and of measurements. As my teacher, Erwin Stresemann, used to say in his habitually sarcastic manner, "Some people seem to think that those characteristics which prove most resistant to the attacks of moths and the destructive beetle, Anthrenus, must also be regarded as those most resistant to evolutionary change." The skulls of all the raptors mentioned above are indeed surprisingly similar to one another because, to quote Stresemann again, "Bones are just like wax in the hands of evolution."

A. E. Brehm (1890), who as a taxonomist did not otherwise shine at all, naively but with justification relied on his own gestalt perception and boldly asserted that the harpy was "the hugest of all goshawks" and that the hooded eagles *(Spizeatus)* were "large slender goshawks with relatively short wings." The correctness of his opinions and the taxonomic errors that still persist in the *Tierenzyklopädie* are both caused by neglecting the fact, mentioned in One/II/3, that the natural computer of our gestalt perception can take in and evaluate a much greater number of data than our rational computation can. Many truths become falsified and many obvious facts become invisible if one restricts his methods to quantification alone.

Quantification, however, has the last word in verification, and all that our perception can tell us becomes "science" only if and when we succeed in confirming it by rational verification. In order to accomplish this difficult task with regard to our phylogenetic considerations, we have no other method but that of tracing back the way by which our perception came to its results. In other words, we must try to find out, and try to describe, what were the single characteristics evaluated by the computation that our gestalt perception has performed. We are very far indeed from regarding perception's function as a miracle, so we can be quite certain that all these data must have, in some way, been "fed into" the apparatus of perception. As I have already said: if anywhere in biology man-made computers are more than a mere model, it is in the physiology of perception.

So it becomes our task to find out which characteristics link the golden eagle to the buzzards, the bald eagle to the kites, and the harpy to the hawks. These characteristics must be exclusively distinctive of the group concerned; they must not be a common possession of the next larger taxonomic unit, in our case, of the raptors; if they were, they would not support our assumption. Our attempt to compute the relationship between the numbers of group-specific characteristics and those of a more generalized kind raises the difficult problem of what has to be regarded as "one" or a "single" characteristic. There are many characteristics which superficially seem independent of one another, as parts of the same adaptation. Streamlined bodies and sickle-shape fins or wings are virtually always part of the same adaptation to swift movement, so they ought to be regarded, in our computation of analogous versus homologous characteristics, as only one characteristic. The closer to each other, on the genealogical tree, the two points are situated from which two courses of convergent evolution have taken their departure, the smaller is the number of group-specific characteristics in relation to those created by the convergent adaptation. With regard to the three groups of raptors mentioned above, it is just possible for people with a gift for gestalt perception to reach an unequivocal classification.

There are, however, cases in which the criterion of relative numbers fails us completely. There is, for instance, a species of waterfowl in Abyssinia, the blue-winged goose (*Cyanochen cyanopterus*), which unambiguously belongs to the subfamily of sheldrakes (*Tadornini*). Like many other waterfowl, these birds have, through adaptation to feeding on grass, evolved a goose-like toothed bill. So have the South American members of the genus *Cloephaga*, which also clearly belong to the Tadornini. Being members of the same subfamily, *Cyanochen* and *Cloephaga* have so many distinctive marks in common, and so few exclusively specific ones, that no one can tell whether *Cyanochen* is a *Cloephaga* which, through a freak of windstorms, was blown over from South America, or whether an independent kind of Tadornini has "invented" the grass-eating bill on its own in Abyssinia. No one has yet undertaken an investigation of the two genera in detail, searching for *Cyanochen*-specific and *Cloephaga*-specific characteristics. This type of diligent search for distinctive characteristics is the never-ending chore of the phylogeneticist endeavoring to disentangle the most recent steps of evolution; it will be discussed in detail in Section IV/12.

11. The Changing Value of Single Characteristics

For judging genealogical relationships it is not only necessary to assess the relative numbers of homologous and analogous characteristics; one must also draw into consideration the rate at which every distinctive mark to be used in one's computation is apt to change during the course of evolution. The rate at which one and the same characteristic changes can be very different in different taxonomic groups. The same distinctive mark can be very similar or practically identical in all members of a large group, and it can be highly variable in another. The deduction is justified that, during the evolution of the latter group, such a distinctive mark tends to change very quickly. Having four legs is a tolerably conservative characteristic in tetrapods, yet in one lizard family, the Scincidae, we find closely related forms of which some have four legs, some two, and some none at all. Among parrots (Psittaci), the coloration and markings of the plumage are extremely different, often even in closely allied forms, while the form of the bill is nearly identical throughout. Conversely, in the Galapagos finches (Geospizidae) and also in the Hawaiian Drepanidae, the plumage of all genera and species is closely similar, while the form of the bill is subject to extreme variation. Obviously, if one were to ascribe to the coloration of the plumage, or to the form of the bill, a constant "taxonomic dignity" throughout the class of birds, this would give rise to very erroneous conclusions. There is no such thing as a constant taxonomic value for any characteristic.

In his contribution to *Bronn's Klassen und Ordnungen des Tierreiches* (1891), Hans Gadow has made an interesting thought experiment. He chose thirty distinctive marks whose importance was generally recognized by ornithologists and, ascribing the same value to each of these characteristics, he constructed a taxonomy of birds based exclusively on those thirty characteristics. The result was surprising: while it showed some striking points of agreement with current taxonomy, it diverged on others in the most blatant way. Gadow himself clearly recognized that the "intuition" of gifted taxonomists attributed a different weight to the same characteristics in different branches of the genealogical tree. He was also aware that this "intuition" evaluated a much greater number of characteristics than a mere thirty.

The multiplicity of data fed into and interpreted by our gestalt perception enables that great computer to ascertain the relative speed with which a certain distinctive mark is evolving in different groups of animals, and to attribute a corresponding significance to it with regard to every group. The prerequisite for this tremendous accomplishment is, of course, that an equally tremendous number of data has been "fed" into the computer, innumerable data concerning each species and also concerning a huge number of different species. The speed with which a certain characteristic changes in a certain group can only be computed from a comparison with the speed of change in many other characteristics of many other groups. The correctness of the end results would only be a certainty if the taxonomist could evaluate *all* characteristics changing through evolution in *all* the members of the group investigated. This is obviously utopian, but it is certain that the probability of correct genealogical interpretation rises with every new characteristic and with every new species drawn into consideration—possibly even in a geometric curve.

Comparative evaluation of the relative changeability of many distinctive marks contributes to furnishing a criterion of homology which certainly enters into what is called "taxonomic intuition," although it is consciously and rationally used only in rare cases. It is a matter of course to all taxonomists that the existence of homologous characteristics is a sign of phyletic relationship. The inverted conclusion seems banal: of course, the likelihood of two characteristics being homologous in two forms of life increases with the number of other homologous characteristics both possess. This trite statement gains in significance as investigation advances to more detailed questions concerning the "microsystematics" of a group. The farther this endeavor proceeds, the more the difficulties arising from homoiologies increase. In this field, and quite particularly in behavior research, it becomes a help that there is a relationship of "mutual elucidation" between ascertaining the homology of two single characteristics and that of the phyletic relationship between two species. As Dagmar Kaltenhäuser (1971) has shown in her study of homologous motor patterns in dabbling ducks *(Anatini)*, the proof of phyletic relationship is often less dependent on a demonstration of the homology of two motor patterns than, conversely, the proof of the homology of two complicated behavior patterns hinges on a demonstration of the relation between the two species in question.

12. The Difficulties and the Importance of "Microsystematics"

All our assertions about the phyletic relationship of animals, extinct or extant, are based on a consideration of probabilities. The probability of our being correct is in direct proportion, not only to the number of characteristics evaluated, but also to the number of forms of life bearing these characteristics. All that has been said in this chapter proves just this. The recognition of these facts makes it evident that our reconstruction of the great genealogical tree of vertebrates possesses a vastly greater probability of being correct with regard to the branching of the old, large taxa. It becomes equally evident that this probability diminishes in proportion to the number of distinguishing marks setting off one group against the other. In addition, the documentation by means of fossils leaves us completely in the lurch as far as the most recent steps of evolution are concerned.

All this constitutes a severe obstacle to a very important breakthrough in modern natural science, to the synthesis of phylogenetics and genetics. It is only the most extensive knowledge of the most subtle marks distinguishing a great number of living forms that can help to surmount this obstacle. Yet the investigator who concentrates all his life's work on the study of one seemingly unimportant group of animals is often regarded as a crank, if not a monomaniac. The man who seems inordinately enamored with such a group, counting the bristles on legs of different Cladocera, or describing one particular vein in the wing of some tiny midge, is all too easily ridiculed, yet it is he who helps to accomplish the great breakthrough here under discussion. As Erwin Stresemann tells us, even the great ornithologist Ernst Hartert met with the disapproval of his colleagues when he insisted "on the most meticulous distinction of local forms" and justified his contention by writing, as early as 1899: "Forms that are difficult to distinguish from one another must be observed as they occur in nature, and there is nothing in nature that we may neglect" [my translation]. One feels tempted to speculate that this great systematist may have felt intuitively that a comparison of forms that can hardly be distinguished from one another could elucidate some of the most essential problems of evolution.

To the best of my knowledge, Erwin Stresemann was the first to grasp this and was the first to take the necessary steps for utilizing the great amount of detailed knowledge gathered by ornithologists, as well as the huge amount of material accumulated in ornithological collections, for the study of evolution. By being a *scientia amabilis*, ornithology has attracted a great number of "amateurs," in the sense defined in One/II/4, with the result that no class of vertebrates has ever become nearly as well known, with regard to its systematics, its geographic distribution, its ecology, and the breadth of variability occurring within each species, as have the birds. Stresemann emphatically opposed the opinion, then current among ornithologists, that the continuity of transitions between adjacent and very similar species of birds was due to the inheritance of characteristics that were caused by climatic or other environmental influences. This opinion was then held by such great scientists as Charles Otis Whitman and Bernhard Rensch. As Stresemann demonstrated in his classic study on discontinuous variation, a gradual transition between two closely allied, yet clearly distinguished species occurs exclusively when their habitats are adjacent to each other so that, *secondarily*, hybridization takes place. Stresemann's exploitation of the hoard of ornithological material brought a result of the utmost importance in the history of biological science. It proved the mutation theory to be correct and proved the assumption of the inheritance of acquired characteristics to be false.

These new finds opened the way for a new branch of biological science, population genetics, represented in America by Sewall Wright and in England by Ronald A. Fisher. Among geneticists, it was Theodosius Dobzhansky who most successfully combined the methods of genetics with those of phylogenetics. It was an ornithologist, and a pupil of E. Stresemann's, Ernst Mayr, who in 1942 wrote *Systematics and the Origin of Species*, a book which really effected a major breakthrough by bridging the gap existing between two hitherto unrelated branches of science. Every student of ethology ought to read this book because, as Stresemann said, " . . . for a long time to come, it will be an unerring guide to the systematist, guiding him through the complex maze of phenomena from which our predecessors, 150 years ago, vainly sought a way out."

13. The Origin of Ethology

Not only this new bridge uniting the study of phylogeny with that of genetics has its factual fundaments in the findings of the modest and pedestrian search for more and more comparable characteristics in more and more related species—a search that was, and still is, looked down upon by people lacking an understanding for the great historical facts of evolution. Another new branch of biological science, a side branch that sprouted in an altogether unexpected direction, has the same factual foundation, and is the subject of this book: comparative ethology. As has been explained in Chapter II, the cognitive functions of gestalt perception are absolutely indispensable in biological science. It has also been demonstrated that being an "amateur" is, rather surprisingly, the prerequisite for the full unfolding of these functions. It is easy to understand why "amateurism" and gestalt perception play a supremely important role in systematics and particularly in the microsystematics discussed in Section 10 of this chapter. It is equally easy to understand why ornithology, looked down upon by fools as a *scientia amabilis*, has given birth to population dynamics, to population-genetics and to ethology, three sciences whose importance is increasingly recognized. The joy experienced in the beauty of organisms leads to collecting; the joy of collecting leads to systematics; systematics leads to the recognition of the great laws prevailing in the genesis of the organic world.

The discovery which may be equated with the origin of ethology is a simple one. It was made by microsystematists occupied with their insatiable hunt for more and ever more comparable characteristics. It was by no means a coincidence that the two men who, independently of one another, made that discovery, Charles Otis Whitman and Oskar Heinroth, were both ornithologists and both unmistakably true "amateurs," both aviculturists and both collectors of live creatures. Entomologists, too, enjoy the beauty of organisms, but they tend to collect carefully preserved specimens rather than live ones. Most ornithologists, on the other hand, assiduously observe live birds, either in the field or in captivity. The passion for collecting assumes an important part as well; Whitman kept a collection of doves and pigeons (Columbae) in aviaries; Heinroth had at his disposal the rich collection of waterfowl kept at the Berlin Zoo. As has been explained in One/II/5, the observation of captive animals has the important advantage of stimulating comparison by showing, side by side, different species normally inhabiting far distant countries.

Under these circumstances a microsystematist on the lookout for comparable characters can hardly fail to notice that there are behavior patterns which represent just as reliable—and often particularly conservative—characteristics of species, genera, and even larger taxonomic groups, as do any morphological characteristics. In his short paper, "Über bestimmte Bewegungsweisen bei Wirbeltieren," (1930) Heinroth clearly demonstrated that the concept of homology is applicable equally to motor patterns and to morphological characteristics.

As the history of science shows, it is often necessary for a natural law to be revealed in a particularly simple and striking form in order to draw the attention of the research worker. Gregor Mendel discovered the Mendelian laws when he had the good luck to stumble on their simplest possible realization in hybrids differing only with regard to one gene. Both Whitman and Heinroth discovered the fact that motor patterns can be homologized when they observed the most constant and unchangeable sequence of movements existing in the animal world, that is, ritualized motor patterns of fixed intensity. There are in many animals motor patterns which act as signals and which, under the selection pressure of this function, have evolved in a direction of becoming less ambiguous, as will be discussed in Two/II/3. It suffices to say here that motor patterns of fixed intensity lack the degree of variability which, in others, is correlated with the variations of specific excitation. Some courtship patterns in pigeons and in waterfowl are typical of this type of signal movement.

14. Chapter Summary

Ethology, or the comparative study of behavior, is based on the fact that *there are mechanisms of behavior which evolve in phylogeny exactly as organs do, so that the concept of homology can be applied to them as well as to morphological structures.* As all behavior is based on the function of structures which have phylogenetically evolved, the statement of this fact is (or ought to be) redundant. Nevertheless, it was left to two zoologists to discover. They did so while searching for distinctive marks that could be used in the detailed systematics of the group they were investigating.

When used by biologists, the verb "comparing" means using the similarities and dissimilarities of extant forms of life in an attempt to reconstruct their descent from a common ancestor. Such a reconstruction can be accomplished by means of a diagram into which no hypothesis needs to enter. If one symbolizes, by the use of vertical lines, the species of animals living today, and subsequently connects them by horizontal lines representing characteristics common to a number of them, all that is necessary to give the resultant diagram the form of a *tree* is to order the symbols of common distinguishing marks in such a manner that those which connect the greatest number of living species are marked at the lowest level (at the bottom of the diagram), and to arrange the others in a sequence corresponding to the width of their distribution among animal forms. This has been done in the diagram of Figure 6, using the chordates as an example.

Practically everywhere in nature that we perceive the well-known form of a tree, the assumption proves correct that what is found has *grown*, in other words, that the parts now representing the tree top are youngest and that, at the first stages of growth, the whole tree was represented by what now forms the lowest part of the trunk. Even without the documentation stemming from other sources, such as paleontology and animal geography, the data brought to light by comparison alone would render the hypothesis of common descent a near certainty.

Complete certainty is attained by the testimony of paleontology. The fossils characterized by unmistakable distinguishing marks as being ancestral are found in the lowest strata of the earth, and in the resultant sequence of the earth's layers we find fossil organisms in exactly the same sequence as that which has to be postulated on the basis of a comparison. In the diagram of Figure 6, the geological epochs can be represented by horizontal lines which coincide, without constraint or the least contradiction, with the conclusions drawn from comparisons concerning the sequence in which new characteristics first made their appearance.

Organs and characteristics which owe their similarities to descent from a common ancestor are called *homologous*. There is one other way by which similarities can come to be: two or more forms of life, which need not be related to each other, can evolve organs amazingly similar in almost every detail by becoming adapted to the same function. The classical example for this process of convergent evolution is represented by the camera eyes independently evolved by vertebrates and cephalopods *(Octopus)*. Similarities arising from convergent adaptation are called *analogies*.

For correctly assessing genealogical relationships, it is of the utmost importance to distinguish clearly between homologies and analogies. A consideration of probabilities is the surest way to this end. A porpoise *(Delphinus)* and an ichthyosaurian are strikingly similar to each other with regard to the streamline forms of their bodies and to the organization of their flippers, but these similarities are few in number while, on the other hand, hundreds of distinguishing marks prove the ichthyosaurus to be a reptile and the porpoise to be a mammal. Any attempt to explain the similarities between the two by the assumption of common descent would have to explain the innumerable mammalian characteristics of the porpoise and the reptilian characteristics of the icthyosaurian on the basis of convergent adaptation—which would obviously be abstruse.

The nearer to each other, on the genealogical tree, the two starting points of convergent adaptation are situated, the less confidence can be placed in this calculation of probability. For example, the marks distinguishing a small group of raptors from each other, such as the hawk-like (Accipitrini) and the kite-like (Milvini), do not appreciably exceed in number those marks which both groups have evolved through convergent adaptation when each developed so-called eagles. The fewer the characteristics distinguishing two groups, the more difficult it becomes to separate homologies from analogies. This is why we know more about the older and greater divisions of the genealogical tree than we do about the smaller and more recent ones, although the latter are much more interesting to those concerned with population dynamics and with genetics.

In order to acquire more insight into the most recent events of phylogeny, the microsystematist is forever searching for more and more comparable characteristics. The results of his patient search made possible the important breakthrough on which the unification of phylogeny, population dynamics, and genetics is exclusively based. An unexpected and additional result of this search is ethology, that is, the comparative study of behavior, which also originated through microsystematics. In the diligent search for comparable characteristics, Whitman and Heinroth hit upon the fact that behavior patterns could be just such characteristics. Thus the comparative study of behavior, called ethology, has arisen from systematics as an unexpected new branch of science.

The discovery of behavior patterns which, in phylogeny, "behave" exactly as morphological characteristics do, is of the greatest importance for one particular reason: it proves beyond a reasonable doubt, and on the basis of all the mass of evidence proving evolution as such, that fixed motor patterns, comparable in their minutest detail, owe their special forms to genetic programs that came to be such as they are through the processes of evolution in exactly the same manner as did the programs for all morphological structures.

Part Two
Genetically Programmed Behavior

Chapter I
The Centrally Coordinated Movement or Fixed Motor Pattern

1. History of the Concept

To give an exact definition of what we mean when we speak of a fixed motor pattern or a fixed action pattern is difficult because one should not include any working hypotheses in the definition of any biological function or structure that has not already been thoroughly analyzed. Still, it is possible to confess that we believe that the hard core of what we call fixed motor patterns consists in centrally coordinated sequences of endogenously generated impulses, and that this coordination has evolved phylogenetically and is very resistant to any individual modification. A fixed motor pattern's most important distinction from motor patterns that are not fixed and, simultaneously, the cogent argument for its being genetically programmed, consists in its taxonomic distribution. Fixed motor patterns show, from species to species and from genus to genus, similarities and dissimilarities that concur strictly with those of morphological characters. The discovery of these facts of similarity and dissimilarity is due to the work done by C. H. Whitman and O. Heinroth. They discovered that the concept of *homology* could be applied to motor patterns in certain "ritualized" movements of courtship in pigeons (Columbidae) and in waterfowl (Anatidae). It is typical for discoveries constituting major breakthroughs that they are made with objects in which the newly found laws of nature are represented in the simplest possible ways. The classic example of this, as already mentioned, is Gregor Mendel's hitting upon monohybrids, that is, hybrids between races of plants which differ in only one gene. The courtship movements in question also obey the simplest possible laws. They obey the so-called all-or-nothing law of nervous discharge; in other words, their identity is not veiled by the great variability of the forms in which other motor patterns appear in correlation with the varying intensity of their specific excitation. As will be discussed in the following section, even a low excitation can elicit barely noticeable "intention movements," and with rising excitation, a gradual scale of transitions leads from this "intention" to the fully intensified motor pattern achieving its teleonomic function. In some particular motor patterns which function as *signals*, this intensity-correlated variability has been abolished in the interest of unambiguity: when they are performed at all, it is always with the same "typical intensity," as Desmond Morris (1957), who discovered the phenomenon, has described it.

These kinds of motor patterns of courtship, always performed monotonously and with the same intensity and, furthermore, hardly overlaid and veiled by simultaneous orientation responses, were the object of study through which Whitman and Heinroth discovered, independently of one another, first, that they were highly *characteristic for each species*, and second, that their similarities and dissimilarities from species to species, from genus to genus and, indeed, from one taxonomic group to another, were most exactly correlated to the similarities and dissimilarities of all morphological characters. This meant that the concept of homology could be applied to these behavior patterns just as well as to morphological properties. Historically, as has been explained in the introduction, it was the search for characteristics classifiable as homologous that led Whitman and Heinroth to their truly epoch-making discovery.

Neither of them ever formed a hypothesis concerning the physiological nature of their discovery. It is, therefore, worth extensive consideration that, in their endeavor to collect motor patterns that could be used as characters in taxonomy, they unequivocally chose processes of one single physiological type. This chapter and most of the second part of this book will be dedicated to this particular physiological process—the endogenous, centrally coordinated movement, which is also called the *fixed motor pattern.*

Being not particularly interested in the physiological aspects of the process, Heinroth defined it exclusively by the function of the whole program. Thus this concept embraces what we now know to be three physiologically different functions: first, the "drive" to search for a certain stimulus situation; second, the selective response to it-its "innate recognition"; and third, the discharge of an equally innate motor activity coping with the situation. Behavior systems integrating these three parts are indeed very common in nature, which explains and almost excuses Heinroth, as well as myself, for the length of time we believed that the *arteigene Triebhandlung* (species-characteristic drive action) was the most important, if not the only element of which all animal behavior is built up. At a time when the reflex was generally thought to be the most important, if not the only element of behavior, it is not surprising that the reflex-like response to a certain stimulus situation was not conceptually separated from the equally specific motor activity that followed.

The scientists who at that time were investigating orientation responses tended to formulate similar, all-embracing concepts. Even when Alfred Kühn, in his classic book, *Die Orientierung der Tiere im Raum*, spoke of a positive or negative phototaxis, his conceptualization of this term included not only the organism's turning in space toward or away from the source of light, but also the locomotion in those directions.

The combination of the unlearned "knowledge" of an object with an unlearned "skill" for coping with it is striking to the observer when, for instance, a hand-reared, totally inexperienced young goshawk catches a pheasant flying across the room in midair and alights on the corner of a wardrobe with the prey already dead in its claws. Heinroth writes: "This first 'professional' act of the hawk made an unforgettable impression upon us."

Frequent as the functional unity of a releasing receptor mechanism and an innate motor pattern is, it is far from being the only way in which these two elements can collaborate in organized behavior. For this reason it is not quite correct when, in Bullock's new textbook on neurophysiology (1977), it is counted as a constitutive characteristic of the innate motor pattern that it can be selectively released by certain specific combinations of external stimuli. There are other ways in which these elements can be put together in organized systems of behavior, one of which has been analyzed by Prechtl and Schleidt (1951). In some young mammals a motor pattern serving the search for the mother's teat is continuously at work as long as the baby is awake and is inhibited only when it has found the teat, as will be discussed in detail in Two/IV/2.

The innate ability to "recognize" a biologically relevant stimulus situation on one hand and, on the other, the innate "skill" to deal with it in the teleonomically correct way, are based on two physiological organizations which are entirely different from each other. As has been mentioned in the Introductory History, Charlotte Kogon was the first to grasp the necessity of further analyzing Heinroth's concept of the *arteigene Triebhandlung*. In 1941 she wrote: "In consistent continuation of Lorenz's terminology, it is not possible any longer to speak of an instinctive 'action', but only of instinctive movement, a consequence which, however, he fails to draw." As has been mentioned, the conclusion was indeed drawn immediately afterwards. The dynamics of the interaction between the "instinctive movement"—now termed *fixed motor pattern* in English—and the innate releasing mechanisms were fully understood only after the experimental analysis accomplished by Seitz, as will be discussed in Section 14 of this chapter.

A fundamental prerequisite for the success of this analysis was a really thorough familiarity with the different forms in which a motor pattern can appear at different levels of specific excitation. This knowledge could never have been acquired by any other methods than those described in the second chapter of Part One.

2. Differences in Intensity

The so-called "all-or-nothing" law, so well known as a part of early neurophysiology, does not hold true with regard to instinctive movements, except for those movements performed with typical intensity, as described on page 108. Quite the contrary, when the specific excitation activating a certain fixed motor pattern begins to rise even by minimal degrees, this finds its expression in movements: slight indications, "hints" of the motor pattern appear. Although their amplitude is so small as to be hardly discernible, the "impulse melody," as von Holst called it, becomes recognizable to anyone familiar with the pattern. These phenomena reveal what actions are to be expected from the organism in the near future; in other words, they indicate the organism's "intentions," and for this reason Heinroth called them intention movements. A hawk in which the specific excitation to take flight begins to awaken, performs aiming movements with its head and neck, treads alternately on one foot and then the other, crouches in preparation for jumping off, and even half opens its wings. When in a night heron the specific excitation for nest-building begins to well up, it will assume the attitude of standing in a nest, while, in fact, still standing on a branch or on the ground. Its shoulders are lowered and its tail is raised; it fixates for a moment on a dead stick or some other potential building material, only to relapse in the next second into its former, relaxed sitting position. The faculty of recognizing these kinds of hints or indications is indispensable to the ethologist trying to predict behavior.

An increase of action-specific excitation, first noticeable in the intention movements, can level off at any value of intensity already attained, or it may begin to wane again at any given moment. A greylag goose, in which excitation for taking wing has stopped just short of the threshold for actually doing so, can come to a full stop in a deep crouch preparatory to jumping with its wings half extened—a position that makes it look like a badly stuffed bird—only to stand up again and carry on with whatever it had been doing before it had begun to want to fly.

Still, if one is sufficiently familiar with the series of different forms that the goose's preflight movements take at different degrees of mounting excitation, one is perfectly able to foretell, and with tolerable exactitude, whether or not the bird will finally fly. I can always impress visitors by saying: "Look at that goose. It thinks it is going to fly, but it won't," and have my predictions come true. And I could do this long before strenuous self-observation revealed to me which were the data I was using to derive that information: these were the speed with which the goose passed from one state of intensity to the next higher one. If the bird proceeds slowly through stage one (raising its neck and uttering preflight calls) and then gets stuck at stage two (which is bill-shaking) for a long time, often then relapsing to stage one (calling without bill-shaking), it is certain that the intensity will not rise to stage three (moving the wings out from under the flank feathers) nor to stage four (crouching for the jump), and least of all to the stage of jumping into the air and taking wing. If stages one, two, and three are passed in quick succession, one can be sure that the curve of mounting excitation will not flatten out suddenly and that the following stages are going to be reached. The waxing as well as the waning of excitation seems to contain a sort of inertia within itself; the curve which excitation describes cannot break off sharply and can, therefore be safely extrapolated so that, after having registered a portion of its course, the actions which are to follow can be predicted.

Quite another question concerns the criteria by which an observer can recognize a fixed motor pattern when all he can see of it are but slight hints, which are very different from its full performance. The answer to this question has been given by Schleidt in his paper, "How 'Fixed' is the Fixed Action Pattern?" (1974), which will be discussed in more detail in Section 14 of this chapter. What remains constant during the whole series of transitions leading from the slight intention movement to the full performance of an innate motor pattern are first, the relations between the *phases* of the elementary movements of the pattern and second, the equally unchangeable proportions between the *amplitudes* of these movements. By means of these characters the gestalt perception of the observer recognizes the "impulse melody"—as von Holst has called it—of the behavior pattern, just as a melody can be recognized even if only parts of it can be heard and it is played so softly that it is hardly perceptible.

Erich von Holst demonstrated that the difference in the forms which a fixed motor pattern takes at different intensities is to be explained in the following manner. The automatic cells generate the impulses which are coordinated by central coordination, as will be described in Section 13 of this chapter. These impulses activate motor cells in the anterior horn of the spinal cord, and these cells respond with slightly different thresholds to the same quality of excitation. At a low intensity, only a fraction of the motor cells are responding, and their number increases with rising excitation "by recruitment," as von Holst has termed it. The margin between the highest and the lowest thresholds of the motor cells involved differs with different motor patterns. For those patterns serving as signals, it is in the interest of unambiguity that their form should be held as constant as possible, and this is achieved by narrowing the margin between the thresholds of motor cells, so that even with changing intensities the motor pattern can vary only within narrow limits. For such instances Desmond Morris (1957) speaks of a "typical intensity" or, when the patterns actually obey the all-or-nothing law, of a "fixed intensity." As has been mentioned, motor patterns of courtship, which are the paradigms of signals as well as of fixed intensities, have become important in the history of our science because it was through them that Whitman and Heinroth discovered that motor patterns could be acknowledged as homologous (One/I/1).

3. Qualitatively Identical Excitation Activating Different Motor Patterns

The phenomenon of recruitment is not always sufficient to explain the differences in the movements that are successively activated by the escalation of one specific excitation. There are many cases known in which an excitation of obviously identical quality calls forth, by its gradual increase, a series of motor patterns which, though unambiguously correlated to that same kind of excitation, are quite different from each other in the form of their movements. If the specific excitation of fighting is elicited in a male of the genus *Haplochromis*, a cichlid that was one of the main objects of Seitz's investigations (1940, 1941), the fish first responds by spreading its median fins and assuming "nuptial" (more correctly, "displaying") coloration. Then the fish approaches the releasing object— a dummy or a live rival—and orients in such a way that the largest contour of its body is presented at a right angle to the adversary's line of sight. This is called a broadside display. In this position, the fish extends the gill flap or branchiostegal membrane downward so that it forms a broad, black crest enlarging the fish's contours when seen from the side. After this, with mounting excitation, there follows a simultaneous contraction of all the muscle segments on the side nearest the enemy. This synchronous movement is completely different from the metachronous action of the fish's muscle segments, the undulating movement of swimming forwards. The simultaneous contraction does not result in locomotion but in an extremely strong, sideways sweep of the widely-spread tail fin in the direction of the rival. This movement causes an abrupt and strong pressure wave which is certainly perceptible to the other fish through the organs of the lateral line, and perhaps conveys a measure of the antagonist's power. Up to this stage the changes in the displaying fish's motor patterns can be explained by recruitment, because all the muscle activities which occur at the lowest steps of mounting excitation have continued; none has been "switched off." Now, however, with excitation rising still higher, the fish suddenly changes its orientation and relinquishes its stiff, broadside display in order to bite or, more correctly, to ram. The mouth is protruded so that the teeth point forward, and these are thrust forcefully against the antagonist toward which the fish has necessarily had to turn. Frequently both combatants turn simultaneously so that mouth is thrust against mouth. This is accompanied in many cichlids by a frontal display during which the gill membrane assumes a position different from the one shown during the broadside display: the membrane is extended at a right angle to the longitudinal axis, increasing the body contour when seen from the front. This phase is very short and even rudimentary in *Haplochromis*, while in other cichlids it has become ritualized into an elaborate pattern of mouth fighting. In *Haplochromis*, the adversaries almost immediately change orientation so as to be able to ram one another on the unprotected flank. From this moment on the real, damaging battle is joined; the fish swim around each other in narrow circles, a movement which has been called the "carousel" by Seitz. The ramming thrusts find their mark again and again; fins are torn and soon scales are floating around.

Under normal conditions these motor patterns follow one another precisely and in the sequence just described. Only when an abnormally high degree of excitability prevails, for instance, after very long isolation, does it happen that, when presented with a releasing stimulus situation, the fish might show the described movements out of their regular sequence, that is to say, the fish might skip the movements correlated to low intensities of excitation and proceed, almost from the very beginning, to tail beating or biting. Except for these very rare occurrences, one might say that the fish is unable to show its lateral display before having assumed nuptial color, nor to deliver a tail beat before having oriented broadside to the antagonist, and so on. The motor patterns just mentioned are connected by gliding transitions and it seems safe to assume that their intensity-correlated differences can be explained on the basis of recruitment of motor cells. For the same reason it is equally safe to assume that they are the expression of *one* kind of excitation, different only in quantity and not in quality.

4. Unity of Motivation

In the cases of motor patterns not grading imperceptibly into one another but separated by sudden cessations of certain movements and equally sudden emergences of others, as are tail beating and biting, this is a problem of whether excitation changes in quality or only in quantity. To the naive observer, it would seem obvious that the latter were true, but this intuitive assumption must be supported by rational confirmation. The first verification consists of the absolute predictability of the subsequent stage of intensity—once the preceding stage has been gone through. When Seitz demonstrated cichlid fighting to our students in Königsberg, he accompanied the actions of the fish with a running commentary, in much the same way a radio announcer would do for a boxing match. But just as he was wont to do when showing one of his own beautiful films, he made allowance for the reaction times of his listeners by anticipating, by a few seconds, what the fish were going to do. Often he had already mentioned the tail beat, and had to stop a second or so, waiting for the fish to do what he had just said they would do. It was remarkable how few students noticed this and were surprised by his prescience.

In addition to the possibility of reliably predicting the movements correlated to the next, higher stage of intensity by means of observing a precedent step, another argument for assuming one qualitatively constant excitation is the frequent occurrence of mixtures, and of extremely quick switches from one pattern to the next and back again. Also, genuine intention movements associated with the next higher stage of intensity can be observed while lower intensity patterns are still being performed. In a *Haplochromis* male, the first hints of turning towards an adversary while still in the phase of broadside display are just as much intention movements as are the first beginnings of preflight movements in a quiescent heron.

A third argument for assuming that it is a qualitatively identical excitation activating the graded scale of different intensities lies in the complete lack of "inertia" shown by the transitions from one motor pattern to the next. As will be discussed in One/V/4, an animal needs a considerable amount of time to change its "mood" (*Stimmung*, Heinroth), that is to say, to switch from one system of instinctive behavior to another. The required period is that much longer the more complex and integrated the two systems are and, also, the stronger the inhibitive influence they exert on one other. There is one exception to this rule: as will be explained in Two/VIII/2, the so-called maximum selecting system can effect lightning-like switches between two competing motivations, for instance, between attack and flight. Otherwise, a quick transition from one motor pattern to another argues for the assumption that one motivation is activating both.

A fourth argument for the unity of excitation is the fact that one and the same releasing mechanism, in other words, the same stimulus configuration, elicits all of the motor patterns correlated to different intensities. This is in perfect agreement with the fact found by Erich von Holst: typical series of motor patterns, gradated in correlation to intensities of excitation, can be elicited from the same locus by electrical stimulation of gradated strength, and in exactly the same sequence in which they appear in an intact animal reacting to external influences of appropriate stimulus configurations.

Lastly, the strongest argument for assuming a common physiological factor is this: The organism's readiness to perform any one of a set of innate motor patterns fluctuates parallel to its readiness to perform any other. If an activity correlated to a low intensity of excitation can be elicited with very slight stimulation, it can be predicted with absolute certainty that those correlated to the higher grades of intensity will be equally facilitated. If such a "weak" motor pattern can be elicited only by strong stimulation, it becomes predictable that the high intensity pattern will prove impossible to elicit at all. These parallel fluctuations of threshold could not have been discovered without simultaneously discovering the laws prevailing in the function of the releasing mechanism. Both discoveries are due to research done by Alfred Seitz (1940, 1941).

5. The Method of Dual Quantification

In the preceding section I was forced to treat some facts as if they were already known, although they really become clear only through the investigations conducted by Seitz, which now will be described. In this description and for similar reasons, I shall be forced to anticipate some discoveries that will not be dealt with until the next chapter. Analogous difficulties are present in the analysis as well as in the didactic representations of any complex system in which each part is interacting with every other part. The methods of coping with these difficulties have already been explained in One/II/2.

Before we had grasped the laws prevailing in the imperceptible gradations of the forms which motor patterns assume in correlation with the gradated intensities of one and the same quality of specific excitation, it was, in principle, impossible to discover the fact that quite a number of stimulus configurations exert a qualiatively identical but quantitatively different releasing influence. An inversion of this sentence is equally true. In other words, the laws prevailing in the different intensities of specific excitation and those governing the function of innate releasing mechanisms could only be discovered simultaneously. This is exactly what Seitz did. His work can be regarded as a model of analysis, doing justice to the systemic character of its object.

The primary and naive aim of Seitz's undertaking was to discover the quantitative relationship between the impinging stimulus and the motor activity elicited. His subject was the fighting behavior of a *Haplochromis* species then called *Astatotilapia strigigena*. Male fish of this species respond easily to rather simple dummies. The first and, at that time, disappointing result was that any dummy presented to the fish did not elicit the same response even twice in immediate succession; during the second presentation the response was already perceptibly weaker, and still weaker during the next. In such a situation the experimenter quite unconsciously tries to increase the effectiveness of the dummy by the simple means of waggling it a bit—and behold! the response regains some of its former intensity!

This simple and unintended result may be regarded as the basis of Seitz's further procedure: he grasped the essential fact that, in any dummy experiment, he had to deal with *two* variables. First, with the internal readiness of the animal to perform a certain motor pattern, a readiness which obviously decreased with every performance; and, sec-

ond, with the varying efficacy of different stimulus situations, the waggling dummy being obviously more effective than the motionless one. It
also became clear that *the same activity* could be elicited by a strong internal readiness and a weak external stimulation and vice versa. All of the
subsequent experiments conducted by Seitz were already based on the
hypothesis that *one* sort of action-specific excitation appearing in *one* set
of intensity-gradated motor pattern was released by *one* receptor mechanism responding to a specific configuration of key stimuli. On the basis
of this hypothesis he devised the elegant method of dual quantification.

To find the degree of effectiveness inherent in a dummy, he presented
it to the fish and recorded the strength of the response. Then he confronted the experimental animal with the strongest stimulation at his
disposal, that is to say, another fish he had first induced to assume full
fighting coloration, and again recorded the strength of the response. In
this way he determined the decrease of readiness caused by the presentation of the dummy; in other words, he ascertained how much readiness
was "still left" after the first part of the experiment, the presentation of
the dummy. The greater the effect of the dummy, the weaker was the
subsequent response to the maximum stimulation. Repeating this experiment with a series of dummies, Seitz was able to determine the differences between the effects of the several dummies independently of the
state of excitability in which the experimental animal happened to be at
the time of each experiment.

Seitz's investigations of the varied effectiveness of different dummies
showed, as an unexpected result, that the similarity between the dummy
and a real fighting male was irrelevant to the releasing effect, at least as
similarity appears to our human perception. My own former term for the
perceptual mechanism releasing instinctive behavior had been *angeborenes auslösendes Schema*—innate releasing scheme. The word *Schema*—
scheme—suggests an *image* which, although much simplified, still conveys an overall idea of the *whole* unit that it represents. As early as 1935,
I had pointed out that the innate recognition of any fellow member of
the species did not depend on perceiving and recognizing this other
animal as a unitary whole. Quite the contrary, each of the stimulus configurations which were effective as "key stimuli," evoking a certain
behavior pattern, acted independently of each other; a tuft of the red
breast feathers evokes the fighting response of a robin redbreast in a
manner qualitatively indistinguishable from the bird's reaction to a tape
recording of its own song. Still it was surprising to find that the reaction
of *Haplochromis* males to the dummies which elicited rival fighting did
not depend at all on their similarities to the real rival. An elongated
block of grey plasticine attached to a glass rod holder evoked intense
fighting if it were moved in such a way as to imitate the tail beat of a
rival—an easy thing to accomplish by simply rotating the glass rod
between the fingers. Even if this simple dummy were oriented so as to

be parallel and close to the fish, as a rival would be during a broadside display, it evoked a fighting response, although of less intensity than the response to the imitation of the tail beat. Seitz conducted a series of experiments in each of which another character of the conspecific rival was tested separately, and its releasing value determined by the method of dual quantification. The single characters, such as the blue gloss of the flank, the black oblique line across the eye, the black crest below the head imitating the extended gill membrane, the black margin along the upper edges of the median fins and the reddish margin below, each had its own releasing effect when represented on a dummy that otherwise did not resemble a rival male at all. Signal movements, on the whole, proved more efficacious than characters of form and color. The effect of orienting the dummy parallel to the fish was proved to be greater the larger the vertical surface presented was, but if the surface were too large, the male reacted by fleeing, as it would normally do when confronted by a much larger rival. The effect of imitated tail-beating proved stronger than that of any single morphological character, and was inferior only to the effect of a ramming thrust that could easily be simulated by prodding the fish's side with the glass rod. This usually provoked an instantaneous counterthrust by the experimental animal.

In another series of experiments, Seitz investigated the *cumulative* effects of stimuli whose efficacy he had previously ascertained. Always maintaining the method of dual quantification, that is to say, compensating constantly for changes in the fish's internal readiness, Seitz was able to compare the releasing effects of different combinations of stimuli and to formulate some very interesting equations. For example, the effect of all morphological signals plus parallel orientation was the same as that of a grey square dummy performing the tail beat. Through patient experimentation of this sort, Seitz was able to formulate the following highly important conclusion: Any character possessing a releasing value in itself, retains that same value in any combination with any other character releasing the same activity. The releasing effect of the dummy is dependent on the *sum* of the releasing characters which it embodies. This is now called the *law of heterogeneous summation*. The validity of this law was later convincingly confirmed by Heiligenberg (1963) and Leong (1969) who used an entirely different method. Most importantly, they could show that the relationship between key stimuli was truly additive and not multiplicative, as stimulus effects often are. They also showed that Seitz was justified, on the basis of his data, to exclude the multiplicative effect of the stimuli investigated.

In cannot be sufficiently emphasized that the quantification of stimulus effects was only possible on the basis of a very complete knowledge of the particular form which a motor pattern assumes at a certain intensity of specific excitation. This particular form furnished the scale by which the effect of stimulation was measured.

6. Action-Specific Fatigue

All that has been said concerning the law of heterogeneous summation, and concerning the constant releasing value of the stimulus configurations involved, proves clearly how reliably one can infer, from one single response to a stimulus of known efficacy, the animal's present state of readiness to perform a certain action pattern. The same intensity of motor response can be kept constant throughout a number of performances if one increases the strength of external stimulation so as to compensate for the decrease of internal readiness. This is demonstrated when, for instance, at the first presentation of a square of grey plasticine a fish has reacted with a broadside display and tail beating and, at the second presentation, it only reached a mere broadside orientation, but on being confronted at a third trial with a similar model with blue gloss added, the fish regained the intensity shown during the first presentation. By adding further stimulus configurations the action-specific excitation could be kept at the same level for even a few more trials.

On the receptor side, the decrease of the internal readiness to perform a certain motor pattern finds its expression also in an increase in the threshold values of releasing stimuli. Both phenomena together may be described as action-specific fatigue or exhaustion. That which is fatigued or exhausted corresponds exactly to the entity called species-characteristic drive action, in other words, to a system consisting of appetitive behavior, an innate releasing mechanism and a consummatory instinctive motor pattern. As we already know, each of these constituents is the function of an entirely different physiological apparatus and, therefore, we are confronted with a problem: Which of them is exhausted? In which of them is the process of fatigue situated?

Action-specific fatigue or exhaustion has one character in common with a process called habituation (which will be discussed later in Three/ II/2). Both action-specific exhaustion and habituation concern only one specific activity and the equally specific stimulus situation which releases it. This parallel could lead to thinking that the whole process of fatigue takes place on the receptor side alone. Seitz and I, at the time of his classic experiments, tended to believe the opposite: our impression—influenced perhaps by the hypothesis held by Erich von Holst—was rather that it was on the side of the motor activity that "something" was used up, which determined the degree of excitability. Von Holst suggested a specific neurohormone which was consumed or eliminated by the performance of the act. As shall be explained soon, this simplistic assumption was not quite correct, but it was legitimate and heuristically valuable insofar as the fatigue of the whole complicated afferent system, which comprises everything from the peripheral sensory cells to the highest levels of the central nervous system, did not play a decisive role in the processes we were investigating.

Our assumption, that some sort of motor excitability was accumulated while the motor pattern was not performed and then used up by its performance, was supported by one important observation: When the readiness to perform a certain motor pattern has been exhausted as completely as possible by the use of the strongest stimulation attainable, it takes some time for the specific excitability and the releasing thresholds to reach their "normal," that is to say, their average values. If, however, stimulation is withheld still further, neither the rising of excitability nor the concomitant lowering of thresholds will stop at any certain predetermined "normal" value, but will go on until the animal is ready to respond to extremely slight stimulation, that is to say, to stimuli which are very far from characterizing the biologically adequate situation in which the activity would accomplish its teleonomic function. Lissman studied the effect of this phenomenon on the agonistic movements of the Siamese fighting fish *(Betta splendens)* and drew the correct inferences through measuring the process of *threshold lowering* which will be discussed further in the next section.

Seitz and I assumed that these regular fluctuations of internal readiness could be explained on the basis of a "damming up" of a specific excitability, which is subsequently "consumed" during the motor activity. This explanation seemed convincing because of some results obtained with spinal fish in which an analogous phenomenon, the so-called spinal contrast, was observed, in which no specific receptor organizations were involved. This will be described in Sections 12 and 13 of this chapter. The lawful fluctuations of readiness for a certain instinctive motor pattern are mainly dependent on processes taking place in the motoric sector of the system, although there are very similar ones which concern the receptor side. It was rather fortunate that we did not know about the latter at the time of Seitz's experiments on dual quantification; they can be neglected in the fighting of *Haplochromis* without constituting a serious source of error.

When H. Prechtl later (1949) investigated the receptor organization releasing the gaping movements of young chaffinches *(Fringilla coelebs)*, he demonstrated that a number of stimulus configurations combine their several releasing effects according to the role of heterogeneous summation. They consisted of a) a slight percussing of the nest, b) a very high chirping tone, and c) the optical effect of the parent bird—or, for that matter, the hand of the human experimenter—approaching the nest from above. Furthermore, gaping can be released by a slight tapping on the nestling's head. When Prechtl presented one of these stimuli until the response to it had ceased completely, any one of the other stimuli would still be able to evoke gaping. The longest series of gaping movements was obtained when any one of the effective stimulus combinations was exchanged for another one just before the effect of a prior combination had expired. The general effect was exactly analogous to that which an experienced chef strives to achieve by means of a cleverly devised sequence of dishes. Heterogeneous summation was clearly demonstrated by simultaneously presenting two or more of the aforementioned stimulus configurations. Prechtl's experiments showed that not only processes of fatigue on the motor side, but equally those on the receptor side of a species-characteristic drive action could be responsible for changes in the organism's readiness to perform.

It was Ludwig Franzisket (1953) who succeeded in analyzing and differentially quantifying the effects both of motor and of receptor fatigue. He investigated a comparatively simple instinctive action, the back wiping movements of the frog *(Rana esculenta)*. He transected the frog's medulla oblongata in such a way that breathing remained undisturbed while spontaneous movements of the limbs were eliminated. The "wiping reflex" by which anurans remove disturbing stimuli from their dorsal side could still be elicited, although it was slightly weakened immediately after the transection. Some "training" was necessary before the fixed motor pattern had regained its former response level. Using the frog thus prepared as object, Franzisket examined the question as to what extent the readiness to perform a certain motor pattern is specific to that pattern; in other words, to what extent can it be influenced by fatiguing similar and functionally analogous movements. Two different motor patterns were investigated: first, the common and well-known wiping reflex, in which the hind foot is brought onto the back at the rear end and moved forward so that the toes scrape along the entire back as well as over the head; second, the heel wiping, in which the heel of the foot is moved as far forward as it will go on the frog's back and is then scraped over it in a caudal direction. The fatiguing of one of these motor patterns proved to have no effect whatever on the readiness to perform the other, as is shown in Figure 10.

The second important question put by Franzisket was "whether the amount of excitability is generally correlated to a type of movement, or whether it is a phenomenon inherent to the nervous pathway along which the response takes its course" [my translation]. The two wiping movements just mentioned offer a good opportunity to examine this problem because both of them can be elicited by stimulation at two physically and neurologically distinct body areas. These areas are divided by an externally visible ridge and each is supplied with its own sensory nerves, the nervi cutanei dorsi mediales and the nervi cutanei dorsi laterales.

Franzisket first released a series of toe-wiping movements through stimulation of the dorsal locus until, after a number of responses, the wiping movements became rarer (Figure 10). Then he transferred the point of stimulation to the lateral part of the frog's back and obtained a much smaller number of responses, yet slightly more than he would have got without changing the locality of stimulation. The reverse exper-

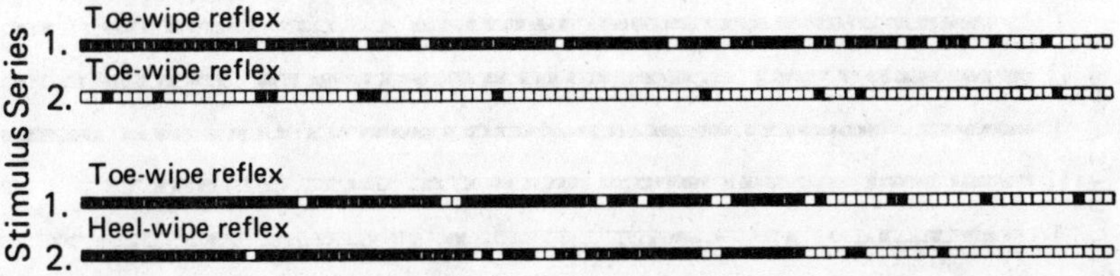

Figure 10. 200 scratch stimuli, applied to the same place on the back, elicit many toe-wiping responses among the first hundred and only a few such responses among the second hundred (two rows at top). When, however, the second hundred stimuli are applied to the caudal area at the tail end of the trunk for a release of the heel-wiping reflex, the large number of heel-wiping responses (bottom row) indicate that the preceding toe wiping movements have not influenced the amount of the capacity for excitation available for the heel wipe. (Franzisket, L.: "Untersuchungen zur Spezifität und Kumulierung der Erregungsfähigkeit und zur Wirkung einer Ermüdung in der Afferenz bei Wischbewegungen des Rückenmarksfrosches.")

iment, stimulating first laterally and afterwards dorsally, brought the same results. It is to be concluded that the motor pattern itself possesses a specific amount of excitability, as the change of receptor pathway cannot appreciably increase the number of movements released. Still, the slight increase of response caused by the change of locus seems to indicate that receptor fatigue could play its part, too.

For a clearer demonstration of receptor fatigue, it was necessary to render the motor sector of the wiping movement "indefatigable"; Franzisket achieved this by allowing the frog to rest for ten days instead of two days—as had been done during the earlier experiments. Given this much rest, the motor sector for the pattern was not exhausted after 100 stimulations, the number which had become standard during the preceding experiments. But now fatigue on the receptor side became apparent. If stimulation was given only at the same locus, at the standardized interval of ten seconds, the response began to wane after 50–80 performances, at a time when the motor readiness was not yet diminished, as could readily be demonstrated by changing the stimulus locus, as is shown in Figure 11.

When, instead of changing the locus of stimulation, Franzisket interposed a pause of 30 minutes, he obtained the same effect as that achieved by changing the receptor pathway. Obviously, recovery from complete exhaustion takes a much shorter time on the receptor side of the wiping response than on its motor side. At the same time, the excitability of the motor pattern can be accumulated and preserved over a much longer period than that of the receptor mechanism. From his study of fatigue and recovery which, in the afferent and the efferent sectors of the system proceed with characteristically different speeds, Franzisket has drawn the following conclusions: The quantity of excitability of the motor pattern is a function of central nervous structures (supposedly a trophic state

Figure 11. Seven consecutive stimulus series, one following immediately after another, which were alternately applied to the back (Stimulus Area I) and to the flank (Stimulus Area II) for a release of the toe-wipe reflex. Because of a rest period of ten days prior to the initiation of this experiment, the appearance of numerous wipe responses, up to about the middle of the fourth stimulus series, is indicative of the accumulation of the capacity for excitation. (Franzisket, L.: "Untersuchungen zur Spezifität und Kumulierung der Erregungsfähigkeit und zur Wirkung einer Ermüdung in der Afferenz bei Wischbewegungen des Rückenmarksfrosches.")

in the connecting neurons coordinating the motor patterns), while fatigue is inherent to the afferent pathway (supposedly a function of synapses between the afferent path and special groups of connecting neurons which achieve the coordination of the wiping movement). An argument for assuming that the excitability of the wiping movement is due to a trophic state of the connecting neurons coordinating it lies in the fact that the speed of its recovery after complete exhaustion is dependent on temperature (1953). The most important conclusion is that the concept of a specific quantity of excitability obviously corresponds to a physiological reality.

The organism has at its disposal a limited amount of excitability specific to a certain motor pattern. The quantity of this amount is as different in homologous patterns of different animals as it is in different motor patterns of the same species. The metachronous coordination of segmental muscles that effects the swimming movements of a mackerel or of a a pelagic shark is as indefatigable as are the contractions of a bird's heart. The beating of the pectorals of a wrasse *(Labrus)* is practically inexhaustible as long as the fish is awake; the homologous movement made by a sea horse *(Hippocampus)* can be sustained, at the most, for a number of successive minutes only. The "supply" available for these movements is correlated exactly to the "demand" made on the organism, and this is expressed as the average amount of time it has to spend performing them. It is obvious why locomotion must be difficult to exhaust in so many creatures. In the pelagic fish already mentioned, locomotion is so constant that they can afford to abolish the mechanisms which, in other animals, serve for breathing: their unceasing forward movement causes a constant stream of water, sufficient for oxygenation, to pass through their gills. These fish suffocate if their forward locomotion is prevented.

Another teleonomic reason for having an inexhaustible supply available for locomotion is its importance for escape. For a majority of instinctive motor patterns, specific exhaustion sets in long before the organism, as a whole, is completely exhausted. Very few instinctive motor patterns can be repeated right up to the limits set by the basic functions such as breathing, heartbeat, or general muscular fatigue. Yet the readiness to flee, the overpowering urge to get away, is still at work even when the peripheral organs fail to obey. From the teleonomic viewpoint, the primacy of escape is obvious.

As will be discussed in Section 12 of this chapter, locomotion is subordinate to quite a number of superior "commanding instances," each of which puts it to the service of another teleonomic function. A roebuck must run in order to escape from the wolf, in order to pursue a doe, in order to chase away a defeated rival, in order to seek a better pasture, and so on. A similar dependence on multiple motivations is found in many instinctive movements. A mouse must gnaw in order to open hard seeds, to excavate a burrow in compacted soil, to free itself from a trap, et cetera. I have suggested calling these kinds of motor patterns "tool activities" (Werkzeugbewegungen) because, like simple tools, they can serve more than one function. Perhaps the term "multipurpose movements" would be preferable.

The fact that these activities are, for the most part, performed under the influence of a superior motivation does not by any means imply that they are lacking in a spontaneity proper to themselves. On the contrary, they possess a particularly strong endogenous production of specific excitability which is indeed very necessary because they must be available at any time and at short notice. More than other instinctive motor patterns, multipurpose movements show a quick lowering of thresholds whenever they are not used for a time. Also, they tend to be performed in vacuo more often than any others. The wolf running endlessly and aimlessly to and fro within its enclosure, the ostrich incessantly plucking nonexistent grass, the rodent gnawing all objects within reach, are familiar to every zoo visitor.

7. Threshold Lowering of Releasing Stimuli

While in Section 5 of this chapter I described the experiments made by Seitz, I have not as yet placed sufficient emphasis on one of their most important results: When the fighting movements of Seitz's *Haplochromis* had not been elicited during a period considerably exceeding the average intervals between experiments, the fish would not only be ready to perform fighting movements with greater intensity and continue to do so a greater number of times, but it would also respond to a much weaker stimulation. Franzisket would probably have found the same thing if he had investigated a gradation of stimuli possessing a quantifiable releasing effect. Working as he did with a single standard stimulus, he demonstrated only the increase in internal readiness and not the concomitant lowering of releasing thresholds.

The recovery of internal readiness to perform a certain instinctive motor pattern after exhaustion does not, as in other cases of recovery after fatigue, stop at a certain predetermined level, but continues to build up as long as the experimental animal is deprived of adequate stimulation under otherwise biologically desirable circumstances. Wallace Craig (1918) was the first to describe this phenomenon in the motor patterns of courtship of the blond ring dove *(Streptopelia risoria)*. A male of this species, after having been isolated from conspecifics for some time, was ready to court a domestic pigeon, something he had refused to do earlier. After isolation had been continued even longer, the bird was ready to court a human hand; still later, he directed his courtship activities toward the rear corner of his box where the convergence of the three edges offered at least a point for fixation. In most cases of alleged "vacuum activities" a similar substitute can be found if one looks for it. Most intentional crossings of different species are achieved by breeders through the simple method of isolating the animals long enough to cause the thresholds of their sexual responses to be lowered sufficiently to accept a nonconspecific partner. In dummy experiments Lissmann studied the process of threshold lowering of fight-eliciting stimulus configurations in the Siamese fighting fish *(Betta splendens)*, with results analogous to those obtained by Craig in his investigations of courtship in doves.

The thresholds of all stimulus configurations releasing the same set of motor patterns fluctuate parallel to each other, exactly as does the readiness of the several activities belonging to that set. In many cases the intensity of appetitive behavior directed at their performance also fluctuates in parallel. There is hardly any doubt that these three kinds of phenomena are consequences of an identical physiological process. In our institute's jargon it has become customary to describe the complex of these phenomena of accumulation as the "damming up" *(Stau)* of an instinctive action. This is, of course, a rather inexact conceptualization, because to what extent the observable phenomena are due to processes in the afferent, and to what extent in the motor section of the system, ought to be investigated in every individual case. The experimental results of the work done by Seitz, Franzisket, H. Prechtl, and others tell us that both may be the case. We also know that the endogenous production of excitability often takes place in the receptor itself, but we do not know to what extent this may be specific for an instinctive action.

With regard to the accompanying subjective phenomena, it is trivial to state that the "damming up" of accumulated readiness first becomes noticeable on the receptor side. If, while on holiday in the south of Europe, we pass by a butcher's shop when we are hungry, we perceive the appetizing smell of raw beefsteak; but when we pass the same shop after having dined well, we unambiguously smell carrion. A tramp steamer captain who was a friend of Oskar Heinroth once asked him to explain the following experience: Wherever he returned to Hamburg after a very long voyage, all the women in that city appeared to him to be very beautiful, but after he had been in port for some time, most of them seemed quite ugly. Goethe, in *Faust*, comments on the same phenomenon by saying: "Du siehst mit diesem Trank im Leibe bald Helenen in jedem Weibe." ("With this potion inside you, you will soon see Helen of Troy in every woman.")

It seems to be an unanswerable question whether it is possible to remove or lower accumulated action-specific thresholds by repeated presentation of releasing stimuli without any consumption of motor readiness, since the latter is influenced by many kinds of stimulation.

8. Effects Obscuring the Accumulation of Action-Specific Excitability

If, in order to study the increase of appetitive behavior, motor readiness, and threshold lowering, one keeps an animal under conditions that prevent the arrival of specifically releasing stimuli, it is not so very easy to avoid two side effects obscuring the phenomena.

The first of these is a true atrophy of the activity caused by its remaining unused for too long a time. After Heiligenberg kept a male *Pelmatochromis cribensis* isolated for a very long time, the fish, on being presented with a conspecific rival, at first appeared to be extremely ready to fight, but contrary to all expectations and unlike Franzisket's frog, it was exhausted more quickly than it would have been after a shorter period of stimulus deprivation. This lack of stamina, however, disappeared after a short period of training.

A more lasting atrophy of a motor pattern caused by long disuse is exploited by aviculturists to induce full-winged waterfowl to stay where one wants to keep them. If one clips the wings of such a bird before it has fledged, one renders it incapable of flight until the next wing molt. After such treatment and for the rest of its life, the bird will be less ready to fly than it would have been if allowed to fledge normally. By clipping the wings of the bird again before it can fly after the molt, the effect is even more pronounced and more lasting. A female greylag that had been kept clipped by her former owner until she had reached her third year always flew much less than any of the other healthy geese. She was never seen circling high in the air; she flew only in order to get from one place to another. With regard to muscular power and flying technique she was in excellent form and she demonstrated this by "whiffling" and also by coming down steeply and landing in difficult places.

A second effect which tends to obscure the accumulation of action-spe-

cific excitability is the *waning* of *general arousal*. For a long time I doubted
the validity of the concept of general arousal, but there can be no doubt
that higher organisms are subject to threshold fluctuations which concern not one, but many or all of an animal's responses to external stimulation; a human can be sleepy when overtired, or generally aroused
after having drunk too much coffee. When subjected to what are conventionally called constant and controlled laboratory conditions, an animal
is usually deprived of a great part of the kind of stimulation that does
not specifically elicit any particular response, but which still contributes
to keeping the animal awake. At an early date I recognized the fact that
the constancy of the environment in which most or all captive animals
must live is a dangerous pathogenic factor because it tends to slow down
metabolism as well as all nervous processes. In my attempts to keep tame
animals in perfect condition, I long ago devised adequate methods to
keep them sufficiently "amused"—which is to say, generally aroused.

In her experiments on the marine Jewel Fish *(Microspathodon chrysurus)*, O. A. E. Rasa (1971) made a special study of the phenomena of de-
arousal occurring under constant conditions. She had to do this in order
to demonstrate the accumulation of specific excitability that was being
counteracted by the unspecific waning of general excitability. In the
small tanks in which the fish were experimentally isolated, their general
excitability diminished rapidly, that is to say, *all* thresholds, even those
of mutually exclusive responses, rose parallel to one another. The resulting states were, in their higher degrees, strongly reminiscent of *sleep*. All
locomotion became rare and was slowed down; the coloration of the fish
paled in so exact a correlation to the other phenomena of de-arousal that
it was proved that color could be used as a measure of the state of excitability prevailing at any moment. Unspecific changes in the environment, such as a new piece of coral in the tank, stronger lighting, water
currents caused by a pump, or even a Christmas tree ornament hung
before the front pane of the tank, all had the effect of temporarily eliminating the de-arousal, that is, of lowering all threshold values.

The assumption of a variable state concerning general excitability is
not new to physiology. Stellar (1954) supposed that general arousal
might be controlled by a certain area within the hypothalamus; R. Jung
demonstrated by electrical stimulation that, in the cat, the *formatio reticularis* can cause a rise of general excitability. And although it was Rasa's
work that caused me to realize the existence of this important phenomenon, I have since been told that H. W. Magoun was the first to express
these ideas in 1950.

Rasa's demonstration of the influence which unspecific stimulation
exerts on the general state of excitability is of great theoretical importance because it draws attention to a similarity in the functions of stimuli
which generally "charge up" the readiness to act and those of stimuli
which specifically release activity. Later, in Two/IV/4, I shall discuss

these problems further and I will try to show why the concepts of excitability and of excitation are difficult to define.

9. Vacuum Activity

If one keeps an experimental animal under tolerably good conditions that do not cause any great loss of general excitability but which, at the same time, are so contrived as to exclude the stimulation that, under normal conditions, would be adequate to release a certain instinctive behavior pattern, the phenomena already described appear, that is, increased appetitive behavior, the lowering of stimulus thresholds, and an increase of readiness to perform the pattern in question. With some species and with some motor patterns this process can reach an extreme, and the pattern can "go off" without any noticeable external stimulation. It is obviously impossible to say "without any stimulation" because, as in the case of Craig's ring dove which directed its courtship behavior at the meeting point of three straight lines, a substitute object is easy to find, even if it is an extremely weak one. Also, as has already been mentioned and as will be fully discussed in Two/III/3, 4, it is not possible to draw a sharp line between those stimulus configurations that "charge up" readiness for a certain pattern and those that set it going. So our definition of what we call a "vacuum activity" remains, necessarily, inexact.

Vacuum activities are most striking when they involve motor patterns which, under normal circumstances, are directed at an object. I shall never forget the behavior of a starling I kept when I was a schoolboy. One day while sitting on the head of a bronze statue in our dining room, the bird kept scanning the white ceiling in an excited manner. From time to time it took off, flew up to the ceiling, snapped at something, came back to its perch, performed the movements of beating an insect against the perch, then swallowed and appeared satisfied for the moment. I had to climb up on pieces of furniture and even then I had to fetch a ladder before I had really convinced myself that there were no flying insects in that room. At the age of 17, Bernhard Hellmann and I fully realized the importance of this observation. It may be of historical interest that our German term, *auf Leerlauf*, did not mean 'in vacuo' at all, but was a term taken directly from motorcycling parlance, from the expression of letting the motor run 'in neutral'. In fact, this is a much better metaphor for what actually happens. Another striking example of a vacuum activity is the weaverbird's *(Quelea)* nest building. If the males of this species are kept in a cage devoid of anything that can be used as nest-building material, they will still perform the very complicated motor patterns of tying blades of grass to the twigs they perch on.

In these cases of a motor pattern obviously directed at a certain object but performed in spite of its absence, the naive observer definitely receives the impression that the animal is *hallucinating* the missing object. This interpretation is not as farfetched as it may seem. What happens in the central nervous system of an animal performing a vacuum activity may differ from the teleonomic performance of the same pattern only with regard to a few, obviously dispensable reafferences. How then should the poor creature know the difference between dream and reality?

There are cases in which an animal cannot be deprived of releasing situations because, if all others are lacking, parts of the animal's own body can be used as substitute objects. A female canary *(Serinus canarius)* which I isolated for quite different purposes performed the actions of collecting nesting material, carrying the material to the nest site, and of building there by grabbing her own breast feathers in her beak, carrying them to a corner of the cage, and performing the "tremble–shove" movements that will be described later. Young rats, which Eibl-Eibesfeldt isolated in order to study their nest-building activities, used their own tails as nesting material: they searched for material to carry, "found" their own tails, carried them to the nest location and carefully deposited them there.

From my own observations I know of three cases in which aggressive behavior patterns were directed at an animal's own body, using it as a substitute object. Bankiva cocks *(Gallus bankiva)*, reared in total isolation by Kruijt (1971), persisted in attempting to hit their own tails with their spurs. They kept squinting backwards at their long tail feathers; suddenly they would jump round by 180° to strike the air where their tails had just been. Mallard drakes *(Anas platyrhynchus)* treated in exactly the same way by Schutz (1965) also tried to attack their own tails and they persisted in this stereotyped activity for a long time even after having been liberated on the Ess-See. A test question for visiting ethologists then was how the crazy circlings and bitings backward of these drakes should be explained. I once possessed a Moorish idol *(Zanclus canescens)* which used to attack its own tail whenever it made a sharp turn and its tail came into its field of vision. Then it would circle for a time, in much the same way that the mallards did. Normal fighting in this species involves a circling of the adversaries around each other, and this differs from the behavior just described only in its larger radius.

The frequency with which a motor pattern occurs as a vacuum activity is clearly correlated to the frequency with which it is normally performed. This has to do with the question of "demand for" and "supply of" a certain instinctive movement and will be discussed later. Gallinaceous birds of various families have a motor pattern consisting of scraping with their closed beaks to uncover food particles, and captive birds do this almost incessantly on the floors of their cages. Bankivas and other members of the crested family scratch with equal persistency with their toes. Rodents, mice for instance, are forced by their endogenous impulse production to spend much of their time gnawing, quite independently of whether gnawing is necessary or not.

The behavior patterns most frequently appearing in the form of vacuum activities are, for obvious reasons, those of locomotion. Interestingly enough, in birds as well as in mammals, the readiness for locomotion is closely bound to the readiness for escape. From the point of view of internal readiness, flight appears as the highest intensity of locomotion—which again is teleonomically understandable. As every equestrian knows, an "accumulation" of locomotion through keeping a horse stabled for some time increases not only its readiness to bolt, that is, to run fast, but also its readiness to buck, jump sideways, stop suddenly with head lowered, and every other stratagem that has been programmed in the phylogeny of horses for throwing off large predatory mammals. The exuberance which calves, lambs, kids, or young rabbits show after being liberated from close confinement is closely akin to the behavior of the horse that has been stabled for too long: they not only indulge in some fast running, but they also perform zig-zag and sideways jumps and other motor patterns that serve in escaping from predators. Birds of very different taxonomic orders show the same gradations of motor patterns beginning, at a low intensity, with mere locomotion, and culminating, at the highest degree of intensity, in motor patterns whose teleonomic function indubitably is the avoidance of flying predators, in particular of raptors stooping toward the bird from above. Birds as different as ravens, swallows, and geese fly off faster and faster when liberated after a period of captivity and, having gained sufficient altitude, perform the same and probably homologous motor patterns of turning on their backs, presenting the supporting areas of their wings upwards to the air current, and dropping earthwards with an acceleration exactly double that which could be achieved through the use of gravity alone. This motor pattern is probably common to all carinate birds and is regularly seen during states of "exuberance."

These dramatic effects of a short period of "damming up" locomotion should remind us once again of the fact that the motor patterns involved, although often "commanded" by other motivations, possess a very high production of their own action-specific excitability.

10. Appetitive Behavior

At a time when I myself had fully grasped the implications of what had been observed with regard to threshold lowering, to endogenous accumulation of excitability, and to vacuum activities, I had not yet quite realized the importance of another essential consequence of stimulus deprivation. It was Wallace Craig who first drew attention to the fact that a motor pattern which the animal had not been able to discharge for

some time not only causes threshold lowering and an increase of excitability, it actually creates an excitation of its own which activates the
whole organism and causes the animal to search for releasing stimuli. In
the simplest case, this kind of disquietude causes the organism to move
aimlessly and at random, but even this undirected restlessness serves to
increase the probability of the animal's meeting the stimulus configuration that can release the undischarged motor pattern. In its most complicated forms it involves learning and purposive behavior. In fact, we do
not know any instance of learning by reward—conditioning by reinforcement—which does not take place within the context of searching
or striving behavior that is always determined by a phylogenetically
evolved program. In his classic paper, "Appetites and Aversions as Constituents of Instinct," Wallace Craig (1918) called this ubiquitous phenomenon *appetitive behavior*.

As an opposite to appetitive behavior or appetence, Craig conceptualized *aversion*. While appetence continues until a certain stimulus is
reached, aversion continues until a certain stimulus has been got rid of,
a stimulus that Craig, following Thorndike, called the "original
annoyer." Craig's concept of aversion is not quite as clearly defined as
his concept of appetence. As Meyer-Holzapfel (1956) has shown, the
avoidance behavior embraced by Craig's term must be separated into two
concepts, a) that of true aversion, and b) that of an appetitive behavior
aimed at quiescence. Because the differences between these two processes
lie mainly in their effects on conditioning, they will be discussed in more
detail in Three/IV/3, 4. Here it suffices to say that true aversions play an
important part in all conditioning by punishment.

At present we know only a very few innate motor patterns which do
not give rise to appetitive behavior when the animal is deprived of the
releasing stimulus situation for an appreciable period. One such is the
guttural gobble noise made by the male turkey: even in a stage of strong
threshold lowering, the bird does not show any searching for releasing
stimuli. A motor pattern which does not lead to threshold lowering
when "dammed up" is not known to us; no behavior with a constant
threshold has ever been observed in animals.

11. Threshold Lowering and Appetitive Behavior in Avoidance

The consequence of withholding the adequate object of an instinctive
motor pattern for an unusually long time can have a teleonomic effect:
intensified searching must improve the probability of finding adequate
stimuli and the lowering of thresholds must diminish selectivity so as to
make it possible for the organism to accept, in a pinch, an object that is
not quite up to standard. There is a proverb in German: *In der Not frißt*

der Teufel Fliegen ("Other food lacking, the devil eats flies.") At least this is obvious for all action patterns that commence with organisms *turning toward* the object of the instinctive activity.

With behavior patterns of avoidance, the phenomena described in the last section appear, at first sight, to be dysteleonomic. Particularly the incessant fluctuating of thresholds seems to serve no sensible end. Working in the field with tame full-winged wild geese, one is made most painfully aware that the thresholds of the stimuli that elicit wild panic and escape in these birds are subject to the wildest fluctuations. At one moment a slight rustling of dry grass or a small downy feather drifting along on a breeze may cause a great flock of geese to rise thunderously into the air, while, at another time, a dog running through brushwood or the supernormal dummy of a flying predator, a hang glider rushing by at low altitude, may cause an alarm of much lesser intensity, such as a stretching-up of necks and a following of the object with the eyes. If one considers the enormous waste of energy these birds can ill afford to expend, which is incurred by the repeated and unnecessary taking wing of a great flock and, on the other hand, the equally enormous danger of reacting in too leisurely a way to an approaching danger, one cannot help wondering why it is apparently impossible for the mechanisms of evolution to construct, in the greylag goose *(Anser anser)*, a releasing mechanism responding with a constant threshold to the stimuli emanating from the only flying predator endangering their species, the white-tailed eagle *(Haliaetus albicilla)*.

Intraspecific aggression is generally counted among avoidance responses because it serves, under normal conditions, the *dispersal*, that is, the regular distribution of individuals over the habitat available to the species. The defenders of stimulus-response psychology tend to deny spontaneity of behavior in general, and strong ideological reasons demand that this denial should be emphasized with regard to aggressive behavior. In particular, the existence of appetitive behavior aimed at the discharge of fighting has been grimly negated by authors who should know better. A man "looking for trouble" is, perhaps, not too familiar a sight in civilized circles, but a greylag gander or a zanclus *(Zanclus canescens)* in this mood is a spectacle that can be seen practically every day.

Many years ago Lissmann demonstrated the lowering of the threshold releasing fighting behavior in the Siamese fighting fish *(Betta splendens)*. A really active search for a situation for fighting first caught my own attention through the fish already mentioned, *Zanclus canescens*. In a large tank a dominant fish had intimidated a weaker fish so completely that the weaker fish was constantly hiding behind a rock wall at a place where it was not only invisible to the dominant fish but also unreachable except by means of very steep detour that, moreover, led very close to the water's surface where it crossed the upper edge of the rocks. Coming close to the water's surface constitutes a strong deterrent to most fish.

The dominant zanclus moved around quietly in his home range near the tank's front pane. From time to time his intention to attack became visible through the laying back of the dorsal and anal fins in preparation for a strike and, at almost the same moment, he would rush toward the invisible victim to harass it still further. I have seen this very same seeking a fight with an invisible opponent innumerable times in the same species and under much more favorable conditions in my very large tank at Altenberg.

On these observations of the appetite for agonistic behavior in *Zanclus*, Rasa (1971) based her study of the same phenomenon in the marine Jewel Fish *(Microspathodon chrysurus)*. She showed that the appetite for agonistic encounters could be used just as well as the appetite for food as a reward situation for teaching a fish to swim through a simple maze. The fish were made to learn a simple L-shaped maze at the end of which the reward consisted of being able to see a conspecific antagonist through the diaphanous walls within a plastic chamber. The fellow member of the species put into the chamber was chosen so as to be slightly smaller than the experimental animal in order to invite attack. To get measurements of motivation it proved necessary to limit the size of the experimental chamber so as to make staying in it sufficiently disagreeable for the attacker; otherwise the fish would remain in it indefinitely, glaring at its unattainable opponent.

The amount of time the fish spent in the chamber was clearly correlated to the intervals during which it had previously been prevented from entering the chamber. In the evaluation of these experiments, the effects of general de-arousal (mentioned in Two/II/8, and to be further discussed in Two/III/4) were either prevented or taken into consideration and compensated for.

As Hogan and Adler (1963) also demonstrated in the fighting fish *(Betta splendens)*, the presentation of a fighting opponent has exactly the same effect, as a reinforcement for the learning of a maze, as has the presentation of food. Even without any systematic experimentation, anyone who is sufficiently familiar with the natural behavior of fish or of birds knows how strong the appetite for agonistic behavior can be in very many species. In the swordtail *(Xiphophorus helleri)* Franck and Wilhelmi (1973) studied the effects of "damming up" agonistic behavior patterns and found all the typical phenomena of increasing readiness and decreasing thresholds, as well as clearly defined appetitive behavior. Polemics should be kept out of a textbook, but it must be mentioned here that the editor of a well-known German journal specializing in popular science thought it fitting to head the publication of Franck's and Wilhelmi's results with the title, *Spontaneität der Aggression—Nein!* (Spontaneity of Aggression—No!), thus implying the exact opposite to what was being demonstrated by their paper. The ideological bias against all spontaneity that emanates from stimulus–response psychology is surprisingly strong in itself, and this bias rises to something resembling religious fervor the moment the spontaneity of aggressivity enters into the consideration. This is exasperating to anyone who, through lifelong observations devoid of any underlying hypothesis, has become familiar with higher animals such as fish, birds, and mammals and has encountered, innumerable times, unambiguous evidence of the spontaneity of agonistic behavior. Why indeed should it be less spontaneous than any other kind of behavior? It would be extremely surprising if it were.

12. Driving and Being Driven

In principle, all instinctive motor patterns are capable of furnishing their own autonomous contribution to the multiple motivations which keep an animal going. Equally, all processes based on endogenous generation of impulses, including complex instinctive action patterns, are susceptible to additional stimulation coming from other sources of motivation. This is true at many different levels; even the excitation-producing loci of the heart are spontaneously driving and, at the same time, susceptible to being driven. The pacemaker producing the excitation that causes the atrium and the ventricle of the heart to contract possesses its own rhythm in discharging endogenous impulses. Nevertheless, the heart still beats at a considerably higher rate because impulses coming from another superordinated pacemaker, situated on the sinus, always arrive a fraction of a second before those coming from the atrioventricular pacemaker are discharged. The rhythm of the superordinated, faster pacemaker is, in its turn, subject to accelerating and inhibiting influences exerted by the nervus accelerans and the nervus depressor cordis.

In this respect the instinctive activities of animals "behave" very much like the pacemakers of the heart: although possessing their own endogenous production of excitation, each of the motor patterns hitherto investigated in this respect acts as a drive, in the accepted sense of the word. At the same time, each of the motor patterns is subject to "being driven" by other factors. Some motor patterns, however, are more resistant to being driven than others. Highly differentiated specific motor patterns, those of copulation for instance, which are performed rarely and only in one equally specific stimulus situation and only in the service of one function, are largely independent of other motivations and are never performed except for their own sake, that is to say, never in the service of, or activated by, any other system. Unless one conceives of hormonal states as stimulus situations, they are very resistent to "being driven." As will be discussed later in Three/IV/5, these one-purpose activities are also very difficult to condition. The other end of a long scale of increasingly "driveable" motor patterns is represented by the multipurpose activities which, as already mentioned, are programmed in such a way as to serve very different motivations.

In principle, all instinctive motor patterns are exactly what A. F. J. Portielje, in his book, *Dieren zien en leeren kennen* (1938), has called "action-and-reaction-in-one." This term, although rather lengthy even without the Dutch double vowels, fits the facts as no other. The quantity of impulses endogenously produced during any time span (as already mentioned in Two/I/6), is adapted to the average demand which the species in question has for that particular motor pattern. This is not only true on the low level of fin movements in fish; a small bird such as a tit *(Parus)*, which uses its wings every few moments as long as it is awake, commands an almost unlimited supply of flight movements that, therefore, appear as "voluntary" to the human observer. A greylag goose, in contrast, takes wing comparatively rarely and can easily get into a situation of "wanting" to fly, but being unable to do so because its internal readiness is insufficient at that moment. If, when returning from an extensive flight, a goose has the bad luck to land within a narrow enclosure from which it can escape only by taking wing again, it shows at once that it possesses full insight into the situation. The goose does not try to find an exit through which it might walk out; it incontinently proceeds to perform preflight movements. But it cannot take off simply because it is not able to raise its specific excitation for flying above the necessary threshold. The observer is strongly reminded of a man very near the threshold of sneezing but who fails to bring off the relieving explosion; the man tries to reach the threshold through self-stimulation—for instance, by looking at a strong light. The goose, in the situation described, also resorts to self-stimulation, to calling, and to bill-shaking; but often a long time elapses before it can finally take off. The bird is unable to make a *decision* (the German word *Entschluß* is even more descriptive etymologically), and the movements of flying obviously are not "voluntary" in the sense discussed in Three/V/2.

Paul Leyhausen has studied the endogenous impulse production of the several motor patterns pertaining to prey-catching in catlike carnivores *(Felidae)*. He put a hungry cat in a room that was completely devoid of any cover but filled with an abundance of live mice, thus maximally facilitating prey-catching. In every one of these experiments, the cat first caught, killed, and ate half a dozen of the mice, then killed a few more without eating them, then proceeded "playfully" to catch some more without executing the killing bite. After reaching this stage, the experimental cat would sit quietly in the attitude of lying in ambush, with its head lowered and intently watching some of the mice running about on the opposite side of the room while others were actually crawling, unnoticed, over its paws. The number of performances after which each of these motor patterns proved to be exhausted corresponds exactly to the relative frequency with which each of them is "in demand." A cat often has to spend a long time sitting in ambush before being offered an opportunity to stalk a mouse, and usually it must do a lot of stalking before it ever gets into a position from which the long leap at the prey has any likelihood of success, and the leap can miss so that several leaps must be programmed in relation to each killing bite. Even this can fail to accomplish its end, so the cat must have more killing bites at its disposal than the number of mice it can eat.

In the complex hierarchical systems serving various animals during the acquisition of food, it is by no means the process of actually eating that invariably constitutes the most important consummatory act. In birds of prey, as falconers know, the main motivation of food acquisition is the catching and not the eating of the prey. There seems to be a gap in the innate program between the sequence of catching and that of eating: Having caught its first prey, a naive peregrine falcon *(Falco peregrinus)* appears emotionally exhausted and rather at a loss over what to do next. Then it begins plucking the prey in a tentative, haphazard way. Actual pecking, that is, the beginning of eating, seems to set in only under the influence of the optical stimulus of seeing blood. In dogs, hunting and killing are similarly independent of the motivation of eating: As everyone knows, it is impossible to wean a dog from its passion for hunting through abundant feeding. The consummatory act toward which the hunting appetite is striving is the killing, particularly the shaking of the prey, and not the devouring of it.

Neweklowsky (1972) studied the manner in which the prying movement of the starling *(Sturnus vulgaris)* is dependent on internal and external influences. The starling thrusts its bill into clefts or into soft material and then opens it with considerable muscular force, thereby enlarging or making a cleft into which it is able to peer. In birds possessing this prying movement, and in adaptation to this motor pattern, the cleavage between the mandibles is positioned so as to be in an exact straight line with the pupil of the eye, so that the line of vision leads unimpeded into the fissure opened by the prying movement, however narrow this may be. This organization has evolved at least three times independently: in some starlings (Sturnidae), in some icterids (orioles, blackbirds, meadow larks) and, curiously enough, in the penduline tit *(Remiz pendulinus)* which uses the movement only for the building of its elaborately woven nest.

The prying of the starling is strongly stimulated by the sight of a narrow cleft and by the touch of soft edges offering only limited resistance to being widened. Tame starlings seem to enjoy it enormously if one permits them to thrust their bill between two fingers that offer only a little resistance to being pried apart. Also, the starling quickly learns to recognize objects soft enough to be torn by prying, such as a newspaper lying on a soft support. The frequency of prying is increased only to a small degree by hunger; the increase is just at the borderline of being significant. On the other hand, exploratory behavior (Three/V/2) contributes appreciably to the motivation of prying: Any new object offered to a starling elicits long bouts of prying. Otherwise, the external stimulus situation has little influence on the number of prying movements performed within the time unit. In a cage completely devoid of fissures or clefts to pry into, and with abundant food openly offered, the frequency of prying is not significantly lower than when the starling has to acquire all of its food by prying into cups closed by rubber diaphragms that have slits in them and are not too easy to pry open. In a species that, like the European starling, acquires most of its food by performing one single motor pattern, the autonomous motivation of the latter is obviously sufficient to ensure adequate feeding and needs no appreciable additional drive from the side of tissue need.

The cactus finch (*Cactospiza pallida*) of the Galapagos Islands acquires a considerable part of its food by means of an extremely complicated behavior pattern that includes the use of "tools": the bird grabs a sharp cactus spine of suitable length in its bill and thrusts this into holes and crevices to poke insects out of them. Like the prying movement of the starling, this motor pattern is performed most persistently even when no prey can be acquired by it and when sufficient food is offered in open dishes. A strong appetitive behavior is demonstrably aimed at the intermediary goal of the spine, the particular releasing properties of which Eibl-Eibesfeldt has investigated. A tame cactus finch will greedily grab at a nice spine and immediately begin to poke it into clefts even when some favorite food, such as a wax moth larva, is offered simultaneously. Given the choice between a good spine and a fat larva, even a rather hungry cactus finch will unhesitatingly grab the former. Eibl-Eibesfeldt has even observed one of his finches put a larva into a hole, search for a spine and then poke the larva out again—in a way similar to a sportsman stocking his "shoot" with pheasants.

13. Neurophysiology of Spontaneity

In 1935, when I gave that lecture at the Harnack House in Berlin, I was already aware of all the salient facts concerning the spontaneity of instinctive motor patterns although not of their quantitative verification, which has been mentioned here. I discussed all the effects of threshold lowering, of vacuum activities and of appetitive behavior, and I even quoted from the letter written to me by Wallace Craig in which he said that it was "obviously nonsense to speak of a re-action [*sic*] to a stimulus not yet received." All this knowledge notwithstanding, I still stubbornly upheld the theory that instinctive movements were based on chain reflexes, although not on simple linear ones but on complicated polysynaptic networks of reflex processes. I assumed that the phenomenon of spontaneity—which I had conscientiously described—could be explained by an auxilliary hypothesis.

In those amazingly unenlightened assertions, to recapitulate briefly what has been written in the Introductory History, I was motivated by two prejudices. One was the belief that the obviously mechanical performance of an instinctive movement and the equally reflex-like reaction to a very specific stimulation were arguments in favor of the chain reflex theory. The second was an almost subconscious antagonism to the theories of vitalists such as McDougall (1923) and Bierens de Haan. I stupidly felt that relinquishing the chain reflex theory of instinctive actions meant a concession to purposivistic, that is, vitalistic psychology, and such a concession was something I was unwilling to make.

Nowadays, as I have already explained, it seems obvious that I should have asked the following question: Do we know any physiological processes that, though certainly as mechanical as instinctive movements and, like these, certainly not requiring any vitalistic explanation, but which, nevertheless, are not reflexes, which in fact are demonstrably independent of external stimulation and tend to recur rhythmically at regular intervals? The obvious answer would have been that processes of this kind have been known for a very long time in the excitation-producing loci of the heart.

Production of impulses within the heart was by no means the only process of endogenous generation of stimuli known at that time. In particular, the results obtained by Erich von Holst on the endogenous production and coordination of motor impulses within the ventral cord of the earthworm, as well as in the spinal cords of fishes, were quite unambiguously analogous to those obtained by Craig, Seitz, and myself on intact organisms. In fact, all of the phenomena discussed in the previous sections—with the exception of appetitive behavior—have been demonstrated by von Holst on a lower level of neural organization. It is surprising that his work is hardly ever mentioned in some of the very recent books on ethology.

Paradoxically, the very first investigation by von Holst that was destined to explode the explanatory monopolism of the reflex concept was originally aimed at analyzing an alleged "chain reflex." At the time, the following experiment was regarded as the paradigm and final proof for the concatenation of reflex processes and was even quoted by Jakob von Uexküll despite his fundamental antipathy to mechanistic explanation. An earthworm was cut in two and the pieces were subsequently tied or sewn together with thread. The worm then continued to creep along with well-coordinated movements, the waves of successive contractions running over the segments of its body and passing over the cut without any apparent hindrance. This was regarded as proof that the passive stretching which each segment underwent because of the contraction of the segment preceeding it caused its own contraction by way of a reflex. It was assumed that the swimming movements of a fish, for instance those of an eel, were coordinated in the same way; the contraction or relaxation of one muscle segment was believed to influence the muscular tension of the following one by means of proprioceptors which released reflexes. The way in which von Holst proceeded shows, most surprisingly, that he must have known that all these explanations were wrong even before he started experimenting.

His first experiments were based on the following considerations. If the conduction of excitation really consists of a chain of successively released reflexes, it must fulfill a number of conditions. Excitation must always reach one segment *after* the other just as, in a row of standing bottles, one must fall after the other when the first has been knocked over. But this is not always the case; under the influence of ether all the segments of a worm's body extend simultaneously. Furthermore, excitation should prove incapable of passing over a stretch of the ventral cord from which all peripheral nerves have been cut, since the path of the reflexes has been interrupted. What actually happens is that the excitation passes over such isolated stretches of the ventral cord with even greater rapidity than it does over the intact ones.

After these preliminary experiments, von Holst completely isolated a worm's ventral cord from its body, removed the supra-esophageal ganglion, suspended this preparation in Ringer's solution, and connected every single one of the ventral ganglia to a highly sensitive voltmeter. These instruments showed spikes of a tension, but not randomly—which would have been important enough in itself—but in a regular sequence; beginning at the front end, the wave of excitation passed over the entire length of the preparation at approximately the same speed and with the same rhythm in which the wave of contraction passes over the intact worm's body while it is creeping. Von Holst went on to prove that the impulses made visible by means of the instuments were indeed identical to those causing segmental muscle contractions: he made similar preparations in which a few segments of the ventral cord were not isolated and connected to voltmeters but were left in connection with the muscle segments. These then contracted in perfect coordination with the segments whose ganglia were connected to voltmeters.

Similar experiments on spinal fishes had similar results. Using a tench *(Tinca tinca)* with all posterior sensitive nerves cut away from the spinal cord so that reflexes could no longer be released from the skin, the fish could still react to optical and static stimulation and could swim with normal, well-coordinated movements.

An eel treated the same way also retains a normal coordination of the swimming movements. If the middle part of its long body is immobilized by cutting not only the sensitive posterior roots but the anterior motor roots as well, the wave of the swimming undulation, beginning at the fish's front end, disappears into the paralyzed part as a train would into a tunnel, only to reappear at the non-paralyzed tail end of the fish with the phase relationships nearly unchanged—not quite unchanged because, for reasons unknown, the processes of the centrally coordinated wave of excitation pass through the immobilized part of the body at a rate slightly faster than normal. The same effect is attained if a part of the eel's body is immobilized, not by cutting nerves, but by putting it into the strait jacket of a narrow tube.

As all these experiments show, none of the motor patterns investigated

is based on a chain of reflexes but on processes of spontaneous generation and of coordination of impulses; both take place within the central
nervous system itself, through processes independent of extero- or proprioceptor stimulation and of segmental reflex arcs.

With regard to the normal undulating swimming movements of fish,
simple observation could have pointed out the fact that, when a fish
starts swimming, its movements involve, from the very beginning, all
the segments of its body simultaneously, and that stopping is accomplished in the same way when the fish arrests all its swimming movements. According to the reflex theory, undulation ought to begin at the
front end when the fish starts swimming, and gradually pass along and
out at the tail end when the fish stops.

After having demonstrated to his own satisfaction the spontaneity of
endogenous stimulus generation within the central nervous system, von
Holst went on to investigate the factors responsible for the coordination
of movements. Since movement coordination is independent of afferent
nerves, the problem for investigation was obvious but there were some
difficulties in achieving its solution. One of these lay in the fact that the
motor pattern presented itself as a fully integrated whole the very
moment it was initiated. As soon as an organism changes from a state of
quiescence into one of motion, coordination is perfect and, as von Holst
says:

> ... it is as impossible to draw any conclusion concerning its genesis as it is
> impossible for the experimental embryologist to obtain any information
> concerning the factors causing and directing its ontogenetic development
> by the study of the mature organism. This difficulty forces us to look for
> objects in which the finished, absolute coordination of the several motor
> organs does not represent the only relation that is possible between them,
> but rather represents an extreme limiting case—the other extreme being
> represented by complete lack of any mutual influence between motor pro-
> cesses. Perhaps such objects could show us all transitions, all grades of
> mutual influence, ranging from very slight interactions to the strongest
> obligatory linkages [my translation].

Von Holst found the desired object for his investigations in the swimming movements of those fishes which, for propulsion, use rhythmical
skulling movements of the fins rather than the more common method of
undulating the whole body so that the tail fin serves as the main pro-
pellent. Wrasse and some other percoid fishes use tail fin swimming only
during emergencies demanding maximum speed; otherwise they propel
themselves by means of a rhythmical paddling of their soft fins while
keeping the body stiff. Analyses of films taken of intact fish show that
the fins often beat synchronously and in absolute coordination for a long
time, and then this coordinated connection is broken quite abruptly and
the fins beat completely independently of one another, each fin having
its own rhythm; that is to say, there is no coordination at all. The most
frequent and, at the same time, the most interesting relationship between

the rhythmical beating of two fins is the following: Each fin tends to maintain its own frequency but each exerts a certain quantitative influence on the the beating of the other, both with regard to its frequency and to its amplitude. The physiological mechanism effecting this phenomenon has been termed "relative coordination" by von Holst.

Von Holst developed a simple method for recording the fin movements under the influence of relative coordination. After transecting a fish's medulla oblongata and arranging for artificial respiration, he connected each fin to a lever writing on a rotating drum. The lever, constructed from extremely thin slivers of straw, was connected to only a few rays of a fin, the others having been cut away in order to eliminate the effects of water resistance. "By this procedure," von Holst says, "an unpredictable creature is suddenly transformed into an apparatus of high precision which performs movements of complete regularity as long as external and internal conditions are kept constant, but which reacts to each external influence with a definite change in its activity."

To evaluate the curve obtained by this method, von Holst used a procedure based on the principle of Fourier's sequences, a discussion of which here would lead too far afield. Every biologist and particularly every student of behavior interested in the physiology of the central nervous system is urgently advised to read the papers by Erich von Holst (1973) listed in the index of this book; they are available in paperback editions.

For a majority of cases in which the rhythms of two fins stand in a relationship of relative coordination, these rhythms affect each other mutually, although one of them often has a stronger influence than the other. In such a case, one can speak of a dominant and of a dominated rhythm. In an extreme case, one rhythm can exert a very one-sided domination over the other without, in turn, being appreciably influenced by it. In labrids and probably in many other perch-like fish, the rhythm of the pectoral fins dominates all the others. The two pectorals stand in a relationship of absolute coordination with each other. This is so regular in a majority of fish that the one known exception strikes every observer familiar with fish behavior as humorous: the pectorals of the Moorish idol (Zanclus canescens), by moving without any coordination at all, convey the compelling impression of an inebriated fish. In most perch-like fish, the pectorals have two motor patterns and both of them are executed in absolute coordination on both sides. In one motor pattern, both fins move in a skulling movement, pressed broadside against the water and pushing the fish forward while, during the return stroke, they move edge on. In the other pattern, the fins also move in absolute coordination but alternately and with an undulation taking place among the single fin rays, producing a downward directed stream of water. The first coordination serves to propel the fish forward, the second allows it to hover in one place. It is only this second coordination of the pectorals that influences the beat of the other two fins.

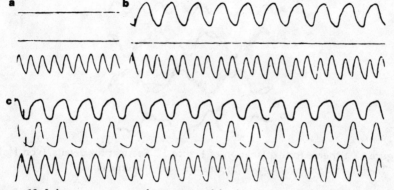

Figure 12. *Labrus:* movement of one pectoral fin (upper trace), the second pectoral fin (middle trace) and the dorsal fin (lower trace). In *a*, the two pectoral fin rhythms are inhibited by pressure on the sides of the body; in *b*, only one pectoral rhythm is inhibited; in *c*, the two pectoral fins oscillate in alternation. (von Holst, E.: *The Behavioural Physiology of Animals and Man*, Volume One.)

The influence which the pectoral fins exert on the subordinate rhythms of the caudal, of the soft dorsal, and of the anal fins can be demonstrated with particular clarity through the trick of excluding the pectoral rhythms for a time. This can be done quite simply by compressing the anterior part of the fish's body. The effects of the re-awakening pectoral rhythm can be observed as it gradually takes charge again. As Figure 12 shows, the dominated rhythms beat in a regular sinusoidal curve as long as the dominating rhythm is excluded. This demonstrates what form the dependent rhythms would assume if left to themselves and also what changes are caused by the dominant rhythm when it assumes command again.

The influence of an absolutely dominant rhythm may here serve to explain this effect because it is the simplest form of relationship between two or more endogenous rhythms. As already stated, the influences which two rhythms exert upon each other are, as a rule, mutual. Each rhythm has the tendency to maintain a constant frequency of the fin under its command—it shows a tendency to persevere *(Beharrungstendenz)*, as von Holst called it. The effect of the dominant rhythm on the dependent rhythm can be described as an attraction exerted by the peaks of the dominant one on those of the dependent one: If the culmination of the dominant fin movement is reached just before that of the dependent fin, the latter is speeded up; if the dominant fin lags behind, the beat of the dependent fin is slowed down. This effect gives the impression that the dominant rhythm is "trying" to force its own frequency on that of the dominated rhythm. The force of this influence is dependent on the span between the culminations; the nearer they are to one another, the stronger is the attraction—much like the effect a magnet has on iron filings, and for this reason von Holst coined the term "magnet

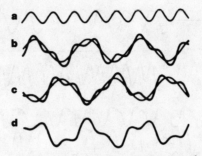

Figure 13. Scheme for explanation of Figure 12. See text for details. (von Holst, E.: *The Behavioural Physiology of Animals and Man*, Volume One.)

effect" *(Magneteffekt)*. Necessarily, with two rhythms beating at different frequencies, the phase relationships change periodically. When the phase of the dependent rhythm precedes that of the dominant rhythm, the latter has the effect of slowing down the dependent rhythm while, on the other hand, the frequency of the dependent rhythm will be accelerated if it is just a little behind that of the dominant one. The strength of this influence—and this is essential—is changing periodically with the periodic changes of phase distances between the two rhythms; it is always increasing when the distance between culminations decreases and vice versa.

Obviously, the quantity of this influence must be the greater the more often the culminations of the two rhythms coincide or are near each other, and this happens most often when the frequencies stand in a relationship that can be expressed in whole numbers, for instance, if every second beat of a dependent rhythm comes near to a beat of the dominant rhythm. At a certain, very small distance, the dependent rhythm often catches up with the dominant one by making a little jump—which is exactly what is so strongly reminiscent of the effect of a magnet.

Besides, and together with, the magnet effect, there is another form of mutual interaction between two endogenous rhythms—one that is more easy to understand and to explain. This is simple superposition. Again, and for simplicity's sake, the rare case of absolute one-sided dominance of one rhythm over the other is chosen as an example. As Figure 13 shows, the amplitude of the dependent rhythm increases whenever it beats in the same direction as does the dominant one, and exactly to that extent corresponding to the peak of the excursion made by the dominant rhythm at that very moment. Therefore, the fin activated by the dependent rhythm describes a curve corresponding to a superposition of the two curves of both rhythms.

Relationships between two rhythms based exclusively on superposition are just as rare as those based on the magnet effect alone; in the great majority of instances both effects are at work simultaneously. Also, a purely one-sided dominance is just as rare with regard to superposition as it is with regard to magnet effect; in fact, it is only the rhythm of the pectorals which, in the fish species investigated by von Holst, proved to be absolutely dominant.

An interesting detail is the following. As already mentioned, the pectorals of a labrid and acanthurid fish beat alternately as long as the fish is standing still, but synchronously when it is swimming forward. It is only in the former case that the rhythm of the pectorals exerts a dominant influence on the other fins. When the pectorals beat synchronously, the rhythm of the dependent fins becomes regular, freed from superposition and the magnet effect, not because the influence emanating from the pectoral rhythm ceases, but because the effects of the two pectorals now beating in opposite directions neutralize each other. To the best of my knowledge, von Holst never discussed the question of which influences are at work between the two pectoral rhythms: They always beat synchronously (except in *Zanclus*); it is only the sign of their excursion peaks that changes.

There are all kinds of possible intermediates and transitions between relative and absolute coordination, but the phenomena of magnet effect and of superposition are quite sufficient to explain them all. It is easy to understand why, for aquatic animals like fish, relative coordination is sufficient to produce tolerably regular motor patterns of locomotion; even in an untrained swimmer, relative coordination between arm and leg movements is a common occurrence. For locomotion on dry land, less changeable phase relationships between limb movements are desirable for the simple reason that there, in addition to propulsion, the functions of supporting the body and of maintaining equilibrium become important. Nevertheless, relative coordination occurs in terrestrial animals more often than one would suppose. Dogs, for instance, besides their absolutely coordinated paces of galloping, trotting, and walking, often show transitions into relative coordination when they change from one pace to another. When changing from walking to trotting, some dogs show the normal trotting coordination, in which contra-lateral legs are moved simultaneously, but they regularly fall into the coordination of the "ambling" trot, in which ipsilateral legs move together, when they change from galloping to trotting. They do not continue ambling for very long, however; they soon return to normal trotting by way of an interposed period of relative coordination.

These and other phenomena are in agreement, down to the smallest detail, with our assumption that identical physiological processes underly relative coordination in aquatic and absolute coordination in terrestrial organisms. The magnet effect appears to have a still wider distribution. It has been demonstrated in the aguish movements of patients afflicted with Parkinson's disease and it is almost banal to state that it also prevails in voluntary movements; everyone knows how difficult it is to play 4/4 with one hand and 3/4 with the other on a piano.

In Two/I/2, 3, when speaking of intensity differences of instinctive motor patterns, it was mentioned that two different central nervous processes cooperate in centrally coordinated movements. By a method and a reasoning whose discussion would lead too far afield here, von Holst has shown that there is a duality of functions, one sort of cell producing rhythmic impulses and several kinds of motor cells, each of which responds to these impulses with a slightly different threshold. The cells producing endogenous impulses determine the rhythm and its frequency, while the amplitude of the movement is dependent on the number of motor cells which are activated, "recruited" by these impulses. An explanation of the phenomena here described would indeed be most difficult if one should assume that the motor elements which send their impulses directly to the muscles were identical to those responsible for the endogenous generation of impulses as well as for their coordination. On the other hand, says von Holst, "the facts are easily explained if one assumes that two kinds of elements are contained within the spinal cord, one of which generates endogenous rhythmical impulses to which the other kind, the motor cells proper, respond by being alternately excited and inhibited and by sending corresponding motor impulses to the muscles." When the relative coordination of two rhythms is at work, the amplitude of the fin movements activated by the dominant rhythm fluctuates parallel with the influence it has on the dependent rhythm, in other words, parallel with the measure of the latter's periodicity. This influence becomes noticeable even when, for instance, the pectoral fin, after having been inhibited, begins to beat with a very small amplitude, although with the characteristic frequency which it will retain later. The gradual increase of amplitude is caused, as already explained, by the "recruitment" of motor cells which, owing to their different thresholds, respond in increasing numbers to the increasing intensity of endogenous impulses. Because of this the interaction of several rhythms can produce a constant phase relationship, in other words, a "gestalt" or a "melody" of the overall movement that remains recognizable even at very different intensities, as has been mentioned in Two/I/2, 3. All these complex and harmonious movements are produced entirely without the help of proprioceptors and even without the help of afferent processes in general.

Endogenous production of impulses has since been demonstrated to exist in very many different organisms, in very different parts of the central nervous system and even in non-nervous tissues, such as in tissue cultures taken from the heart of chicken embryos, in the body wall of coelenterates (Batham and Pantin 1950 a,b) and in the muscles of polychaete worms (Wells 1950). It exists in the central nervous system of the crayfish *(Astacus)* (Prosser 1961), in that of mantids, grasshoppers and cockroaches (Roeder et al. 1960), in isolated pieces of the brain cortex of cats (Kristiansen and Courtois 1949), in cell cultures made from the ganglion cells of *Aplysia*, and in all sensory epithelia that have been investigated hitherto.

14. Analogies of Function in Neural Elements and Integrated Systems

The central nervous system plays what may be called the "dirty trick" of accomplishing, on very different levels of integration, analogous functions in so perfectly similar a manner that even a highly sophisticated scientist can be misled into thinking them to be physiologically identical. The classic example of such a mistake was made by Helmholtz in assuming that the abstracting functions of perception mentioned in One/II/3 were based on rational, although unconscious deductions. The greatest caution is necessary whenever one attempts to find a connection between properties inherent in neural elements and those properties found in complex systems into which these elements are built.

This necessary reserve notwithstanding, it remains an important fact that even the smallest neural elements, down to isolated nerve fibers, show a very similar spontaneity as do whole animals. The old reflex theory propounded, and some modern stimulus–response psychologists assume that nerve cells and whole organisms, like well-bred children of Victorian times, "don't speak unless spoken to," in other words, that they remain passive and silent until a stimulus of sufficient strength impinges on them. As Bullock remarked, "somehow it did not impress behaviorists that the fly on the table sometimes takes off without any apparent stimulus" (1977). The neural element is regarded as a rather mechanical contraption that does not possess any more "behavior" than an electric switch.

The stimulus–response doctrine is all the more surprising since it is by no means certain that a neural element possessing the properties postulated by the doctrine exists at all. In every single instance in which a neural element has actually been investigated it has, as Kenneth Roeder pointed out, "been shown to have an elaborate intrinsic behavior determined by membrane properties, cell geometry, ion concentration, neurohumoral processes, and the spatial and temporal configuration of extracellular impacts" (1955).

Even in isolated neurites it can be demonstrated that the same element can be alternately reactive and spontaneously active. Figure 14 shows a comparison between the fluctuations of excitability in a spontaneously active and in a reactive element. On the ordinate axis is indicated the excitability prevailing at the moment. Its value can only be measured by the strength of the stimulus necessary to cause the element to discharge a nervous impulse. The upper horizontal line represents the threshold which must be reached for this to happen, the lower horizontal indicates the value of the rest excitability at the moment, for instance, in the neurite of a mammalian sciatic nerve suspended in Ringer's solution. The drawn-out curve shows the fluctuations of excitability which follow on the impact of the stimulus S. After a quick rise of excitation, the neurite

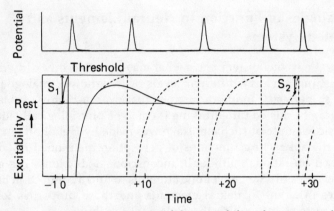

Figure 14. *(Lower graph)* A comparison of the excitability changes in stable (stimulus-response) and unstable (spontaneously active) neural elements. Solid curve represents excitability sequence in elements such as mammalian A fibers following stimulus S_1. Broken curve represents predicted excitability sequence in elements with a lower threshold and, hence, repetitively active following stimulus S_1. S_2 is the stimulus interpolated at some point in the spontaneous excitability change and causes premature discharge. *(Upper graph)* Nerve impulses that would arise from the excitability changes shown below. Time units would have different values for different types of excitable tissue. In the case of mammalia A fibers, the units would be milliseconds. (Roeder, K.: "Spontaneous Activity and Behavior.")

"fires off" an impulse and then its excitability sinks to the value of zero; in other words, no stimulus whatsoever can make the neurite discharge an impulse again for a certain duration. This time span is called the absolute refractory period. Subsequently, excitability rises again, in an undampened curve, overshooting the mark of rest excitability by far, regaining its value only after some time and by way of a dampened oscillation.

A small change in the value of rest excitability, easily effected by diminishing the calcium content of the Ringer's solution, has the consequence that the excitability which follows on the refractory period not only exceeds the value of rest excitability but actually reaches that of the threshold, thus causing another discharge and, therewith, a sequence of spontaneous, rhythmically discharged impulses.

As will be discussed later in Two/III/2, it has been demonstrated that sensory cells—formerly regarded as paradigms of elements passively waiting for stimulation—are characteristically spontaneously active units. Pumphrey has convincingly indicated the teleonomy of this fact (1950); the spontaneously active element does not have a threshold in the conventional sense of the word. A stimulus may arrive at any time and be of any strength; even if it is extremely small it will cause a *modulation* of the frequencies sent out by the receptor element. Today we know that the signals of all sensory cells hitherto investigated do not consist of a single impulse but always of modulations on the frequency of the impulses they produce spontaneously. Even for the neuron, and even for a neurite separated from its neuron, Portielje's old assertion made for intact animals remains equally true: Its function is "action-and-reaction-in-one" (1938).

In higher multicellular animals all spontaneous activities, down to those of the smallest elements, are influenced by those of superordinated loci which, in turn, are effected by exterior factors. It is only in organisms devoid of a centralized nervous system that all spontaneous activities are directly influenced from without. It is worth some contemplation that mobile unicellular animals behave so very much as metazoa do.

If stimulus–response processes really played the role they are supposed to play according to the old reflex theory, one should expect that an organism which happens to be in an environment offering too little stimulation would get stuck at dead center, as Roeder says, and stay quiescent until a change in the environment could offer further stimulation that would set it going again. Very few animals actually wait for stimuli or remain quiescent until stimuli arrive, although some highly specialized and cryptically colored predators seem to lapse into a natural kind of "akinesis" while lying in ambush waiting for prey. The larva of the ant lion (Myrmeleon) and some bottom-dwelling fish offer examples of this, but even they will move spontaneously if they must wait too long. For the vast majority of free-moving organisms, William McDougall's old saying is perfectly true: "The healthy animal is up and doing" (1923).

On the basis of their investigations of the behavior of sea anemones, Batham and Pantin conclude that "whatever may be the origin of these activities, it appears to lie in the animal itself and not to be caused by external stimulation" (1950 a,b). There are any number of motor responses which we are wont to describe as "reflexes" because the sequence of their muscle contractions is as short as their coordination is simple and, also, because their reactivity is much more evident than the participation of spontaneous elements. In my opinion, it is permissible to speculate that some of them, such as blinking, swallowing, stretching, sneezing, and others, may be constructed in a way similar to fixed motor patterns. Many of them, such as blinking, swallowing, and others, can appear as displacement activities in situations of conflict. Stretching, sneezing, and yawning, like some typical instinctive activities, are built on the "orgasm principle," which is to say that action-specific excitation rises to a climax, then the consummatory act is discharged, after which the act cannot be repeated. As F. Beach demonstrated in the chimpanzee, a retrograde inhibition is exerted by proprioceptors reporting the consummation. Having stretched or yawned, one cannot do either again immediately. Sneezing even has its own appetitive behavior, as is demonstrated by people buying snuff.

This is not true of other reflexes such as the optomotoric, muscle stretch, vestibular-ocular, and many other responses serving to supply instant information concerning body position and equilibrium. Many of these *must* have a constant or well regulated gain (input: output function); also, their functioning should not leave any lasting engram because what they report must be open to being countermanded within the next fraction of a second. Many of these, such as the allegedly monosynaptic tendon reflex, are based on complicated regulatory systems.

Apparently, responses which are not "action-and-reaction-in-one" are rather rare. Still, the element which lacks spontaneity and "does not speak unless spoken to " does exist. One such element, which W. Heiligenberg told me about, is the constricting muscle around the outflow opening of sponges. Also, the giant fibers which in many phyla cause extremely fast startle responses may, for long perods, show no vacuum activity, although the threshold is often quite labile (personal communication from T. Bullock, 1981).

What holds true, on the lowest level of integration, for the functional properties of neural elements and also, on the highest level, for the instinctive behavior of higher animals, is equally valid for the intermediate level of integration represented by the endogenously generated and centrally coordinated movements investigated by Erich von Holst. All attempts to explain fixed motor patterns and their properties on the basis of reflexes (however complicated and polysynaptic the hypothetically chosen patterns may be) are so obviously constrained and farfetched that their ideological motivation becomes apparent at once. If, on the other hand, one assumes that endogenous impulse production and central coordination form the basis of most animal activities, one finds the most natural explanations for just those phenomena which present the greatest difficulties to the chain reflex theory; threshold lowering and vacuum activities cease to be paradoxes and become effects which would have to be postulated if they had not already been observed. As W. Schleidt has pointed out in his paper, "How 'Fixed' is the Fixed Action Pattern?" (1974), some of the changes of form which an instinctive motor pattern undergoes through fluctuations of intensity find an unconstrained explanation on the basis of von Holst's assumption of the duality of stimulus-production and motor function and on the basis of his theory of recruitment of motoric elements: what remain constant are the relationships of phase and amplitude which constitute the harmony of the pattern recognizable even at the lowest intensities.

15. Chapter Summary

1. There are unchangeable, easily recognizable sequences of movements which, as properties of species, genera, families, and greater taxonomic units, are as reliable as criteria of evolutionary relationships as are any morphological characteristics or combinations of such. To these *fixed motor patterns* the concept of *homology* is equally

applicable. The distribution of fixed motor patterns within the taxonomic system, as well as the degrees of their similarities and dissimilarities within different taxonomic groups proves, beyond the necessity of any further confirmation, that these motor processes, in every detail of their forms, are anchored in the genes in exactly the same way as bodily properties are.

These genetically coordinated movements often, but not always, form a functional unit together with the releasing mechanisms that, without previous experience, respond selectively to stimulus situations in which the motor patterns are apt to fulfill their teleonomic functions. This type of functional unit has been called *arteigene Triebhandlung*—an instinctive action, or literally, a "species–characteristic drive action"— by Oskar Heinroth. Fixed motor patterns and innate releasing mechanisms are, however, entirely different physiologic mechanisms which can be incorporated into complex behavior systems independently of each other and in varying combinations.

2. Far from obeying an "all-or-nothing law", fixed motor patterns can appear in forms of all the possible transitions from a very slight indication, called an "intention movement" by Heinroth, to the full teleonomic performance that occurs at the high intensity of specific excitation. What remains constant throughout all fluctuations of intensity are the phase relationships as well as the proportions of their amplitudes. This makes the "melody" of the movements recognizable throughout all of their intensities.

3. In some instances, the same quality of specific excitation elicits different motor patterns, each of which is correlated to a particular degree of excitation.

4. It is assumed that these motor patterns, correlated to stages of intensity, are indeed activated by the same kind of qualitatively uniform excitation. This assumption is based on the following facts: a) all of these movements are elicited by the same configurations of external stimuli, in other words, by one IRM; b) they can also be elicited through electrical stimulation at the same loci of the hypothalamus, as von Holst has demonstrated with the chicken. Their scale of intensities, correlated to electric stimulations of different strengths, corresponds exactly with the scale of intensities observed in the intact organism; c) the thresholds of all the motor patterns of such a "set" fluctuate strictly parallel to each other; the exhaustion of one of them raises the thresholds of all the others; d) the transition from one such motor pattern to the pattern of next higher or next lower intensity is achieved without any time lag, while the change from one independent system of motor patterns to another independent system is subject to an "inertia" which causes a measurable pause between the activities.

5. The intensity with which a fixed motor pattern is performed depends on two factors: a) on the internal readiness of the organism,

and b) on the effectiveness of the external stimulation. The observation of a motor pattern being released by a certain stimulus situation furnishes us, therefore, with an equation containing two unknowns. Alfred Seitz added a second equation by offering an animal, after each dummy experiment, a stimulus configuration known to exert the maximal releasing effect. In this way he ascertained how much specific readiness was "still left" after the first presentation of the dummy. This he called the method of dual quantification. The laws which determine the decrease of internal readiness caused by each performance of a fixed motor pattern, and those other laws which determine the releasing effect of a stimulus configuration, could only be found by investigating *both simultaneously*.

6. Each performance of a certain motor pattern decreases the organism's readiness to perform it again *without*, at the same time, fatiguing the animal as a whole, that is, without affecting its readiness to perform other motor patterns. One of the few exceptions is represented by the motor patterns of locomotion that pertain to escape; these can be released until the entire organism, particularly with regard to its respiration and circulation, is exhausted.

7. The action-specific fatigue of one motor pattern, or of one "set" of motor patterns, is different from fatigue in general with regard to one important point: After general fatigue, the restitution of normal readiness to act reaches a definite level and stops there, while the experimentally enforced quiescence of a fixed motor pattern causes an almost unlimited lowering of the threshold values of releasing stimuli; this makes possible the acceptance as stimuli of inadequate substitute objects.

8. If an experimental animal is kept for a long period under constant and strictly controlled conditions that prevent the arrival of releasing stimuli, the above-mentioned phenomena of increasing readiness for a certain motor pattern can be obscured by two effects. One of these is an atrophy which can affect an unused motor pattern in much the same way it affects an unused muscle; the second is a gradual waning of "general arousal," that is to say, a general raising of all thresholds, a condition that is closely akin to that of sleep. The study of general arousal and, more particularly, of its opposite, general "de-arousal" caused by a deficiency in unspecific stimulation, has contributed considerably to our understanding of the relationship between stimuli which "charge up" the readiness and those which directly release a motor pattern.

9. If the experimental animal is kept under conditions that exclude directly releasing stimulus configurations but still supply the organism with sufficient unspecific stimulation to prevent de-arousal, the threshold lowering for certain motor patterns can reach the extreme value of "zero," that is to say, the motor patterns can be discharged

in vacuo without discernible releasing stimuli. This is particularly striking for object-directed motor patterns.

10. A long-enduring state of quiescence of a fixed motor pattern not only leads to a lowering of the thresholds of releasing stimuli but also induces a state of general restlessness in the organism as a whole. In its simplest form, this phenomenon, by causing the animal to move about randomly, increases its chances for encountering a releasing stimulus situation, while in its most complex differentiation, the same phenomenon constitutes the motivation for *purposive* search. This type of behavior has been termed *appetitive* behavior by Wallace Craig (1918). *All conditioning by reinforcement occurs within a context of appetitive behavior*, at least in non-human species.

11. Threshold lowering and appetitive behavior also occur in motor patterns which, because of their teleonomic function, must be considered as constituting *avoidance* behavior. In some instances such as intra-specific aggression and in some patterns of escape, this may lead to effects which are clearly dysteleonomic, particularly if, as in some types of aggressive behavior, *intraspecific selection* plays a part that is very dangerous to the survival of the species. In escape behavior, too, the phenomena of spontaneity often appear to be distinctly dysteleonomic. It would seem that evolution has been unable to construct an IRM possessing a constant threshold. This is all the more surprising as a number of other cases are known in which thresholds can be remarkably constant. Otherwise, constancy of perception is largely dependent on a highly complicated feedback mechanism sensing and regulating blood sugar, body temperature and many other factors. The fact that the motor patterns of fighting are subject not only to threshold lowering but also give rise to virulent appetitive behavior has met violent, ideologically motivated denial.

12. Every motor pattern that is striven for by its own appetitive behavior constitutes an autonomous source of motivation for animal and human behavior. On the other hand, hardly any fixed motor patterns are known which cannot be "driven," that is, activated or facilitated by motivations coming from outside the realm of their own autonomous spontaneity. This rule holds equally true for the lowest levels of motor patterns such as the rhythmic contractions of the vertebrate heart as well as for motor patterns demonstrably caused by endogenous generation and central coordination of impulses, and also for the most complex systems of instinctive behavior. A. F. J. Portielje's rather long term, "action-and-reaction-in-one," is perfectly fitting for all of these cases. It is only the quantitative measures of driving and of being driven that vary in the different cases. The amount of a motor pattern's susceptibility to "being driven," in other words, its "availability," is dependent upon the quantity of its endogenous generation of "readiness," of excitability.

13. All the facts stated and described in the preceding sections find an unconstrained explanation through the research results of Erich von Holst who demonstrated that, in the ventral ganglion chain of the earthworm *(Lumbricus)* and in the spinal cord of many fishes, the processes of endogenous generation of impulses and their coordination occur within the central nervous system itself without afferent stimulation taking any part in shaping the coordinated "melody of impulses." This explodes the chain-reflex theory of instinctive movements.

14. An important way in which two primarily independent processes of endogenous production of impulses can become coordinated has been called the "magnet effect" by Erich von Holst. Each rhythm influences the other in the sense that the peaks of the movements produced attract one another. This effect is the stronger the nearer the peaks are to each other. In consequence of this, the rhythms tend to force upon each other those frequencies which stand in a tempo relationship that is "harmonious," in other words, that can be expressed in simple whole numbers. If the frequencies of two rhythms are sufficiently close to a harmonious relationship, the magnet effect forces them into keeping step permanently. Thus "relative coordination," found more often in aquatic animals, is turned into "absolute coordination" which prevails in organisms moving along on dry ground.

15. Notwithstanding the great caution that is indicated when applying conclusions drawn from the properties of the elements to properties of the system into which they are integrated, it is still permissible to point out that even the smallest units of nervous tissue, including even neurites (Roeder 1955), are far from conforming to the idea of the purely reactive elementary process postulated by the reflex theory. Slightly more integrated functions of central nervous systems, such as centrally coordinated movements (von Holst), show an even more impressive similarity to the behavior of intact animals. All the phenomena of spontaneity which cannot be accounted for by the reflex theory become not only explicable but must be postulated if one assumes that the spontaneous generation and central coordination of impulses, as demonstrated by Roeder and von Holst, form the basis of the fixed motor patterns observed in intact animals.

16. The essence of everything that has been said in this chapter can be condensed into Erich von Holst's analogy: "The central nervous system is not like a lazy donkey that must be whipped or, to make the comparison closer, that must bite its own tail every time before it is able to move a step; the central nervous system more closely resembles a spirited horse as much in need of the bridle as of the spurs."

Chapter II
Afferent Processes

1. The Innate Releasing Mechanism (IRM)

As has been emphasized repeatedly, the functional unit of the instinctive action now called the species-characteristic drive action consists of two fundamentally disparate physiological processes. The active, spontaneous part was the first to get our attention; therefore, as I have tried to reconstruct the genesis of our own ideas in this book, the fixed motor patterns have been discussed before the afferent processes. As long as the whole of the motor activity was regarded as a chain of reflexes, the first link of this chain did not seem to be different from the subsequent ones nor did it seem to demand any special attention. With increased insight into the physiological nature of spontaneous motor patterns, however, it became clear that it must indeed be a physiological apparatus of a very different kind, an apparatus which selectively "recognizes" the biologically correct situation and, thereupon, removes the inhibition which otherwise blocks the performance of the fixed motor pattern.

In the last sections of the preceding chapter I was forced, for reasons already explained, to anticipate some of the facts concerning the mechanisms which enable the animal to "recognize," without any previous experience, a biologically relevant situation—in other words, to respond to it selectively by a teleonomically "correct" and equally unlearned action pattern. At first I called this selective afferent mechanism the *angeborene Schema*—the innate scheme—because the organism seemed to have some sort of simplified, sketchy information about what the biologically relevant situation was like. Later, Tinbergen and I relinquished this term because its connotations suggested that something like an outline or an image of the whole situation or object was innate. In discussing the methods of dual quantification, I was forced to anticipate the important fact that it is by no means an image of the whole object or situation which is innately "known" to the animal, but a number of independently effective, very simple stimulus configurations whose releasing functions, obeying the law of heterogeneous summation, add up to a qualitatively unitary effect. For this reason Tinbergen and I (1938) abandoned the term *Schema* and decided to call the neural organization here under discussion the *innate releasing mechansm* (IRM)—in German, *angeborener Auslösemechanismus* (AAM).

This concept is defined exclusively by its function. It is obvious that in organisms differing with regard to the complexity of their nervous organization as well as to the levels of integration attained by their cognitive faculties and their behavior, very different demands are put upon the *selectivity* of their responses to external stimulus configurations. It is equally obvious that very different physiological mechanisms have evolved to cope with these demands.

Even with the lowest organisms, the question arises concerning whence the animal obtains the information telling it what to do under which circumstances. In Two/VI, I shall describe in detail the mechanisms evolved to receive and exploit instant information. The IRM is to be regarded as one of these, yet the problem of its selectivity must be discussed here. How can we explain that, for instance, an amoeba does not ingest all corpuscles of suitable size but refuses—though with some pardonable errors—to eat undigestible material? We know that a flagellate, obeying a kinesis (Two/IV/5), accelerates its locomotion when traversing unfavorable conditions and slows down on entering more favorable ones and, by these simple reactions, achieves the goal of spending most of its time within the latter. But how does the flagellate know which environmental conditions are favorable and which are not? The system of actions, the repertoire of behavior patterns at the disposal of these protozoans comprises but a few possibilities for motor activities, among which the avoidance of danger and the approach to food are predominant. Therefore, no excessive demands are made on the selectivity of the releasing mechanisms. Still, if an amoeba responds to quite a number of quite different stimuli in a manner which—at least statistically considered—is sufficiently teleonomic to assure the survival of the species, this fact needs an explanation, all the more so since the motor response to all these stimuli, the amoeboid movement, remains virtually the same throughout, changing only in intensity and in symbols. All an amoeba can do is to creep, with varying intensities, toward or away from a source of stimulation, the extremes being represented by creeping "all over" an object, and thus engulfing it, or, in the opposite case, by thickening the ectoplasm of its entire surface, in other words, by capsulating. The identity of the motor mechanisms makes it all the more remarkable that a multitude of different stimuli evoke either approach or avoidance in the teleonomically correct situation. The mechanism underlying this selectivity is little known; chemical stimuli are predominantly responded to, but thermical and tactile ones are, too.

A little bit more is known about the releasing mechanisms by which ciliates, particularly paramecium and related forms, are guided. The most important criterion by which the environment is "judged" to be favorable or not, is its pH value. The mechanisms of phobic and of topic responses, to be discussed in Chapter VI, have the effect of keeping the animals in water with optimal acidity. The acid found much more frequently than any other under natural conditions is CO_2. It is regularly found in the vicinity of decomposing organic material as a product of bacterial activity. This regularity is sufficiently reliable so that the ciliates can "afford" to be programmed to respond to certain concentrations of acid as a sign of the presence of bacteria on which they can feed. Under normal conditions all other acids are so rare that the survival of no species of ciliates is threatened by their reacting dysteleonomically to oxalic or another poisonous acid. The experimenter who drops oxalic acid into his culture of paramecium is so rarely encountered in nature that the behavioral program of this species need not provide for him.

There are natural enemies which exploit the limited selectivity of the paramecium's response to acid. At certain optimal concentrations, paramecia will react specifically to tactile stimulation by soft substances; they stop their forward movement and "anchor" by pressing gently against the soft obstacle. Large amoebas excrete just the right amount of CO_2 to make the vicinity near them attractive to ciliates, and they present to an approaching paramecium a surface of exactly the right, soft consistency to entice it to "anchor." Then the amoeba quite slowly extrudes pseudopods that surround the paramecium and finally enclose and capture it. I once observed a paramecium which, when it was all but enclosed in such a net of pseudopods, went into reverse and slipped out of the trap. To do this it had to resort to a special motor pattern at the disposal of the species, that is, constricting the tip of its body sufficiently to allow it to enter a narrow passage and then causing the constriction to pass along the length of its body in a peristaltic movement. This, of course, pushes the body in the opposite direction, thus forcing it through the narrow aperture. When that particular paramecium was completely out of the cavity formed by the amoeba's pseudopods, that ill-advised animalcule shifted into forward movement and went in again, reversing the peristaltic trick. In the next instant the amoeba had closed the trap and the paramecium gave a few last violent, jerking escape responses which made the thin membrane closing the trap bulge visibly. Then it expelled its trichocysts and died, which in these protozoa is visible through the sudden dissolution of the internal plasma structures. The whole incident most dramatically illustrated the danger of "erroneously" responding to the "wrong" stimulus configuration, a danger incurred by the limited selectivity of all IRMs—and not only the simple ones of the lowest free-moving organisms.

This danger is minimized by the "choice" of stimulus configurations made during the evolution of IRMs. These configurations always represent a compromise between the greatest possible simplicity and the greatest attainable improbability of any external stimulus situation, other than the teleonomically adequate one, eliciting the specific response. A paragon of this combination is the classic example cited by Jakob von Uexküll (1909), the stinging response of the common tick *(Ixodes rhizinus)*. The female of this species, after the last molt, can wait a very long time before finding a final host, any mammal. The IRM responding selectively to this host object consists of a reaction to only two key stimuli: first, a body temperature of roughly 37°C and second, the smell of butyric acid. Furthermore, finding the proper object is helped by the tick's sitting patiently on low branches and allowing itself to drop down, when these are shaken, so that there is a good chance of its falling onto an animal moving below. The probability of all these conditions being fulfilled by anything *but* a mammal is negligible. On the occasion of an institute carnival party, one of my students composed a wonderful epic in hexameter describing how, on a sunny slope covered with boulders, a wild boar rubbed its back against one of them and set it rolling downhill, and how the boulder, striking and shaking a bramble, and smelling of butyric acid acquired from the rubbing and secretions of the boar's skin, seduced a tick into trying to sting it, and how the poor tick, having irreparably bent its proboscis, died of depression. Nothing could better illustrate the strength and the weakness inherent in the IRM.

The problem of how and when the function of selecting is performed by the IRM must be separately investigated for every single instance. The questions how and when are easiest to answer when a sensory organ is responding to only one single sort of stimulation to which the animal responds with but one single behavior pattern. As Regen (1924) has demonstrated in the common cricket *(Acheta domesticus)*, the auditory organ of the female responds exclusively to the pitch of the male's courtship song, and the insect reacts to it by turning towards and approaching the source of the sound. In one of the experiments, the female jumped right into the loudspeaker Regen was using. Similar one-to-one linkages of stimulus perceived and behavior pattern released have been shown in the males of some mosquitoes responding to the frequencies of the female's wing beats.

The same questions of how and when must obviously receive very different answers if an animal possesses a large repertoire of different behavior patterns, each of which is released selectively and teleonomically by one of an equally large number of stimulus configurations, all of which are received by way of the same sense organ, for instance, the eye. In such a case one cannot avoid assuming the existence of a physiological mechansm situated between the sense organ and the motor activity that performs a function comparable to that of *filtering* incoming stimuli, and that permits only certain configurations to pass and to affect the locus in command of one particular motor pattern. Several physiologists have grasped the necessity of postulating such a stimulus-filtering mechanism. One of them was Pavlov; he very aptly named it the "detector," a term which is, perhaps, preferable to that of the IRM. More than half a century ago, the American ornithologist, F. Herrick, made the important statement, "The instincts of a species fit like lock and key," and therewith compared the function of impinging stimulus configurations to that of keys. The term *key stimuli* is accepted in ethology as denoting those stimulus configurations that, as has been explained in Two/I/5, add up to their effects according to Seitz's law of heterogeneous summation.

When I said that the term "detector" is, in a way, preferable to that of innate releasing mechanism, I did so because the releasing of a fixed motor pattern does not by any means represent the only function of the mechanism here under discussion, just as the instinctive action, the species-characteristic drive action, is not the only behavioral system into which IRMs and motor patterns are found integrated. Still, if the term IRM implies that releasing is one of the most common functions of the mechanism thus described, the implication is not altogether misleading, and I propose to retain Tinbergen's term although it must be remembered that, as I shall describe later in Three/IV/3, the most common function of IRMs consists in switching from one link in a hierarchic chain of behavior to a subsequent one. Cases are known as well in which a typical IRM "releases" nothing but a specific inhibition!

At the moment, very little is known about the physiologic processes which achieve the function essential for the IRM, that of filtering stimuli. The investigation conducted by J. Y. Lettvin and his co-workers on the retinal functions of the frog (1959) tend to show in what direction the solution of these problems may be expected. In the retina of the frog, groups of sensory elements are connected with one gaglion cell. Each group responds to another form of stimulus configuration reported by the elements. One responds only if all elements simultaneously report a change from light to darkness or the opposite (the on–off effect). Other groups respond only to much more specific sensory inputs, for instance, to a convex contour separating light and darkness and progressing in a particular direction across the group of sensory elements. Each of these sensory elements is a member of several groups, being connected to all adjacent cells in the ganglion retinas. The selective response to such specific configurations as "dark convex contour moving from left to right" is strongly reminiscent of that of the IRM in an intact animal responding to a key stimulus. One is indeed tempted to speculate that it should be easy for a more centrally situated group of nervous cells to integrate the information furnished by the cells of the ganglion retinas into relevant reports, such as "insect flying past from right to left," which could be directly passed on to motor systems.

E. and P. Kuenzer investigated the response of young pygmy cichlids *(Nannacara anomala)* to the optical stimulus configurations emanating from their mother (1968). The young fry clearly differentiate between their mother and other, potentially predatory fish by swimming toward the former and avoiding the latter. The most effective key stimulus configurations eliciting approach proved to be the light and dark color pattern of the parent fish and the sideways jerking head movements made by the female *Nannacara* in the presence of her progeny—at about the same frequency with which a mother hen utters her clucking call. Surprisingly, the black and white coloration of the mother was not only effective through the contrast between both shadings, but also through the contrast between these and the background: the dark markings had to be darker than the background, while the effect of the white markings was dependent on their contrast with both the dark pattern and with the background. Thus the light and the dark elements of the female's color pattern appeared to furnish separate pieces of information. What proved essential for the releasing effect were not absolute quantities of stimulation, but contrasts, in other words, relationships between impinging stimuli. The Kuenzers also examined the physiological conditions which are responsible for the releasing function within the sensory organ itself. On the basis of these results they succeeded in constructing "super-normal" dummies that, with regard to their releasing effect, by far surpassed the natural object and were able to lure the *Nannacara* babies away from their real mother.

When watching the prompt and teleonomically correct response which the normal object calls forth by way of an IRM, the naive observer tends to overrate the amount of information contained in its program. To see a newly-hatched turkey *(Meleagris gallopavo)* hide in cover and crouch at its first sight of a hawk flying over, or to see a young kestrel *(Cerachneis tinnunculus)*, on first encountering water, bathe and preen as if it had done these things hundreds of times, is indeed impressive. To see turkey chicks react in the same manner to a fat fly slowly crawling along the ceiling, or the young kestrel trying to bathe, using the same movements, on a polished marble table, is actually disappointing. Yet these errors are significant and were the first indications which led us to a better understanding of the IRM and of the paucity, or better, the parsimony of the information it conveys.

Tinbergen demonstrated the surprising simplicity of key stimuli and, at the same time, their additive effect in the IRM directing the gaping of nestling blackbirds *(Turdus merula)* towards the head of the parent birds bringing food. If one offers to the nestlings two rods at the same elevation, they will gape at the nearer one; if one offers the rods at the same distance but at different elevations, they will gape at the higher one. If

Figure 15. Any discontinuity in contour acts as "head." With a projecting triangle, it is always the upper corner which attracts gaping. (Lorenz: *Studies in Animal and Human Behaviour*, Volume II.)

one presents two objects, for instance, cardboard discs of different size at equal distances as well as at equal elevations, they will gape at the smaller one. Tinbergen presented to the nestlings a dummy consisting of two cardboard discs differing in size. Offering this dummy at first with the smaller disc up, and then rotating the dummy slowly and thereby lowering the smaller disc, Tinbergen ascertained how far this could go until the gaping ceased to follow the smaller disc and was directed at the upper edge of the larger one (Figure 15). By playing the stimulus config- uration of "higher" against that of "smaller" Tinbergen ascertained the optimum relationship of the discs: the gaping of the nestlings directed at the smaller disc followed this the farthest downward when its diam- eter was one-third that of the larger disc. The relationship was indepen- dent of the absolute size of the model. Analogous experiments with regard to the configurations of "higher" and "nearer" brought analogous results, the first proving much more effective than the latter. The opti- mum difference between the two was not investigated. Two indentations in the contour of a single disc caused the nestlings to direct their gaping at the area between them, provided they were at the right distance from each other to properly simulate a head, but they did not follow this as far downward as they did a more distinctly separated "head" when it was lowered. For her doctoral dissertation Ilse Prechtl investigated the

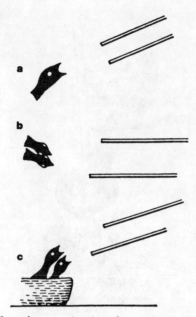

Figure 16. *a* and *b*. The schema orienting the gaping responses of young black-birds. With two rods at the same distance, gaping is directed at the higher (*a*: side view), while with two rods at the same height, gaping is towards the nearer (*b*: overhead view). In *c*, height is offset against nearness; height wins. (Lorenz, *Studies in Animal and Human Behaviour*, Volume II. Adapted from Tinbergen, "The Releasing and Directing Stimulus Situations of the Gaping Response in Young Blackbirds and Thrushes.")

effects of further criteria which constitute properties of the real parent head. First, by using three-dimensional models, she showed that the con-figurations of "higher" and "nearer" when presented simultaneously do indeed have the summational effect predictable on the basis of Seitz's rule of heterogeneous summation. Furthermore, any structures of the head, particularly those which protruded in the direction of the gaping nestling, added to the releasing value of the model's "head." On the whole, Ilse Prechtl's models showed a remarkable similarity to a very crude toy bird.

All these experiments show a number of properties inherent to the IRM which tend to explain why the assumption of a simplified image, of an "innate scheme" of the object seemed promising. On the other hand, they show very clearly that the phyletic information is not given to the organism in the form of a unitary, if simplified, image of the object, but by a number of mutually independent responses to very simple config-urations—to key stimuli—whose effects add up in accordance with Seitz's law.

Although the sum of the key stimuli to which an IRM responds does not, by any means, represent a unitary complex quality, the "gestalt" of its object, nevertheless each of the stimulus configurations that act as "keys" to the response can be regarded as a simple gestalt in itself. Its effect as a signal is never dependent on absolute stimulus data, but always on the perception of *intervals*, of differences and relationships, all of which can be represented by very different absolute values. The only exception is represented by mechanisms whose selectivity is dependent on the narrow margins of receptivity in the sense organ itself, as in Regen's cricket (page 156). The relatively simple stimulus configurations which act as "keys" to an IRM are closely akin to gestalt perceptions in this respect: Christian von Ehrenfels, one of the pioneers of Gestalt psychology, emphasized that "transposibility" is one of the criteria of gestalt perception (1890). The classic example is the recognition of a melody; this is quite independent of absolute pitch, of the instrument which produces the sounds, and so on. Transposibility is equally characteristic of all key stimuli. It has already been mentioned that, for the orientation of gaping in nestling thrushes, the "head" has to be one-third the size of the "body," independently of the absolute size of the dummy. The contrast phenomena that, as the Kuenzers have demonstrated, are essential for releasing following responses in young *Nannacara* (page 158) are another example. A third example is furnished by the response of male mouthbreeders of the species *Haplochromis burtoni* to the markings on the head of the rival. Among these, a dark bar traversing the eye represents one of the most effective key stimuli releasing rival fighting. This bar extends from the pupil of the eye obliquely downward and forward. As Leong showed through dummy experiments (1969), the "transposable" character essential for the releasing effect is not the angle between the bar and the horizontal, which would have been possible to assume since the males, in the typical broadside-on threatening posture, are positioned more or less horizontal, but the angle between this bar and the longitudinal axis of the fish's body.

The overwhelming majority of IRMs that hitherto have been investigated are composed of several responses to key stimuli which are, in principle, independent of each other, and which add up to a qualitatively uniform effect. The rule of heterogeneous summation has prevailed in every case examined. Only two instances are known to me in which one single configuration of stimuli proved to be effective; in both cases this configuration was singularly complicated and, in this respect, gestalt-like. The so-called rattling attack of the jackdaw *(Coleus monedula)* serves to defend a fellow member of the species which has been taken by a predator. To release this behavior pattern it is necessary that an object that is a) black, and b) soft and dangling or fluttering, be carried by a live creature. I discovered the response when I happened to carry a pair of wet black bathing trunks in my hand. As further experiments showed, it is quite irrelevant for the response what sort of a creature is carrying the soft black object; a nest-building jackdaw trying to carry a raven's secondary feather to its nest was furiously attacked by all the jackdaws within sight. An object that was rigid in itself, though black and carried by a live being, as for instance a black camera box carried by myself, elicited no response, but I had to hide from my jackdaws whenever I pulled out the black paper strips which, at that time, served to exchange the films. Whenever the birds saw these fluttering black objects in my hands, I was subjected to mass attack immediately. The number of such experiments I could conduct was limited by the aftereffects of each rattling attack; the birds were severely alarmed and remained distrustful of me for a long time after each such event. A greater number of trials would have spoiled my chances of further observation.

The second example of an IRM which responds to a single but complicated and gestalt-like configuration of stimuli was found by O. Drees in male jumping spiders (Salticidae) (1952). At a certain distance, these animals respond to any small black visible object by running towards it. The initial behavior leading to either catching prey or to courting a female is identical. Which of these two behaviors will follow as the sequel is determined only when the male has approached the object near enough to discern its contours. Near enough is a distance of a few centimeters. Then the object, or a dummy connected to the substratum by short vertical "legs," releases the prey-catching jump. At the sight of an object showing long legs, which, like a spider's, are directed upward from the body at their base and, arching high above it, touch the substratum only at a certain distance, the male will stop and begin to wave its palpi in species-characteristic courtship movements.

These two IRMs, of jackdaws and of Salticidae, represent rare and special cases of an innate response being elicited by a single, but complicated configuration of stimuli. In view of their theoretical importance, these phenomena ought to be investigated further.

2. Limits to the Functions of IRMs

Everything said in the preceding section was intended to show that IRMs are unable to respond to complex qualities in the way that *learned* gestalt perception can. A practically unlimited number of single criteria can be integrated into a single, unambiguously perceived quality by the learning of a "gestalt." At the age of five years my elder daughter proved able to identify as members of the family of rails (Rallidae) all the different species which at that time were exhibited in the Schönbrunn Zoo. This was remarkable for two reasons. One is that the rails include forms adapted to very different biotopes: long-legged wading birds, prairie dwellers extremely similar to gallinaceous birds, and ducklike aquatic forms. The second reason is that the little girl was familiar only with the aquatic forms—the coot *(Fulica atra)* and the moor hen *(Gallinula choloropus)*. When asked how she recognized all these birds as Rallidae, my daughter could only say that they were "somehow like a moor hen." Unlike the few configurations essential to an IRM, the innumerable criteria integrated in a gestalt perception cannot easily be verbalized.

The simplicity and poverty of the information conveyed by an IRM can, as already mentioned, lead to "errors" and can do so even under natural circumstances. Geese can react to a leaf wafted along by a slight breeze as if it were a slowly gliding eagle. I have known incubating turkey hens to roll smooth pebbles or—in one case—a tin cigarette box into their nests because the IRM of egg rolling responds to any object that is hard, smooth, and devoid of projections.

Another weakness is inherent in the IRM for the very reason that the information which it contains is coded in relations and not in absolute values. As a result of this, it is possible to *exaggerate* certain relationships which act as key stimuli and to construct models whose efficiency by far surpasses that of the natural object. Tinbergen has demonstrated with gulls and Baerends with the Oystercatcher that the incubating bird prefers oversized egg dummies painted with a pattern of strong contrasts to its own clutch. When in an experiment involving choice the bird is offered such dummies side by side with its own eggs, it will promptly sit on the former. The presence of the supernormal object effectively prevents the silly bird from normal incubation.

Another example of an IRM that can easily be misled by the exaggeration of one key stimulus is the one eliciting copulatory actions in geese. Besides some pre-copulatory movements, the most effective stimulus configuration consists of the partner's offering a large horizontal plane near the surface of the water, as does the female goose when inviting the male to mount. The effect of this horizontal surface can be very much enhanced by making it larger and by offering it just a few centimeters below the water surface. Unintentionally the human foster parent does just this when going into the water with tame geese. Even juvenile geese not yet able to fly, including females, will try to mount the swimmer's back, scratching most horribly. This is done—as must be emphasized— by individuals that are not sexually imprinted to humans. The information conveyed by the IRM would read when verbalized: "Large horizontal plane near water surface offered by conspecific."

In a manner of speaking, IRMs of this kind are "open to exaggeration in one direction"; verbalized they would read "as large as possible," "as rich in contrast as possible," and so on. There are a number of social parasites which employ the method of exaggerating key stimuli, as does the

European cuckoo, and a number of social parasites among insects. Hein-roth observed that a fully fledged young cuckoo which he put in an avi-ary was fed by birds of quite varied species, not only by adults, but also by juveniles that had only just become independent of being fed them-selves. Apparently the huge gape of the young cuckoo represents a supernormally strong key stimulus to the feeding behavior of many kinds of passerine birds. Heinroth remarks, "The feeding of a young cuc-koo is, in a manner of speaking, a vice of these birds"—a statement of remarkably deep insight.

Human beings also possess a number of IRMs that are "open to one side" and which respond to supernormal stimuli. An American journal-ist, at an ethological conference, having seen G. P. Baerends's film of an oystercatcher trying in vain to sit on an oversized and brightly painted egg, exclaimed, "Why, that's the cover girl!"—which showed complete understanding of the phenomenon. Most measures taken by fashion to enhance female—and male—beauty function on the principle of exag-gerating key stimuli. The same is true of the doll industry. Humans respond with emotions and behavior patterns of parental care to a num-ber of configurational key stimuli that can easily be analyzed—and also exaggerated. One of them is a high and slightly bulging forehead, a brain case large in proportion to the face and the visceral cranium, large eyes, rounded cheeks, short and stubby limbs, and a rounded fat body. Addi-tional key stimuli are uncertain, stumbling movements. A puppy which can keep to its intended direction as long as it walks, but deviates from it the moment it tries to gallop, is surprisingly sweet. It is typical for the unreflecting nature of the IRM that we feel moved to tenderness even by adult animals provided they possess the characters just mentioned. Such creatures are felt to be engaging, sweet, or appealing; in German their species names often end in the diminutive suffix -chen (Figure 17).

T. Tugenhat made an interesting series of experiments with humans, showing them models in which the configurational key stimuli were depicted in different degrees of exaggeration. Her results were somewhat contradictory and I believe this was caused by the kind of instruction given to her experimental subjects: she instructed them to choose the model that was "most babylike." B. Hückstedt, who had no bias against introspection and the recognition of emotions, made the same sort of experiments, but she told her subjects to choose the model they would prefer to cuddle. Her results were quite unambiguous and also demon-strated the validity of the law of heterogeneous summation. As an inter-esting side result, she was able to explain why the teddybear and Bambi can compete with human effigies as effectively as they do. The Kewpie doll represents the maximum possible exaggeration of the proportions between cranium and face which our perception can tolerate without switching our response from the sweet baby to that elicited by the eerie

Figure 17. The releasing "schema" for human parental care responses. *Left:* head proportions perceived as "lovable" (child, jerboa, Pekinese dog, robin). *Right:* related heads which do not elicit the parental drive (man, hare, hound, golden oriole). (Lorenz: *Studies in Animal and Human Behavior*, Volume II.)

monster. The eerie-monster response is elicited whenever a very well-known gestalt perception is disturbed by one or several unknown new characters. The conventional pictures of devils and ghosts illustrate this phenomenon. The eerie-monster phenomenon is the more potent, the better the distorted gestalt is known. For this reason the proportions of cerebral to visceral cranium can be exaggerated to a much higher degree in the picture or in the model of an animal without causing revulsion than it can in the human picture or model. An exaggerated baby donkey was about the most strongly supernormal dummy B. Hückstedt could devise. Of course, the doll industry has for a long time been aware of all this and has successfully exploited this knowledge.

The art of cooking, the competition of chefs catering for the most sophisticated gourmets, long ago inspired the invention of supernormal

food stuffs, much to the detriment of civilized humanity. For our paleo-
lithic ancestors, hungry as they were much of the time, it was certainly
sound strategy to follow the instructions of IRMs telling them what
foods to choose: they should contain as much fat as possible, as much
sugar as possible, and as little roughage as possible. Being "open on one
side," these key stimuli led to an extremely unhealthy preference for
supernormal objects. White flour is causing severe and obstinate consti-
pation in millions of civilized people; chocolate combines all the three
key stimuli mentiond above, being devoid of indigestible fiber and consisting of fat and sugar. Even the most complete insight into the workings of our IRMs does not make it easy to avoid suicide by overeating.

3. IRM and the Releaser

If, in the interest of survival, an animal has to react innately and selectively to a certain object in its environment, the maximum possible
adaptedness is reached when the IRM responds with the greatest possible selectivity to key stimuli which the object is emitting. It is beyond
the powers of any organism's evolution to endow the object of an innate
response with characters rendering it more unambiguously recognizable.
This becomes possible only if the acting subject and the object of its activity are members of the same species. The pike, figuratively speaking, is
not able to affix a little flag to the silvery minnow that will then release
its snapping, and thus keep itself from snapping at any silvery lure. But
a species of songbird, during its evolution, is perfectly able to attach colorful signals to the gape of its nestlings and thus ensure that only its
own progeny will be fed by it. Structures and motor patterns—or combinations of both, as in most cases—that are thus evolved in the service
of emitting key stimuli are called *releasers*. As a stickler for nomenclature
I must here call attention to a current misuse of this term: it is often misleadingly used to denote releasing stimulation in general, more or less
in the sense in which the term 'key stimulus' would be correct. In its
proper sense, the term 'releaser' connotes a structure or a movement,
most often a combination of both, which has *evolved* in the service of
sending a signal, that is to say, of emitting key stimuli.

It has been proposed, with some justification, that the adjective 'social'
be joined to the term 'releaser' because, in fact, the vast majority of key
stimuli emitted by releasers are addressed to fellow members of the same
species. There are, however, many stimulus-sending organs and movements which have been evolved in order to influence animals of other
species. Many insects have convergently evolved means to frighten away
predators: the beautiful eye spots on the wings of moths and butterflies,
as well as on the front legs of many mantidae, have been demonstrated

to perform this function. An octopus uses the enormous motility of its body as well as of its chromatophores to make appear, with really frightening suddenness, a huge pair of eyes on the surface facing an approaching predator; squids (*Sepiotheutis*) "paint" magic eyes on their lateral fins. For obvious reasons, the frightening effect of such eye spots is the greater the farther they are apart, in other words, the larger the head of the simulated predator is made to appear.

Some releasers have evolved to influence not the predator but the prey. The large North American snapping turtle (*Macroclemmys telmincki*) possesses, on the tip of its tongue, a very convincing imitation of a worm that, by its wriggling, entices fish to swim right into the turtle's mouth. Angler fish (Lophiidae) also possess lures attached to the first rays of their spiny dorsal fins, situated near the front of their heads. In the split-lure anglerfish (*Phrynelox scaper*), this lure consists of a wormlike appendage which wriggles exactly like a worm.

The vast majority of releasers, however, serve intraspecific communication. It is hardly an exaggeration to say that every striking or "showy" color pattern or structure found in a vertebrate, as well as any loud and regular sound utterance, or any regular, complicated, and rhythmically performed movement, functions as a releaser. On observing a striking or colorful structure, it is very often possible to predict without any observation of behavior the way in which this structure will be presented to the conspecific. Tinbergen and I happened simultaneously to obtain a species of cichlid (*Cichlosoma meeki*) new to both of us, which had eye spots not, as many other members of this group, on the operculars but on the gill membranes. Our letters, with drawings, in which both of us correctly predicted the form of frontal display peculiar to this species, crossed en route.

A few further examples can suffice to illustrate the principle. Morphological releasers often serve to make a motor pattern more conspicuous; the motor pattern itself must not be changed in the interest of its teleonomic function. Many birds, when taking off, disclose color patterns which remain hidden under their wings while they are grounded. The wing speculum of ducks, the white rump of geese, many finches, and others, and the brightly colored lateral tail feathers of the budgerigar (*Melopsittacus undulatus*) are examples. Morphological releasers totally unconnected with any particular motor pattern are not very common. The only examples I can cite offhand are the color patterns permanently shown by certain coral reef fish. These—unlike the colorful patterns of many freshwater fish—are shown constantly and do not alter with changing moods. Their primary function is the release of aggression against fellow members of the species, in other words, to ensure aggressivity being strictly intraspecific, in still other words, to avoid unnecessary fighting with fish that are not food competitors. The multiplicity of ecological niches concentrated on a reef, and the consequent number of species and of individuals crowding on it, have exerted a selection pressure under which the incredible gamut of coloration has evolved.

In the case of social releasers, the stimulus-emitting apparatus and the stimulus-receiving apparatus are in a position to exert pressure on one another. The releaser obviously "caters for" the particular properties and limitations inherent in the IRM, and the IRM can conform to the ever-growing unambiguity of the key stimuli sent to it. In this way a type of communication can evolve that, functionally, is closely analogous to the use of *symbols*. Motor patterns that have undergone a high differentiation in the service of their releasing function have been described by many observers—who were far from naive—as ritualized symbolic actions.

As mentioned, the great majority of releasers consists of a combination of a motor pattern acting as a signal and a morphological structure enhancing the signal's effect. Very often a comparative study of many closely related species reveals the fact that motor patterns are phylogentically older than the structures serving to make them more conspicuous. The courtship movements of male dabbling ducks (Anatini) furnish many good examples of this. A homologous movement is often very similar, in many species, while the patterns and structures of the feathers that make the movement optically more effective are quite different, although they obviously evolved under the same selection pressure. We know more about the phylogeny of this sort of releasing motor pattern than we do about any other kind of genetically programmed pattern of behavior, because we know quite a number of beautiful series of differentiation and, what is more, we know in which direction they should be read.

Man, too, is in possession of a number of true releasers, as Charles Darwin was the first to point out. Certain expressive movements, such as the smile—studied extensively by René Spitz and Irenäus Fibl-Eibesfeldt—have been demonstrated to be genetically fixed with respect to their motor coordinations, as well as to the responses evoked in the addressee. Like the "poster colors" of coral fish, some bodily structures of humans can be shown to have a releasing effect which is more or less independent of motor patterns. The distribution of fatty tissue over the body surface can cause configurations which demonstrably have the effect of emitting key stimuli. One example is the corpus adiposum buccae, the bunch of fatty tissue in the cheeks of small children. Farfetched assumptions have been made to explain its presence, for instance, that it has played a role in the mechanism of sucking. If so, how it is possible for all other primates to manage without the organ remains to be explained. On the other hand, its function in helping elicit responses of parental care has been demonstrated. Unlike that of the corpus adiposum buccae, the releasing effect of the specific distribution of fatty tissue on the female body does not seem to have struck any observer as problematic.

Releasers of a very special kind have evolved whenever the advantage of being mistaken for another species has exerted a selection pressure. The best known and perhaps also the most common examples are furnished by many "imitating" or "mimicking" species which are, in some way, protected by poisons, repellent taste, or by other means. Most of the species thus protected are colored and marked in a strikingly aposematic way. These marks have the effect of warning off predators either because they possess an innate aversion to them or because they have had individual experience of the repellent agent and have associated this with coloration. Aposematic colors emit stimuli that may be received by an IRM or, in other cases, by a learned response. Any unprotected and tolerably similar species may, of course, enjoy the advantages of this protection by evolving toward even more similar coloration.

One particular kind of mimicry consists of imitating certain social releasers of another species and thereby profiting from being treated in the same way as a fellow member of the species. The parasitic whydah birds (Viduini), which lay their eggs in the nests of waxbills (Estreldinae), imitate the juvenile plumage and particularly the gape of their hosts so exactly that they deceived even J. Nicolai (1970) who, thinking he had brought home nestling whydahs, later found that two of his birds belonged to the species of their host. The closeness of the mimicry in the young both with regard to morphology and to behavior is necessary because the whydahs, unlike the European cuckoo, do not destroy the young of their hosts. As Nicolai could convincingly show, the brood parasitism of whydahs is phyletically rather old; their speciation proceeded parallel to that of their hosts. In consequence of this, there are some species which belong to the same genus and are hard to distinguish as adults, while their neonates and juveniles differ considerably, being adapted to mimic the morphology and behavior of different host species. These species have always been considered by older ornithologists as subspecies, if not as mere races. As Nicolai could demonstrate, they deserve without question the taxonomic rank of a "good" species, since they are sympatric (occur in the same area) and yet never hybridize. To do so would be disastrous for the offspring because the young hybrid, being adapted neither to one nor to the other host species, would have no chance of survival. Under this particular selection pressure, the whydah birds have evolved a barrier against hybridization which, as Nicolai has demonstrated, is based on learning processes of the *imprinting* type, which will be discussed in detail in Three/III/6.

In a very peculiar case of mimicry, releasers can simulate organs of the same species. W. Wickler, who has investigated this phenomenon thoroughly, speaks of "automimesis." When the first specimen of the mouthbreeder *Haplochromis burtoni* had just arrived in Seewiesen, an American guest, John Burchard, Jr., pointed out to me the strikingly shaded orange spots on the anal fin of the males and offered a bet that he could tell me their function. I cut him short by saying that the spots were imitation eggs, and that the female, after spawning, would snap at them while the male discharged his sperm—which was exactly what Burchard had suspected. Wickler proved the correctness of this rather obvious assumption and made an important comparative study of the evolution of the "egg dummies" in African mouthbreeders. It is interesting that so small a selection pressure should produce such a very special adaptation of morphology and behavior. The only advantage gained is that the eggs can be taken into the mouth of the mothers at once and then inseminated while she snaps at the egg dummies, instead of remaining exposed for a number of seconds until the male has inseminated them.

Wickler has drawn attention to some other cases of automimesis: in several species of baboons and of vervet monkeys, the male carries on his rump structures and colors imitating the genitalia of the estrous female. They are presented during the appeasement gesture to the dominant male. In the gellada baboon *(Theopithecus gellada)*, a detailed imitation of the rear aspect of the female is shown on the front of the male's chest, and this is also presented during the gesture of submission. An interesting detail is that the structures imitated and the structures imitating need not, by any means, be homologous. The red callosities on the rump of male babooons imitate the labia minora of the female; in some vervet monkeys red hairs cover regions of the male's body which, in the female, show a strongly vasculated skin.

Wickler has pointed out that a comparative study of mimicry furnishes particularly good objects for investigating the evolution of releasers. Since mimicry is caused by a selection pressure exerted by the IRM of another species, it is a *one-sided* process of adaptation, while in all social releasers the stimulus-emitting and the stimulus-receiving apparatus evolve in a complicated process of mutual adaptation.

4. An Important Rule of Thumb

Very different though the releasers are that have evolved among all the phyla of higher animals, they have certain properties in common. This can easily be explained on the basis of what has been said in the preceding section about the functional limitations of the IRM. All releasers emit relatively simple spatial and temporal stimulus configurations and, as far as they are visual, they employ simple, that is to say, nearly pure spectral colors. In other words, they have all been evolved under the selection pressure mentioned in the preceding section, which tends to give them the greatest possible simplicity and, at the same time, the greatest possible unambiguity. It is characteristic of releasers that they can be described in comparatively few and simple words. This fact can easily be made evident by reading, in any ornithological book, the description of the male and the female of the species, in which the male has nuptial plumage, while the female is cryptically colored. A mallard drake with its green head, white neck band, brown breast, et cetera, can be described with very few words, while the description of the female, in order to afford equally detailed information, must fill many pages.

As has been mentioned on page 161, the IRM cannot do what is so easily done by our learned gestalt perception, that is, respond selectively to complex qualities. It is an extremely reliable rule of thumb that an IRM can be assumed to be at work whenever an organism is "taken in" by a very simple dummy or model. Conversely, if the attempt to elicit a certain response by a dummy fails, and it proves necessary to simulate a biologically relevant stimulus situation in all its details in order to release a response, or if even this proves to be impossible, the assumption is justified that the organism has *learned* to respond to a complex quality. This rule was brought home to me in a most unforgettable way by the following experiments made by Alfred Seitz. When he had performed his now classic experiments on releasing fighting in male *Astatotilapia*, he next attempted to elicit, by the same method, the male's responses of courtship. He was quite unsuccessful with simple models. Then he proceeded to build increasingly complicated imitations of the female fish, finally arriving at models made of semi-transparent paraffin fitted with celluloid fins and rendered silvery by the application of powdered aluminum. These models might easily have deceived a human observer when they were suspended in the aquarium by the thinnest of nylon threads. They did not, however, deceive the male fish, not even when these were suffering from a considerable lowering of threshold.

Having more confidence in my theories than I had myself, Seitz concluded that the male *Astatotilapia's* response to the female must be conditioned and based on learned gestalt perception, and he decided forthwith to rear some males in complete isolation, depriving them of any opportunity to learn what a female looked like. The deprivation experiment was not at all easy with a mouthbreeding species whose eggs have to be continously whirled about as they normally are by the breathing movements of the mother. Seitz's patience did not flinch before the task of constructing an egg-whirling apparatus consisting of a number of upward directed jets of warm, aerated water on which the eggs were kept dancing. When he had finally succeeded in rearing to full maturity five males which had never seen their own kind, Seitz invited me to watch the crucial experiment. In order to avoid any possible conditioning influencing later experiments, Seitz began with the most simple dummy possible, a grey sphere of plasticine stuck onto a thin glass rod. When this dummy was shoved into the tank containing one of the males and was gingerly brought near the fish, the latter, which up to then had sat quiescent and cryptically colored within the cover provided by a plant, quickly blushed into full nuptial coloration, erected the median fins, oriented broadside to the model, and burst into a bout of courtship movements of the utmost intensity. It bears witness to a commendable distrust in my own theories that I was utterly surprised by this. The rule of thumb just mentioned had been derived mainly from the observation of birds, and I had not really believed that the learning of complex gestalt perception could play such an important part in the behavior of a fish.

From all that we know about releasers, it is safe to conclude that it is not possible for the evolution of sensory–neural organizations to construct a receptor mechanism which responds selectively to a complex quality composed of a great number of stimulus data. If it were, there would be no selection pressure causing the evolution of all those innumerable stimulus-sending contrivances which gladden our eyes and our ears; there would not be any pure colors of flowers, nor beautiful colors of coral-reef fish or birds, nor would there be any pure notes in bird song.

The IRM obviously cannot do what the learning of gestalt perception finds so easy, that is, to characterize a complicated multiplicity of sensory input so that it becomes umambiguously recognizable. The surprising accomplishment of gestalt perception, of which an example was mentioned in II/2, is by no means granted exclusively to human beings. A tiny greylag gosling, not much more than a day old, has already learned to recognize its parents among a hundred other geese by the physiognomy of their faces as well as the individual qualities of their voices. Curiously enough, the same parts of the face, that is, those areas around the eyes and nose, are essential for recognition in both humans and geese.

The difference between the functions of the IRM and the learned perception of gestalt qualities is indeed impressive, but nonetheless the difference is only quantitative and concerns only degrees of complication. Doubtlessly the same elementary processes of perception take part in both functions and dictate one fundamental similarity: the information received is always couched in terms of *relations*, or *intervals* between two or more stimuli, and not in the absolute values of single stimulus data. For reasons obvious to the cyberneticist, it is much easier to build a receptor apparatus responding selectively to signals consisting of precise and simple relationships between stimulus data, preferably to configurations that can be expressed in whole numbers, in other words, that are "harmonious." On the afferent side of the central nervous system, there seems to be an interaction between elementary receptor processes that is somewhat akin to the interaction which, on the motor side, takes place between processes of endogeneous production of impulses, and which also results in products whose stability is dependent on the degree of harmony attained. Harmony is generally improbable in itself, and thereby contributes to the unambiguity of any configuration perceived. The German psychologist, Felix Krüger, termed this phenomenon, which is common to a gestalt perception, the *Prägnanztendenz*, the trend toward terseness in perception (1948). The urgent need which *all* perceptual processes have for harmonious configurations of stimuli exerts a selection pressure not only on the evolution of IRMs, but equally in the historic development of human signals and, last but not least, of human art. Pure spectral colors, pure sounds in harmonious combinations, geometrical forms easy to express in whole numbers, rhythmically regular temporal sequences and so on, are to be found in releasers as well as in man-made signals and in art. It is, in fact, this property common to all perception which has caused many organisms to become so *beautiful*.

It is perfectly conceivable that there might be releasers, or stimulus-emitting organizations, the signals of which are not addressed to an IRM but are received by learned perceptions, as are the color patterns of our flags. The functions of perception can certainly cause the production of signals catering to the properties just described. While there is an abundance of man-made signals whose properties are clearly dictated by the *Prägnanztendenz* of human gestalt perception, we know only a few examples of phylogenetically programmed stimulus emitters without a corresponding IRM, in other words, a releaser the response to which must be learned. Neonate greylags at first do not respond to the call note of their species, and when they do, it is only the call note of their parents which evokes a response. As Otto von Frisch demonstrated, newly hatched curlews *(Numenius arquatus)* do not respond to their parents' warning call until they have heard it one or two times in connection with the optical perception of a bird silhouetted against the sky. S. Sjö-lander (oral communication, 1977) demonstrated that the zebra finch's *(Taeniopygia castanotis)* response to the red color of the conspecific's bill was not innate, as had been supposed. He succeeded in imprinting young birds on foster parents with a bright green bill. It is doubtful, however, if they could have been imprinted on a grey or a white bill; the verbalized information of the IRM might read just "bill of very striking color."

5. IRMs Rendered More Selective by Learning

The Viennese zoologist, Otto Storch, was the first to draw attention to the fact that adaptive modifications concerning the receptor side of behavior are found on much lower evolutionary levels of the animal kingdom than are modifications of motor activities (1949). He distinguished *Erwerbs-Rezeptorik* and *Erwerbs-Motorik*, which may be translated as receptor and motor learning. One of the most common learning processes in general, and one of the most basic ones, consists of rendering an IRM more selective by learning: further conditions for the release of the behavior pattern concerned are added to those already coded in the

IRM. Like all true learning processes, this represents an *adaptive modification* of behavior and will be dealt with in detail in Three/II/2. However, the adaptive modification of the stimulus-filtering apparatus is so closely interwoven with the function of the IRM that it must be discussed in this section.

The IRM eliciting in our male *"Astatotilapia"* the motor patterns of courtship responds to very few and simple key stimuli. As Seitz demonstrated, any object that is approximately the size of a conspecific and that slowly approaches the male when he is located in his territory instantly releases his courtship movements, which consist of a ritualization of the motor patterns by which a "nest" is swept out for spawning. When, at this signal, the object neither flinches nor approaches any closer, the male proceeds to the next step of spawning behavior: he turns nestwards with a ritualized movement, overaccentuating the undualtion of body and of tail fin. At this, the courtship-eliciting object must swim forward and, arriving over the shallow excavation representing the nest, it must join the male in a circular movement. All of the actions of this sequence can be easily released by means of a dummy if the male has been deprived of previous experience. After circling, the male will approach the dummy's underside, and at this moment his behavior will break off because olfactory stimulation emanating from the female is necessary to release the actions which normally follow. During the circular movement, the dummy must not at any moment present a flat surface to the male; to this he instantly reacts as he would to the broadside-on display of another male and starts fighting. While circling around over the nest, the female presents to the male a concave side; this, however, need not be imitated in the dummy experiment, only the presentation of a plane must be avoided. A spherical model suffices to keep the circling going, showing that no information regarding the body form of the female is contained in the key stimuli.

All this is true only of a fish reared in isolation. In a normally reared fish, all the key stimuli mentioned must emanate from a fellow member of the species. The information programmed in the IRM could be verbalized thus: "Any conspecific, slowly approaching, passively tolerating courtship movements, then following to the nest and joining in circling it, is a ripe female." What a conspecific looks like is not contained in this innate instruction, and this gap must be filled in by a complex gestalt perception which the individual must *learn* to recognize during the course of its individual life. The special learning process which accomplishes this will be discussed in Three/III/3.

In higher vertebrates, such as teleost fish, birds, or mammals, it is difficult to find IRMs which are not made more selective by individual learning of this type, but exceptions do exist. The selectivity of the IRM releasing the gobbling response in the turkey cock does not increase by learning, as M. Schleidt has demonstrated. More usually, IRMs not modifiable by learning are found in invertebrates, particularly in insects and spiders (Arachnidae), and primarily in connection with activities that are performed only once, or only a very few times during an individual's life.

It is a reliable rule of thumb that the function of an IRM is involved whenever it is possible to elicit some innate behavior pattern by a simple dummy, but this rule must not be inverted. As mentioned, the releasing mechanism is often made much more selective by association with a complicated gestalt perception, so much so that it has become quite impossible to release it even with the most sophisticated model—as has been shown for the courtship patterns of male "*Astatotilapia*." The impossibility of evoking a response by means of dummies does not, however, imply that the IRM does not still play a part, nor that the original key stimuli have become dispensable—as is the case in some other kinds of conditioning. The effects of key stimuli and those of conditioned stimulus configurations are added to one another, but their interdependence poses a problem which has not been sufficiently investigated. It is all too easy to offer, quite unintentionally, supernormal stimulation in the dummy. It is always possible that an excessively effective dummy more than compensates for the absence of conditioned stimuli. The observation that the copulation responses of greylag geese can be released by swimming people does not justify the conclusion that conditioned stimuli take no part in normal copulation.

Chapter III
The Problem of the "Stimulus"

1. All-Embracing Conceptualizations

The term "stimulus" is often associated with an extremely broad concept subsuming almost every external influence that could elicit an observable response from any organic system—from a protozoan, from a whole multicellular organism, from a single nerve cell or even from an isolated neurite. We describe as a "key stimulus" that complex configuration of many stimuli to which the IRM of a higher animal responds selectively. A key stimulus elicits a very special and teleonomic response. We make this descriptive distinction in spite of our awareness that the selectivity is due to a most complex "filtering" mechanism through which any stimulation must pass—a filtering mechanism which evaluates a multiplicity of stimuli and reports nothing but a single, reliable signal to the higher loci within the animal's central nervous system. At the same time we speak of a "stimulus" when we cause a single, quantifiable electric shock of a few millivolts to excite a single neuron, or even an isolated nerve fiber, and occasionally the term "stimulus" is used even when an unspecific neural response is released by some change in the environment not "provided for" by phyletic adaptation—when, for example, a deficiency of calcium ions in the blood or in the nutrient solution causes some neurons to fire spontaneously.

2. Stable and Spontaneously Active Nervous Elements

On the comparatively low integrational level of the single neuron, everything causing the membrane to change its ionic conductances, either up or down, therefore to result in either depolarization or hyper-polarization, or contributing to its readiness to do so, can be regarded as a stimulus. The now obsolete expression, a "breakdown" of membrane potential, that we once used, is rather metaphoric; what happens at the moment of nerve discharge is an alteration in the sign of electric charge on either side of the membrane: on its outside, the positive charge is transformed into a much weaker negative one, while the opposite change takes place on the inner side. This process can lead to the "firing" of the cell, although several gradational processes besides firing are known. Receptor cells in particular usually have gradated receptor potentials. Thus a signal is emitted that is addressed to one or more other neurons; the change of potential spreads from the cell membrane along that of the neuron and induces an identical process in the neuron addressed, provided the latter is, at the moment, in a sufficient state of excitability.

At this point we meet with a conceptual difficulty to which Kenneth Roeder has drawn attention (1955). He says:

> The excitability of a nerve cannot be defined in physicochemical terms. The only way in which it can be made manifest and measured is by determining the minimum energy change, within a certain time interval and in a certain direction, that must be applied before the nerve will discharge an impulse. If an electric stimulus is used, the energy change is expressed in terms of electric current and the direction in terms of potential sign. Thus, we can say that the excitability or its reciprocal, the stability, of a nerve is proportional to the energy needed to abolish it, but we are unable to define it as a continuous property of the living tissue. Analogous reasoning is used in describing the stability of a building or other structure. In this case stability is expressed in terms of the force (pounds per square foot, wind velocity) that is just sufficient to cause its collapse, as compared with the force to which it is exposed under normal operating conditions.
>
> The relationship between the excitability changes in a stable nerve and those in a spontaneously active nerve is depicted in the lower graph of [Figure 14]. The vertical axis represents excitability, which in practice would be measured in units of stimulus strength. The lower horizontal line represents the rest excitability of a relatively stable nerve such as the sciatic nerve; it corresponds to the normal operating load in the building analogy. The upper horizontal line represents the threshold excitability or the load at collapse in the building analogy. The solid curve shows the sequence of excitability changes that follow exposure of a stable nerve to a momentary stimulus of the dimension of S_1. It can be seen that the excitability (or instability) increases rapidly from the rest level until threshold excitability is reached. In the building analogy this is the moment of collapse; in the nerve it is the moment of propagation of the impulse, the outward sign of which is the all or none electric change or action potential (upper graph). During the impulse the excitability of the nerve drops to zero, the absolute refractory period; in the building analogy collapse is at this moment complete. From

this point the nerve departs from the building analogy, since its metabolism enables it to return to its former state. The subsequent course of events varies in different nerves, but in large vertebrate A fibers excitability not only returns but overshoots the resting level, leading to a phase of supernormal excitability. As is shown in the solid curve, this is followed by a relatively prolonged subnormal phase of excitability and eventual return to the rest level.

The supernormal phase of excitability is of particular interest, since it provides a link between the stable and spontaneously active states of nerve. There is considerable variation in the relative magnitude of the supernormal phase, or, in other words, in the relative values of resting and threshold excitability. If the supernormal phase is relatively large or the difference between resting and threshold excitability is small, then the sequence of excitability changes must follow the dashed curve. As the rising excitability reaches the threshold level during recovery, the fiber becomes self-exciting, and impulses follow one another at regular intervals ([Figure 14], upper graph). Each impulse is accompanied by absolute refractoriness and followed by relative refractoriness and supernormal excitability rising to the threshold level. Thus, a single stimulus may initiate a sequence of impulses that continues subject only to the counter influences of adaptation and fatigue.

In a sense, this activity could be considered as spontaneous activity, since the original stimulus that triggered a long succession of impulses could readily be overlooked. Strictly speaking, it is repetitive activity. True spontaneous activity can be said to arise when the values for rest and threshold excitability (horizontal lines) coincide. At this point the nerve becomes completely unstable, and a similar succession of impulses begins without the need for any external triggering stimulus.

The suggestion by Pumphrey . . . that a spontaneously active fiber lacks a finite threshold is also illustrated in [Figure 14]. A stimulus, S_2, may be interpolated at any instant during the excitability cycle of the fiber. If the stimulus occurs at the instant illustrated, it must be of the relative dimensions of the double arrow in order to bring the fiber to threshold within the utilization time. This leads to a propagated impulse and accompanying refractoriness somewhat earlier than it would have occurred spontaneously. The later its appearance in the excitability cycle, the smaller the critical size of S_2, and the smaller the effect that it would have on the frequency of the rhythmic discharge. On the other hand, a stimulus of the dimensions of S_2 would be completely inadequate if it occurred at the instant of S_1. Therefore, the sensitivity of the spontaneously active nerve element, frequency-modulated as it is by stimuli of all dimensions, is limited only by the capacity of central nervous mechanisms to detect small changes in the frequency of its rhythmic discharge.

Pumphrey's suggestion also gives a convincing explanation for the fact that some kinds of sensory cells have proved to be spontaneously active elements, their signals consisting in modulations of frequency and not in a single discharge.

3. Analogous Phenomena in Integrated Neural Systems

What has been said in the preceding section about stable and spontaneously active elements, as well as what has been said about the varying
relationship between rest excitability and threshold, abolishes the sharp
borderline between those stimuli which increase the rest excitability and
those which directly trigger a discharge. At least as far as the activity of
single neural elements is concerned, any influence which exerts a
"tonic," long-term stress on the membrane potential increases the rest
excitability and diminishes the stability of the element. A question
important to ethological research is to what extent the relationship
between stimulus strength, excitability, and threshold is analogous to
that existing between the complicated stimulus configuration acting as
the "key stimulus" on an IRM and the fluctuating readiness of the organism to perform the motor pattern to-be-released.

As has been emphasized in Two/I/14, the attempt to explain the functional properties of any integrated system on the basis of the functional
properties of its elements, is an undertaking fraught with danger. The
central nervous system has a deceptive proclivity for accomplishing analogous functions by entirely different means and on entirely different levels of integration, but in ways so similar that even the wary investigator
can be misled into believing them to be identical. Nevertheless, the analogy of functions that can be physiologically investigated justifies the formulation of a hypothesis, and what has been said in the preceding section does justify just as much as what was said in Two/I/14 about the
relationship between spontaneous generation of impulses, central coordination and the properties of the fixed motor pattern.

According to the laws of heterogeneous summation (Two/I/14), the
key stimuli to which an IRM responds produce, on a higher level of
integration, strictly analogous results, as do stimuli of varying dimensions with nervous elements: those too weak to cause an immediate discharge still serve to increase the state of readiness for a certain motor
pattern, much as electric stimulation stresses membrane potential and
thus facilitates its final breakdown or switch. Even the effect of those
complex configurations of stimuli which must pass through a highly
selective "filter" in order to exert a specific influence on equally specific
efferent processes is dependent not only on the quantitative dimensions
of the key stimulus, but also on the state of readiness prevailing, at the
moment, in the stimulated system. It depends on this state of readiness
whether the key stimulus immediately releases the specific efferent
response, or whether it merely increases the readiness to discharge it by
raising the present level of action specific potential, in other words, by
increasing its value so that the threshold value is approached. The complicated afferent sector of this kind of process "behaves," in many cases,
in a manner strictly analogous to that of the membrane potential of a

single nervous element. Neither the absolute value of rest excitability nor that of the threshold can be measured directly any more than they can in the A fibers investigated by Roeder. The only value that can be measured is the distance between rest excitability and the threshold represented in Roeder's diagram by the varying dimensions of S.

My old, much ridiculed "phycho-hydraulic" thought model, represented in Figure 18a, shows the steadily rising level of ASP (action-specific potential; see below) during the quiescence of a fixed motor pattern and also the effect of external stimulation opening the discharge valve. However, this model misleadingly implies a qualitative difference between those stimuli which fill up the reservoir of ASP and those which finally release the motor pattern; it fails to show that the charging and releasing stimuli differ only in quantity. It is a well-known fact that stimuli, each of which alone is too weak to call forth a motor response, will finally do so if applied repeatedly in a long and persevering sequence. This is called "summation of stimuli," and is analogous to the loading of the cell membrane at the elementary level.

It is Kenneth Roeder's well-founded assumption that the increase in readiness to discharge is brought about, not by a lowering of the threshold—as we are wont, rather inexactly, to say—but by a raising of excitation. This solves a problem that for years was a subject of long discussions at the institute Erich von Holst and I directed. Then as now we, hypothetically, assume that relationships analogous to those which Roeder demonstrated as existing on the elementary level—those between rest excitability, stimulus effects, and threshold—also prevail on more highly integrated levels of the central nervous system, and we symbolize them in a thought model (Figure 18b) which does justice to the new discovery that readiness-increasing stimuli and instantly releasing stimuli are not qualitatively different but only quantitatively, that is, in respect to the time period between their arrival and their taking effect in the efference. This model represents the threshold as being constant: it is symbolized in the spiral spring whose tension is, in this model, not influenced by an external agent. The opening of the cone valve depends exclusively on the pressure of the liquid, in other words, on the present level attained by the internal readiness to perform the fixed motor pattern. Immediately releasing stimuli are different from those which latently increase readiness only with respect to the time that is necessary for them to take effect motorically (Figure 18). A simulation of the real process at which the model aims could be made more exact by building an element of inertia into the opening and the closing of the valve.

This is exactly the hypothesis Walter Heiligenberg formulated on the basis of his experiments with crickets *(Gryllus)* and fishes *(Pelmatochromis kribensis)* (1974). He says:

It could be assumed that a certain behavior pattern always occurs when a specific concomitant hypothetical physiological state exceeds a certain minimal value, that is, a critical threshold X_0, and also that this occurrence becomes the more probable the higher the average basic level of this X value is. Spontaneous behavior patterns, like the chirping of a cricket, would be characterized, on the basis of this assumption, by the fact that the concomitant X value reaches the dimension of the critical threshold X_0 even without the influence of any external stimulus. The occurrence of non-spontaneous activities should be dependent on an external stimulation capable of raising

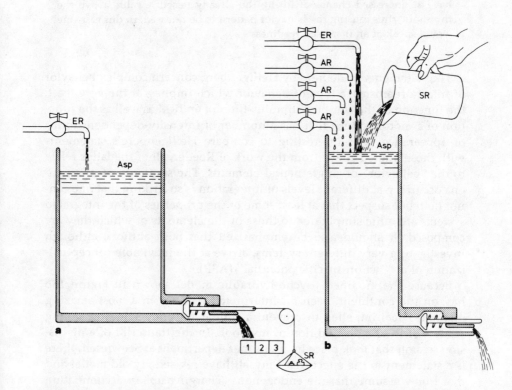

Figures 18a. and 18b. In the old "psycho-hydraulic" model (*left*), the spigot *ER* represents the source of endogenous and automatic generation of stimuli; the line *Asp* symbolizes the present level of action-specific potential. The spiral spring at the outlet represents what Roeder called the "stability of the system." The traction exerted by the weights *SR* stands for the effect of the releasing stimuli. In Figure 18b, the additional effect of unspecific readiness-releasing stimuli is represented by the outflow of the spigots *AR*. This new model is meant to account for the fact that the effect of the specifically releasing key stimulus *SR* is different from that of the endogenous stimulus *ER* and that of the additional readiness-increasing stimuli *AR* only with regard to its time curve. The difference in the height of the two reservoirs containing *Asp* in the two models is meant to suggest that, according to the new hypothesis, the opening of the valve is effected only by the necessary pressure from within the reservoir. The simulation could be brought closer to the real physiological process by adding a few gadgets, for instance, by a mechanism imposing the phenomenon of inertia on the opening and the closing of the valve.

their X value enough to exceed the critical threshold. On this assumption, the type of stimulus effect—whether increasing readiness or immediately releasing—depends exclusively on the temporal curve of the increment X value caused by it. A strong and rapid increase causes the behavior pattern to follow immediately after the stimulus; one should say, in this case, that the behavior pattern has been released by the stimulus. A gradual and enduring increase would have the effect of allowing later stimulation to have an increased chance of lifting the already raised X value above the threshold, thus causing the behavior pattern to be released; in this case one would speak of an increased readiness.

The statements made here by Heiligenberg concern complex behavior of intact organisms, a type of behavior which implies, at the very least, the function of the complex stimulus-filter of an IRM as well as the function of a motor pattern that has a number of intensity-dependent forms of appearance. It is interesting to compare Heiligenberg's statements with those quoted above from the work of Roeder; all of the latter relate to the "behavior" of single neural elements. The similarity of phenomena occurring at different levels of integration is so striking that one cannot help but suspect that at least some of the properties of the integrated systems are quite simply due to those of the elements of which they are composed. It should also be emphasized that both authors, although investigating very different systems, arrive at the inevitable conceptualization of an "action-specific potential" (ASP).

Because the modified psycho-hydraulic model shown in Figure 18b has, on the continent, been misinterpreted recently in a most amazing manner, I feel impelled to prevent a similar misunderstanding among readers of the English edition of my book. In the transcript of a discussion session that took place in my former department at Seewiesen, there is a statement to the effect that I myself have revised my old model and that I now assume that the endogenous "charging up" or accumulation of ASP is very small and that, hence, even in the absence of releasing key stimuli, no "damming up" of the internal drive need occur. ("Lorenz geht davon aus, daß die endogene Aufladung eines Triebes nur gering ist, das heißt, auch beim Fehlen bedingter Außernreize kommt es nicht zwangsläufig zum Triebstau.") I am thoroughly taken aback that this gross misinterpretation went unchallenged and uncontradicted during the discussion itself. Anyone with any sense for quantification who looks at the model must be able to see that the endogenous production of excitation represented as a thick spout is discharging at least ten times the quantity of the three dripping spigots of unspecific "charging up" stimuli taken together.

In consideration of this falsification of my true opinions, it seems advisable to emphasize here, once again, what a very crude simplification of the actual physiological process my model—in fact, any model—represents. The physiological process could, of course, be simulated much more closely by a few additions which have been left out for simplicity's sake. The most important of these would be a qualification of the symbolic valve to indicate an element of inertia, as I have already mentioned above. The valve "sticks" when opening as well as when closing—a phenomenon to which Seitz drew attention nearly half a century ago. The valve opens very slowly at first, even under strong stimulation, and once open it stays open and allows the level of ASP to sink far below that level at which it was when the valve first opened. This is precisely why instinctive motor patterns tend to "break out" in bouts and not to "dribble out" constantly.

The statements quoted from the writings of Roeder and Heiligenberg show that there is one way in which the functions of the integrated systems differ sharply from those of their elements, and this is the *speed* with which the changes of readiness caused by stimulation take place. Heiligenberg speaks of a strong, but quickly evanescent effect of some stimuli as well as of an enduring, slowly fading effect of others. I doubt that stimulus effects of similarly long duration can ever be demonstrated in isolated neural elements. In complex neural systems, Erich von Holst demonstrated that the duration of any change of readiness in a behavioral system was correlated with its level of integration. Through brainstem stimulation experiments with chickens he found that if a highly integrated system had been stimulated, the stimulus-induced increment in a readiness for some specific types of activity took a longer time to fade away, while the effect of stimulation disappeared almost at once when only a subsystem of low integrational level was concerned. If, for example, the electrode was positioned so that it activated the entire series of motor patterns pertinent to escape from a terrestrial predator, beginning with a raising of the head, scanning the environment, uttering a specific warning call, and finally taking wing, the bird required several minutes to quieten down enough in order to be ready for other types of behavior. If, however, the electrode was situated so as to release only head-raising and a warning cackle, the aftereffects were of a much shorter duration, disappearing quickly after the cessation of the stimulus.

In intact animals it can be demonstrated that the "inertia" of integrated neural systems is correlated to their complexity, in other words, to the number of subsystems between afference and efference. When Seitz offered a strongly fight-eliciting dummy to a male *Astatotilapia* that had spent some time in isolation, the fish, in spite of its high internal readiness to fight, took quite some time to run through the sequence of behavior patterns correlated to the rising stages of fighting excitation, as has been described in Two/I/3.

This kind of inertia seems to be due to the number of afferent and efferent mechanisms that have to be activated in sequence, one after the other, between the arrival of the releasing stimulus configuration and the appearance of the activity released. In order to compare the effects of readiness-increasing and of directly releasing stimuli, Heiligenberg kept a *Pelmatochromis kribensis* adult male in the company of a number of juveniles of the same species. By using a suitable number of fish in a tank of a suitable size, it was possible to quantify the average number of attacks launched at the juveniles by the adult male in the course of a certain amount of time and to gain, in this way, a good measure of the latter's readiness to attac... When, within this experimental arrangement, the adult male was shown a rival or a dummy for a period of thirty seconds, no immediate response in the form of typical agonistic behavior was seen during this short time, but after the removal of the stimulus and in the course of the next three or four minutes, the number of attacks on the young fish increased by more than half. This is a typical example of the "inertia" of specific excitability.

When Seitz had enticed one of his *Astatotilapia* males to fight a rival or a rival dummy with great intensity, the sudden removal of the object did not abruptly terminate the combative behavior. The fish then regularly attacked inadequate substitute objects, such as the small plastic tube joining the air-disperser to the pressure piping inside its tank. Analogous phenomena are observed in many behavior patterns released by complicated IRMs which obey the law of heterogeneous summation. In some cases the inertia of excitation causes displacement activities (the so-called "after discharge displacements") to appear after the sudden cessation of a stimulus.

On the other hand, it would seem that behavior patterns released by very simple IRMs are better able to respond on very short notice, the obvious example being those of escape. In some escape reactions it is possible to demonstrate, with particular clearness, the difference as well as the similarity existing between readiness-increasing and releasing stimuli. When flocks of sparrows *(Passer domesticus)* or yellowhammers *(Emberiza citrinella)* accumulate on an open field or road, having been lured far away from any cover by a supply of food, they appear to be struck by blind panic at regular intervals, flying back as fast as they can to the cover, only to return again to their feeding place almost at once. The stimulus situation presented by exposure to flying predators, particularly the sparrow hawk *(Accipiter nisus)*, is definitely not directly releasing these escape reactions, although it does exact extreme watchfulness. In other words, being so exposed increases readiness to an extreme, and to such an extent that the escape threshold is reached again and again, at short intervals, even though the typical releasing stimulus, represented by a fast-moving object silhouetted against the sky, never appears. This also explains (as was mentioned in Two/I/7) why it is impossible to measure a constant threshold of escape reactions.

4. Action-Specific Potential (ASP)

Erich von Holst discovered and analyzed the effects of the spontaneous generation of impulses and their coordination within the central nervous system of spinal fishes. He also studied another important phenomenon in the spinal sea horse *(Hippocampus)*, a phenomenon which had previously been described by Sherrington and termed by him the "spinal contrast." A spinal sea horse kept alive by artificial respiration shows no movements of the dorsal fin, the main locomotor organ of this fish. The fin remains quite still, but not in the position it assumes in an intact sea horse during repose, when the fin rests completely folded at the bottom of a groove along the fish's back; in the spinal preparation the dorsal fin remains partially unfolded. By applying certain stimuli, simply by exerting, for example, pressure on the "neck" region of the fish, it is possible to cause the dorsal fin to fold down completely into its groove, just as it does in the intact organism when at rest. When the stimulus is stopped, the fin not only unfolds, but extends further than it had before the stimulation was applied. The longer the stimulus causing the fin to fold is applied, the higher it rises after the stimulus has been removed. If, through a sustained application of the stimulus, the fin is forced into its folded position for a much longer period of time, it will not only unfold completely when the stimulus is removed, but it will also—if only for a very short while—begin to perform the undulating movements of locomotion. After ceasing to undulate, it sinks down gradually in an asymptotic curve to the "half-mast" position it usually assumes in the spinal seahorse.

These phenomena von Holst interprets hypothetically as follows: While the centrally coordinated motor pattern of locomotion is at rest, an action-specific exciting agent—perhaps in the form of a specific neurohormone—is being continuously produced, and a performance of the motor pattern consumes part of this accumulation. The quantity of consumption is dependent on the intensity of performance; even the slightest intention movement uses up a little of it. The quantity of endogenous production of excitability specific to a certain motor pattern is correlated to the average rate at which it is used by the organism. In a wrasse (Labridae), the endogenous production of impulses keeps the fish swimming more or less continuously during the hours of daylight; in a seahorse, which normally swims but a few minutes each day, a much smaller production is sufficient. As long as the inhibitory mechanisms at work in an intact seahorse keep the dorsal fin completely folded in its groove, all of the centrally produced excitability is accumulated so that, on the sudden removal of the inhibition, enough of it is available to permit the fish to swim away. In the spinal preparation, the central inhibition is lacking and the endogenous production of impulses finds its way to the motor cells unimpeded, causing a movement of low intensity that takes the form of a partial raising of the fin; this consumes exactly as much excitation as is continuously furnished by the endogenous impulse production. In order to accumulate the amount of excitability to the threshold level at which the undulating swimming movements set in, it is necessary to prevent the excitability from "seeping out" through the pathway of a low-intensity movement. This is achieved by substituting an artificial stimulus for the central inhibition that is lacking in the spinal preparation.

These functions of the spinal cord of a fish, described by Erich von Holst, are strictly analogous to those processes observed in the behavior of intact animals that were discussed in Two/I/ 6, 7.

I do not see how the assumption can be avoided that all these phenomena are caused by the spontaneous and continuous production, during the quiescence of a motor pattern, of "something"—whatever it may be—that is consumed or otherwise eliminated by a performance of the pattern. This hypothesis is strongly supported by the fact that we find exactly the same changes in readiness, the same relations between internal readiness and external stimulation, in some other activities which depend on the accumulation of "something" that we know and that we can measure quite well. Examples of such activities are those regulating the contents of hollow organs, as well as those controlling tissue needs.

The motor patterns of urination performed by a male dog show all the phenomena here under discussion. A very strong releasing stimulus situation, such as the smell of a rival's mark in the dog's own territory, will cause him to lift his leg even when the amount of urine at his disposal is, at the moment, negligible. Even under the pressure of a much higher urinating potential, the dog will still look for releasing stimulus situations, such as upright objects, preferably on exposed corners, at which to lift his leg. Under extreme internal pressure he will forgo every external stimulation and even forget the conditioned inhibition of house training and urinate on the carpet—in this pitiable situation usually without even lifting his leg. Adherents of stimulus–response psychology have contended that sexual behavior in male mammals and in man is similarly dependent of the pressure within the seminal vesicle and, on the basis of this assumption, have coined the term "detumescence drive." As we have just seen, this assumption is not entirely correct, even with regard to the urination activities of the male dog.

With motor patterns that supply tissue needs, such as eating, drinking and, quite particularly, breathing, a deficit in the concentration value of the required chemical within the tissues acts analogously to the pressure within hollow organs or, for that matter, to the level of the hypothetical liquid accumulated in the tank of our thought model. But things are more complicated than this because, besides the signals emitted by the tissues needing supply, the endogenously produced readiness to perform each of the motor patterns concerned is adding its own contribution to the organism's general state of readiness—as de Ruiter (1963) and Dethier and Bodenstein (1958) have demonstrated. Moreover, the proprioception of the contents of hollow organs may also contribute. None the less, it is a perfectly justifiable assertion to say that the intensity of appetitive behavior, as well as that of the consummatory acts released, rises relative to the extent to which the chemical in question is deficient; to a comparable extent, the selectivity of the IRMs concerned decreases.

Breathing also serves to supply tissue needs, and since the processes regulating it are simpler than those governing eating and drinking, the analogy to our thought model, to which Haldane (1932) has drawn attention, is even more striking. Carbon dioxide is continuously produced in the body and stimulates the breathing center whenever its concentration rises above a certain threshold value. The motor pattern then released eliminates the carbon dioxide.

We do not yet know of what that problematical "something" consists, that "something" which is produced while a motor pattern is at rest and which is consumed when it is in action, but we do know that it *does exist* and we know that it is specific, in every single instance that has been investigated, to one particular motor pattern—in other words, specific to one of those sequences of movements which is species-characteristic and which, as Whitman and Heinroth discovered, can be homologized just as definitively as morphological characters. We know that the effects of external stimulation and of the endogenous build-up of excitability combine in a manner that produces qualitatively identical effects independently of the proportion each of these apparently so different factors has contributed to the total sum: strong internal readiness and weak external stimulation add up to exactly the same result as a very strong stimulation impinging at a time when excitability is at a low ebb. The *quality* of the motor pattern released remains the same independently of the value attained by this addition; it is only its *intensity* that fluctuates in proportion to this value, ranging from hardly perceptible intention movements to the full teleonomic performance of the motor pattern. As has been explained in Two/I/2–6, the prerequisite for discovering these demonstrable relationships was knowing about all the stimulus configurations acting as key stimuli on the same IRM and, furthermore, being completely familiar with all the forms which a motor pattern could assume at different intensities. Stimulus configurations that are known to act as key stimuli on one IRM and to exert one qualitatively identical and quantifiable influence, add their effects to those of an equally specific and qualitatively identical and quantifiable state of endogenous excitability; the sum of this addition is indicated by the intensity of the motor pattern performed, which varies only unidimensionally along a single scale of intensities, which again permits perfect quantification: thus can Seitz's law of heterogeneous summation be restated.

In the terms of our hydraulic model, the quantity of discharge at the outflow is determined by the sum of endogenous and exogenous factors, while its quality is constant and quite independent of the proportions in which they contribute to the sum. This constancy of specific quality is remarkable in view of the heterogeneity of the influences contributing: no matter how they are mixed, they find their exclusively quantitative expression in the unidimensional variation of the action's intensity. This unidimensionality implies the existence of a firmly integrated system that ensures the discharge of highly differentiated motor patterns in the exact environmental situation to which they are adapted. The function of this system does indeed fully merit Portielje's old term, "action-and-reaction-in-one."

The heterogeneity of afferent influences on the one hand and, on the other, the unity of internal readiness as well as the unity of the subsequent motor discharge, appear to imply that the specificity of the whole process is dependent less on the specificity of the contributing factors than on the "reservoir" in which they are "collected." We do not know what, physiologically, represents that reservoir, nor, indeed, what it is that is collected in it. But as has already been pointed out, we find the most detailed analogy of function with those of processes regulating the contents of hollow organs or of supplying tissue needs. However one tries to construct a flow diagram or a thought model simulating the processes just discussed, one will find it impossible to avoid the assumption of an accumulating action-specific "readiness" or excitability. The accepted expression, "action-specific potential," (ASP) seems to me to be a neutral and useful term. The only danger of misunderstanding consists of a possible confusion of the ASP of a fixed motor pattern with the membrane potential of a single neural element. Great as the analogies are, it is not permissible to equate the two concepts.

Chapter IV
The Behavior Mechanisms Already Described Built into Complex Systems

1. Appetitive Behavior Directed at Quiescence

As has been explained in the Introductory History and in One/I/1, and mentioned again in Two/II/1, both Oskar Heinroth and I regarded the *arteigene Triebhandlung*, the species-characteristic drive action, as the smallest and ultimate, indivisible unit of behavior. But this unit is actually a quite complex mechanism comprising appetitive behavior, the function of an IRM, and the performance of a consummatory action. The conceptualizations of appetitive behavior, the innate releasing mechanism, and the fixed motor pattern have been proved applicable in many cases in which these functions are built into sequences of a kind that are very different from, and more complicated than, the species-characteristic drive action. If Heinroth and I regarded the tripartite sequence of appetitive behavior, IRM, and the consummatory act as a single, and the only element of animal behavior, this must be regarded as a simplification that is not only forgivable, within a new and developing branch of science, but also unavoidable and heuristically fertile. For, after all, when drawing flow diagrams, biocyberneticists intentionally rely on similar simplifications. Flow diagrams representing these kinds of complicated behavior systems, that is, appetitive behavior, IRMs, and consummatory acts, are so similar to each other that it is permissible to speculate that the mechanisms underlying their functions are not only analogous but physiologically akin to one another.

In his classic treatise on appetites and aversions as constituents of instinct, Wallace Craig (1918) was the first to demonstrate that the very same elements, such as goal-directed appetitive behavior, innate releasing mechanisms, and fixed motor patterns can be joined together in quite different ways to form teleonomic systems of behavior. He defines appetites and aversions in the following manner: an appetite is a state of arousal which continues as long as a specific stimulus situation, which he calls an "appeted" stimulus, is not reached. When this specific stimulus situation is reached, however, the consummatory action is set free, the appetite is assuaged, and a state of satiety, that is, of relative quiescence is achieved.

Aversion, on the other hand, has been defined by Craig as a state of agitation which continues as long as a certain specific stimulus, referred to as the disturbing stimulus, is present, but which ceases and is replaced by a state of relative rest when the stimulus has ceased to act on the animal's sense organs. As an example of aversion, Craig cites:

> . . . the so-called jealousy of the male dove, which is manifested especially in the early days of the brood cycle before the eggs are laid. At this time, the male has an aversion to seeing his mate in the proximity to another dove. The sight of another dove near his mate is an "original annoyer" (Thorndike, Chapter IX) [1911]. If the male sees another dove near his mate, he follows *either of two* courses of action: namely a) attacking the intruder with real pugnacity; b) driving his mate, gently, not pugnaciously, away from the intruder. When he has succeeded either in conquering the stranger and getting rid of him, or driving his mate away from the stranger, so that he has got rid of the disturbing sight of another dove in the presence of his mate, his agitation ceases. If we prevent him from being successful with either of these methods, as by confining the pair of doves in one cage and the third dove in plain sight in a contiguous cage, then he will continue indefinitely to try both methods. Or if we leave all three doves free in one pen, the mated male will try the mettle of the intruder and conquer him if he can; if he fails, he will turn all his energies to drive his mate away from the intruder. Or if in former experiences he has learned to gage this individual intruder, if he has conquered him before, he will promptly attack him now, but if defeated by him before, he will now choose the alternative of driving away his mate. In sum, the instinctive aversion impels the dove to thoroughly intelligent efforts to get rid of a disturbing situation."

An essential difference between appetites and aversions exists with regard to the reinforcing and to the extinguishing function of releasing stimuli. In the case of appetites, the finding of any slight stimulus which adds to the stimulus situation, releasing the consummatory action, has the effect of a reinforcement. Any addition to the stimulus situation that helps to increase the readiness for a specific act, as discussed in Two/III/ 4, will "encourage" the animal in its efforts. Conversely, in aversions, every diminution of the disturbing stimulus situation will reinforce the kind of behavior that has led to this relief.

The concept of aversion, as defined through these points of view, does not seem very satisfactory when applied to a certain, rather common type of behavior which may be classed among the aversions because it serves to make the organism *avoid* certain detrimental stimulus situations. All the physiologic mechanisms that cause the animal to choose the sort of habitat to which its species is adapted, in other words, that cause it to search for a special optimum of humidity, temperature, or illumination and the like, obviously are in complete accordance with Wallace Craig's definition of aversions. There are, however, very many other instances in which appetitive behavior is striving for a very special stimulus situation that, far from releasing any consummatory action, is just what the animal requires in order to come to rest. Thus, the mere *absence* of such a stimulus situation acts as an "original annoyer," but no gradation of stimulus-strength leads the organism along the correct path for getting rid of it. What the animal does, in this case, is the purest form of blind searching. An example is afforded by the behavior of many birds dwelling in dense masses of reeds, such as the bearded tit *(Panurus biarmicus)* or the least bittern *(Ixobrychus minutus)*. These birds are content only in an environment which permits them to sit within dense cover, both feet turned outwards with claws clasping, on either side, the vertical stems of sedge. A fully fledged young greylag goose which has strayed from its family will most strenuously search for it, wandering about restlessly, sounding distress calls, and never coming to rest until it has found its loved ones again.

To describe this kind of appetitive behavior as aversion seems somewhat strained: to say, for instance, that the bittern has an aversion to all landscapes that are not a dense growth or mass of reeds, or that the young goose has an aversion to all environments not containing its parents. Monika Meyer-Holzapfel has proposed describing this kind of behavior as appetite directed at quiescence (1956). Physiologically it is different from the true aversion in that there is no gradient leading the animal away from the disturbing stimulus and towards the situation in which it can find rest. The term "quiescence" must never be misinterpreted to mean that the animal, having got rid of the disturbance, will now lapse into a state of complete rest or fall asleep. On the contrary, being liberated from the disturbance, it will proceed to perform any of a great number of behavior patterns which, up to that moment, have been suppressed by the disturbing stimulus.

Transitions and intermediate stages between aversions and appetites for quiescence are, of course, numerous. When we go indoors on a cold winter's day, it remains questionable whether we do so because we feel an aversion to the cold, or whether we are moved by the longing for a warm stove.

2. Searching Automatism

Monika Meyer-Holzapfel's conceptualization of appetitive behavior as a striving for quiescence (1956) called attention to the fact that Heinroth's species-characteristic drive action (Two/I/1), that is, a system composed of appetitive behavior, an IRM, and a consummatory act did not, by any means, represent the one and only way in which these three elements could be combined.

Prechtl and Schleidt (1950, 1951) demonstrated a very special system composed of these three parts. As long as a newly born kitten is awake and not sucking at one of its mother's teats, it performs a constant, to-and-fro sideways sweeping movement with its head and the foreparts of its body. All the while it is doing this it is also creeping slowly forward and, when it touches a solid vertical surface, will snuggle up to this and maintain contact with this while continuing on its way. If the kitten comes into contact with fur, it will stop its forward motion and orient the sweeping movements so that its nose remains pressed against the fur while moving to and fro in it. When by doing this the kitten happens to touch a spot bare of any fur, the sweeping movements cease and are replaced by repeated snapping movements of the mouth, which under normal conditions will find the teat. When this is accomplished, all movements hitherto described come to a standstill and, while the upper jaw and the tongue enclose the nipple, the kitten now begins to suck and to perform a new motor pattern, thrusting its nose rhythmically against the mother's breast and massaging the breast gently with its fore paws— a movement termed "milk treading" that is found in many mammals, including man.

The beginning of the chain of activities is, in this instance, the *uninhibited* performance of a fixed motor pattern that continues until a specific stimulus situation is reached which inhibits it while, at the same time, others are released. In this chain of processes, fixed motor patterns play the role of appetitive behavior insofar as the stimulus situation which terminates them at the same time serves to release another fixed motor pattern which forms the next link of a functionally consistent chain.

H. Prechtl (1955) has shown that the activities of searching for the mother's breast performed by the human baby, and the reaction at finding the nipple, are programmed in a very similar way, except for an additional orienting mechanism: if one gingerly touches the cheek of the baby while it is moving its head to and fro in the automatic movement, it interrupts this rhythm suddenly to perform a well-oriented snap in the direction from which it has been touched.

The program of these activities accomplishes a highly teleonomic sequence in which fixed motor patterns and innate releasing mechanisms are linked together to form an *adaptable* program. The sequence begins, in this instance, with the performance of a fixed motor pattern which is not under any constant inhibition and does *not* stand in need of an IRM to be liberated. One motor pattern in this chain of activities plays the role of an appetitive behavior striving for the next motor pattern: the stimulus situation achieved not only terminates it, but, at the same time, corresponds to the IRM setting off the next action of the sequence.

3. Hierarchical Systems

Chains of behavior mechanisms such as the one analyzed by Prechtl and Schleidt (1950, 1951) are extremely common; in fact, they are much more common than actions consisting of only a single link of appetitive behavior, one IRM, and one comsummatory action. It is perfectly legitimate— it even constitutes a mark of genius—to discover the simplest possible instance in which a natural law is realized, as, for example, are the Mendelian laws in monogene hybrids. Yet one must not commit the error of believing that the simplest instance is also the most frequent one—as Oskar Heinroth and I admittedly did in the case of the species-characteristic drive action. Further analysis has shown that much more complex systems are much more common; at the same time, this analysis has demonstrated the value of our first conceptualizations: all these complex systems have been proved to be based on the very same three elementary mechanisms that we assumed in our provisional flow diagrams.

Only rarely does the primary appetitive behavior, with which an animal begins an activity, lead directly to a stimulus situation releasing the consummatory act terminating that activity. Much more commonly the primary appetitive behavior leads to a situation in which the first form of appetitive behavior is switched off and a subsequent one is switched on, just as in the case of the kitten finding the nipple area. The program of such a chain is much more adaptable than the single tripartite action, not only because the time spent performing each phase is variable, but also because every step of appetitive behavior usually includes orientation or other mechanisms exploiting instant information—as will be discussed in Chapter VI.

Tinbergen describes this type of chain as the *hierarchical organization* of instinct. One simple example is found in the behavior of the hobby falcon *(Falco subbuteo)*, which generally directs its hunting flight to areas promising prey. On discovering a flock of potential prey—for instance, a flock of starlings—the falcon approaches and thereby causes the starlings to cluster close together. This formation releases in the falcon a "sham attack," that is, a motor pattern which is not adapted to catching prey but is adapted to stampeding one starling out of the swarm. If this is successful, the new situation releases true prey catching, a motor pattern calculated to hit the prey with great impact, usually from below. This action bears the character of a consummatory act, indeed much more so than the subsequent consummation, that is, eating the prey. After striking and making the kill, the falcon stands on the dead bird, often for quite a while, before beginning to pluck; afterwards, the eating it

does with unhurried movements provides the impression that these dis-
passionate actions do not really belong to the same behavioral system as
those of the catching and killing.

Tinbergen has represented the principle of such a hierarchical organization in a diagram which intentionally simplifies matters but, nevertheless, very ably demonstrates the interactions conceptualizing the
duality of the endogenous generation of excitability on one side, and of
the exteroceptor function of the IRMs on the other. He uses the concept
of a "central excitatory mechanism" (CEM), as proposed by Frank Beach
(1942), though he specifically opposes the notion of monocausality, that
is, of regarding the CEM as the single, or even as the main source of
stimulation. Concerning this, Tinbergen (1951) says:

> ... it seems that the single CEM postulated by Beach is rather a system of
> CEMs of different levels. Each 'centre' in our system is a CEM in Beach's
> sense, as each of these centres has its own afferent and efferent connexions.
>
> Of no less importance is the difference between motivational and releas-
> ing factors. For, as we have seen, the motivational factors influence the CEM
> itself while the releasing factors activate a reflex-like mechanism, the IRM,
> removing a block that prevented the outflow of impulses along the efferent
> paths.
>
> The system C(entral) E(xcitatory) M(echanism)–I(nnate) R(eleasing)
> M(echanism) is tentatively presented in Figs. [19a and 19b]. Let us first con-
> sider Fig. [19a], which represents one centre of an intermediate level.
>
> The centre is 'loaded' by motivational impulses of various kinds. First it
> receives impulses from the superordinated centre of the next higher level.
> Impulses from this higher level flow into other centres as well, in fact to all
> the centres controlled by the higher centre. Second, centre 1 may receive
> impulses from an 'automatic', self-generating centre belonging especially to
> it ([compare] ... the dual nature of centres as found by von Holst ...). Third,
> a hormone might contribute to the motivation, either by acting directly on
> centre 1, or through the automatic centre. ... Fourth, internal sensory stim-
> uli ... may help to load centre 1. Fifth, external sensory stimuli might also
> act directly upon the centre and contribute to its motivation.
>
> This system together represents a CEM in Beach's sense, belonging to one
> level of the hierarchical system.
>
> Outgoing impulses are blocked as long as the IRM is not stimulated. When
> the adequate sign stimuli impinge upon the reflex-like IRM, the block is
> removed. The impulses can now flow along a number of paths. All but one
> lead to subordinate centres of the next lower level. However, all these
> centres are prevented from action by their own blocks, and most of the
> impulses therefore flow to the nervous structures controlling appetitive
> behaviour. This appetitive behaviour, as we have seen ..., is carried on until
> one of the IRMs of the lower level removes a block, as a result of which free
> passage is given through the corresponding centre of this next lower level.
> This 'drains away' the impulses from the appetitive behaviour mechanism
> and conducts them to the appetitive behaviour mechanism of the lower
> centre.

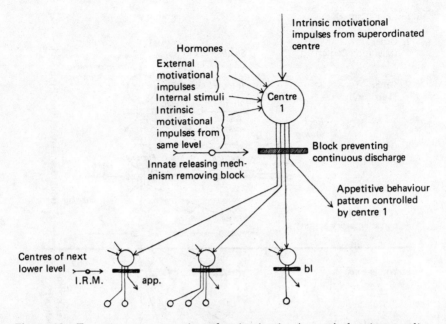

Figure 19a. Tentative representation of an instinctive 'centre' of an intermediate level. Explanation in the text. (Tinbergen, N.: *The Study of Instinct*.)

Fig. [19b] suggests how centres of this type might be organized within one major instinct. The reproductive instinct of the male three-spined stickleback has been taken as a concrete example. The hormonal influence, presumably exerted by testosterone, is acting upon the highest centre. This centre is most probably also influenced by a rise in temperature. These two influences together cause the fish to migrate from the sea (or from deep fresh water) into more shallow fresh water. This highest centre, which might be called the migration centre, seems to have no block. A certain degree of motivation results in migratory behaviour, without release by any special set of sign stimuli, which is true appetitive behaviour. This appetitive behaviour is carried on—the fish migrates—until the sign stimuli, provided by a suitable territory (shallow, warm water and suitable vegetation) act upon the IRM blocking the reproductive centre *sensu stricto*, which might be called 'territorial centre'. The impulses then flow through this centre. Here, again, the paths to the subordinated centres (fighting, nest-building, etc.) are blocked as long as the sign stimuli adequate to these lower levels are not forthcoming. The only open path is that to the appetitive behavior, which consists of swimming around, waiting for either another male to be fought or a female to be courted, or nest material to be used in building.

If, for instance, fighting is released by the trespassing of a male into the territory, the male swims towards the opponent (appetitive behaviour). The opponent must give new, more specific sign stimuli, which will remove the block belonging to one of the consummatory acts (biting, chasing, threatening, etc.) in order to direct the impulse flow to the centre of one of these consummatory acts.

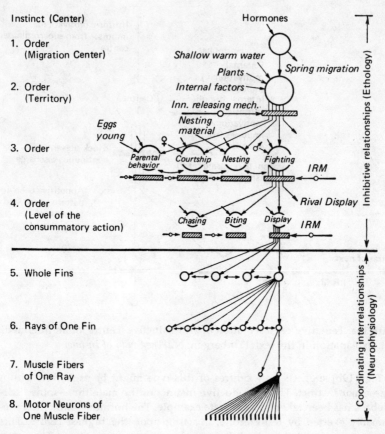

Figure 19b. Hierarchical centers of the major reproductive instinct of the stickleback male. Motivational impulses are represented by straight arrows which 'load' the centers (shown here as circles). These impulses may come from the external environment as well as from superordinated centers, or they may occur spontaneously within a center (this is not considered in the schema). The shaded rectangles indicate inhibiting influences, which prevent a continuous discharge of motor impulses. These blocks are removed by innate releasing machanisms. When this has occurred the animal will show a specific appetitive behavior until more specific releasing stimuli activate the next subordinated instinct and the still more specific appetitive behavior. The concave, two-headed arrows between centers of the same level indicate inhibiting relationships and the existence of DIS-PLACEMENT ACTIVITIES. Below the level of the consummatory acts a number of centers come into action simultaneously. The relation between subconsummatory centers of the same level is indicated by horizontal lines. (Additional explanation in the text.) (Eibl-Eibesfeldt, I.: *Ethology: The Biology of Behavior.*)

The various centres located at the various levels are, therefore, not organized in exactly the same way. The very highest centre has no block. If there were blocks at these very highest centres, the animal would have no means of 'getting rid' of impulses at all, which, as far as we know, would lead to neurosis. The next centre responds, in comparison to the lower centres, to a relatively higher number of motivational factors.

The next centres of the male stickleback's reproductive behaviour pattern, represented, for example, by fighting and nest-building, are loaded primarily by the impulses coming from the higher centre. Whether there are special motivational factors for each of these centres besides those coming from the higher centre is not certain, but I think there are, because the fighting drive displays the phenomenon of after-discharge, and, moreover, seems to be motivated (not merely released) by external stimuli. In general it seems, that the lower we go, the more pronounced the influence of external releasing stimuli becomes.

Arrows between the centres of one level indicate interrelationships suggested by the existence of mutual inhibition and of displacement activities. It should be emphasized that it is quite possible that these interconnexions do not in reality run directly from one centre to the other, but go by way of the superordinated centre, and that the 'inhibition' of one centre by the other may in reality be competition, the 'inhibiting' centre by decrease of resistance 'draining away' the impulse flow at the expense of the 'inhibited' centre.

Thus the motivation is carried on through a number of steps, which may be different in different instincts, down to the level of the consummatory action. Here the picture is changed. When the block of the consummatory centre is removed, a number of centres come into action simultaneously, between which horizontal co-ordinative forces are effective. With fish, these centres below the consummatory level are arranged in two or three planes, the lowest of which is the centre of the right or left fin-ray muscle, which is a relatively simple type of nervous centre. The relation between sub-consummatory centres of the same level are represented by horizontal lines.

Tinbergen stresses that, in his opinion, "these diagrams represent no more than a working hypothesis of a type that helps to put our thoughts in order"; also, he emphasizes that the diagram does not take into account the great number of feedback effects and regulating cycles connecting the lowest and the highest levels of any hierarchical organization of instinct. It is certain, for instance, that a high ASP of a motor pattern at the lowest level can exert a decisive influence on the highest "centers." These qualifications notwithstanding, it is necessary to state that Tinbergen's diagram is indeed much more than a mere working hypothesis. The stratification of superimposed levels of integration, as well as the IRMs shunting behavior from one to the other, are *realities*. Their number can and has been ascertained and the specific stimulus situations causing the switch from one level of appetence to the subsequent one have been experimentally analyzed.

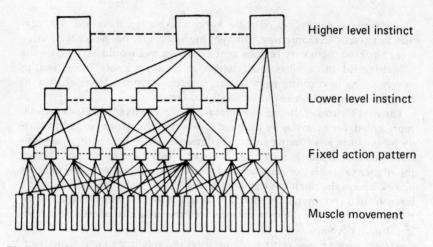

Higher level instinct

Lower level instinct

Fixed action pattern

Muscle movement

Figure 20. The hierarchical scheme of G. P. Baerends (1956), clearly showing the interrelationships of the centers. Especially noteworthy is the fact that lower centers are often controlled by several higher ones. Dotted lines represent inhibitory relationships between mechanisms of the same order. (Eibl-Eibesfeldt, I.: *Ethology: The Biology of Behavior.*)

In his analysis of the parental care exhibited by the female diggerwasp *(Ammophila campestris)* (1941), Baerends found that subsystems of the hierarchy, which are situated on a lower level, are quite often governed by more than one locus belonging to a higher level. It is hardly worth mentioning that this is frequently the case on levels below that of the fixed motor pattern, since, obviously, the contraction of a certain muscle can occur in the service of many functions. An analogous relationship on the level of motor patterns appears more interesting. As has already been mentioned in Two/I/12, there are a number of fixed motor patterns which can be performed in the context of many different systems of behavior. These "multi-purpose activities" are, for the greater part, rather simple tools such as those of locomotion, et cetera. Baerends discovered highly differentiated motor patterns, each of which was adapted to a special function, but, in this function they recurred again and again in different parts of the temporal sequence determined by the hierarchical organization. Baerends's diagram, represented in Figure 20, takes into account all the pertinent aspects observed in the behavior of the female diggerwasp *(Ammophila campestris Jur.).* Baerends writes:

During the first bright days in June the males leave the cocoons. The females appear some days later. Mating takes place within a few hours after the female has hatched. Shortly after coition the female begins to dig her first nest (nest A). As nesting sites flat, sandy areas with a compact soil are selected. The nest consists of a vertical shaft about 2-1/2 cm long and one elliptical cell about 2 cm in length. Having finished the nest, the shaft is temporarily closed by loosely filling it up with some clods, and the wasp then disappears into the heather. She usually returns within a few hours, carrying a paralyzed caterpillar. She reopens the nest, carries the caterpillar down and lays an egg. Then she closes the nest with much more care than before. After she has finished, it is impossible for the human eye to distinguish the entrance from the surroundings. She now leaves nest A and it may be some days, before she provisions it again.

Soon afterwards the wasp begins to dig a new nest (B).

It appeared to be a general rule that once a nest was begun, the work at this nest was continued without interruption, until an egg was laid.

The first series of activities, therefore, constituting the first stage of the care for every nest made, will be called the first phase.

After completing the first phase of nest B, which takes her one or more days, dependent on the amount of sunshine, the wasp returns to nest A and, before fetching a caterpillar, opens the nest. After a brief visit, she closes it again and flies off to the heather. Such a visit, in which no caterpillar is brought, will be called a "solitary visit", in contrast to "provisioning visit". As a rule the wasp, after this solitary visit brings one or more fresh caterpillars, before she leaves the nest alone for the second time. This phase I shall call, therefore, the second phase; it consists of a solitary visit followed by storing 1–3 caterpillars. Occasionally this phase consists of a solitary visit only, namely when the egg has not yet hatched at the time of this visit.

After having finished this second phase in nest A, the wasp carries through the same phase in nest B. Now she again pays a solitary visit to nest A and there enters into the third and last phase, consisting of one or more solitary visits and the storeage [sic] of another 3–7 caterpillars. This phase is concluded by closing the nest in an especially careful manner, the wasp pressing down the contents of the shaft with her head, during which a loud humming sound can be heard.

She now goes to nest B to accomplish the third phase here. After having finally closed this nest she begins to dig a new nest.

As we see from the above, in each nest provisioning occurs in three phases. During every phase the wasp is occupied with one particular nest exclusively, interrupting work at the nest only for foraging on her own behalf, for hunting caterpillars or for sleeping, but never for any work concerning another nest.

Having finished one phase she goes to another nest and works through an entire phase there. If there is no other nest to provide for, she makes a new nest. Occasionally, in very favourable weather, the wasp, after having completed the second phase in nest A, digs a new nest C before beginning the second phase of nest B. In this way a wasp sometimes has three nests under her care.

The second and the third phase always begin with a solitary visit; sometimes a phase consists of even no more than that one solitary visit. This may occur when the nest has been disturbed shortly before this visit, or, in the case of the second phase, when the egg has not yet hatched. This suggests that the solitary visit serves as an inspection, that is to say that the wasp during this visit receives stimuli from the contents of the cell which determine whether she will leave the nest alone or go and fetch fresh caterpillars.

An experimental test of this hypothesis is possible on the following basis. If the solitary visit actually has a regulating function, it should be possible to influence the wasp's subsequent behavior by changing the contents of the nest just before the solitary visit. This could not be done in the real nests but it appeared that the wasps did not interrupt their provisioning activities, when I replaced their nests by artificial nests, provided certain precautions were taken. These nests were made of gypsum and consisted of a lower part, containing the cell, and a lid that could easily be lifted so that I could reach the cell and change its contents at will.

I carried out the following experiments:

1. Nests which according to preceding observations, should be provisioned immediately after the solitary visit, were disturbed by removing the larva just before that visit. The result was that the nest was abandoned after the first solitary visit.
2. In similar nests, I replaced the larva by a paralysed [sic] caterpillar with an *Ammophila's* [sic] egg, taken from another nest. Now the wasp did not start provisioning immediately after the solitary visit (as she should have done), but she waited until the egg was hatched.
3. Before the wasp paid her first solitary visit of the third phase to the nest I added some paralysed caterpillars to the contents of the nest. The result was that the wasp either stopped provisioning altogether, or at least brought less caterpillars than the smallest amount ever stored under normal conditions.
4. In nests containing one caterpillar with an *Ammophila's* egg, nests, therefore, that should not be provisioned immediately, I replaced the egg by a larva. In these cases the wasp brought fresh caterpillars soon after the solitary visit.
5. Occasionally a wasp pays a solitary visit when the third phase is halfway concluded. A few times I succeeded in taking all caterpillars away just before the visit. Normally the wasps should have brought only a few more caterpillars, but now they again stored a considerable number of caterpillars, making the total amount of stored food larger than ever observed under normal conditions.

The same experiments were carried out just before provisioning visits. Under these circumstances the wasps did not react to any change in the contents of the cell. They even continued provisioning when the larva was removed together with the food.

These experiments conclusively show, therefore, that the solitary visit is a real inspection, during which the wasp learns how to act in the following hours or even days.

Apart from having a function as a regulatory principle, the solitary visit also demonstrates a most remarkable phychological fact: although the external stimulating situation is exactly the same at a solitary visit as at a provisioning visit, the wasp's behaviour is profoundly influenced by it at the first occasion, whereas at the second occasion not the slightest influence can be traced.

In one case, however, the contents of the nest does influence the wasp's behaviour during a provisioning visit. When I put certain objects into the cell just before the wasp would pay her very first visit, during which she had to lay her egg, the wasp did react. If the object was a caterpillar with an *Ammophila's* [sic] egg or a cocoon, the wasp pulled it out of the cell and threw it away. If it was a larva, she immediately brought in her caterpillar but failed to lay an egg. Often she even captured some more caterpillars and stored them, still postponing the laying of the egg. It appeared that the presence of a young larva stimulated the wasp to bring 1–3 caterpillars (corresponding with the second phase) and that an older larva stimulated the wasp to bring 3–7 caterpillars (corresponding with the third phase).

Whereas, as we have seen, it is, the amount of food present at the solitary inspection visit which determines the wasp's behaviour in the second and third phase, the wasp is stimulated at her first visit by the age of the larva.

Now the two series of experiments that served to investigate the part played by the solitary visit revealed the regulatory system, at work within the second or the third phase. They did not answer the questions as to the factors that bring the wasp from one phase into the next phase in the same nest.

Here the third series offers a suggestion. The age of the larva, which the wasp happens to find in her nest at her first visit, determines whether she will be brought into the second or into the third phase. This and other arguments, which cannot be treated in detail here, render it probable that the age of the larva has the same influence during the solitary visits.

The following may be illustrated by the narrative of the activities of wasp GO. . . .

The wasp was marked shortly before she finished the third phase in nest A. After having closed this nest she paid a solitary visit to nest B. As the egg had not yet hatched, she closed this nest again without bringing a caterpillar and began to dig a new nest C. Next morning she brought in a caterpillar and laid an egg in this nest. Then she paid a solitary visit to B again where the larva had just hatched. Provisioning, therefore, is started (third phase) and is continued for 2 days. After she has finally closed nest B, the wasp pays a solitary visit to C. The egg in C has not yet hatched whereupon the wasp leaves C alone and starts digging (D). As this was begun at a late hour, nest D was not completed before the end of the day. Next morning the wasp brought [sic] a solitary visit in C, nest D apparently being abandoned. In C, the larva has hatched and the wasp brought one caterpillar. Then a new nest E was started, an egg was laid, whereupon, next day, the third phase in C is completed, which took 2 days. Next morning a solitary visit was paid to nest E where the larva had hatched. As a consequence one caterpillar was brought soon afterwards. After that the wasp again began a new nest which is not taken into account here, because of incompleteness of my observations. Next day the third phase in nest E was completed.

It is on these observations that Baerends's diagram (Figure 20) is based. As the diagram illustrates, the hierarchical organization endows a sequence of behavior patterns with great plasticity and adaptability to

changing environmental conditions—despite the fact that all its subsystems, as well as the interactions among them, are phylogenetically programmed and modifications by learning play hardly any part in it at all.
Modification by learning is restricted to the acquisition of local orientation and otherwise has no influence on the stupendous adaptability of
the hierarchical system. This makes it possible for the wasp to take care
of four nests simultaneously, when each nest contains progeny at a different stage of development requiring different actions pertinent to
parental care.

4. The Relative Hierarchy of Moods

As already mentioned, a fixed motor pattern retains the character of a
consummatory act, something striven for for its own sake by its own
appetitive behavior, even if, in the sequence of a hierarchical organization, it plays the role itself of an appetitive behavior striving for the stimulus situation that will release the next link in the behavioral chain.
Action-specific appetence for a behavior pattern can be so strong that its
motivational power exceeds by far the stimulation coming from the next
higher center, as represented in Tinbergen's diagram (Figure 19). One
example is sufficient: A motor pattern common among ducks and geese,
while they are swimming in shallow water, is that of "upending," that
is, of stretching the neck straight down into the water and groping for
food at the bottom. Usually this pattern forms a part of the system of
feeding behavior and is motivated "from above" by an appetite for food.
If, however, geese are kept on a pond that is devoid of vegetation, so that
upending consistently fails to provide anything edible, the geese will
still, nevertheless, from time to time, indulge in the motor pattern of
upending for its own sake. Geese kept constantly in such an environmental situation and fed exclusively on corn that is strewn on dry
ground and fed there to the extent that they refuse to eat any more, will
begin again to feed when offered the same food thrown into the pond at
the right depth for upending. In this case it is quite correct to say that
the geese are now feeding for the sake of upending instead of upending
for the sake of feeding—as is usually done.

Another amusing example of two appetites swapping roles in this way
was discovered by Ursula von Saint Paul and myself during our investigation of the ontogeny of "impaling" behavior in shrikes of the genus
Lanius (1968). These birds hoard their prey, insects and small vertebrates,
by impaling them on thorns. On an earlier occasion I had observed that
in red-backed shrikes (Lanius collurio) the motor pattern of pressing the
prey onto a thorn is innate, but that the orientation to the thorn must be
learned. It soon became apparent that this lack of orientation was due to

inadequate rearing, as mentioned in One/II/9. Saint Paul reared shrikes using a perfect technique; these birds oriented to a thorn at the first sight of it without any fumbling. Birds which had never been in contact with either a thorn or with prey for impaling were first offered a thorn in the guise of a nail of adequate size driven through one of their perches. The birds investigated the nail at once, examining it closely and then nibbling it. Then they went in search of pieces of food to impale. Not finding any bits of food, they resorted to tiny and most inadequate objects. One greater shrike (Lanius excubitor) grabbed a small piece of dry butterfly wing and carried it straight to the nail-thorn. The orientation of the impaling movement to the point of the nail was so exact that the bird succeeded in splitting this small object right through its middle—which may, of course, have been mere chance. In the complementary experiment, each of the inexperienced shrikes was presented with an object extremely suitable for impalement—a whole, dead, newly-hatched chicken. Each bird at once grabbed it and very obviously went in search of a thorn, wiping the object along the perches and on the bars of the cage and performing impaling motions in vacuo. Thus the presence of one of two objects belonging to the temporal sequence of the shrike's impaling behavior awakened appetitive behavior directed at the other, in spite of the fact that, in nature, grabbing prey must precede impalement on a thorn.

Thus the temporal sequence in which activities follow each other in the normal performance of a hierarchical system need not necessarily be identical with the direction in which a "higher" center (in Tinbergen's diagram) is supplying excitation to a lower one. In the impaling behavior of our shrikes, as well as in the upending of our geese, the "eating drive," which might be assumed to be exerted by the highest center of the hierarchy, plays but an inferior role as a source of excitation, while motor patterns situated at the low level of consummatory acts exert a decisive influence on the animal's behavior.

Among higher mammals, in whose behavior learning plays a much more important part than in that of birds, a much more complicated interaction takes place between the levels of a hierarchical organization. Paul Leyhausen, who investigated these phenomena in carnivores of the cat family (Felidae), speaks of a "relative hierarchy of moods" (relative Stimmungshierarchie). The acts of lying in ambush, stalking, catching, killing, and finally eating prey, form a sequence which is obligatory only with regard to their common teleonomic function. Physiologically, each of the motor patterns involved retains the character of a consummatory act that possesses its own appetitive behavior independently of whether it is performed under the pressure of the higher level of tissue need or acted out in play, for its own sake.

As has been explained in Two/II/4, Leyhausen has demonstrated that the endogenous ASP production of any motor pattern is strictly correlated in its quantity to the frequency with which the performance of the movement is needed in the daily life of the species.

It is to be assumed that, even in felines, a primarily linear sequence of appetite and IRMs exists in ontogeny and that this sequence serves to guide the inexperienced kitten along the right route from stalking a prey to eating it. Leyhausen says:

> After the cat has caught, killed, and eaten several prey animals and has thus experienced the connection between these three activities, it learns gradually to substitute learned, or at least partially learned appetitive hahavior for the initial links of the chain of prey-catching motor patterns. Species as well as individuals differ considerably in regard to the methods used in these learned movements. As in the case of the orientation of the killing bite, the fixed motor patterns themselves are in no way modified by learning (as are IRMs by the increasing of their selectivity), nor is there any transformation of instinct through experience, as assumed by Bierens de Haan (1940). The fixed motor patterns remain autonomous and unchanged, side by side with newly acquired learned motor skills. In neurophysiology the existence of these two kinds of "motoric templates" has been known for a long time.

5. The Locus of "Superior Command" (Übergeordnete Kommandostelle)

As has been described in Two/I/13, when the abdominal nerve cord of the earthworm (Lumbricus) is separated from the supra-esophageal ganglion, it continues to send out the incessant coordinated impulses for the worm's creeping locomotion; the decerebrated spinal cord of a wrasse (Labrus) continues to send out impulses that move the fish's fins until the death of the preparation. All tissues that are endowed with endogenous automatic production of excitation and that are normally subordinate to a central inhibiting influence, perform, on its removal, a continuous activity lasting as long as the preparation lives. Excitation-producing tissues of animals that lack a central nervous system, such as the neuroepithelia of coelenterates, represent intermediate forms between nervous, muscular, and epithelial tissues and, as Batham and Pantin (1950) have demonstrated, are constantly and unceasingly automatically active, quite independently of any external influence.

Whether excitation-producing tissues which are similarly independent exist in any organisms possessing a centralized nervous system is doubtful. It seems justified to suppose that, in higher animals, excitation-producing organs are always subject to higher loci within the central nervous system which exercise those inhibiting, as well as those excitatory functions symbolized in Erich von Holst's analogy of the bridle and the spurs (Two/I/16). Even the sinus ganglion of the vertebrate heart is controlled by the nervus accelerans and by the nervus depressor cordis which perform these two antagonistic functions.

The coelenterates investigated by Batham and Pantin are far from being the only organisms whose uncentralized nervous systems are devoid of superior, "commanding" loci. In sea urchins *(Echinus)*, concerted action of the peripheral organs, such as the ambulacral feet and the pedicels, is brought about by means of a direct mutual influence on each other and not via nervous pathways leading to a "center" and back again to the periphery. When a sea urchin moves hurriedly away from a starfish *(Asterias)*, this movement is caused, anthropomorphically speaking, by a panic spreading among the spines. Jakob von Uexküll used to say: "When a dog runs, the dog moves its legs; when a sea urchin runs, the legs move the sea urchin." This assertion was based on the following experiment reported by von Uexküll. A sea urchin was broken in half and the inner sides of both halves of the shell were scraped using sandpaper. The whole of the ambulacral system as well as the nervous system was thus completely removed. Then the two halves were joined together again by means of a spring clasp. The spines of the sea urchin still worked in coordination with one another. In this special case, the riderless horse of von Holst's parable does indeed exist; the sea urchin's reaction of fleeing from a star fish still functioned. And in this sense, von Uexküll's description of a sea urchin being a "reflex republic" is justified, provided one keeps in mind that the "reflex" no longer plays the all-important role ascribed to it during von Uexküll's time.

The different roles performed by the loci of superior command are well exemplified by the functions of the central nervous systems in various echinoderms. In sea urchins, the function of a superior commanding locus is hardly discernible by direct observation. In star fishes of the class Asteroidea, it is clear that messages are passed from one arm to the other arms. For instance, the animal finds its way back into sea water immediately, walking on its ambulacral feet, if one of its arms touches the water surface with its tip. What is so remarkable in this is that the star fish "walks" by means of coordinated movements that, necessarily, must pull at different angles to the longitudinal axis of each arm.

If the star fish is turned over onto its back, a coordinated movement of its arms serves to right it. In brittle star fish, Ophiroidea, the central nervous system can effect coordinated, undulating movements in the arms themselves, so that the animal "walks" much more quickly than any other star fish can and in any "desired" direction, which generally means toward cover.

Some Holothuraidea have developed into virtually bilateral animals, particularly the genus *Synapta* which lacks ambulacral feet and "walks" by means of peristaltic movements of its entire body. It certainly is the most lively of all echinoderms and, in its behavior, gives the impression of a bilaterally symmetrical animal.

All true bilaterally symmetrical animals, in other words, all those animals having a front end and a rear end and, therewith, a preferred direction of locomotion, possess, near their front ends, a central commanding locus as part of their nervous system, that is, a "brain." This is also the case even in those animals not possessing a "head," as, for instance, clams (Lamellibranchiata). The "invention" of a "head," that is, of a concentration of sense organs and nervous tissues at the end, which precedes during locomotion, brought with it such obvious teleonomic advantages that the invention has been made twice, independently, during the history of animals. Arthropods, (crustacea, centipedes, insects, arachnomorphs) as well as mollusks, may have inherited their heads from their mutual ancestors, the annelid worms. In all members of this great taxon, the mouth develops out of the blastopore, which means that it is homologous to the "protostome," the single body apperture of coelenterates, wherefore these creatures are termed 'protostomata.' Vertebrates and a few others have a mouth of different origin, and are termed 'deuterostomata.' Exaggerating for effect, it can be said that vertebrates and insects have their heads at opposite ends of their bodies. Both protostomes and deuterostomes possess a surprisingly similar, if only analogous organization of the head; nobody could ever have a moment's doubt about where a wasp or a squid has its head, its eyes, or its mouth. The functions of the two kinds of independently evolved brains also appear analogous.

A superior command locus obviously becomes necessary at the stage of evolution when an organism has developed more than one system of behavior patterns of which only one can function at any given time. Such a juncture becomes imperative in order to prevent incompatible motor patterns from "meshing gears" by being discharged simultaneously. An earthworm (Lumbricus) can creep forward and backward; it can eat, roll up dead leaves, and draw them into its burrow; it can copulate, draw back with lightening speed into its burrow, and, finally, it can—this I have never seen—move away quickly, on the surface of the ground, by executing a vertical undulating movement. As simple observation confirms, each of these movements is performed by itself, neatly separated from and never combined with any of the others. In an epileptic fit, mixed discharges can occur pathologically. This demonstrates that such a dysteleological occurrence is possible, in principle, and must be prevented by special mechanisms. A comparatively simple physiological organization achieving this purpose is what biocyberneticists call a maximum selecting system. It is represented in Figure 21. The mechanism is built in, like a filter, between the several sources of specific excitation and the motor pathways through which ASP is discharged. By causing a "backward-directed subtraction," it effectuates a simple mutual inhibition among the action patterns involved. The principle of "lateral backward inhibition" makes certain that the behavior pattern possessing, at

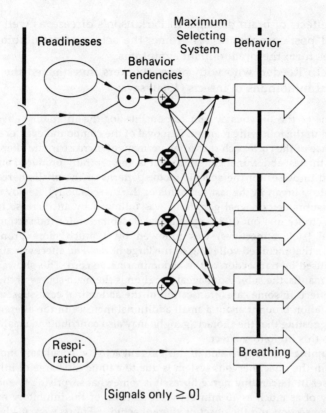

Figure 21. Functional diagram representing the reciprocal inhibition among behavior tendencies in accordance with the principle—plausible for such cases— of retroactive inhibition. Respiration is usually not included in this system; breathing continues unaffected by other forms of behavior. (Czihak, Langer, Ziegler in *Biologie*.)

the moment, the highest ASP value has free access to its consummatory action unobstructed by any competing motivation.

It can be hypothesized that the primary function of the simplest possible brain-like organs of bilateralia has been based on two functions. The first is that of a maximum selecting system serving to pass motor patterns one at a time; the second is that of IRMs serving to decide which of these behavior patterns should be discharged in a given situation.

All motor patterns not in use at a particular moment are kept under constant restraint by central inhibitions. It has been demonstrated by Erich von Holst, Kenneth Roeder, and by many others, that in annelid worms, in insects and in vertebrates, superior command loci within the nervous system are exerting a constant inhibitive influence that prevents the subordinate processes of endogenous impulse production from having a continuous influence on motor activity. The same functional principles prevail in the human brain, too, as is demonstrated by the multi-

farious effects of brain damage. In Parkinson's disease, as well as in the
so-called post-encephalitic syndrome, the action of disinhibited motor
processes form the predominant symptoms.

Kenneth Roeder, who with his co-workers investigated the function
of central inhibitions in insects (1960) says:

> Regions of the nervous system responsible for the inhibitory effect were
> located in the following manner. Removal of the compound eyes, ocelli, and
> antennae of the cockroach caused no permanent increase in the efferent out-
> put of the last abdominal ganglion [that is, the centrally produced and coor-
> dinated impulses for the specific motor·patterns of the phallomeres of the
> copulatory organ in the last segments of the insect's body]. Removal of the
> brain (supra-oesophageal ganglion) was followed by an increase in small
> spike activity in 4 out of 8 preparations. Decapitation (or transection of the
> cercival [sic] connectives) was followed by a much more pronounced
> increase that included volleying in the large fibres. The effect was similar to
> that caused by transection of the abdominal nerve cord. This shows that, as
> in the mantis, the sub-oesophageal ganglion is the main source of the inhib-
> itory effect. In some cases transection of the abdominal cord subsequent to
> decapitation brought about a small additional increase in the efferent activ-
> ity, suggesting that the thoracic ganglia may also contribute in smaller mea-
> sure to this inhibitory effect.
>
> Assuming that suppression of this efferent activity [copulatory motor pat-
> terns] in the intact nervous system is due to a tonic discharge of inhibitory
> impulses in descending nerve fibres, it is somewhat surprising to encounter
> a delay of as much as 15 min between removal of the inhibitory effect by
> cord transection and the onset of efferent activity. Efforts were made to find
> out whether the duration of this delay is determined by the site at which
> the inhibitory pathways are interrupted. There was no evidence that the
> delay differed when transection of the cord was made in the neck as com-
> pared with the abdominal region. However, since the delay was so variable,
> ranging from a few seconds to as much as 15 min, its duration in relation to
> the site of transection could have been obscured in the small number of
> observations that have been made.
>
> The method of cord transection permitted only one release of endogenous
> activity per preparation, so attempts were made to establish a reversible
> block of the inhibitory effect. An electronic method was first tried. The pas-
> sage of direct current through the nerve cord via an anode placed on the
> cord pitted against an indifferent cathode brought about a small increase in
> the efferent activity in nerves IX and X in 3 out of 11 cases, but this action
> was not sustained for the duration of the polarizing current. In the other
> cases there was no change in efferent activity. In 6 of the 11 cases the nerve
> cord was transected subsequent to treatment with the polarizing current and
> in each of these there was the usual increase in efferent activity.
>
> Localized ionic block of descending inhibitory pathways in the nerve cord
> was attempted through the application of isotonic potassium chloride and
> sodium-free (sucrose substituted) Hoyle's saline. Isotonic potassium chloride
> applied locally to the intact nerve cord takes about 30 min to block conduc-

tion in the ascending giant fibres, but if the sheath surrounding the cord is removed before potassium chloride application the block occurs in a minute or so (Twarog and Roeder, 1956). These agents were applied to intact and desheathed portions of the abdominal nerve cord while monitoring the output of efferent activity in nerves from the last abdominal ganglion. Difficulties were encountered in restricting the potassium chloride to a limited region of the nerve cord, and attempts were made to prevent it from reaching the last abdominal ganglion by submerging the latter in mineral oil. Of 7 experiments in which efferent activity continued in the last abdominal ganglion throughout the rather involved procedure 1 showed no change, 4 showed a slight increase not comparable with that achieved by cord transection, and in 2 there was an immediate increase followed by cessation of all efferent activity. In the latter activity was restored after 5 min by washing with saline, and the cessation could have been due to leakage of potassium chloride to the region of the ganglion.

The failure of these two attempts to block the inhibitory action caused some surprise, and is interesting in itself. Three possible explanations come to mind. First, the methods were technically inadequate. However, the same method of producing a potassium chloride block was successful with the giant fibres (Twarog and Roeder, 1956). Second, the inhibitory fibres have a small diameter and are in some way protected from agents that block the giant fibres. Third, the inhibitory action of the higher centres is exerted by agents other than nerve impulses. The last two possibilities remain entirely open, and the mode of inhibition will be considered further in the discussion.

In higher vertebrates, the "superior command locus" has a much more complicated function than those investigated by Roeder and von Holst, as it has to act as a connecting link between phylogenetically programmed and individually acquired behavior. Also, its function is quite certainly not limited to merely inhibiting unwanted activities; it obviously acts just as frequently as the initiating source of activity in general. It uses the spur as often as the bridle. Although "multi-purpose" activities do possess a sufficient and even an abundant supply of endogenous impulse production (Two/I/12) there is no doubt that quite often a very energetic active impulse emanates from superior command loci—I have been trying to avoid the word "center." As is to be explained later in the chapter on motor learning (Three/IV/1–3), the so-called voluntary movements have especially evolved in order to be at the beck and call of active superior command loci, and to be built into complicated systems in which not only learning, but also "insight" in the form of exploiting instant information takes a decisive part (Two/VI/12).

Even though in the highest animals and in man the superior command loci still retain their primary function of keeping motor patterns under inhibition and of liberating them only at the right moment, direct observation makes it obvious that, additionally, the very highest loci of most warm-blooded animal's brains are spontaneously active as long as the animal is awake. Unlike a worm or a snail, a lively creature such as a songbird or even a small coral fish is constantly moving receptor organs in different directions, actively searching for stimuli during the hours of its wakeful activity. It is primarily in organisms of this type that the state of wakefulness is clearly distinct from that of sleeping.

This wakeful searching for stimulation can be regarded as a precursor of true exploratory behavior, to be discussed in Three/VI. A stickleback while remaining motionless in the water moves its eyes about, "feeling out" its surroundings prior to moving in an appropriate direction. The same is true for many small songbirds, whose eyes are never still for a moment—as every photographer comes to realize with regret. In man, the movements of the eyes, focusing on one point of the ambient environment after the other, are so continuous that their cessation immediately draws our attention: we then say that a person "stares into space," which expresses the fact that these movements serve to maintain spatial orientation.

This activity certainly is based on endogenous impulse production rather than on reflex processes. It is also an obvious assumption that superior commanding loci of higher vertebrates perform an exciting as well as a bridling effect on the subordinate processes. A strong argument in favor of this assumption is that the voluntary movements which are known to exert the strongest influence in driving multi-purpose activities are, at the same time, more directly obedient to superior commands than any other kind of neural process, in fact, obedient until complete exhaustion of the organism as a whole has set in.

Chapter V
How Unitary Is "An Instinct"?

1. The Danger of Naming Instincts by Their Functions

A "system," according to Paul Weiss's somewhat aphoristic definition, "is everything that is unitary enough to deserve a name." In choosing any name one must avoid following the example of medieval pseudo-science which confused effect and cause. When air was streaming into a vacuum, a "horror vacui" was made responsible for that effect; the "phlogiston" was assumed to explain burning, and so forth. In exactly the same way, vitalistic psychology, rampant at the turn of the century, used terms such as the "escape instinct," the "reproductive instinct," and even the "instinct of self-preservation," deeming this to be a sufficient explanation of behavior. This seemed legitimate as long as an "instinct" was regarded as a preternatural factor, neither standing in need of nor accessible to a causal explanation.

To call a function by a name stemming from its teleonomic effect is, in itself, permissible, provided that one remains aware of the danger that this name may, as John Dewey pointed out, insidiously raise the false pretension of being an explanation for the function it describes. When dealing with a complex behavior system fulfilling a unitary teleonomic function, we are justified in naming it according to its function and to speak of a "reproductive instinct," or an "aggressive instinct," as both Tingergen and I have done (1938), but when doing this we must never forget that the system thus embraced by a functional concept represents a very loosely tied unit within which the teleonomic cooperation of very many autonomous parts is calling, if not screaming, for a causal explanation. The name, far from furnishing such an explanation, is nothing but a challenge to physiological analysis. The justification for providing a name depends exclusively on the success of this analysis.

Even if one remains fully aware of all these facts, it is still dangerous to name a somewhat larger behavior system by its function. Even though an expression like "reproductive instinct" or like "aggressive instinct" no longer implies postulating a preternatural factor, remnants of teleological thinking still tend to suggest, at least to some, the assumption of a single, if natural, source of causation. The reproach of assuming a "mono-causality" of instinct, particularly of aggressive instinct, has often been raised against me, although in my book on aggression I devoted an entire chapter, "The Great Parliament of Instincts," to the way in which a multiplicity of independent motivations are interacting in aggressive behavior.

2. The Multiplicity of Motivations

Tinbergen's diagram of the hierarchical organization of instincts (see Figure 19b) tends to further the conception of a one-way causation, but quite erroneously, since no one was or is more acutely conscious than Tinbergen that innumerable important feedback causations stem from the lowest levels of the hierarchy and take effect at the highest ones. As Heiligenberg and others have shown, a high pressure exerted by the ASP of one motor pattern, even at the lowest rung of a hierarchy, demonstrably exerts a decisive influence on processes taking place at the highest level.

In his 1959 article, "Unitary Drives," Robert Hinde has convincingly argued against the assumption of a mono-causality of instincts and against the concept of unitary drives. "One feature of behaviour which drives are postulated to explain is the temporal correlation between related activity. Most behaviour consists of sequences of activity and it is often suggested that these occur together, because they are governed by the same drive." Neither Tinbergen nor Baerends ever thought so; both saw very clearly that the teleonomically correct temporal sequence of activites within a hierarchical organization is programmed by its structure. In other words, the sequence is determined by the fact that each temporally preceeding link of appetitive behavior is switched to the succeeding one by one particular IRM. The function of each of these IRMs has been experimentally demonstrated by both authors.

Robert Hinde has investigated the multiplicity of the motor patterns which are integrated into the unitary function of the nest building of canaries (Serinus canaria). He showed that the single motor patterns are very independent of one another and, on the basis of this fact, Hinde argued correctly against the assumption of their being caused by a unitary drive. However, he ignores the fact that every single one of the motor patterns concerned in nest building possesses its own appetitive behavior as well as its own IRM. He also refuses to accept the fact that every motor pattern is a systemic unit which in itself is much more closely integrated and forms a much better defined unit than the super-imposed, much more loosely connected hierarchical system which, following Tinbergen, we are wont to call "an instinct." Hinde avoids our assumption of an action-specific potential (ASP) which can be accumulated and exhausted. For this, an unavoidable assumption in my opinion, he substitutes the following argumentation: External stimuli can exert a specific as well as an unspecific influence on behavior. Unspecific stimulation is necessary to sustain a sufficient measure of general nervous excitation, while specific stimuli determine the intensity of behavior. According to Hinde, it is sufficient to assume a continuous general activity within the nervous system, while there is no necessity to postulate specific motivations of behavior.

I fully agree that unspecific stimulation is necessary to keep up an adequate measure of general excitation (Two/I/8). However, I strongly object to the second assertion that the intensity of response is dependent only on specific stimulus situations. Hinde refuses to acknowledge not only the banal, ordinary, everyday experience of anyone who knows animals, but also the irrefutable results of the experiments made by A. Seitz (1940, 1941), H. W. Lissmann, D. Franck and U. Wilhelmi (1973), and many others. I refer to what has been said in Two/I/5 on the method of dual quantification.

Hinde's failure to acknowledge these facts is all the more surprising since he correctly, and in detail, describes the several fixed motor patterns of nest building and does not neglect the stimulus situations which release them. In doing this he cannot help mentioning spontaneity, appetitive behavior, and the threshold fluctuations concerned with these elements of behavior. Nonetheless, he concludes, " . . . are we then to postulate a separate drive for each of these activities? If so, where do these processes stop, for each of these activities can be analyzed into constituent movements?"

The first of these questions has been answered correctly by Leyhausen:

> The extent of the complexity of the constituent movements in question is quite inessential. If a pattern can appear for itself, independently of its context in the whole of the teleonomic sequence and if, furthermore, it is striven for by a specific appetitive behavior directed at its releasing situation, these very phenomena *are* its own independent motivation, it is not necessary to postulate one!

The second question concerning the level of integration, at which our search for a unit of motivation has to stop, receives an equally clear answer. It has to stop at the level of those patterns which show the phenomena of threshold-lowering, intensity fluctuations, in short, all the phenomena of spontaneity discussed in Chapter Two/I. All these phenomena are not shown by single muscle contractions or even by movements of whole limbs, in other words, not below the third level, that of the consummatory act in Tinbergen's diagram. The fact that it is the unit of the fixed motor pattern which has its own motivation is just what makes its discovery by Whitman and Heinroth so very important. The whole science of ethology is based on this discovery.

The multiplicity of motivations entering into the functional entity of a so-called instinct corresponds to the number of independent motor patterns taking part in the system. The analysis of these many independent motivations is indeed quite as important as Hinde has urged. Our aim, however, is not the elimination of the concept of a unitary and teleonomically functioning system of autonomous motivations, but the physiological analysis of their interaction which makes the system a unit. The idea of a hierarchical organization of instincts as developed by Tinbergen, Baerends, and Leyhausen may represent a great simplification of reality, but it uneqivocally shows the way which causal analysis has to take.

The methods of approach dictated by these considerations are important even in those cases in which the functional, teleonomic unity of the single motor pattern is unquestionable, though a hierarchical temporal sequence cannot be shown. One behavior pattern of nest building, incidentally not described by Hinde in the domesticated canary and more familiar to me in some of the bird's wild relations (Carduelidae), consists in salivating on nesting material, treading on it with one foot and trying to fasten it onto branches by a certain complicated movement of bill and tongue. Simultanously with this motor pattern, female Carduelidae show a second pattern, the function of which is the molding and smoothing of the nest cup. It consists of simultaneously pushing forward the chest by kicking backward with both feet and pressing the shoulders of the wing outward. This pattern is obviously very old; there does not seem to be a carinate bird in which it is lacking. Among the small songbirds here under discussion, this motor pattern has acquired another function. By performing the movement in a crotch of branches chosen as a potential nesting site, the bird acquires information about how favorable or unfavorable the locality in question is. The greater number of branches which the bird touches in performing the cup-molding pattern, the more favorable the location obviously is for the building of a nest cup, the shape of which is largely preformed and supported by the branches touched. Learning processes, presumably in the form of conditioned appetitive behavior, play a role in the choice of a nest site, since the females of many tree-nesting birds regularly try out different possibilities by performing the cup-molding pattern before they begin to build. On the other hand, and in contrast to the nest building of rats (One/II/9), learning does not seem to improve the temporal sequence of the motor patterns used in building a nest.

3. Integrating Effect of the Instinct Hierarchy

Tinbergen definitely underestimates the value of his diagram (see Figure 19b) when he says that his hypothesis of a hierarchical organization of instincts represents nothing more than a diagram designed to bring some provisional order into our theorizing. This statement might make us underrate the number of experimentally proved facts explained by the hypothesis. These facts are:

1. The number of IRMs taking part in the system.
2. The specific stimulus situations releasing each of these IRMs.
3. The form and function of the motor patterns released.
4. The interrelations of these behavior patterns, the mutual facilitation and inhibition as indicated by the arrows and double arrows.
5. The teleonomic function of these experimentally analyzed processes which consist in creating adaptive sequences out of motor patterns rigid in themselves.

In spite of the unavoidable simplification which comprises primarily an omission of the manifold feedback effects contributing to the functional integration of the system, Tinbergen's diagram nonetheless shows very clearly in what way the interaction between its parts serves the integration of the whole. It makes sense from the point of view of teleonomy that, for instance, a male stickleback is not able to develop nest-building motivation before having satisfied appetitive behavior of the first order by reaching shallow, warm water with vegetation. Even more striking is the adaptive order-producing function of the sequence of different actions in the system of nest building and parental care which Baerends investigated in the diggerwasp *(Ammophila)* (1941).

As has already been said, one fixed motor pattern can constitute the appetitive behavior which aims at the release of a subsequent one. Hence, one motor pattern can receive motivational energy from another one. Conversely, driving power can also be exerted from the higher level in the direction of the lower in the sense of the arrow in Tinbergen's diagram (see Figure 19b). As discussed in Two/IV/4 in connection with the relative hierarchy of moods, the relationship between action patterns that are driving and those that are being driven can reverse itself according to the ASP of the several action patterns, as well as to the general stimulus situation and the state in which the organism finds itself at the moment. This reversibility helps to achieve an even greater adaptive variability of the system.

Furthermore, learning processes in higher animals can act as another integrating factor by setting a common goal to a great number of behavior patterns taking part in a hierarchical system. Highly adaptive "short cuts" to the teleological end can thus be achieved.

4. Interaction Between Motor Patterns

As indicated by the horizontal double arrows in Tinbergen's drawing (see Figure 19b), motor patterns on the same hierarchical level tend to inhibit each other. Obviously a stickleback occupied at the moment with fighting cannot simultaneously build a nest or court a female. Motor patterns of the same hierarchical level can be based on a common state of readiness characteristic for their level, but they are prevented from breaking out simultaneously by a specific mechanism which is akin to that of the maximum selecting system mentioned in Two/IV/5. Simple superposition of the endogenous impulses stemming from two motor patterns, as will be described in Two/VII/2, would obviously be unadaptive in this case.

If one wants to decide, by statistical evaluation of observational data, whether mutual inhibition or mutual facilitation prevails between two motor patterns, the answer would depend on the time span one chooses. If one judges from samples taken only seconds distant from each other, the result will be a relationship of absolute mutual inhibition between motor patterns lying on the same level. If, however, one chooses samples taken one or several days apart, it will appear that these motor patterns are activated simultaneously and by the very same motivations. This corresponds generally with what has been said in Two/I/4 on the greater inertia of change characteristic for the "moods" of higher and lower levels.

The closeness of two motivations within a hierarchical system finds its expression in the time that must elapse before the organism is able to change from one motor pattern to the other. In the stickleback, rival fighting and courtship can follow each other within a few seconds. In cichlids, in *Hemichromis bimaculatus* for example, the high general excitation elicited by fighting can be channeled directly into a correspondingly high excitation in courtship. After having been mated for a long time, old specimens of this species show courtship activities only of a remarkably low intensity. Even spawning and fertilization are performed as a matter of routine; the lack of excitation gives the impression that the entire performance is running along a path smoothed by habit. If one confronts such a tired and long-married couple with a highly colored fellow member of the species, both mates will attack it furiously, and it is quite surprising that in the general mix-up the mates hardly ever hit each other rather than the intruder. If the latter is now suddenly removed, both mates, still in high fighting mood, are for a moment in obvious danger of attacking each other, but immediately afterward their excitation is channeled into the path of sexual behavior and the fish perform courtship movements of the highest intensity such as they have not evinced since the first phases of pair formation at the time of "young love." By a more exact analysis of the motivations underlying agonistic and sexual motor patterns we are confirmed in our supposition that both have similar conditions of internal hormonal readiness.

Generalizing, it is permissible to say the following: The time necessary to change from the readiness for a certain action pattern to that of another becomes the longer the higher the levels of the readinesses in question are placed within the hierarchical organization embracing both. Should one try to switch the behavior pattern of a pair of *Hemichromis* by changing their external stimulus situation—not, as described above, from fighting to courtship, but from an escape reaction of corresponding intensity to courtship or to agonistic behavior—one would find that the fish requires not seconds, but nearly half an hour to perform the necessary change of "mood."

In the experiments of electrical brainstem stimulations performed by Erich von Holst on chickens, he encountered the same phenomenon. A motor pattern of low integrational level released by itself can very quickly disappear or be replaced by another. If, for instance, of the whole system pertaining to alarm and flight, von Holst released only one motor pattern belonging to the lowest level of integration, for example the raising of the head and looking about in all directions, this motor pattern disappeared almost simultaneously with the ending of the stimulus and, in an equally short space of time, the chicken was ready for motor patterns belonging to other systems. If, however, the electrode was positioned in a way to activate the whole alarm-and-escape system, the arousal of which actually begins with the motor pattern just mentioned, but, with stronger stimulation, escalates to uttering the warning cackle and, finally, to flying away, the bird, after the cessation of the stimulus, takes much longer to quiet down, let alone to perform behavior patterns belonging to an altogether different system. The larger the system activated and the higher the level of its activation, the longer it takes for the disappearance of the inhibiting effect which its excitation exerts on comparable neighboring systems.

The results obtained by Erich von Holst agree very well indeed with the hypothesis developed by Tinbergen and Baerends concerning the hierarchical organization of motor patterns belonging to "an instinct." It may be, however, that the abnormally strong stimulation of the system investigated causes an apparent "mono-causality" which is not normally characteristic of the function of the system in the intact animal. In any case, the findings of von Holst do not constitute an argument for the mono-causality of instinct.

5. Motor Patterns Not Specific to the System

There is a particular, rather well-defined type of fixed motor pattern which can be built into very different systems, into hierarchical ones as well as into less integrated mosaics of behavior. As discussed in One/I/ 12, describing the way in which all fixed motor patterns can exert a driving function just as well as they can allow themselves to be driven by other motivations, I have already explained that there are certain multipurpose activities, for example, fixed motor patterns that can be used for different purposes and activated by very different neural mechanisms. The same principle exists at lower levels of neural integration: the same retinal element can simultaneously act as a member of several different organizations. As Lettvin and his co-workers have shown, one cell in the retina's layer of ganglia can subsume the report of several receptor cells and abstract from it a definite report and convey it towards the center. One reports only a simultaneous change from light to darkness and the reverse (the so-called on–off effect), others abstract more specific messages, for instance, the progression of a dark, convex contour in a direction from the left to the right side, and so forth. On the highest level, a man can be a member of several organizations, of a club, an army, and of a political party.

Some of the "multipurpose actions" here under discussion are found built into not only several, but practically into *all* the more highly integrated systems. Locomotion, for instance, forms an indispensable part of most existing hierarchical organizations of instinct. The existence of multipurpose patterns precludes our defining "an instinct" through an enumeration of the motor patterns functioning within its context.

Even motor patterns that have very obviously originated in the service of a quite particular system which, in turn, serves an equally specialized function, can be phylogenetically transferred, in an apparently rather sudden change of function, into an altogether different system performing an altogether different teleonomic function. Teeth and jaws have evolved to catch and eat prey; the "invention" of using these organs for self-defense, though seemingly obvious, has not "occurred" to all gnathostome vertebrates. Very few teleost fish try to bite when caught or cornered, even if they possess a great gape with sharp teeth; neither pike (Esocidae) nor salmon (Salmonidae) do. Among the great family of blennies, only the giant *Anarrhichas lupus*, called the "sea wolf" in German, bites most vigorously, and so does the barracuda *(Sphyraena barracuda)* and the characin *Hoplias malabaricus*, which in its external appearance and ecology is very like a pike. The heavily armed piranha, also a member of the order of Characinidae, apparently does not bite in self-defense. All Plecostomidae, in particular the large triggerfish, bite most viciously. It seems not to be known whether sharks bite during rival fighting; some, but by no means all, bite when caught by the tail. Very few amphibians bite; only the horned toad (Ceratophrys) does. And even among reptiles there are many, such as the grass snake *(Natrix natrix)*, which have not grasped that hunting weapons can be used in self-defense. Young alligators *(Alligator mississippiensis)* do not bite, while young crocodiles *(Cro-*

codilus niloticus) not only bite, but at the same moment start to twist side-ways—as I have learned the hard way.

We know two kinds of fish, quite unrelated to each other, which have a very special organization of organs and motor patterns that serves pri-marily to scrape algae from the substratum, but has secondarily been transferred into the behavior system of rival fighting. Both the "kissing" gourami *(Helostoma temmincki)* and the blenniid *Escenius* have jaws and teeth adapted to scraping, and each of the two contending fish "scrapes" at the mouth of the other with exactly the same motor pattern. In the gourami, this gives the impression of passionate kissing.

In the above, the expressions I employed to describe a motor pattern which "originated in the service" of one system and later was "used by" another could give the impression that these "multipurpose" activities tend to be motivated exclusively by the influence of the higher levels, or "centers." This certainly is not the case. Even the activities of locomotion, more susceptible than any of the others to being driven by motivation coming from "above," contribute by their autonomous production of impulses to the excitability of the whole system. In the cichlid fish *(Pel-matochromis subocellatus kribensis)*, Heiligenberg has shown that the readi-ness to move exerts a decisive influence on the system of escape behavior (1964). The same standardized stimulus causes the fish to dart away if it possesses, at the moment, a high readiness to swim, yet when impinging on an individual which, at the moment, possesses a low readiness to move, the stimulus will cause the fish to develop cryptic coloration and to hide. Anyone who has ever ridden a horse that has not been out of the stable for a long time is aware of the way in which the "damming up" of locomotor activities can influence the entire behavior of an animal.

6. Chapter Summary

1. Under the name of "an instinct" or "a drive" we conceive a spontan-ously active system of behavior mechanisms sufficiently connected by a common function to deserve a name. Choosing a name for such a system corresponding to its function should not be misinterpreted. We neither believe in an extranatural factor guiding the organism to a teleologically determined goal, nor do we believe that there is a sin-gle "mono-causal" physiological process which is responsible for the spontaneity of the system.
2. Systems of instincts, as we understand them, are always activated by a multiplicity of motivations independent of each other. The best known of these motivations are the appetites for the performance of the several fixed motor patterns participating in the system. Any motor pattern that, independently of the teleonomic context of the

system, can be shown to possess its own spontaneity and to cause appetitive behavior directed at its release, *is* a motivation.

3. A number of independently spontaneous motor patterns and innate releasing mechanisms (IRMs) are integrated into a functional whole by the structured program governing their interaction within the hierarchical organization of the "instinct." Tinbergen, Baerends, and Leyhausen have demonstrated the structure of this program by conclusive experiments.

4. These interactions consist partly of mutual inhibition, partly of mutual facilitation, and often in obligatory temporal sequence, one motor pattern bringing about the releasing situation for the next.

5. The unit of an instinct cannot be defined by enumerating the motor patterns taking part in it, because many of them can be built into, or "used by," several independently functioning systems. Although these "multipurpose" activities can be driven by strong impulses stemming from higher strata of the hierarchy, they represent, by their autonomous production of excitation, an essential motivating power for the whole system.

Chapter VI
Mechanisms Exploiting Instant Information

1. Receiving Information Does Not Always Mean Learning

The fact that an organism receives information does not imply unconditionally that it *learns* something, although of course the receiving of
new information is an indispensable prerequisite for learning. As will be
discussed in the third part of this book, learning, in the widest possible
meaning of the word, is defined as an *adaptive modification* of behavior,
in other words, an improvement of the physiological "machinery"
whose function is behavior. As in any other adaptive process, adaptation
to a certain given in the organism's environment invariably means that
information *about* this given must somehow have been fed into the
organic system. In phylogeny this is achieved by the age-old, trial and
success method of random genetic change and subsequent selection, but
in ontogeny this is achieved by learning. Both processes have one faculty
in common; both can acquire and store information. The first process for
gaining information is as old as life itself; the second could only come
into being after a more or less centralized nervous system had evolved.

In addition to and independent of these two mechanisms for acquiring
information, there exists a third great category of processes, similar to
the two just mentioned with regard to the faculty for gaining and for
exploiting information, but quite unlike them in another important
aspect: the processes of this category cannot *retain* the information; in
fact, they must not, because they must maintain a readiness to counter-
mand any of their own prior messages at a moment's notice.

While we are walking we are receiving and exploiting, at any single
moment, a vast amount of information. Our proprioceptors keep us
informed about what our legs are doing, exteroceptors report the prop-

erties of the ground on which we are stepping, our gravity and acceleration receptors keep telling us the position of our center of gravity in relation to our support, by optical means we are informed about the speed of our movement, optokinetic responses keep us going straight and tell us about any deviations, and so on. Every single piece of information thus received is evaluated and exploited, to be erased immediately afterwards. The messages *must* not leave any vestiges whatsoever—so that they cannot impede any contrary response which may be demanded at the very short notice of a hundredth of a second.

Mechanisms exploiting instant information are omnipresent. An adaptive change of behavior achieved by the method of genetic change and selection requires, as a minimum amount of time, the duration of one generation. An unimaginable environmental constancy would be required for the survival of organisms devoid of mechanisms enabling them to adjust to any small deviation from the norm of external conditions, and thus to keep constant the functions of their internal processes. Regulating mechanisms must have come into existence when life did.

Many students of behavior are of the opinion that "learning" takes place during every type of complex behavior. This error is probably based on their confusing the function of learning with that of the mechanisms exploiting instant information. Perhaps this confusion is furthered by the ubiquitous expression, "I have just learned that . . .," meaning "I have just been informed." There are innumerable highly complex and even highly adaptable mechanisms of behavior in which learning plays no part at all, but there are none which can dispense with the function of innumerable mechanisms exploiting instant information. Even while a mallard drake performs the grunt whistle, the most rigid, fixed-intensity motor pattern I can think of at the moment, his gravity receptors continue to function and his orienting mechanisms keep his spatial relation to the courted female constant.

The functions under discussion are not experience, but they are the prerequisite for making experience possible, thus strictly conforming to Immanuel Kant's definition of what is "a priori."

2. The Regulating Cycle or Homeostasis

The simplest and probably the phylogenetically most primitive form for acquiring instant information is the regulating cycle or homeostasis. It enables the organism to regain and maintain the equilibrium of its life processes after they have deviated in some way or been made to deviate from the desirable state. When an animal, under the influence of a lack of oxygen, begins to breathe faster, or when, surrounded by abundant food, it stops eating for a while, this means that the organism is informed, not only about its internal need for certain materials, but also about their present availability in its environment—about the condition of the "market." The genetically programmed structure of regulating cycles makes it possible to maintain, approximately constant, certain "values of reference" *(Sollwert)* within the organism. Regulating cycles are the most common type of mechanisms exploiting instant information. They range from rather simple chemical processes to the most highly differentiated organizations of neural and sensory organs—as will be discussed in Section 7 of this chapter.

3. Excitability

Excitability in general, not the action-specific excitability discussed in Two/III/3, is usually defined as the readiness of living matter to respond to a stimulus. However, neither the concept of "response" nor that of a "stimulus" can be defined exactly. Basically, any chemical change within the organism caused by an external influence is a "response," and any such influence can be thought of as a "stimulus." Conventionally, physiologists think of a stimulus as an external agent causing the organism to react by movement or by secretion, and the conceptual division of stimulus and response is derived from the functional division of labor between the nervous system, which receives stimuli, and the muscles or glands, which respond to them.

But this duality of organs should not enter into the definition of excitability because not only in all protozoans, but in very many of the lower metazoa as well, it is the same cell which receives the stimulus and responds to it. In sponges there are the contractile cells surrounding the outflow apperture. What ought to be included as part of the definition of excitability is the energetic relationship between stimulus and response: the stimulus supplies incomparably less energy than is liberated through the response. The term "trigger causality" contains an elucidating description of the process.

The only response to stimuli in many sessile metazoa is a contraction of the whole body that results in a minimizing of the vulnerable surface and, in some cases, a thickening of the protective outer layers. An analogous behavior is found in some protozoa, as in amoebas. There seems to be no unicellular animal or plant known in which locomotion is not correlated to excitability. Both together are programmed in such a way as to bring the organism into the best possible environment and to maintain it there.

4. Amoeboid Response

The most simple and probably the most ancient movement is the plasma flow as it is known in amoeboid cells. Rather surprisingly, it shows a faculty which otherwise is found only in the movements of much higher animals: the faculty of orientation within the three dimensions of space. Orientedness in all possible directions is possible to the "naked" amoebas for the simple reason that, "as yet," they do not possess head or tail, nor any differentiated parts of body surface and can therefore extend a "pseudopod," that is, a hernia-like extrusion of their ectoplasm, in any desired direction in space.

Formerly it was believed that these extrusions were caused by changes in the surface tension of the protoplasm, which was visualized as being liquid in all of its layers. In reality, this process is brought about by the capacity of the ectoplasm to change, through the influence of a stimulus, from the jellied state to the liquid state and back again—something I asserted a long time ago, purely on the basis of observation. This has since been proved by L. V. Heilbrunn (1958). Normally, that is to say always, except at the moment of ingesting some object such as food, the surface is covered by a thin film of jellied ectoplasm. On the impinging of a stimulus eliciting a negative response, this layer is very rapidly thickened and, because the protoplasm in the state of gel occupies a slightly smaller space than in the state of sol, this thickening results in a contraction of the surface, which in turn exerts a pressure on the interior of the cell—that much of the surface tension theory is correct. Conversely, the positive response to a stimulus consists primarily in a thinning of the jelled ectoplasm layer, which causes the body to bulge in the direction of the stimulus. At lower intensities of response this stimulation merely determines the direction in which the animal will move. The motion itself has other and not yet analyzed causes. In the most intense form of positive response, as in that of taking food, a break in the jelled skin permits the liquid endoplasm to spout like a geyser, quickly enveloping the object. The liquid endoplasm then jells on the outside, remaining liquid where in contact with the object, and in this way the object is received into the interior of the cell.

The information telling the amoeba which objects to ingest and which to reject is contained exclusively in the objects' chemical properties that cause the ectoplasm to dissolve. The selectivity of this archaic releasing mechanism is none too great. The negative response is elicited by an even greater range of stimuli, among which tactile and thermic ones play an important role. A needle prick is responded to in much the same way as a locally applied heat stimulus.

In its natural environment, in other words, in a culture in which it can live and propagate, the behavior of an amoeba appears so adaptable and plastic that the observer tends to forget that all he is seeing are but variations in intensity of one and the same process. The animalcule "placidly" wanders about "searching" for food; it moves hurriedly to avoid an unfavorable situation, it escapes from damaging stimuli by "fleeing as in panic"; it rushes "hungrily" at prey and engulfs these most "greedily." H. S. Jennings, who knows protozoa better than anybody else, says that were an amoeba as large as a dog, one could not hesitate ascribing to it the faculty of subjective experience. Yet it is only the change from sol to gel and back again that causes the whole gamut of highly teleonomic responses whose adaptiveness rests on the selectivity of response to specific stimulus situations.

5. Kinesis

All unicellular creatures that, in the interest of swimming speed, have evolved an elongated and more or less streamlined form as well as a preferred direction of locomotion and, therewith, a front end and a rear end to their bodies, stand in need of steering mechanisms which guide the fast, though rigid, form teleonomically within the three dimensions of space. Most freely moving metazoa are faced with the same problem. There are but few among them that are radially symmetric and can move, if only on one plane, in any direction they choose.

One of the most primitive behavior mechanisms, which accomplishes the task of keeping swiftly moving organisms as much as possible out of unfavorable and within favorable conditions, does so by the simple means of slowing down their movements when traversing favorable environments and speeding them up while going through unfavorable ones. Many of the flagellates and ciliates are more or less continuously moving through the water, much the way pelagic fish, such as mackerels, do. The behavior just described results in their being found in greatest density at favorable locations. By an analogous process, cars are crowded in an undesirable density along bad stretches of road that enforce slow driving. This mechanism of spatial orientation, according to G. S. Fraenkl and D. S. Gunn, is termed *kinesis* (1961).

Most organisms do not move in an absolutely straight line; the protozoans mentioned above usually swim along the line of a screw—regularly and wrongly described as a spiral. When orienting to favorable localities, the effect of kinesis can be improved by increasing the angle of the random deviations from the straight line, and these are inherent to locomotion in any case. By this means, the organism is kept in the desirable environment longer and is made to exploit an increased part of its area. This process, termed *klinokinesis* by Fraenkl and Gunn, is found not only in swimming protozoa but also in higher crustacea, in grazing mammals, and in man when, for example, he is searching for mushrooms.

6. Phobic Response

Phobos is the Greek word for fear, and the name of the orienting mechanism here under discussion is derived from its function, which in most cases causes the animal to flee from unfavorable stimulus situations.

However, phobic response is by no means the only process achieving this teleonomic effect, nor is escape the only function of all phobic responses. The essential character which defines phobic response is found in the fact that the *angle* at which the animal changes course is *not dependent* on the direction from which the impinging stimulus comes. A paramecium which, while swimming forward, moves into rapidly deteriorating environmental conditions, first reverses the direction in which its cilia are beating so that it retraces, for a certain stretch, the path along which it has come. Then it stops for a time, moving neither forward nor backward, by making the cilia on one side of its body beat in reverse while on the other side they resume their forward beating. As an effect of this, the animal's front end swings around in a circle, the longitudinal axis of its body describing the mantle of a cone. After some time, the duration of which depends on the strength and not on the direction of the stimulus, the cilia are again switched to full speed ahead and the animalcule resumes its travel in a direction which depends exclusively on the position of its body at the moment of the switch.

This direction is chosen at random, in the sense that it has nothing whatever to do with the direction from which the stimulus has come. It happens often enough that the circle described by the front end measures exactly 360° and that the animal resumes its forward motion in the former direction, swimming a second time straight into the releasing stimulation. If this is not a solid obstacle but a gradient of temperature or of a chemical solution, it often happens that the paramecium resumes swimming forward in a direction still less favorable than the former one, so that it enters into an even steeper gradient than before. In this case, it simply repeats the response until its new direction avoids the stimulus.

The phobic response furnishes the organism with a much greater amount of information than does kinesis. It causes the organism not only to shorten its stay in an area having unfavorable conditions, but to avoid the area altogether. It conveys to the animal not only the message that environmental circumstances are bad, but also in which direction they lie. It does not, however, give any report on an improvement in environmental conditions. No reaction is elicited when the paramecium enters optimal circumstances; it continues its straight, though "screwy" path until it leaves the favorable area on the other side. Having done this, the animal gives the phobic response. A long time ago, when his mastery of English was deficient, Otto Koehler once compared this with human behavior, saying: "That is just like man; you give him more money, he says not anything; you take away money, he cry awful." In Figure 22, a diagram by H. S. Jennings (1910) illustrates the phobic response.

It must be stated that a paramecium possesses other orientation mechanisms in addition to the phobic response. The latter is most often seen when the animal is observed within the very narrow space of a "hanging drop." Under comparably confined spatial conditions a bird, too, would

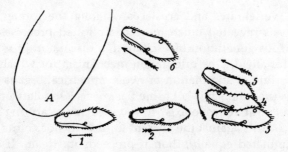

Figure 22. Schematic representation of single phases of the escape reaction of a paramecium which encounters a solid object or some other stimulus in its path. (From Jennings's adaptation of Hempelmann, *Tierpsychologie*.)

fail to show the more differentiated orientation responses otherwise at its disposal. Waltraut Rose has shown incontrovertibly that a paramecium possesses orienting mechanisms of the type described in the next paragraph (1964). In the larger space of a cuvette, in which no sharply angled changes of course are forced upon it, a paramecium avoids unfavorable situations and remains within favorable environments by means of topical responses. One single individual, observed for more than three hours, traversed the optimal area in the middle of the cuvette many times and turned back into it without once showing a phobic response. The observation time was limited not by the activites of the paramecium but because Waltraut Rose fainted at her post.

7. Topical Response or Taxis

In his classic book on the orientation of animals in space, Alfred Kühn (1919) has described a number of orientation mechanisms which can be defined by their common effect of turning the animal in a direction directly determined by that of the impinging stimulus. The angle of the turn is directly determined by the one between the longitudinal axis of the animal's body and the direction of the arriving stimulus. The names Kühn has chosen for the different types of orienting mechanisms are derived primarily from their most common function, just as that of the phobic response, which he also called "phobotaxis" in the first editions of his book; later he reserved the term "taxis" for topical responses. Some of the terms he chose also suggested physiological explanations, working hypotheses that have since proved incorrect. Because of this the terms should be abandoned.

The simplest topical response known is termed tropotaxis and consists, according to Kühn's definition, of the animal's turning sideways until two symmetrically situated sense organs report equal stimulation. This was assumed by Kühn to be the case in the orientation to gravity observed in vertebrates and crustacea. Among the former, Erich von Holst's analysis revealed much more complicated processes, including the spontaneous generation of excitation, a discussion of which would lead us too far afield. One orientation mechanism for which the theory of an equilibrium of stimulation of two symmetrical organs holds absolutely true is the "rheotaxis" of some flatworms. One flatworm, *Planaria*, reacts with a "positive tropotaxis" to water currents carrying the scent of food. *Planaria* turns against the current until both sides of its tricornered head are stimulated equally; then it proceeds upstream. If the head is stimulated symmetrically by two jets of water, the worm works its way through the resultant rush between the two currents.

All topical responses are vastly superior to the phobic in regard to the amount of information procured. While phobic responses tell the animal only in which direction *not* to proceed, the topical response informs the organism unequivocally, which one to choose among all the directions possible in space.

Here is not the place to summarize the results which research on orientation has brought to light since the noted writings of Alfred Kühn were published. The part played by complicated regulating processes within the sensorineural apparatus of orientation can well be shown in the light-compass orientation of insects, which Kühn defined as a *menotaxis* (from the Greek *meno*—"I remain"), those orienting mechanisms through which a constant direction is maintained by steering a course at a constant angle to the incidence of the stimulus. This is achieved by feeding the output of the regulating cycle back into its input, thus enabling the organism to sustain constant values of reference *(Sollwert)*. This principle of negative feedback is essential to regulating cycles.

An analysis of the regulating cycles functioning according to this principle is complicated by the fact that the choice of a given value of reference is subject to higher levels within the central nervous system which can, at any time, "command" a new value (see Two/IV/5). An insect steering by the angle of light incidence may, of course, arbitrarily change to another course; in fact, it does so every few moments when, for instance, it is following a learned path habit. However, it could not stay on any course for even one second if it were not for the light-compass orientation. That the latter is indispensable becomes apparent when the prerequisites for its functioning are lacking. One of these prerequisites is that the source of light be at a very great distance so that its rays are practically parallel to one another. As we know, lights at a lesser distance are a danger to insects. If insects choose for their light-compass a value of reference having an angle less than 90°, they necessarily describe a spiral ending at the light itself, just as we see them doing at every street lamp. The lucky ones that have chosen an angle greater than 90° are not seen by us at all because they have disappeared into the darkness.

8. Telotaxis or "Fixating"

Kühn (1919) defines telotaxis as those orienting mechanisms which are akin to menotaxis insofar as they function to keep a certain stimulus constantly at the same place on a certain receptor organ, in most cases the eye. The animal turns its eye, its head or its whole body in the direction of the stimulus. If, colloquially, we say that we "fixate" on an object, we mean that we turn our eyes so as to get the image on the fovea centralis, the place of sharpest vision on our retina. There the image is retained, even if the object moves quite fast. Our eyes and our head and, if necessary, our whole body move in such a way as to keep the image at that place on the retina. Although it remains stationary there, we perceive the movement clearly. Amazingly, our perception reports a smooth and continuous movement of the bird we see flying across the sky, notwithstanding the disparity of the receptors reporting it. Only during the very first moments, just when the bird "catches our eye," is there a succession of retinal elements reporting the movement of the bird's image. The next instant, when our eyes have fixated on the bird and are following its movement across the sky, the message informing us about those movements stems from the motor organization, studied extensively by Erich von Holst and Horst Mittelstaedt, that keeps the eyes fixated on the object. In particular, it is the "efference copy" of the motor impulses going to the eye muscles that conveys the information about the changing direction of the eyes and, therewith, the direction in which the object pursued by the eyes is moving. When finally we turn our heads to keep that bird in sight, the task of reporting its movement is passed on to the neck muscles. Marvelous enough is the fact that all of these messages are integrated into one continuous perception of the bird's flight.

For the catching of prey by the "praying" mantis, a subject particularly suitable for this kind of research, Mittelstaedt has demonstrated the function of the regulating cycles that enable this curious insect to capture prey by a stroke of its clawlike front legs (1957). As far as I know, this is the most clearly analyzed example of a telotaxis. The mantis fixates on prey by turning its head towards an intended victim and, by doing this, follows the prey's movements. This, in an insect, is so very unusual as to be extremely striking when first observed. If the mantis must creep forward towards its prey, it turns not only its head in the direction of the prey, but also its prothorax to which the catching claws are affixed. Finally, if it has rather far to go, it turns its whole body. On the other hand, when the prey is so near that no locomotion is needed, the mantis can capture it by moving the claws sideways, in a direction not lying in the plane of symmetry of the prothorax. The information underlying the insect's very exact aim must be supplied by messages coming first from the eyes and then from afferent processes which tell the mantis the exact position of its own head at the moment of striking.

As Mittelstaedt has shown, this positional information is furnished by the "neck organs," cushions of sensory hairs situated on both sides of the joint connecting neck and head. At each turn of the latter, these sensory hairs are bent and report the degree of bending. When Mittelstaedt cut the nerve leading from the left neck organ, the mantis missed the prey by striking too far to the right. If he disconnected both organs, the mantis could hit its prey, but only when it happened to sit exactly along the median plane of the prothorax. If it was situated to the right of the plane of symmetry of the prothorax, the mantis would miss on the left side, and vice versa. So the function of the neck organs is to aim. At first it seemed plausible to assume that orientation of the striking movement was determined by a summation of the optical stimuli coming from the eyes and the proprioceptor reports furnished by the neck organs. If this hypothesis of a simple addition of optical and proprioceptor stimulation were correct, it should not have made any difference for aiming if the head were immobilized in a sideways position by a droplet of glue. Since this fixed position of the head would be recorded by the neck organs, the calculation should still give a correct reading. A mantis with this kind of immobilized neck can still fixate by turning its prothorax, or even its whole body, in such a way that the prey lies along the plane of symmetry of the head. However, having done the turning, the mantis still misses the prey by striking on the side opposite to that in which the head is turned. As Mittelstaedt says, it acts as if it did not know that its head is turned.

To be concluded is that the aiming mechanism of the mantis can achieve a correct report on the position of its head only when the head is able to move freely. The neck organs report the position of the head relative to the prothorax, but this report is not fed directly into the mechanism aiming the strike of the anterior legs, but into the motor apparatus of the neck muscles. Figure 23 is a diagram of the processes involved in the aiming done by the mantis. Mittelstaedt observes that the mantis fixating on a fly sitting to its right aims its claws according to the amount of innervation expended to effect that position of the head—or to put it in an anthropomorphic way, the mantis directs its strike in that direction it believes its head is aiming. The information concerning the actual position of the head contained in the reports of the neck organs is not passed directly to the apparatus of localization; instead, this information is fed into a lower motoric center whose task it is to make the normal position (the "zero" position) of the head independent of deviation caused by any drag on the neck musculature. This can be proved experimentally: if minute weights are attached laterally to the head so as to twist it sideways, a considerable amount of torque can be applied without any decline in aiming accuracy.

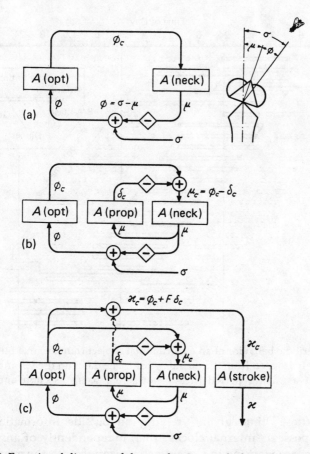

Figure 23. Functional diagram of the mechanism underlying localization in mantids. The hypothesis is developed by steps from (*a*) via (*b*) to (*c*). (*a*) Optic feedback loop only. As indicated by the arrows, information flows from the optic unit (amplification factor: $A_{(opt)}$) to the neck motor unit (amplification factor: $A_{(neck)}$) and again to the optic unit. (*b*) Optic and proprioceptive feedback loops. The neck motor unit is controlled by the difference between the optic (ϕ_c) and the proprioceptive (δ_c) center messages. (*c*) Complete hypothesis. $A_{(stroke)}$ amplification factor of the central unit which determines the direction of the stroke (κ). For full explanation, see text. (Mittelstaedt, H.: "Prey Capture in Mantids.")

9. Temporal Orientation

Like everything else in the universe, behavior proceeds within space *and* time. Behavior must occur not only in the right place and with the right orientation, but also at the right moment. Quite generally, releasing mechanisms, whether innate or acquired, are programmed so as to set off adequate behavior at the teleonomically correct time. In this respect IRMs can be regarded as mechanisms exploiting instant information.

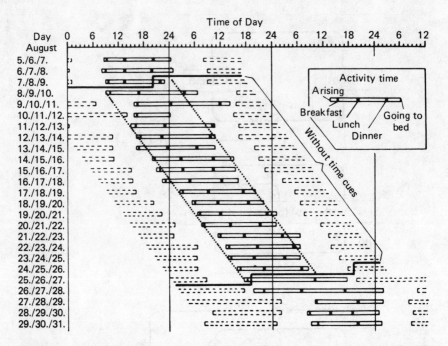

Figure 24. Periodic behavior of an experimental subject (human) in a bunker that was completely isolated from the outside world. The dates on the left indicate the beginning of a waking period (heavy horizontal bars). (Aschoff and Wever, 1962b.)

Besides these "time givers" relying on outside information, most organisms possess "internal clocks" that, independently of any outside information, are working in close synchronization with the great cosmic cyclical processes. They are able to tell the organism, with greater or lesser exactitude, "when the bell has tolled," whether it is day or night, summer or winter. Many marine organisms are, furthermore, informed about the runs of the tides.

C. Pittendrigh (1958) and J. Aschoff (1965) concentrated most of their temporal investigations on the "circadian" rhythms, e.g., those which correspond to the turning of the earth on its axis. Internal clocks attuned to these rhythms were found to keep time much less exactly than any tolerably precise, man-made chronometer. There are some internal clocks which are "fast" or "slow" by a certain amount of time, and this amount remains surprisingly constant over considerable periods, as shown in Figure 24. Within its natural surroundings, the organism corrects the error of its clock every day using external "time givers." The necessity of this correction is so widely spread that Pittendrigh and Aschoff tend to suspect the existence of unrecognized time givers whenever one of these internal clocks appears to be absolutely exact. No organism is known to be capable of exploiting the information received from external time givers in order to speed up or to slow down the running of its own clock. It cannot resort to any kind of correction analogous to that which the clock-maker would perform by adjusting the length of the pendulum, thus making the clock run faster or slower. All it can do is what a person who is not an expert does to his watch or clock, that is, advance or set back the hands each day.

There are internal clocks with "hands" that are easily adjusted and others that are very resistant to such "settings." This is true not only for circadian rhythms but also for those covering longer periods of time. The annual rhythms of two birds belonging to the same order of Anatidae represent both extremes. Canada geese, *Branta canadensis*, transplanted to New Zealand, have been reliably reported to be nesting and breeding during their first southern spring; black swans, *Cygnus atratus*, natives of Australia, when brought to Europe persist for years and, in some cases, for generations in breeding during the northern autumn. Among humans, the circadian clock can be very "soft" and adjustable in some people who, even when travelling halfway round the globe, still find it easy to adapt; it can prove to be extremely "hard" in some less fortunate people who suffer for many days from such a need to reset their clocks. Aschoff and his co-workers have shown that time changes of this type are not always harmless to the organism: in some insect species the normal duration of life is considerably shortened if they are forced to undergo repeated "resettings" of their circadian clocks.

10. Navigation by Sextant and Chronometer

As anyone who has read South Seas stories knows, a navigator whose chronometer has gone wrong can "fetch" an island by "sailing down its latitude," for example, by using the polar star as a point of reference. In order to steer a straight course by the sun, however, its movements have to be taken into consideration and to do this a chronometer is indispensable. Furthermore, from the chronometer readings and observations of the sun's movements ("shooting the sun"), longitude can be computed. Some social insects which always return to their nests after an absence of very short duration can afford to neglect the sun's movements. They navigate, on the way out, by means of the light-compass orientation described in Section 7 of this chapter, and return by simply reversing the process by 180°. If, as shown in Figure 25, one covers with a cup or bowl a worker of the ant species *Lasius niger* on its way out and keeps it in darkness for a period of time, it will, on being liberated, return home deviating from the correct course at an angle corresponding to the extent which the sun has travelled during the period of imprisonment.

For trips of longer duration, obviously this method of orienting could

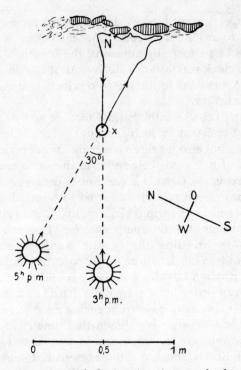

Figure 25. Time experiment with *Lasius niger*, journey back as a reverse of the journey out. The sun-compass orientation alone, which does not take into account the sun's movement, leads to a corresponding aberration. (Brun, adapted from Kühn, in Hempelmann, *Tierpsychologie*.)

not be used. Many phyla of animals, vertebrates such as fish and birds, as well as some arthropods have, independently of one another, evolved highly differentiated computing mechanisms enabling them to include the sun's azimuth in their computations and allowing them to steer straight courses even on long journeys.

A starling hand-reared from the egg by Klaus Hoffmann (1960) which had never seen daylight, let alone the sun, was kept in a dark room illuminated by an artificial sun. In order to make the bird "accept" this light as the sun, it proved necessary to simulate risings and settings by moving the light along the vertical. The bird was kept in a radially symmetrical cage and was trained to look for its food in trays also arranged symmetrically all around the enclosure. For a pilot study, the bird was taught to feed at six o'clock in the morning from the tray lying directly under the artificial sun which had just "risen." After completing this conditioning, the starling was tried at noon, and it promptly went to that tray situated ninety degrees to the left of the sun now standing at the highest point of its up and down movements. In other words, the bird had learned to search for food "*east of*," and not "below the light source." Within a dark room, the starling could have been used as a clock; out in the open, it could have been used as a compass.

11. Taxis and the Fixed Motor Pattern

As has already been explained in Two/VI/1, it is a fundamental error to believe that learning processes take part in all the action patterns of higher animals. On the other hand, the mechanisms exploiting instant information discussed in this chapter actually do participate in practically all behavior. As was shown in Section 2, regulating cycles are practically omnipresent and orienting mechanisms function wherever locomotion occurs. In organisms sufficiently evolved to possess a central nervous system and centrally coordinated motor patterns, it is all but impossible to find examples of behavior in which topical responses do not play a role. At least those responses maintaining equilibrium are always present. I can think of only two behavior patterns in which orientation to gravity might be said to disengage. In the spawning of the fighting fish, *Betta splendens*, both partners seem to "faint," drifting in the water for a few seconds devoid of all orientation; the male rabbit does something analogous during copulation—he falls sideways off the female.

Terrestrial vertebrates which move their legs in absolute coordination for locomotion (as was discussed in Two/I/13, 14) add or subtract, by means of the orienting mechanisms, a certain amount of motor impulse at every step, just enough to adapt the movements to the irregularities of the terrain. In Three/IV/7, 8, I elaborate on these processes. The whole system of orientation mechanisms superimposed on centrally coordinated movements has been called by Erich von Holst "the mantle of reflexes."

As already mentioned, the early literature often includes the processes of locomotion as part of the concept of taxis. Thus, "positive phototaxis" does not only mean that the insect turns toward the light, but also that it flies towards it; "negative geotaxis" implies that the organism strives to move upwards, and so on. The very same reasons that impelled us (Two/I/1) to divide Heinroth's concept of the species-characteristic drive action into its component parts make it advisable to formulate the conception of turning in space as something separate from the conception of locomotion. As in a ship, the apparatus for turning the rudder to port or starboard is expected to be different from, and rather independent of, the apparatus for switching the motor power on and off, and certainly different and separate from the machinery of the engines turning the propellers. The "positive Europotaxis" of an ocean liner is brought about by the functions of the turbines, of the steering apparatus, and, last but not least, by the functions of the navigator. This example delineates rather well the limited influence the higher levels exert upon the lower ones. The highest levels of the nervous system cannot change the basic functions of fixed motor patterns any more than a captain can influence the possible movements of his ship's engines. He can command only their intensity and signal slow ahead, full speed ahead, or, when necessary, reverse.

The multiplicity of the constantly participating orientation responses tends to conceal somewhat the rigidity of fixed motor patterns. In this respect they can have an effect similar to the changes in intensity already discussed in Two/I/3. It is certainly not a coincidence that Whitman and Heinroth first discovered fixed motor patterns through examples in which both of these effects were absent, that is, in those activities barely overlaid by any orientation responses and, furthermore, with fixed intensities.

Using the egg-rolling behavior of greylag geese, Tinbergen and I attempted to analyze the way in which a fixed motor pattern cooperates with an orienting mechanism (1938). Egg rolling is conducive to analysis because it permits an experimental separation of the two components. The behavior is released in an incubating goose when it sees an object situated outside and near the nest and having a number of releasing characteristics. The object must have a smooth outline devoid of all protuberances, and it must have a hard surface. Its form is irrelevant; wooden cubes are treated as if they were eggs, and the size can vary from a few cubic centimeters to the maximum that can be encompassed by the goose's neck. The fixed motor pattern used in the action consists of a stretching forward of the neck, bending the head downward so as to touch the egg with the underside of the bill, and then rolling it toward the nest by means of a slow bending of the neck. Concomitant compensatory movements of head and bill to each side keep the egg in balance and prevent its deviating from the intended path. The fixed motor pattern can be isolated by deftly snatching away the egg after the movement has been released. The movement then continues to run smoothly all the way through to the nest cup, staying strictly within the median, that is, along the bird's plane of symmetry. Once the movement has been released, it can only run its way through to the end and can be changed neither in its coordination, nor in its strength. If one offers the goose an object much too large, such as a huge cardboard easter egg, the movement literally "jams"; the goose proves unable to move the object in any other than the prescribed way—for instance by walking backward. If the object is not heavy enough, it is lifted off the ground; if it is too heavy by even only a slight amount, the movement fails to budge it. This is remarkable because a goose's neck is capable of producing a prodigious amount of power, for instance, enough to pull a table cloth loaded with a complete tea set off a table or, in a more teleonomic way, to tear heavily rooted plants out of the bottom of a pond. However, the power at the disposal of the fixed motor pattern is strictly measured to serve its single function.

As can easily be demonstrated, the movements to each side, which during the whole procedure keep the egg balanced on the underside of the bill, are elicited by tactile stimuli emanating from the object. Whenever the egg deviates to one side, the bill immediately follows it and guides it back into the right direction. It is possible to make the egg "run on rails" during the rolling process by arranging a bundle of reeds obliquely across its path. Then the movement tries to overtake the egg in order to correct the "wrong" direction and sometimes succeeds at the moment when the pressure of the bill acts at a right angle to the obstacle. If the goose "rolls" a square object that facilitates the establishment of a stable contact with both branches of the mandible and thus not diverging from the straight line either to the right or to the left, the balancing movements cease altogether and the fixed pattern alone predominates, just as it does when the object being rolled is removed altogether.

12. Taxis and Insight

Conventionally, insight behavior is defined by exclusion; the organism is acting through insight, it is said, whenever an instant solution is found to a problem for which the organism possesses neither a phylogenetically programmed answer nor one acquired by learning during the course of its individual life.

A better definition of insight behavior can be given. When a fish perceives a desired object behind an obstacle, for instance a chironomous larva behind a finely branched bush of myriophyllum, through which it cannot swim although it can see the larva, even the most stupid goldfish will swim around the bush to reach the tidbit. This detour can be explained as the result of a positive telotaxis directed toward the prey and of a negative thigmotaxis causing the fish to avoid contact with the branches.

Between this simplest discovery of a detour and the most complex functions of insight in animals, such as those investigated by Wolfgang Köhler in chimpanzees (1963), there exists a continuous gradation of intermediates bridging the gap. *Methodos* is the Greek word for "detour," and the expressions which our natural language has found to describe our highest intellectual achievements bear the ineradicable marks of their provenience from the mechanisms of orienting behavior in space. We gain "insight" into a "maze" of circumstances that can be very "complex," just as an ape does into a tangle of intertwined branches through which it has to wend its way. The "concept" we form of a thing cannot become "clear" before we have thoroughly "grasped" it. In the latter expression the priority of tactile perceptions becomes apparent. Through insight we understand only that which can be represented or "visualized" in the spatial model our perception projects in our central nervous system—and in our consciousness. W. Porzig knew this more than a quarter of a century ago (1950). He wrote then:

> Our language translates everything that cannot be visualized into spatial concepts. This is not done just by our own language, or by a certain group of languages, but by *all* of them, without exception. It is a property (an "invariant") inherent to human language as such. Temporal circumstances are expressed spatially: "before" or "after" Christmas, two years have "passed," a "space of time" of several minutes has "elapsed," etc. Concerning subjective processes we speak not only of the "innermost soul," of a "threshold" below which our consciousness is not affected, of the "sub"-conscious, of "layers" of consciousness, and so on. Space serves as a model for everything that cannot be visualized. "Besides" his professional work, he occupies himself with poetry, "between times" he did something else, by this act he "covered" his real intention—it is redundant to add further examples which can be found in any number of samples of written or spoken language. The phenomenon under discussion derives its importance from its wide distribution and from the part it has taken in the history of language. It is apparent in the use of prepositions which originally have a spatial connotation and equally in that of adjectives and verbs. (Translated from the German)

I once explained all of this in a lecture and, afterwards, one of the discussants asked a Chinese student who was conversant in ancient Chinese to write on the blackboard "before Christmas" and "after Christmas" and "an oak is growing in front of the house and a fir behind it." The ideograms for temporal and spatial prepositions proved identical.

I want to add that these considerations of linguistic phenomena are in full agreement with the expectations of anyone who has examined orienting mechanisms. All orientation, including our own, is always concerned with space *and* time. We are quite incapable of perceiving or even of visualizing space without simultaneously visualizing something happening, in other words, movement in space, nor are we capable of visualizing movement without a space within which it can occur.

We define as "directed by insight" any behavior the teleonomy of which is based on the function of mechanisms exploiting instant information. It proves quite impossible to draw a sharp distinction between the simplest detour of that goldfish and the most complex insight-directed behavior of Wolfgang Köhler's chimpanzees, nor can we give a definition capable of setting human insight apart, or the "methods" governed by insight, as something essentially different. The fact that learning always participates in the more complicated processes of insight cannot be used in a definition, since sometimes it is just as involved in quite simple solutions to detour problems. Even for these solutions the reports of one mechanism exploiting instant information must be remembered long enough to be integrated with the messages of another or several others, so that a response which takes all of them into account can be organized.

There is a special type of learning, often termed "insight learning," the most primitive form of which is found in organisms whose processes of orienting in space do not take place simultaneously with the movements they are directing—as they do in the egg-rolling movements performed by geese. Instead they achieve their effect *before* the movement is set off as, for example, in taking aim before firing a shot. The processes orienting the locomotion of fish furnish examples of both types. Many fish, particularly those living in open water, orient by the parallactic shift of the images projected onto their retinas. We can do the same while riding on a train at night, when we can see nothing outside except the lights of the lamp posts. Our perception is perfectly capable of calculating not only the distance from us each lamp post is, but also the speed of the train's movement which makes the posts shift on our retinas. This kind of spatial orientation can obviously function only as long as the organism is in motion. A goldfish can come to a stop at a place where an obstacle is situated directly in front of it. Though it must have received information concerning the obstacle while approaching it, the fish, on resuming its forward motion, does so directly toward the obstacle, veering off only *after* it has got underway.

Other fishes, notably those living in an environment full of complex spatial structures, gain information about these forms while standing still, moving their eyes in all directions, fixating on one object after another, thus optically exploring the vicinity. When they move, they start at once in the "chosen" direction. As they never collide with an obstacle, they obviously must have marked and, for a short span, remembered the direction in which the way was open, where obstacles were located and where there was desirable cover. The stickleback is a typical example of an animal orienting by looking around and fixating on objects successively. Among insects, the praying mantis furnishes the only example of an analogous process. Some birds orient by parallactic shift, as the goldfish does, but, unlike the latter, they acquire their information prior to moving. Typically these are large-eyed birds with restricted eye movements. In order to make the images of the objects in their vicinity shift on their retinas, some of them, like the red-breasted robin, move their heads up and down or left and right; some—as, for instance, kestrels, small owls, and others—make both movements.

A naive human might find this method of gaining information about the spatial structure of the surroundings extremely funny, while even a more sophisticated observer could not help feeling that organisms orienting by fixating are more "intelligent" than those orienting by parallactic shift. In fact, this impression is not too far wrong, as the telotactic or "fixating" method of orientation observed in the "intelligent" stickle-back presupposes the participation of a learning process, if only a very short-lived one, while the parallactic orientation of the goldfish does not.

The sequence of events, first orienting and acting only after orienta-tion has been achieved, as is found in all "fixating" organisms, is encoun-tered once again in very high animals, in monkeys and apes. In these, the temporal separation between the processes of gaining insight and of acting on it is even more clearly marked. As Wolfgang Köhler most graphically described (1963), chimpanzees approach a new problem by first "studying" the situation, for example, by exploring it visually as extensively as possible. This is most beautifully shown in a film produced by the primate laboratory at Sukhumi in the Soviet Union. A young orangutan is confronted with a problem represented by a banana sus-pended from the middle of the ceiling and by a wooden box standing in a corner. The ape has never met with this particular problem before, but he knows that in this lab the solving of problems is, in general, rewarded. He obviously has a preformed association between the appeted goal and the presence of objects to be manipulated. He looks up at the banana, then at the floor directly underneath the banana, and back up at the fruit. Subsequently, he shifts his glance to the box, then back again to the banana, his eyes moving diagonally across the room. Now he seems to know that a) the banana is too high up for him to reach it from the floor, and b) that the box, unfortunately, is not under the fruit. At this point the orangutan goes into a temper tantrum, exactly like that of a human child, throwing himself onto his back, kicking his legs, and screaming. After a while he quiets down, begins to scratch himself vio-lently, in conflict concerning the attraction of the goal and the apparent impossibility of reaching it. After this he concentrates anew on the prob-lem, at first by again looking back and forth between the box and the fruit. Then something happens that is really impressive: the ape looks up at the banana, down at the spot below it; from there his glance switches across the lab to the box and back to the place under the banana and now up to it again. In the next moment, with a somersault motivated by pure joy, the young orangutan rushes across the room to the box, shifts it, and gets the banana within seconds. The gaining of insight has required many minutes (probably longer than shown in the film); acting on it suc-cessfully has taken but a few seconds.

What this ape has been doing is *thinking*. By gaining and exploiting quite a large amount of instant information, and with the help of some insight learning, he has built up within his central nervous system a *model* of his spatial surroundings and he is *acting* internally and within this visualized representation of space—and he has done so without moving anything except his eyes. Acting in visualized spaces precedes bodily action and it can, within limits, comprise genuine exploratory behavior employing the trial and error method. Some higher mammals, primates in particular, are thus able to act within a visualized three-dimensional model of their spatial surroundings and solve the problems presented by these surroundings. I maintain that all human thought processes are based on the same kind of acting in visualized space.

The sameness of the principle ruling the simplest functions of orienting mechanisms as well as the highest achievements of human insight is strikingly expressed in the concomitant subjective phenomena. Karl Bühler has called attention to the fact that an identical and unmistakable subjective phenomenon—termed the "Aha-experience"—always occurs at the moment when a state of disorientedness gives place to that of being oriented (1922). This is true for the simplest tropotaxis, as I know from an unforgettable experience. While I was sound asleep on the deck of a motorboat, a jocular friend had what he thought was a good idea: that of rolling me overboard. It was a dark night and the Danube is a very turbid river so that, when I awoke, I found myself in absolute darkness. I happened to be suspended exactly upside down and, for a few panic-sticken moments, I swam downward. When my statoliths took over, telling me unequivocally which way was "upward," I experienced an unforgettable "Aha-experience." Phenomenology is—contrary to the opinions of some—a legitimate source of knowledge and I am in a position to assert that, on solving a scientific problem, the experience of "Aha" is qualitatively identical to the one accompanying the clicking of gravity orientation.

With full justification we feel that our capacity for directing our actions by insight represents one of the highest values. Our attitude to the question, what is to be regarded as a "higher" and what as a "lower" animal, is strongly influenced by this inescapable value judgment.

In order to keep the organism constantly oriented and informed about the never-ending changes within its environment, and in order to judge the priority of incoming insight information, a special control center is needed, superimposed on all these orienting mechanisms. The function of this center is to *watch over* the interactions of subordinate processes. "Watching" implies staying awake and, I suppose, there must be some wide-awake, in other words, some spontaneously active processes underlying the function of this highest control in our central nervous system. As a mere speculation, I would say that the thread of our consciousness, spun without interruption as long as we are awake, is the subjective concomitant of this very central function, of a function whose competence by far exceeds that of the disinhibiting mechanisms discussed in Two/VI/5.

Chapter VII
Multiple Motivation in Behavior

1. The Rarity of Unmixed Motivation

For reasons of didactic simplicity I have not, until now, mentioned the fact that behavior can be, and in very many instances is, activated by more than one motivation. Only in Two/I/13, 14 have I described how, on a lower level of integration in which the processes of endogenous rhythms investigated by Erich von Holst hold sway, two or more impulse-producing rhythms can compete with one another for the mastery of muscle activity and achieve, by mutual interaction, what Erich von Holst has called relative coordination. I have not yet mentioned that phenomena comparable to these can be found at the higher level of fixed motor patterns. The "classical" old ethologists were not aware of this. Many years ago my teacher, Julian Huxley, used to express the difference between animal and human behavior by means of a parable. He likened the animal to a ship commanded by many captains who, however, were not on the bridge simultaneously, but had a gentlemen's agreement that each of them would cede his command at once if one of the others climbed onto the bridge. Huxley likened the human to a ship also commanded by many captains, all of whom stay on the bridge continuously, each giving his own commands without consideration of any of the others. Sometimes the conflict caused by their countermanding commands leads to complete chaos, but sometimes they jointly succeed in choosing a course which none of them would have arrived at alone.

In a discussion about progress in science, Jakob von Uexküll once said: "The truth of today is the error of tomorrow," whereupon Otto Koehler replied: "No, the truth of today is the *special case* of tomorrow." In the history of science this assertion can be supported by a great number of examples among which the most impressive are the developments that led from classical physics to quantum theory. At the time Julian Huxley used the parable quoted above, it was perfectly legitimate to cling to the simplest example available. Discovering the simplest example available has played an enormous role in the history of science; the Mendelian laws would not have been discovered—at least not when they were—if Gregor Mendel had not hit on monohybrids, the simplest possible case. The simplest form of interaction between two behavior patterns is indubitably that of mutual inhibition. This most often functions in the way mentioned in Two/IV/5, on the principle of the maximum selecting system, and the particular case Huxley's parable illustrates is the one of mutually inhibiting action patterns represented in Tinbergen's diagram (see Figure 19b) as those lying on the same level of integration.

Widespread is the erroneous belief that the cases most frequently cited in textbooks are also those which are most often found in nature. In nature, behavior activated by a single motivation is found at least as rarely as hybrids differing in only one gene. A higher animal in its natural habitat must always be ready to undertake a great number of different and—as often as not—mutually exclusive actions, and what it finally does is almost always a compromise made among several necessities.

2. Superposition

The simplest form of interaction between two simultaneously activated motivations is "superposition." Even at the level of endogenous rhythmic production of impulses, we have already encountered simple superposition of excitatory effects in the sense of addition as well as of subtraction. At the higher level of fixed motor patterns, additive superposition is more frequent than subtractive, possibly because subtraction tends to be replaced by complete mutual inhibition. Additive superposition is found even in cases in which the two independent motivations activate antagonistic muscles. We all know how humans become quite literally "tense" under the influence of conflicting motivations. A conflict between motivations in Anatidae, one demanding a forward extension of the neck, the other a retraction, which can occur in a goose wanting to eat grain offered in a human hand and not quite daring to do so, produces a violent trembling of the neck.

In most of these cases of simultaneous activation by conflicting motivations, it remains doubtful at what level the conflict actually takes place. From the investigations undertaken by Erich von Holst, we know that this can happen at a very low level of automatic rhythms contending for supremacy and becoming superimposed upon one another in every muscle contraction. The "trembling neck" of the goose probably is effected by conflicting innervation of the antagonistic muscles, but we cannot be

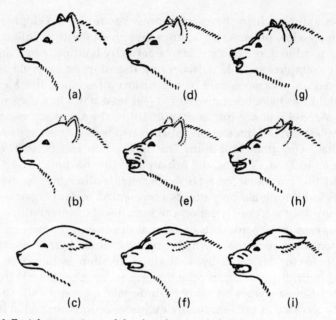

Figure 26. Facial expressions of the dog that result from a superposition of various intensities of fighting and flight intentions. *a-c:* Increasing readiness to flee; *a-g:* increasing aggression and the corresponding superpositions. (Lorenz: *On Aggression.*)

certain about this. There are cases in which different motivations rule units as large as different locomotor organs, fins for example. In territory disputed, certain cichlids *(Etroplus maculatus)* position themselves opposite one another, threatening across the border separating their territories. As in every threat, aggressive motivation is contending with that for escape. Whenever one of the adversaries moves a short distance forward into enemy territory, it appears as if he were swimming into a current, the speed of which rapidly increases as one proceeds upstream. This effect is produced by the action of the pectoral fins, which are sculling in reverse, and doing so more and more intensely the farther the fish moves into the other's territory. The tail fin is under the control of aggressivity and the pectorals under that of escape, and the observer cannot help feeling—ridiculously—that the pectorals are more afraid than the tail, because they are nearer to the enemy. The old adage about fearing one's own courage fits this situation perfectly.

In very many animals, gestures of threat have originated from such superpositions of aggression-motivated and escape-motivated behavior patterns. An old example illustrating the complicated gradations of movements which can arise in this manner is that of the facial expressions of threatening dogs (Figure 26). The intensity of each of the two conflicting motivations can actually be calculated by measuring the linear extent of the movements of lips and ears. The figure legend serves well as an explanation.

Very complicated effects are produced by the superposition of the several vocal expressions of the greylag goose. The signals of alarm, of the intention to move, of calling for company, and of distress, as well as some utterances the meaning of which is as yet unclear, can be superimposed on each other in an indefinite number of ways and proportions. Curiously enough, all of these combinations are directly intelligible to the initiated human observer. In this way a goose can express that it is going to move on because it feels lonely, or because it feels that the environment has become dangerous, or simply because it does not like the present situation. The fact that some utterances *cannot* be mixed, for instance, the sound of displeasure and the eating sound, or the expressions of love and danger signals, and so on, needs a very special study and gives rise to interesting speculations about subjective experience in animals, particularly about the pleasure–displeasure problem.

Provided they do not demand simultaneous contractions of antagonistic muscles, any two motor patterns can be superimposed on one another. As we have seen, superposition is possible even if the motivations of the two patterns are apparently opposed to each other, as are aggressivity and escape in the goose's tremble-neck, in *Etroplus*'s territorial fighting, and in the dog's threatening. If there is no functional relationship between the motor patterns, the possibilities of superposition are virtually unlimited. One example, given in Figure 27, should suffice. The precopulatory movement of the mallard—and of many other ducks— consists in a vertical up-and-down pumping of the head, the bill being held horizontal all the while. An important courtship movement of the female, the so-called "sicking," consists of alternately facing the male and pushing the head in a threatening movement in the direction of a "symbolic enemy." Both movements are highly ritualized and their derivation is well known from comparative studies, but this does not concern us here. The film from which Figure 27 has been drawn is of a pair of mallards. The female is shown alternating between the fixed motor pattern of pumping and sicking. Once the peaks of the two movements happen to come so near to each other that the attraction of the "magnet effect" discovered by Erich von Holst sets in, the two patterns "stick" to each other in superposition and are thus performed, for a few strokes, synchronously and in absolute coordination.

3. Mutual Inhibition and Alternation

Only a few instances are known in which the activation of one behavior system excludes absolutely the activation of any other. Fleeing from a predator is an example of such an activation having priority. It is obvious

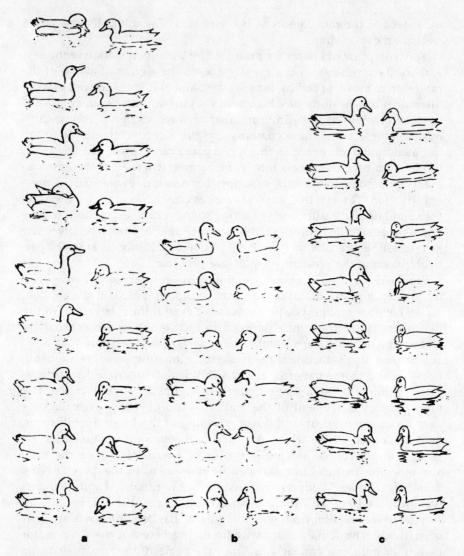

Figure 27. *a* The so-called "inciting movement" of the female mallard is released by the "symbolic" drinking and preening movements of the drake. The movement of the duck pointing her head backwards over her shoulder is repeated several times. *b* The "pumping movement" of the head is a species-characteristic pre-copulatory movement. *c* The culmination points of both movement patterns come near to coinciding and remain tied to and superimposed on one another in the same phase relationship—by virtue of the magnet effect—for the duration of several cycles.

that running even the slightest bit slower, when traversing a field of tempting pasture, would be highly disadvantageous for the hare pursued by a couple of greyhounds. Escape motivation of high intensity not only suppresses all other instincts; occasionally and in a distinctly dysteleonomic manner it suppresses all the functions of learning and insight as well. Not even humans are exempt from the absolutely stultifying effects of panic.

There are few examples of instinctive systems other than that of escape having a similarly absolute priority. There are, however, some instances in which even escape is suppressed by the influence of another motivation. In young eels ascending into fresh water, the motivation to migrate all but extinguishes escape. So does sex in spawning toads, salmon, and some other animals.

A special case of suppression of escape by another motivation is what H. Hediger has termed the "critical response" (1934). When further flight is blocked in some way, for example, when the pursuing predator has come too close, or when there is an unsurmountable obstacle to escaping, the pursued animal quite suddenly turns and attacks the pursuer. "Fighting like a cornered rat" has become proverbial in English.

Mutual inhibition between two conflicting behavior systems appears to occur most frequently among action patterns which, in Tinbergen's diagram of hierarchical organization (see Figure 19b), are positioned on the same level of integration. This was discussed in Two/VI/3. It would obviously be dysteleonomic if activities of this kind were either superimposed or exerted an inhibitive influence on one another. It is of obvious advantage if either the one or the other is performed with undiminished intensity. This "either-or" presupposes a sort of "filtering" mechanism deciding which of the two is to be given priority over the other. This mechanism ensures that the motivation which happens to be the strongest at the moment is allowed to pass through undiminished, in spite of weaker rivalling impulses. As B. Hassenstein has pointed out (1973), a comparatively simple interconnection of nervous pathways can accomplish this filtering. He says:

> A branching-off of *inhibiting* effects must lead from every pathway to every other, so that whichever path is conducting the strongest flow of impulses at a given moment is in a position to block those of all others. There are two possibilities: the inhibiting connections leading to neighbouring pathways can branch off *before* or *after* the comparable connection stemming from neighbouring pathways are received. The second of these accomplishes the desired effect of letting the strongest motivation pass undiminished while inhibiting all others.

The principle of this neural network, the "lateral backward inhibition" *(laterale Rückwärtsinhibition)* was discovered by H. K. Hartline and coworkers (1956).

The principle of the "maximum selecting system" can ensure that, even among more than two competing pathways, the one conducting the strongest flow of impulses is let through. It is probable that a great number of behavior systems that must be prevented from functioning simultaneously are connected in this manner. As Hassenstein emphasized:

This functional part of the behavior system ensures that, at any time, an activity whose motivation is the strongest suppressess all others. It is not the readiness for certain activites that is either suppressed or given free rein, but the actual motivation dependent on the internal readiness as well as on the momentary stimulus situation impinging on the animal. Therefore, if one motivation is damaged, the next strongest is at once able to take over.

Within the organism, the principle of a double quantification [not the one discussed in Two/I/5] and of a maximum selecting system [*Extremwertdurchlaß*] are combined in the way represented in [Figure 21]. The two-part systems modify the tendency toward simultaneous activation of incompatible behavior patterns into a temporal sequence. Many motivations increase *gradually*, as do those for defecation and micturation. At some moment one of them becomes stronger than all others and pushes through *completely*, to subside to zero after having fulfilled its need. The system represented in the diagram accomplishes three functions: it prevents a mixing of behaviors; it ensures that all necessary behavior systems get their turns; it also guarantees that the organism performs, at any given time, the activity most needed at the moment." (Translated from the German)

Occasionally the physiological mechanism just described can have a dysteleonomic effect when it causes a very quick alternation of two conflicting motor patterns. Even in ourselves we can, under certain harassing circumstances, observe alternating intention movements when we feel "torn between" two conflicting motivations. In some fish, intention movements alternating between attack and flight become very marked when two individuals of the same species are positioned opposite one another and threatening. Each of them does the opposite of what the other is doing at the moment, and the interaction between their intention movements can give rise to a self-amplifying oscillation.

Like other non-teleonomic byproducts of neural organization, this oscillation can, by way of ritualization, attain the function of a signal. As Marler and Hamilton pointed out, the oscillation between fleeing and attacking has been ritualized in many small songbirds to form autonomous motor patterns functioning as a signal of alarm or as one releasing the mobbing of a predator (1966). Fire-mouth cichlids, *Cichlasoma meeki*, often perform a ritualized ceremony when positioned opposite one another and going backward and forward across the border marking their territories. This ritual is different in certain characteristics from the unritualized actions from which it is derived. For one, it is beautifully rhythmic in a way that always makes the initiated observer suspect a degree of ritualization. This is confirmed if one of the fish suddenly loses interest and turns away while the other continues to oscillate backward and forward, thus demonstrating the autonomy of the new motor pattern. After the female pigmy cichlid, *Nannacara anomala*, has decided on a nest site, she attracts the male first by attacking him and then by switching to the behavior pattern used to guide him to the nest. At higher intensities, an alternation of these two movements can escalate into a rather irregular oscillation. In the stickleback, the beautifully rhythmic "zigzag dance" of the male has originated in the same manner from the alternating intention movements of attacking the female and guiding her to the nest. This origin, however, is not immediately apparent because the ritualization has progressed much further than it has in *Nannacara*.

4. Displacement Activities

When two conflicting motor patterns are activated simultaneously, it can happen that the organism performs a third pattern which may belong to an altogether different system. This curious effect was first described in avocets, *Recurvirostra avisetta*, by G. F. Makkink, the Dutch ornithologist who called the movements thus elicited "sparking-over activities" *(Übersprungbewegungen)* (1936). The accepted English translation is "displacement activities." Although "displacement" means something entirely different in the psychoanalytic literature, this term, displacement activities, will be used here. Some time later and independently of one another, Tinbergen (1951) and Kortlandt (1955) both studied this phenomenon. Tinbergen says:

> An examination of the conditions under which displacement activities usually occur led to the conclusion that, in all known cases, there is a surplus of motivation, the discharge of which through the normal paths is in some way prevented. The most usual situations are (1) conflicts of two strongly activated antagonistic drives; (2) strong motivation of a drive, usually the sexual drive, together with lack of external stimulation required for the release of the consummatory acts belonging to this drive.

Elsewhere Tinbergen says that displacement activities also occur when the normal outlet for a certain motivation is "blocked." As a stickler for terminology, I must emphasize that the function of "blocking" here under discussion must not be confused with that of the blocks marked in Tinbergen's diagram of the hierarchical organization of instincts (Two/IV/3). Using the terminology of this diagram, one would have to say that a certain motivation must become "de-blocked" and subsequently "reblocked" by some obstacle situated a little farther "downstream" along

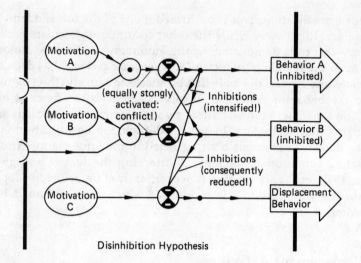

Disinhibition Hypothesis

Figure 28. Explanation in text. (Czihak, Langer, Ziegler in *Biologie*.)

the path of stimulus conduction. The excitation of an antagonistic activity is one special case of such an obstacle; the lack of a stimulus situation necessary for the release of a final consummatory act is another.

To explain displacement activities physiologically, A. Sevenster-Bol, P. Sevenster, and J. van Iersel have developed the following hypothesis. Each of two motivations activating incompatible behavior patterns exerts an equally inhibitive influence on a third one. Being elicited simultaneously and with equal intensity, they neutralize each other, not only in regard to the activation of the motor patterns which they elicit normally, but also in regard to their inhibiting effect on the third action pattern. Thus the latter is disinhibited whenever these two motivations are active with equal force. This "disinhibition theory" of the displacement activity has been represented by B. Hassenstein (1976) in the diagram shown as Figure 28.

An argument for the correctness of this theory is the fact that the effect of the stimulation, which normally releases the "autochthonous" activity, can be added to that of disinhibition. Sevenster-Bol investigated this additive effect in the bill shaking of Sandwich terns, *Sterna sandvicensis*. The activities of incubating as well as those of escape inhibit bill shaking in these birds. Autochthonously, this action pattern is released by small objects, such as drops of water, adhering to the bird's bill. In the conflict between alarm and incubation, bill shaking appears regularly as a displacement activity; autochthonously it is performed with equal regularity when a fine drizzling rain is falling. Sevenster-Bol first counted the displacement activities performed in a standardized situation of conflict, then those observed without any conflict during a rain, and, lastly, those in the same situation of conflict plus the rain. The result was a very neat addition of both effects.

Another argument in favor of the disinhibition hypothesis is the fact that a vast majority of motor patterns appearing as displacement activities are common, "everyday" activities, in other words, are motor patterns that, because of their abundant endogenous impulse production, are constantly available. The so-called comfort activities of birds and mammals, such as scratching, preening, and shaking, furnish the most common examples of displacement activities; when embarrassed, even humans tend to scratch behind an ear—and in other places. Locomotion, too, is often disinhibited in conflict situations; some people tend to walk restlessly to and fro while delivering a speech, and so on. In all of these cases the disinhibition theory fits convincingly.

Yet some typical and indubitable displacement activities have properties which the disinhibition hypothesis fails to explain. The intensity of the motor patterns appearing as displacement activity should, according to the theory, be dependent only on the *equilibrium* between the two motivations canceling each other, but we know a great number of examples of displacement in which the intensity of the displacement activity is clearly correlated to the intensity with which the two conflicting motivations are excited. In any case, the displacement activity should never reach levels of intensity surpassing those reached in autochthonous motivation. If one approaches the nest of black-capped warblers, *Sylvia atricapilla*, the birds mob the apparent predator with loud alarm calls and the alternating movements of turning towards and away from the enemy, as described in Two/VII/3. This ritualized and, in this situation, autochthonous behavior is constantly interrupted and suppressed by bouts of violent preening and wing shaking. These activities, normally occurring after bathing, reach an intensity never observed in their autochthonous performance. The intensity borders on frenzy and gives the impression of something pathological. The same is true for other displacement activities, and some of these will be mentioned in a subsequent section.

Another phenomenon left unexplained by the disinhibition theory is the high specificity of certain displacement activities that, although they are common, everyday activities, appear exclusively in the conflict between a particular pair of motivations and between no others. If the conflict between the incubating and the escape motivations gives rise to displacement bill shaking in the Sandwich tern, we must ask why other comfort activities, equally common and equally suppressed by either incubation or escape, do not also appear in the conflict situation. I, myself, do not know a single case in which the same conflict causes more than one action pattern as a displacement. As the readiness for each of these activities is demonstrably fluctuating, a different one should appear at different moments, and it should be the one possessing the greatest readiness.

Displacement activities are not only often characteristic of a certain conflict, but also of a certain species. In the same conflict between escape

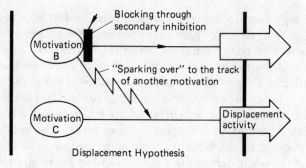

Figure 29. Functional diagram of the "displacement" hypothesis relative to displacement behavior. (Czihak, Langer, Ziegler in *Biologie*.)

and nest defense, each of the ganders of three species belonging to the same genus perform a different kind of displacement activity. The greylag, *Anser anser*, performs a wing shaking, the intensity of which surpasses by far that which the same movement ever reaches when it is autochthonously motivated; the pinkfoot, *Anser brachyrhynchus*, goes through the preening movements that distribute fat from the oil gland, located among the upper tail-cover feathers, over the flank feathers; the greater snow goose, *Anser coerulescens atlanticus*, goes through intensive bathing movements while remaining on dry ground. The correlation shown by the intensity of displacement with that of the conflict and also the specific dependence of a certain displacement activity on a certain conflict both argue in favor of the original hypothesis expressed by Makkink (1936). The hypothesis suggested by the term "sparking over" contains some truth; it is represented in Hassenstein's diagram (Figure 29).

Whether displacement activities have or do not have any teleonomic value has repeatedly been discussed. Tinbergen and others have suggested that displacement activites may serve as a safety valve discharging superfluous motivation. Some displacement activities have been called by Tinbergen "an outlet of the fighting instinct." This interpretation is probably correct for those cases in which a sudden cessation of external stimulation leaves the animal with an excess of specific excitation which has to be got rid of in some manner. The displacement activities observed under these circumstances have been termed "after-discharge activities."

I do not believe in the necessity for finding, at any cost, a teleonomy in displacement activities; it is altogether possible that they represent an a-teleonomic byproduct of neural organization. One argument for this supposition is the fact that displacement activities, through a process of ritualization, so very often attain new functions as signals. Obviously it is advantageous to the species if the conflict within one individual can be communicated to the others. It is actually difficult to find examples of displacement activities that are *not* at least slightly changed by ritualization; in other words, they have undergone changes under the selection pressure of their new function as "releasers" or as signals.

It has been suggested that in German, too, the term *Übersprungbewegung*—literally "sparking-over activity"—should be abandoned. It is correct in principle to postulate that the term chosen for a certain phenomenon should not suggest an explanatory hypothesis. Still, as we have seen (page 252), Makkink's primary hypothesis seems to contain some truth, at least for certain cases. Names are inessential and, rather than create confusion through new terms, I propose, with admitted inconsistency, to retain the term *Übersprung* in German, and the equally unsatisfactory term "displacement" when writing in English.

Part Three
Adaptive Modification of Behavior

Chapter I
Modification

1. Modification and Adaptive Modification

External influences always effect the way in which an organism develops. The genetic program, the *genotype*, stakes out the limits within which changes can be effected by environmental influences. Because the external circumstances that happen to influence each organism's development are never ever quite identical for two individuals, the form in which an organism actually appears is never exactly the same as that of others with the same genotype. This individual form is called the *phenotype* (from *phainomai*, "I appear" in Greek). The changes wrought by external influences, that is to say, the deviations of the phenotype from the genotype, are called *modifications*. The realization of any genetic program that has evolved during phylogeny is dependent on innumerable external conditions influencing the organism during its individual development, during ontogeny. A modification is any more or less lasting change brought about in an organism by the circumstances of its environment during the course of its individual life. Modifications are omnipresent. There is hardly any small change in environmental conditions that does not cause a slight modification which may last only as long as a few minutes or as long as a lifetime. Two individuals growing up in slightly different environments will always show small differences in their phenotypes.

A significant and widespread error is the assumption that any modification brought about *by* a certain environmental influence must necessarily constitute an adaptation to that influence. Modification as such is not directed at adaptation any more than mutation and other genetic changes are. Modifications take place at random, although they are generally more determined and less stochastic than mutations are. Mutations brought about by the mutagenic poison, colchicine, are not adaptations increasing the organism's resistance to this poison, nor are bones deformed by rachitis an adaptation to a deficiency of vitamin D or of calcium.

If we find that a certain change in the environment *regularly* causes a modification which *does* constitute an adaptation to this change, we may assume, with an overwhelming probability, that this adaptedness is founded, as any other is, on phylogenetically acquired information. In other words, an *adaptive* modification is always the realization of a program which has evolved phylogenetically and which has been stored genetically. The modifiability of this program may be regarded as a species-characteristic adaptation to changes in the environment that are to be *expected*, but the direction of which is not predictable. If a mammal's fur regularly grows thicker through exposure to a cold climate, or if a plant grows longer when illumination is decreased, or if a man acquires a greater number of red blood corpuscles when living high up in mountains where the oxygen content of the air is diminished, these teleonomic changes are caused by external circumstances, but they are nonetheless the realization of a genetic program which has evolved as an adaptation to, and as a provision for, the possibility of just these particular circumstances. Verbalized, the information given to the plant in our example would be: When there is insufficient illumination the stem must be lengthened until the leaves receive enough light for photosynthesis.

This kind of genetic instruction enabling the organism to gain mastery over various changes in an unstable environment has been termed, by Ernst Mayr, an *open program* (1942). The physiological mechanism underlying this program enables the organism not only to acquire information not contained in the genes, but to retain and store it for a considerable time span, often for the duration of the individual's life. The open program provides a finite number of possibilities; the stored information enables the organism to choose, from among the options contained in the program, the one that is teleonomically most promising under given circumstances. The choice of the teleonomically preferable option is a process of adaptation; the existence of the open program is a state of adaptedness.

2. Analogous Processes in Embryogenesis

The adapting function performed in the realization of an open program consists of receiving and exploiting information coming from external sources and correctly interpreting this information when opting for the teleonomically correct one among the finite number of possible adaptations. Experimental embryology has thrown considerable light on these important processes. The ectoderm of a newt embryo can develop into simple external skin, into the neural tube, and consequently into the central nervous system, and it can, lastly, form the lens of the eye. In every one of its cells the ectoderm contains information necessary for building every one of these organs. Left to itself, that is, if a piece were cut from the prospective ventral side of the embryo and isolated, the ectoderm would form nothing but skin. If, however, it is placed in close proximity to a piece of the dorsal side of the primitive intestinal tract that later forms the notochord, the ectoderm will develop into a neural tube. When approached from the inside of the embryo's body by the growing eye cup, the ectoderm will be influenced to build a lens. Experimental transplantations have shown that influences emanating from these neighboring organs *"induce"* the ectoderm to form the required structure. If, for instance, a small bit of prospective notochord is implanted under the embryo's ventral skin, the latter will develop a corresponding piece of neural tube.

What happens in all adaptive modifications is, in principle, akin to the processes of embryogeny just mentioned. It does not matter whether the inducing influence is emanating from external factors or from adjacent organs within the embryo. What is essential is that the organism, or the organ, knows "from within," *how* to cope with a number of different eventualities and is informed, "from without," *which* of the eventualities it is that has actually arisen.

3. Learning as an Adaptive Modification

A vast majority of the processes which we are wont to describe as "learning" effect a modification of behavior that is clearly adaptive. The unquestioned teleonomy of all learning processes forces us to assume a phylogenetically evolved program, just as it does in the examples of bodily modification mentioned in Three/I/1. Even the few malfunctions of learning point in the same direction. In this respect, all learning is akin to the embryogenetic processes discussed above: learning selects from many possibilities contained in an open program the one that seems to fit current circumstances best. Environmental influences furnish the information about which possibility this is.

Most learning processes, but by no means all, differ from embryogenetic induction by being *reversible*. Most of what has been learned can be forgotten or "unlearned." Karl Bühler, my teacher in psychology, actually included this characteristic in his definition of learning. There are, however, at least two kinds of important learning processes which cause permanent changes in the machinery of animal and human behavior. These are a) the so-called imprinting processes, and b) what psychoanalysts have termed traumatization. It must be emphasized that these processes are *not* caused by reinforcement and are not self-maintaining through continual relearning, as will be explained in Three/III/ 5, 6.

However one wants to define learning, the definition must include its *teleonomic* function. Surprisingly, even the most brilliant investigators of learning processes have apparently failed to notice that an *explanation* is needed for the indubitable fact that learning practically always results in an improvement of the teleonomic function of behavior. Not only psychologists, but the older ethologists, too, seem to have regarded this as a matter of course! The few exceptional cases in which the function of learning mechanisms miscarries reveal the existence of a highly teleonomic, genetically programmed learning system—in those cases, for instance, in which the relief of tension is afforded not by avoiding the noxious environmental situation but by means of narcotic effects, or in cases in which a supernormal object is more reinforcing than the normal one. Both effects can give rise to vices. Otherwise the only examples of non-teleonomic learning concern the "insatiable" curiosity of man, and even that may serve to sustain and sharpen the human ability to learn.

This rather surprising neglect of an all-important question became obvious only when the heated discussions between ethologists and behaviorist psychologists (described in the Introductory History) were taking place. When D. S. Lehrman in his critique of ethological theory (1953) defended Z. K. Kuo's hypothesis that a mammal embryo could learn *in utero* and that the chick embryo could learn, while still in the egg, to peck by having its head moved up and down passively by its own heartbeat, I answered that in order to avoid the assumption of innate movements Kuo and his followers were obviously assuming the existence of an "innate schoolmarm" who was teaching the animal what to do. Admittedly, this was intended as a reduction of the argument to absurdity, and it did take years for me to realize not only that an innate, in other words, a phylogenetically programmed learning mechanism must indeed exist, but that the major problems concerning all learning processes were condensed in the question of how these inbuilt teachers achieved the task of teaching the organism only teleonomic behavior and of discouraging it from any dysteleonomic actions.

Strict behaviorists who negate the existence of any phylogenetically evolved programs of behavior and who regard the notorious nature–nurture problem as obsolete, regularly assert that the concepts of what is "innate" and what is "learned" are nonvalid, for the simple reason that the one can only be defined through an exclusion of the other (Hebb 1953). The assertion in itself is correct, but the reason given is ridiculously wrong. Recognition of the fact that the innate teaching program must take part in any learning process does indeed preclude any disjunctive conceptualization of what is innate and what is learned, but does so for reasons which are the exact opposite of those for which Hebb and other behaviorists repudiated the "dichotomy" of "innate" and "learned." Their belief that learning processes must be involved in every kind of behavior is entirely erroneous; but conversely, there does not exist a single case of teleonomic learning which does not proceed along the lines prescribed by a program containing phylogenetically acquired and genetically coded information.

The amount of genetic information is the greater the more complex the learning function is. It is hardly possible to quantify, even roughly, the amount of information the "built-in teacher" of a more complicated learning process must possess. However, I dare to assert that, could one count it in "bits," the genetic information needed to establish the neurosensory organization of an open program would prove to exceed by far the information necessary for the mechanisms of a purely innate pattern of behavior. The realization of a closed program can be likened to the building of a house using prefabricated parts whose special forms allow, unequivocally, but one way of putting them together. I have actually seen such houses—sitting on absolutely level lava terraces near Hilo on the large island of Hawaii. But I can hardly imagine any other place where a house could be erected with an equal parsimony of information. It is easy, however, to visualize the enormous amount of additional information that would be needed if an otherwise similar house were to be erected on uneven and irregularly sloping ground. An open program, with its faculty to take in and exploit external information, does not require less, but incomparably more programmed information.

The principle on which phylogenetic adaptation and adaptive modification cooperate to achieve teleonomic behavior is, I think, fairly easy to understand. This understanding, however, is essential to future ethological research. The most important question always is: Whence comes the information that makes the behavior teleonomic? In what elements and structures is it contained, and how does it act in guiding all learning to the goal of reinforcing teleonomic and of extinguishing dysteleonomic behavior? Whoever finds his life's work in this kind of problem will, with amazement and complete lack of comprehension, have to take into consideration the still widespread opinion that the conceptual distinctiveness of phylogenetically programmed and learned mechanisms of behavior is "not only infertile, but actually false," as Robert Hinde has put it (1959). Equally amazing are the following statements made by Edward O. Wilson (1978) in his book, *On Human Nature*: " . . . even in the relatively simple categories of behavior we inherit a *capacity* for certain traits, and a bias to learn one or another of those available. Scientists as diverse in their philosophies as Konrad Lorenz, Robert A. Hinde, and B. F. Skinner have often stressed that no sharp boundary exists between the inherited and the acquired" (page 60). Such statements are as surprising to the ethologist as they would be to a geneticist or to a student of population dynamics, if someone were to tell them that the concepts of genotype and phenotype are "not valid."*

*Similar distortions of my findings and opinions can be found elsewhere in the otherwise admirable writings of E. O. Wilson, and in the publications of others. It is an easy and cheap tactic to ascribe to a scientist witless opinions that he has never held, and then to make him look stupid by disproving them.

Chapter II
Learning Without Association

1. Facilitation and Sensitization

The process of association, that is, forming a connection through individual learning between two or more experiences, was discovered and investigated by Wilhelm Wundt (1922). Since then this kind of process has become the focus of interest of almost all research concerned with learning. The conditioned response, which occupied I. P. Pavlov as well as some important American investigators at the turn of the century, is nothing other than the objective, physiological aspect of what Wundt called association. With some justification, the conditioning of responses was and still is regarded as the essense of all learning.

Thus it is all the more necessary to state that the wide definiton of learning given in Three /I/3 includes a number of processes which definitely achieve an adaptive modification of behavior, although association plays no part in them at all. On the other hand, the nonassociative learning processes to be discussed in this chapter do, indeed, cooperate often enough with association, and in this way form mixtures of, and seeming transitions between the two.

One form of learning which can be considered the most primitive of all is the simple improvement of function by functioning, comparable to the "breaking-in" of a car or any other machine. The process of *facilitation* (*Bahnung* in German, meaning literally "breaking a trail") can be observed in several nervous functions, particularly in that of stimulus conduction. Facilitation is probably caused by changes in synapses and this would furnish a plausible explanation for the fact that the performance of some behavior patterns becomes smoother and faster after a few repetitions. The process of facilitation must not be confused with that of maturation which, in growing organisms, can produce very similar effects.

As M. J. Wells has demonstrated (1962), the prey-catching response of a newly-hatched squid (Sepia) is performed with perfect ease and flawless coordination when it is released for the first time, but much more slowly than after a few repetitions. The improvement of the squid's prey-catching response is very probably due not merely to facilitation but to maturation as well. According to the classical behaviorists' own definition, the concept of operant conditioning (conditioning of the type R) is only applicable in those cases for which, in a situation new to an organism, various modes of behavior are "tried out" and the successful one is retained. This is definitely not the case for the newly-hatched squid; in fact, the typical and unchangeable motor pattern of "shooting out" their tentacles is recognizable 'through intention movements several seconds before the action is actually initiated. In Hess's chicks (see below), it is equally unlikely that conditioning plays a role because its effects, if any, would tend to disturb their aiming mechanism rather than improve it. The diminishing of the scattering of their pecks certainly has nothing to do with information gathering by operant conditioning. When "training" newly-hatched chicks (1956), E. Hess found an effect similiar to that demonstrated by Wells. Hess fitted his chicks with spectacles having prisms; these simulated a sideways shift of all visual objects. The chicks never learned to compensate for this deviation. Their pecking consistently missed the goal on the same side but, none the less, with exercise the scattering diminished considerably.

Processes similar to those of facilitation also take place in the sensory sector of the central nervous system. They are grouped together under the concept of *sensitization*. At the release of a certain behavior pattern, the threshold of its key stimuli is lowered. In other words, the "attention" of the animal is awakened by the first response. This anthropomorphic term already implies that, unlike the motor facilitation already discussed, this type of sensory facilitation is a very short-lived change in the machinery of behavior.

Obviously, sensitization can perform a teleonomic function only when the first impingement of key stimuli permits, with sufficient probability, the prediction that other stimuli will be arriving subsequently. An earthworm (*Lumbricus*) that, most likely due to the sensitization of the giant fiber escape response, has just avoided being eaten by a blackbird (*Turdus merula*) that has taken a peck at it, is indeed well-advised to respond with a considerably lowered threshold to similar stimuli, because it is almost certain that the bird will still be nearby for the next few seconds.

In responses other than those of escape, as in those of catching and eating prey, sensitization for obvious reasons makes sense only when the presence of one prey animal implies the probability of some others being about. As Wells (1962) has shown in impressive examples, marine animals of different kinds, preying on species occurring in swarms or schools, are thrown into a state of extreme excitation by catching one comparatively small prey. The "feeding frenzy" thus induced makes sharks snap at the most inappropriate objects, and the same response in tuna *(Thynnus)* is exploited by commercial fishermen: after having snapped up a few pieces of bait, these fish will snap blindly at unbaited hooks.

However, the "feeding frenzy" of these fish is a function on a slightly higher level. The catching of a single prey lowers the threshold of snapping in general. But still the process is much more complicated. It does not depend only on the eating of one prey animal; it also depends on what is often called "social induction": the stimuli emanating from voraciously feeding conspecifics increase appetite, and this feedback is mainly responsible for the frenzied escalation of a response that is independent of appetite. "Feeding frenzy" can be induced in fish that are too ill to eat normally, for example, and also in healthy fish through the presentation of uneatable objects. The stimulus configuration that consists of many objects of equal size and similar shape massed in one location is what releases the typical darting about and even the aiming at one of the uneatable objects which, then, is rejected only at the last moment.

2. Habituation or Stimulus Adaptation

A learning process found in the lowest as well as in the highest metazoa is habituation to a certain stimulus situation. Habituation can be equated to a desensitization to a quite specific stimulus situation. The situation is thus deprived of the releasing influence it previously exerted.

The fresh water coelenterate, *Hydra*, responds to a number of different stimuli by contracting its body as well as its tentacles. It responds to movements of the surrounding water, to touch, to a shaking of the substrate, and so on. Nevertheless, a hydra can live in a brook sufficiently turbulent that its body and arms wave constantly to and fro. The motion of the water has obviously lost its releasing effect and it can make the hydra sway passively without causing contractions.

Habituation has been termed sensory adaptation by some European physiologists and has been compared by them to sensory fatigue. This is misleading because habituation is, quite on the contrary, a physiological mechanism whose teleonomy consists in preventing fatigue. Yet, I like to speculate that the mechanisms of habituation have arisen phylogenetically by a process of "narrowing in" fatigue to very small sectors in the afferent part of a behavior system. M. Schleidt, trying to create an unpre-

judiced term, spoke of a "throttling down" of afference. Fatigue of the
entire response is avoided by confining the waning of function to specific afferent pathways. What is important about the hydra's habituating
to the stimuli emanating from flowing water is the fact that *the thresholds
of all other key stimuli* eliciting the same response of contraction *remain
unchanged*. While the animal is fluttering and waving about in the current, its reactions to the touch of an enemy or of prey remain as finely
triggered as they ever were when the hydra was hanging motionless in
still water.

As stated above, some physiologists have accepted the term "sensory
adaptation" (*Sinnesadaptation* in German) as a synonym for habituation.
This term should be abandoned for two reasons. For one, habituation
occasionally produces unadaptive dysteleonomic effects; for another, the
term suggests that the process takes place in sensory organs only, as does
the light-and-darkness adaptation of the retina. The process here discussed not only produces more long-lasting consequences than does sensory adaptation, in the strict sense; it is, moreover, by no means confined
to the sensory organ itself, but demonstrably takes place in much more
central parts of the nervous system. Margret Schleidt investigated the
"gobbling" response of the turkey cock (1954). The IRM releasing this
motor pattern is not very selective; quite a number of key stimuli proved
to be effective. This made it possible to investigate habituation to one
particular kind of stimulus. A short sound, produced by an electronic
generator and repeated at constant intervals, at first elicited one gobbling
response each time it was offered. If stimulation was continued patiently
for a longer period, the gobbling gradually became rarer and rarer until,
at last, it was uttered with no greater frequency than it would have been
in vacuo, for example, by a turkey sitting alone in a soundproof chamber.

When the pitch of the sound was changed, the response reappeared at
once, and it was possible to demonstrate that the desensitization concerned only a very narrow range of sound frequencies extending just a
very little above and below that of the original stimulus; on each side of
the peak, the curve of adaptation fell off very steeply. The thresholds to
sounds whose frequencies were more markedly different from that of the
primary stimulus, remained entirely unchanged. The same was true for
all sounds produced by other instruments.

These phenomena could still be explained by an "adaptation" or
fatigue in the sensory organ itself. However, this assumption was dis-
proved by an extremely simple experiment. After the bird had become
completely habituated to a certain sound, Margret Schleidt subjected her
turkey to sounds of the same pitch and duration, at the same intervals
and produced by the same generator, but of a much lower amplitude,
that is, less loud. Surprisingly, this change completely abolished the
desensitizing effects of the preceding habituation; the turkey responded

to the soft tone exactly as it would have done to any other entirely new stimulus situation. This experiment completely precluded the possibility of the process being localized in the sensory organ itself. Also, it cannot be related to any sort of fatigue, otherwise the diminished intensity of stimulation could never have resulted in a new resurgence of response.

Chapter III
Learning Through Association Without Feedback Reporting Success

1. Association

Wilhelm Wundt (1922) defined associations as " . . . connections between contents of consciousness which . . . possess the general character of *non-intentional* processes, taking place in a passive state of conscious attention" (" . . . Verbindungen zwischen Bewuβtseins-Inhalten die . . . den allgemeinen Charakter *unwillkürlicher*, bei passivem Zustand der Aufmerksamkeit eintretender Bewuβtseinsvorgänge besitzen"). Associations are produced when two events happen at once or several times in the same sequence and within short intervals of time. From this Wundt formulated the laws of "succedaneity" and of "contiguity." Both are valid for a majority, if not for all of the learning processes that will be described here.

The welding together or linking up of two subsequent subjective and, accordingly, physiological events has the important consequence that the organism, after having experienced the first, has come to "expect" the second, that is, has come to *prepare* for it. I. P. Pavlov's dog began to salivate when it heard the sound of the little bell it had come to associate with being fed. The experimenter in a laboratory intending to study association naturally applies the stimulus he wants to condition shortly in advance of the unconditioned stimulus, that is, he lets the bell ring before he lets the dog have its food, or before he uses another stimulus that "unconditionally" elicits salivation. The regularity of this sequence, artificially produced by the researcher, should not induce us to forget that, under natural conditions, an equally reliable sequence of two things happening one after the other occurs only *when there is a causal connection* between them. In the mountains of Armenia I often watched herds of half-feral goats gallop wildly towards a sheltering cave whenever they heard the thunder of an approaching storm—a highly teleonomic behavior initiated in preparation for the subsequent downpour. It was dysteleonomic, however, whenever the goats did the same thing after hearing the noise produced by prisoners of war dynamiting rocks.

There can be no doubt about the faculty for association having evolved as an adaptation to the laws of conservation of energy. Energy can take different forms, although always in a strictly lawful sequence. Through its function of preparing the organism for something to be expected in the near future, the faculty for forming associations is analogous to the category of causality in human thought processes. The similarity, even the identity of function has misled great philosophers such as Hume into thinking that they are one and the same. Hume's famous problem arises from this confusion. Logically, the fact that the sun has risen on every day since the beginning of time is in itself not a *logical* argument in favor of the assumption that it will rise tomorrow. It is a built-in mechanism of an altogether different kind that forces us to assume a causal connection between two or more events after they have happened a few times in the same regular sequence; the category of causality, independent of and often contrary to logic, compels us to make this assumption. A lack of logic does not prevent the causal assumption from being teleonomically correct in an overwhelming majority of cases. Like other mechanisms exploiting instant information, it hardly ever errs!

2. Habituation Linked with Association

As direct observations of higher animals in their natural habitats show, there are processes of habituation linked with, and dependent on, very complex functions of *perception*. These functions quite certainly are performed at higher levels within the central nervous system. As every aviculturist as well as every trainer of animals knows, certain responses are bound to a general environmental situation that consists of innumerable stimulus data, none of which may be missing if the response is to remain undisturbed. These stimulus data combine to form a "complex quality," as Karl Bühler called it. The complex quality of stimulus data provides a multifaceted image of the momentary environmental situation and also a context for the multiple interrelationships. A very slight change in the general environmental situation is often sufficient to "break down" an animal's usual and expected response. For instance, a bird that appears to be absolutely fearless of man, taking food from his hand without the slightest hesitation, will be thrown into a panic if the man approaches from the "other" side. A dog that has first learned to lie down on an uphill pathway and responds to the command reliably in this situation, must also learn that this command is just as obligatory when going downhill on the same path. Often the habituation to a complex quality breaks down at small changes not at all obvious to the human observer. If a bird is thrown completely out of phase because the sand covering the bottom of its cage is of a slightly different color, one is in doubt whether to consider the creature as very clever for noticing the change, or as very stupid for being upset or confused by it.

From the physiological point of view, habituation linked with association is a puzzling process: a certain configuration of stimuli *loses* its previous releasing function after having arrived a number of times together with a multitude of other data, which in their turn are selectively perceived and integrated as a single complex quality by the mechanism of gestalt perception discussed in One/II/3. This waning of the original response is sustained only as long as all of the concomitant stimuli integrated into the complex quality arrive together. If any one of them is missing, the complex perception breaks down and the primarily effective "unconditioned" stimulus situation regains in full its former releasing function. A very complex performance of perception has, through association, become the prerequisite for the functioning of the otherwise simple process of habituation. We do not know how this is achieved physiologically, but we are familiar with many examples. What is generally meant by saying that an animal has become tame is, essentially, that it has become habituated to previously flight-eliciting stimulus situations associated with perceiving the nearness of human beings.

Two examples may serve to illustrate the high specificity of this kind of habituation. When we moved our wild geese and other Anatidae to the newly-established institute on the Ess-See, we feared that our birds would become the prey of marauding foxes—beause they were completely unafraid of our externally somewhat fox-like chow chow hybrids, to which they were habituated. As it turned out, their habituation was associated exclusively with those individual dogs. Even a strange chow chow belonging to a visitor was mobbed, and the reaction to foxes was even stronger. Also, the habituation to our own dogs broke down when we arranged for the birds and dogs to be together outside the institute area on the other side of the lake.

A second example of habituation associated with a complex situation is furnished by the aggressive behavior of shama thrushes (*Copsychus malabaricus*). These birds drive the young of an earlier brood out of their territory when those of the next brood are fledging. Once I wanted to keep a young male beyond that time and, in order to protect it against the expected attacks by its parents, I shut it up in a cage. As if by a "creeping in" of stimulation, the older birds habituated to the inevitable presence of this son and paid no attention to the cage and the bird in it— until I made the error of moving that cage to another corner of the same room. From that moment the habituation disappeared completely and both parents attempted to attack the captive bird; they would have let the younger brood die of starvation if I had not removed the disturbance.

In some instances, situation-associated habituation can have dysteleonomic effects. There are a number of responses whose teleonomic function is quite obvious but which still tend to wane after a few repetitions so that, strictly speaking, their full teleonomic effect is accomplished only at their first elicitation.

In the chaffinch (Fringilla coelebs), the warning-and-mobbing response directed at owls loses more than half of its intensity after a few repetitions and, as Robert Hinde has shown, fails to be renewed after a rest period of weeks and even months. According to Hinde, this waning cannot be explained by the absence of reinforcing stimulation; even by allowing the experimental bird to be chased by a real little owl and by having a few tail feathers torn out in the process, the chaffinch's warning-and-mobbing response could not be restored to its original intensity.

The response of hand-reared greylag goslings to an imitation of the parent's warning call showed the same uncontrollable waning. It is inconceivable that responses possessing so clear a teleonomic function, such as the two just mentioned, have evolved only to function but once during an individual's life. For this reason we must conclude that there is something wrong with our experimentation. Possibly part of the waning is due to the experimenter's tendency to keep the conditions "controlled and constant"; yet comparable constancy can occur in nature and I find it impossible to believe that a chaffinch begins to consider a little owl harmless after having seen it twice or three times sitting on the same branch. Perhaps we are ruining the responses by our impatience, releasing them diligently in much too quick a succession—something that would never occur in the wild. However, Hinde certainly did not commit this particular error, and the rapid waning of highly teleonomic responses remains a riddle.

The cooperation between habituation and the associated processes of perception can convey to the organism a very particular form of information. Unlike the ordinary function of habituation, the process here under discussion does not tell the organism that a certain situation is harmless, but on the contrary, calls the animal's attention to a particular danger. Habituation allied to association here develops a function which is otherwise performed by sensitization. As W. Schleidt has shown (1961), the wild turkey's response to flying predators is released by an extremely simple combination of key stimuli. Everything appearing in dark silhouette against a lighter background above the bird and moving with a certain angular speed, that is, a speed correlated to the size of the object, releases intense escape reactions in wild turkeys of all age groups. A fly creeping along the white ceiling of the laboratory releases the same response as a balloon floating across the sky, or as a helicopter, or as a hawk (Buteo buteo). As dummy experiments revealed, the outline of the object was absolutely irrelevant, but habituation to any particular form of the dummy set in very quickly. Any object that had been shown a few times lost most of its effectiveness, and any other object would surpass its releasing value. The strongest releasing objects were always those which the birds had not seen for the longest time. The free-ranging turkeys at our institute in Seewiesen gave the strongest escape responses to a dirigible which, rented by an advertising firm, flew its round over the vicinity about twice each year. Among all of the objects tested, buzzards exerted the weakest releasing influence because they were seen daily flying above our area. This was so in spite of the fact that, of all the objects investigated, they were the ones most similar to the bald eagle (*Haliaeetus leucocephalus*), the only bird of prey that is a real danger to adult turkeys. The information given to the turkeys through the process just described could be verbalized thus: Among the objects slowly gliding across the sky, the most dangerous is the one *which is seen least often*. This would unequivocally characterize the bald eagle.

3. "Becoming Accustomed" or Habit Formation

There is a particular form of learning that is, in a manner of speaking, the antithesis of habituation: while habituation causes an originally effective combination of key stimuli to *lose* its releasing function when associated with the perception of a more complex configuration, the process to be described here has the contrary effect. Key stimuli, originally sufficient in themselves for the release of a certain response, become associated with a multitude of other stimulus configurations and, from then on, retain their function *only* when presented within the context of that complex configuration. Because the behavior thus becomes dependent on primarily non-releasing situations, the process could well be called "habit formation"—if this term were not burdened with the connotations of drug addiction. In common parlance, it means to accustom a person to a thing, "becoming accustomed to something" that, during the process, becomes more and more indispensable. In German, the verb *angewöhnen* has exactly this meaning.

The process is very common and can also be described by saying that an IRM is rendered more selective by an association between innate reactions to key stimuli, on one side, and conditioned responses to complicated gestalt perceptions on the other. It must be emphasized, however, that by getting accustomed to a conditioned stimulus combination, the latter is not transformed into a *substitute* for the original key stimuli—as it is in forming conditioned responses. The key stimuli to which an IRM responds *remain* indispensable even when the associated gestalt perception *becomes* equally indispensable. Henceforth, both can elicit the response only when acting together. W. Schleidt has coined the term

EAAM (E from *erwerben* = acquire, AAM for *Angeborener Auslösemechanismus* = innate and acquired releasing mechanism) for this combination (1962).

An increase in the selectivity of an IRM through the formation of habit is a very common process and has been demonstrated in humans, too. As René Spitz has shown, the smiling response of the human baby can initially be released by an extremely simple dummy—a toy balloon with eyes and a grinning mouth painted on it. A nodding movement is a strong additional key stimulus. The effect of the stimuli obeys the law of heterogeneous summation (Two/I/14); the configuration of the eyes seems to be most important. The effect of the nodding movements is enhanced by a color difference between the face and the top of the head. For a time Spitz, who was bald, wondered why his nodding was so much less effective than that of his dark-haired assistant, until he realized the cause and put on a dark cap.

When smiling first appears, these innate key stimuli are as effective depicted on a crude dummy as they are on the face and head of a live person, but after the baby has smiled only at humans and not at dummies for a few weeks, it begins to fear the dummy and to give the smiling response only to human beings. When the baby has reached the age of five or six months, the smiling response has become even more selective and can be released only by a person familiar to the baby, usually its mother. The baby now reacts to strangers by showing fear and by trying to turn its face away from them.

Even in humans the process of "becoming accustomed" just described does not render the original key stimuli either ineffective or dispensable. Even when the mother is fully recognized by the baby as an individual person, it will still smile at her with the greatest intensity when she bends over it, smiles at it, and nods her head.

In his paper on the history of the concept of IRM (1962), Wolfgang Schleidt has thoroughly analyzed the way in which IRMs are rendered more selective by learning. Otto Storch termed this process "receptor learning" and called attention to the fact that it appears in phylogeny at much earlier stages than does any motor learning (1949). Schleidt says:

The filtering effect of the IRM is often enhanced during ontogeny by the learning of additional characteristics or by habituation to stimulus configurations which have been encountered repeatedly. I propose to separate conceptually from the IRM (in a strict sense) those IRM "modified by experience" and to use the acronym IRME. Releasing mechanisms which either have lost the originally existing structure of their IRM, or which have developed without an underlying IRM, can be separated from the previously mentioned types as "Acquired Releasing Mechanisms" (ARM). If there is no experimental basis for such a classification, or if it is irrelevant whether the linkage between stimulus and response has been established by phylogenetic or ontogenetic adaptation to characteristics of the environment, the term "Releasing Mechanism" (RM) should be used without an additional specification.

I must repeat that this process of increasing the selectivity of IRMs through learning is extremely common, not to say omnipresent. In fact, IRMs which are *not* adaptively modified by experience, thereby having achieved a higher degree of selectivity, are not easy to find in higher vertebrates.

That phase in a baby's life during which it becomes accustomed to contact with individuals and during which it learns to refuse a stranger as a substitute for someone known, represents one of the most important periods in human ontogeny. The very first formation of a bond with an individual is the basis and the prerequisite for the later development of the faculty to form bonds of human love and friendship. A number of organs and a number of behavior systems are susceptible to an extremely rapid process of *atrophy* if they are not used almost at once upon their ontogenetic emergence. In humans, the faculty for establishing personal bonds is one of them. During this critical period, as René Spitz has demonstrated, hospitalized children begin to form a personal attachment to the nurses taking care of them. When the routine turnover of hospital personnel deprives them of these mother figures, attempts to develop a bond with the substitute nurses is already noticeably weaker, after still another turnover weaker still, until, at last, the wretched children give up, turn their faces to the wall and refuse to initiate any further attempts at establishing contact. René Spitz has produced a truly heartrending film of this process. In extreme cases, the poor babies simply die, but even if less damage is done and a child survives and later learns to negotiate with other human beings, its emotional structure is permanently damaged. All of its emotions are eerily blurred and the faculty to love, to become attached to personal friends, is severely diminished. As personal love is the most important antidote against aggressivity, the latter is often dangerously uninhibited in these unfortunate children. Also, curiously enough, their exploratory behavior is very often atrophied together with the reduced capacity for bond formation. A characteristically empty, disinterested facial expression is a symptom of these patients and, in some respects, they resemble those suffering from infantile schizophrenia, with which the phenomena under discussion are often confused. René Spitz subsumed them under the concept of *hospitalization*.

Habit formation, in the sense of becoming accustomed to a stimulus configuration to the point of making it *indispensable*, plays a very important part in the formation of social bonds in many different animals, as well as in man. For those animals in which the process is limited to a strictly definable period during ontogeny, as is the first bond formation in humans, it bears a certain resemblance to the process of *imprinting* that will be discussed in Section 6 of this chapter. One example of the similarity is this: a newly hatched, inexperienced greylag gosling first reacts by "greeting," and a little later by following, any moving object which gives, in response to its "lost piping," a series of rhythmically repeated sounds within a certain range of pitch. After having "greeted" in this manner a human being two or three times, the gosling refuses to react in the same way to any other object, its real mother included. The irreversibility of this "object fixation"—as Freud would call it—is characteristic of imprinting.

One of the great mysteries of imprinting is to be found in the fact that it fixates behavior onto the *species* and not onto the individuality of the object. Once the gosling's following response has been imprinted on humans, the gosling cannot be made to follow a goose, but the human individual fostering it can be exchanged for another without any diminishing of the following response. Also, a gosling hatched by its real mother occasionally changes over to another goose family and remains with that family.

Imprinting of the following response is succeeded by a process of habit or custom formation. During a timespan of roughly twenty hours, the gosling does not reliably recognize its parents as individuals. Interestingly enough, the parents' voices are recognized slightly sooner than are their physical forms. The process of getting to know the parents is demonstrably independent of reward or punishment; if a gosling happens to wander away from its family soon after leaving the nest, it will try to join any strange family with goslings of approximately the same age. If the latter are more than two days old, their parents will take exception to the little stranger and bite it, in a mild and inhibited manner, but still strongly enough to make it utter distress calls and to run away. If one reunites the wayfarer with its own family, it shows that it has definitely not profited by its disagreeable experience; on the contrary, goslings which have once joined a strange family tend to repeat this error. It is as if even a short following in the wake of the "wrong" parents tends to blur the image of the true ones.

In the process of learning to recognize its parents, the gosling's IRM, which releases all filial responses, becomes associated with one of the most complex functions of gestalt perception. In ourselves, the analogous faculty of visually recognizing our fellow humans as individuals is largely dependent upon our perception of the configurations of eyes, eyebrows, and nose. It is surprising how effectively the covering of this area impedes recognition; the small, conventional carnival mask is sufficient to do so quite effectively. Curiously enough, it is the same portion of the head which is essential for personal recognition among geese; a sleeping goose with bill and forehead tucked under its wing becomes completely unrecognizable to its fellows and is occasionally bitten by mistake. One of the funniest sequences is that in which a gander, having thus bitten his beloved mate, recoils with astonishment and switches to abject greeting patterns. Fledged, full-grown goslings, temporarily separated from their parents, search for them most assiduously and, while doing so, respond optimistically to any goose that is not positively identifiable because its head is hidden under its wing or under water—as if it could be one of the lost parents, they rush up to it greeting intensely, and start back disappointed when the head of a stranger appears. Handreared goslings are perfectly capable of transferring their mechanism of facial recognition to the human foster parents in spite of the enormous differences of body proportions. After a time, and somewhat longer than that taken for parent-reared goslings to learn individual recognition, the filial responses of hand-reared goslings, such as greeting, following, and snuggling up, can be released exclusively by the foster mother, no matter how she is dressed. It is the image of the face alone that is relevant, as the following response is in no way diminished if the body of the human, unlike that of a goose, becomes invisible when swimming.

4. The Conditioned Reflex Proper or Conditioning with Stimulus Selection

The term "conditioned response" has been used by I. P. Pavlov and many others rather comprehensively to include some learning processes which are very much more complicated than the one to be described here. As Hassenstein has pointed out, many American behaviorists include within this all-embracing concept learning mechanisms that are very different from one another.

Following Hassenstein, I shall limit the term "conditioned response" to a designation of the result of a simple association connecting an originally ineffective stimulus with a reaction that can be regarded as a "reflex" insofar as its function is not subject to changes of internal readiness (as was discussed in One/I/2). Blinking an eye, a "reflex" which serves to protect the cornea, can be caused to occur by optical stimulation, for instance, by quickly moving an object towards the eye, or by tactile stimuli, such as blowing a fine jet of air against the cornea of an open eye. It is quite impossible to suppress the blinking reaction by willing the eye to stay open.

The time which elapses between stimulus and response, the so-called reaction time, varies between .25 and .40 sec. Acoustic stimuli, if not of overpowering loudness, do not release blinking. If the soft tone of a buzzer is made audible a number of times just before the optical or tactile stimulus is applied, the nervous system responds to this repeated experience by establishing a *new* reflex connection: the tone of the buzzer alone is henceforward able to elicit the reaction, independent of subsequent optical or tactile stimulation. The central nervous system has, in a manner of speaking, taken cognizance of the fact that the acoustic stimulus precedes the releasing stimulus in time with a certain regularity, so that the one may be relied upon to *announce* the other. On the basis of this "assumption," a new "wiring" of the reflex is achieved; this *shortens* the reaction time by putting the reflex on notice and preparing it for what is to come. Hassenstein says:

> On the basis of experience, a new connection is established. The following cogent indirect conclusions are to be drawn from experimental observations. Graphically, they are depicted in [Figure 30]. Between sensory elements and executing organs, the learning process has formed a new and relatively stable signal-conveying connection. The *temporal* sequence between the signals sent by the conditioned and by the unconditioned stimulus must have caused the formation of a new and *comparatively permanent connection between* the two pathways. There must be, within the central nervous system, some loci which, through their sensitivity to temporal sequences in the arrival of signals on two originally independent pathways, are capable of building a lasting new signal-conducting path between them. If the central nervous system does *not* possess this kind of inbuilt mechanism, a conditioned reflex cannot be developed. For instance, it is impossible to connect a tendon reflex with a conditioned stimulus.
>
> . . . Except on the phenomena just described, the conclusion is founded on no other presupposition than that no physical distance effects are at work within the organism.
>
> According to the notion just presented, the information concerning precedent experience is stored in the brain by a process in which two signals, as well as their aftereffects, act *simultaneously and at the same location* and that the result of this is the formation of a new signal-conducting pathway. As far as I can see, no other hypotheses are conceivable. The question *how* new connections are developed within the central nervous system remains as yet unanswered.

The *passive* evaluation of the sequence in which the stimuli arrive performs its teleonomic function quite particularly under conditions and in environmental situations which the organism cannot change by its own activity. Skinner (1938) and others describe this learning process, in which a *new hitherto ineffective stimulus is selected*, as conditioning of the type S, in contrast to those other learning processes by which not a stimulus, but a successful behavior is selected. This latter is called *operant* conditioning, or conditioning of the type R. Conventionally, the concept of the conditioned reflex also includes the so-called classic conditioning represented by the dog's conditioned salivation reflex first investigated by I. P. Pavlov.

As shall be discussed in the section on conditioned appetence (Three/IV/3), Pavlov abstracted a law that is perfectly valid in very many cases from observations of behavior in which it does *not* prevail; in the history of science, quite a number of analogous, productive errors have occurred.

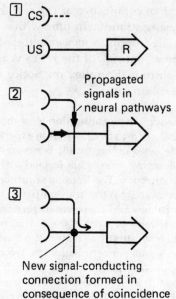

Figure 30. Idealized and simplified flow diagram of the processes indispensable for stimulus conduction and storing of data in the formation of a conditioned reflex. (*CS* = conditioned stimulus, *US* = unconditioned stimulus; *US——R* = original unconditioned reflex, *CS——R* = conditioned reflex.) *Phase 1* represents the state before learning: no connection exists between the stimulus-to-be-conditioned and the reaction *R*. *Phase 2* illustrates the simultaneous arrival of two physiological signals at the locus sensitive to coincidences in the central nervous system. *Phase 3* characterizes the functional state of the new system. The conditioned, as well as the unconditioned stimulus is, by itself, capable of releasing the conditioned reaction. (Hassenstein, B.: *Information and Control in the Living Organism.*)

5. Avoidance Responses Acquired Through Trauma

There are certain acquired avoidance responses which are akin to the conditioned reflex as conceived by Hassenstein. One such response is acquired when an originally indifferent, non-releasing stimulus situation is transformed into the conditioned stimulus by impinging on a passive organism at the same time that an unconditioned stimulus releases strong escape reactions. What is characteristic of this process, which indubitably represents a conditioning of the S type, is that a single experience is sufficient to create the association, and, secondly, that the conditioning is irreversible—probably the effect of the shattering, unforgettable, terror-eliciting nature of the experience. The whole complex quality of the concomitant circumstances under which it was made becomes the "conditioned stimulus." In this respect the process under discussion resembles the learning processes described in Sections 1 and 2 of this chapter.

Conditioned avoidance responses can be observed even in very simple organisms; phylogenetically they have probably evolved from the processes of sensitization discussed in Three/II/1. In some flatworms (Planaria), stimulation by a light does not primarily elicit any escape response, but it can be shown to have a mild sensitizing effect on a subsequent reaction to the unconditioned stimulus of shaking the substratum. By repeatedly applying these two stimuli in succession, the light stimulus can be made into a true conditioned stimulus releasing avoidance responses. By some stretching of the imagination and of the conception, this can be regarded as a transition between sensitization and association. In higher animals and in humans, a superlatively affecting, terror-inspiring stimulation often becomes irreversibly associated with the accompanying situation, thus working irremediable damage. Psychiatrists call this effect a *trauma*.

The conditioned stimulus situation which henceforward elicits uncontrollable terror, can be of varying complexity. One of my dogs once got caught in a revolving door. Because of this single experience she not only meticulously avoided revolving doors wherever they happened to be, but she also fought shy of the whole vicinity of the building in which the mishap had occurred. When forced to pass through the street on which the building was located, she crossed to the opposite sidewalk and flashed by with her ears laid back and her tail between her legs. Trainers of dogs and horses, like psychoanalysts, know all too well how ineradicable conditioned avoidance responses of this type can prove to be.

6. Imprinting

Another learning process, which we call imprinting, is similar to the true conditioned response because it is based on association alone, but, on the other hand, it also resembles traumatic conditioning because it is *irreversible*. Here the association between a certain behavior pattern and a certain stimulus situation also takes place without reinforcement, that is, without the feedback of some rewarding effect of an action. In other words, it represents another example of type S, or conditioning with stimulus selection. One very important criterion of imprinting is its *limitation to a circumscribed ontogenetic phase* during which the organism, in a manner of speaking, "waits" for some very definite unconditioned key stimuli to arrive, only to associate them instantly with a certain part of the accompanying stimulus situation. A phylogenetic program determines precisely when the young organism is to learn what. After hatching and becoming able to look around, a greylag gosling utters its lost piping, to which under normal conditions its mother answers with a rhythmic cackle. To this the gosling responds by "greeting." The mutually releasing sequence of piping–cackle–greeting is predictable with a high degree of probability and the moment at which it will first take place is equally predictable. The program timing the period of sensibility of that irreversible learning process for this particular moment is obviously adaptive. The inbuilt learning mechanism conveys to the gosling information which, if verbalized, would say: "When you first feel lonely, utter your lost piping, then look out for somebody who moves and says 'gang, gang, gang' and never, never forget who that is, because it is your mother." An enormous amount of data is integrated into the releasing mechanism by this process of irreversible instant association.

The teleonomic function of imprinting is to form an irreversible conditioning of a response to its biologically adequate object. Sigmund Freud, who discovered the process independently of ethologists (its first discoverer, according to Eckhard Hess, was the English monk, Saint Cuthbert, 635–687), spoke of "object fixation" (1905, 1916–1917). In most cases of imprinting, a fellow member of the species is the object of the response and the process, thus, is one of the mechanisms guarding against hybridization. In other cases, imprinting can irreversibly fixate reactions on other objects; for instance, the prey-catching responses of predatory birds to a certain species of prey animals.

The temporal sequence of the sensitive periods during which different behavior mechanisms become fixated on their objects shows no correlation to the sequence in which these systems later mature. In jackdaws, the sensitive period for sexual imprinting comes quite a while *before* that for imprinting the following response. In this bird, sexual imprinting takes place while the nestling sits in the nest still half-naked, showing no responses to fellow members of its species except that of gaping at its parents when they arrive to feed it. The imprinting of the responses for following the parents has its sensitive period immediately before fledging. The effect of sexual imprinting does not become apparent until two years later, while the imprinting for the following response is observable after only a few days.

The irreversible association effected by imprinting always concerns *one* behavioral system. It should never be said that a bird is imprinted to humans; it is always only one response which is thus fixated. As early as 1935 I stressed that different responses of the same individual can be imprinted to very different objects. The jackdaw just mentioned was sexually imprinted to humans; its reactions of flocking together were fixated on hooded crows (*Corvus corone*); its behavior of parental care responded normally to young jackdaws. One of the reasons greylag geese are such a glorious object for sociological studies is that their filial and social responses can be imprinted to human beings without affecting in any way their choice of object in sexual behavior.

One of the unexplained properties of imprinting is the association of the unconditioned reaction with a stimulus situation that, though infinitely more complex than the configuration of key stimuli releasing the original IRM, characterizes the species of the adequate object in a *generic* manner. A bird such as a mallard *(Anas platyrhynchos)* or a zebra finch *(Taeniopygia castanotis)* reared in the company of a bird of another, related species, will become imprinted for the purposes of sexual responses to that species but not confined to the individual bird in whose company it was reared. Mallard drakes reared with male sheldrakes by Fritz Schutz (1965) and, after a few weeks, liberated on the Ess-See, flocked with other mallards and showed none of the usual sexual responses to their own species. Instead, in the following spring, they started to court male sheldrakes. In no case did they court the individuals with which they had been reared and which had effected their imprinting. This may have been due to chance because, even if they did not recognize a former companion, this foster sibling was but one among a dozen male sheldrakes on the lake. Still, it is possible that the incest-preventing mechanisms, highly developed in most waterfowl, may have played a role. A jackdaw I hand-reared and thereby imprinted sexually to humans, never responded sexually to me, but it fell violently in love with a petite, dark-haired girl. The surprising thing was that the jackdaw "regarded" her as belonging to the same species as myself.

Some biologists have tried to interpret imprinting as a conditioning by reward, searching assiduously for some stimuli acting as reinforcement. Their rather artificial and complicated hypotheses are not convincing; instead, they show how strong is the ideological bias of the belief that learning by reinforcement is the only learning process extant. In the zebra finch *(Taeniopygia castanotis)*, Klaus Immelmann has shown incontrovertibly that imprinting and learning by reinforcement are two different processes (1965). He demonstrated their independence by setting them against one another. Young males, fostered by Bengalese finches *(Lonchura bengalensis)*, were later given the choice between females of their own species and those of *Lonchura*. They regularly chose the imprinted *Lonchura* species for mating. When Immelmann arranged the rearing of another group of zebra finches by Bengalese, and then kept the males exclusively in the company of females of their own species for weeks and finally for months, the males ultimately mated with their own kind. After these males had successfully reared several broods with conspecific females, Immelmann put Bengalese females in the enclosures with the mated couples. None of the experimental birds left his zebra finch mate immediately, but after they had been exposed to the imprinted objects for some time, they gradually left their previous mates and changed over to Bengalese females. The imprinting process, although followed by no reinforcement whatsoever, vanquished the effects of the strongest kind of reinforcement imaginable. The same phenomenon was demonstrated in an even more dramatic manner by my friend, B. Hellmann, working with budgerigars *(Melopsittacus undulatus)*. He brought together a male and female, both of which were sexually human-imprinted, in a large room where they had no occasion to see humans again since they were fed and watered through a chute. It is well known that, when budgerigars are deprived of normal sexual objects, they easily turn to substitutes, hence the celluloid dolls or mirrors often found in their cages. So it was to be expected that these birds, deprived of the object on which they were sexually fixated, would finally find adequate substitute objects in each other. This they did; they successfully mated and reared their young. Later, just as they again had a brood of young, the birds were exposed to contacts with humans. Hellmann and I entered the garret room. The male and the female rushed towards us immediately and began to court us violently. Although we immediately withdrew, the pair began to fight and subsequently, through neglect, they allowed their babies to starve to death. The engram acquired through imprinting evidently cannot be effaced by any other learning process, not even by the most effective kind of reinforcement known to science.

The effect of imprinting is ineradicable, but so is the phyletically evolved function of IRMs, and the two phenomena can give rise to a conflict, as Schutz has demonstrated (1965). When he was experimenting with mallards *(Anas platyrhynchos)*, he found that males could easily be imprinted sexually to other species, while in females such imprinting was apparently ineffective. Even when Schutz exposed the females to the strongest possible imprinting situation by allowing them to be reared by foster mothers together with foster siblings of another species, they invariably mated with mallard drakes after having been liberated on a lake. Schutz was quick to suspect that this was not due to the absence of any imprinting effect, but to the overwhelming strength of key stimuli emanating from the mallard drake's nuptial colors and courtship movements, to which the female's IRMs were keyed to respond. By means of a very elegant experiment, he proved this suspicion to be correct. It is known from the investigations undertaken by H. Mau (1973) that mallard females, even when given huge doses of male hormones or even after having been spayed, cannot be impelled to perform male courtship movements. The immediately visible effect of testosterone injections is a great increase of female courtship activities, very like that of estrogen injections, but with one important difference: the estrogen-injected birds directed their courtship activities toward males, while those of the testosterone-injected females were invariably addressed to *females*. In other words, it is only the choice of the sexual object which is directly influenced by hormones in the female mallard. Schutz imprinted seven mallard females to muscovy ducks *(Cairina moschata)*. Subsequently, he kept these ducks in a large aviary in the company of an equal number of mallard drakes and muscovy drakes. All the muscovy-imprinted mallard

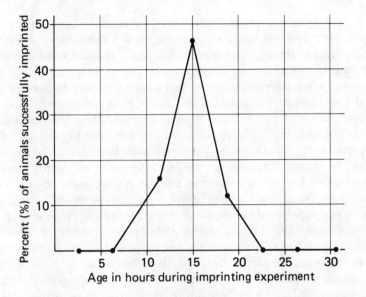

Figure 31. Duration and course of the imprinting phase in ducklings. Every duckling was exposed for one hour to an artificial dummy. Afterwards it was determined in an experiment involving choice whether imprinting on this object had occurred or not. (Hess in Eibl-Eibesfeldt, I.: *Ethology: The Biology of Behavior.*)

females mated normally with conspecific drakes. After this had happened, Schutz implanted the mallard females with testosterone crystals, whereupon all of them left their mallard mates and began violently to court the muscovies, to whom they had paid no attention at all before. As long as these mallards reacted as females, they were susceptible to the releasers of male mallards, but the moment their hormones commanded them to choose a female as a sexual object, they responded according to the imprinting they had undergone, exactly as male mallards would.

A majority of investigations of the imprinting process have been performed on the following response of young, autophagous, precocial birds. In the mallard, Eckhard Hess found that the sensitive period for the imprinting of this behavior extends from shortly before to shortly beyond the fifteenth hour after hatching, but showing a distinct peak at the fifteenth hour (Figure 31).

Many so-called imprinting experiments have been performed on domestic chicks and have led to highly misleading results because, in this species, the following response is not fixated on its object by typical imprinting at all. The imprinting of the following reaction seems to be suitable for research merely because the eggs of domestic chickens and mallards are available at any time. But the most important criterion of imprinting, its irreversibility, can hardly be demonstrated in a response which begins to wane from the first day and which, in chicks and mallards, disappears completely after a few weeks, in geese after a few months. Furthermore, as the response in these animals begins to operate so soon after hatching, it is difficult to prove that no reinforcement is conditioning the following activity.

It should always be remembered that imprinting was discovered in the sexual responses of birds: again and again Heinroth, myself, and, ages ago, Spalding and von Pernau, were disappointed by the impossibility of breeding hand-reared birds; they persisted in courting the aviculturist and persistently refused to pay any attention to members of their own species. In sexual imprinting, the unimportance of reinforcement is made obvious by the fact that the fixation on a certain object is often accomplished more than a year before the response can be released.

There is a superficial resemblance between the imprinting of the following response and the conditioning of appetitive behavior (which will be discussed in the next chapter); the sequence of events participating in both processes is the same. The young bird hears the call note of its parents, or sees the parents' movements, or both, and reacts with the instinctive system of following. While doing so, it learns to recognize the individuality of each parent. To this extent, the prerequisites for forming a conditioned appetence are certainly given. There are, however, reasons to doubt that the satisfaction of a need for contact with the parents really acts as a reinforcement. There have been many debates about imprinting, and also some experiments conducted to explore it. Many of the latter have been performed on the mother-following response of domestic chicks, as noted above. Although easily obtained, this response is not at all ideal for a study of the imprinting process. I repeat that the most important characteristic of imprinting, its irreversibility, so blatantly obvious in sexual imprinting, can hardly be demonstrated in a mother-following response of chickens when, normally, this response lasts only a few weeks and is actually on the wane from the first day onward. E. Hess, in his book (1975), gives an excellent résumé of the work done on imprinting.

7. Conditioned Inhibition

Association alone—that is, association without feedback effects, which are to be discussed in the next chapter—can achieve still another learning process of a particular kind: association is able to create the inhibition of an activity even before it has occurred. As every trainer of dogs knows—or should know—it is quite impossible to dissuade a dog from poaching by punishing it after it has come back. Doing that creates a conditioned aversion not to poaching but to coming back. If, on the other hand, the trainer learns to anticipate the dog's running off—one becomes only too sensitive to the dog's tense attitude and to the particular slinking trot indicative of hunting intentions—and to punish it at once, for instance, by throwing a bunch of keys at the offender, it is perfectly possible to produce an association between the punishment and the intention to initiate a certain behavior, in other words, *a conditioned inhibition* to running away. Even a very slight punishment occurring simultaneously with the offense has a much stronger and more lasting effect than any extinguishing stimuli, however strong, that impinges after the act. In other words, conditioned inhibition is much easier to establish than the conditioned avoidance to be discussed in IV/4.

The intentional production of conditioned inhibitions plays an important role in the training of domestic and of circus animals. Most "teaching" by extinguishing or punishing stimuli acts on the same principle, particularly the so-called breaking of horses, which is customary in some parts of the New World and which appears so atrociously cruel to anybody familiar with the Spanish Riding School and its methods.

Hassenstein has called attention to a possible danger incurred by the forming of conditioned inhibitions. Under their influence a behavior pattern will occur, if at all, much more rarely than is normal, and this can cause an equally abnormal increase in its motivation, particularly if the inhibited pattern represents the only outlet of a certain ASP. Some accidents with circus animals are definitely the outcome of this "damming up" of action-specific potential. E. Zimen has observed in wolves *(Canis lupus)* (1971) and H. van Lawick in African hunting dogs *(Lycaon pictus)* that an individual that has been suppressed for a long period by a dominant pack member, and that has remained passive for a very long time, can suddenly break out in a desperate attack against the suppressor. All mechanisms which normally check aggressivity, such as the reaction to appeasement gestures, remain completely ineffective in that kind of attack, which in the case observed by H. van Lawick, very nearly resulted in the death of the former tyrant. In humans, as Anthony Storr (1968) has reported, the killing of a husband or a wife is by far the most frequent type of murder, and is most often committed by men or women who, up to the moment of the crime, had been abjectly submissive to their wives or husbands and, according to Storr's interpretation, it is the very intensity of love, inhibiting even the mildest utterance of aggressivity, that leads to its catastrophic internal and unnoticeable accumulation, and results in a final and tragic eruption.

Hassenstein has furnished a convincing cybernetic interpretation of conditioned inhibition (1965, 1966). He first delineates the variables of input and output:

The input variables are represented first, as in the case of conditioned action [Three/IV/5], by the central nervous impulse for the activity later to be inhibited; second, as in the conditioned aversion [Three/IV/4], by the message reporting the disagreeable experience as a consequence of which the conditioned inhibition has been developed. The output variable is represented by the activity suppressed by the learning process just discussed.

The formation of a conditioned inhibition is different from that of a conditioned reflex (in Hassenstein's sense, as described in Section 4 of this chapter) in one important aspect: the conditioned stimulus is not associated with a passive readiness to a reaction, not with a "reflex," but with a central nervous impulse, with a "command" in the parlance of biocybernetics.

8. Chapter Summary

1. In all the learning processes discussed in this chapter, the adaptive modification of behavior is caused by the formation of a connection, by an *association*, between a stimulus situation which primarily has no releasing effect—the "conditioned stimulus"—and a second configuration of stimuli—the "unconditioned stimulus"—which acts as a "key stimulus" on a IRM and thus activates a certain behavior pattern. The learning process achieves the *choice of a stimulus situation* in which this behavior pattern performs a teleonomic function.

    This learning process corresponds to B. F. Skinner's concept of conditioning of the type S, which is characterized by stimulus selection (1936). According to Skinner, the following law prevails in this process: The approximately simultaneous presentation of two stimuli—one of which (the reinforcing stimulus) forms part of a reflex that, at a given moment, is developed with a given force—can result in a strengthening of another reflex, the increase consisting of the response to the reinforcing stimulus and to the originally releasing stimulus. As Foppa (1965) suggests, this is just another description of classical conditioning. Skinner also formulated a law of extinction. If a reflex which has been strengthened by a conditioning of the type S is elicited a number of times without being followed by the reinforcing stimulus, its strength will diminish.

2. This latter, rather vague definition fits the one type of learning process discussed in Section 1 of this chapter: habituation is a process by which a stimulus configuration—often a very complicated one—becomes associated with the key stimulus of an IRM in such a manner as to "extinguish" the effect of the key stimulus. This complete suppression of originally effective key stimuli lasts only as long as the *complex* of the associated configuration endures unchanged. The elimination of any small, seemingly unimportant detail of that complex can quite suddenly re-establish the full efficiency of the key stimuli.

3. "Becoming accustomed" to a particular configuration of stimuli is a process that, in a manner of speaking, is reciprocal to the process of

habituation: the originally effective key stimuli are associated with a complex configuration in such a manner that they retain their effectiveness *only* when presented together with that complex.

4. In the formation of the conditioned response—in the strict sense defined by Hassenstein—and also in the formation of an avoidance response brought about by a "trauma," association has an exclusively unilateral effect: the releasing value of the originally effective "unconditioned" key stimulus is in no way changed while, by being associated with it, an originally non-releasing combination of stimuli acquires an efficacy equal to that of the unconditioned stimulus.

5. Like the process of "becoming accustomed" to a complex of stimuli configurations, imprinting results in an increase of the selectivity of an IRM; like the formation of an avoidance response after a trauma, imprinting is irreversible. The most important function of imprinting is to fixate certain activities on their biologically adequate object, in most cases on a fellow member of the species.

6. Conditioned inhibitions are formed when a behavior pattern, at the very moment of its emergence, is countered by a punishing stimulation such as fright or pain. The process becomes teleonomic by suppressing a behavior under the circumstances under which it was followed by these undesirable consequences.

All the paragraphs of this chapter have dealt with learning processes that induce an animal to perform—or not to perform—a particular action upon the arrival of a certain previously irrelevant stimulus, which is the principle of stimulus selection or of conditioning of the type S. In other words, the animal learns by having something *happen to it*. In the next chapter I shall discuss learning processes in which the animal gains information *by doing something itself*. It should be mentioned here, however, that not all processes in which an animal gains information through its own activities represent conditioning of the type R, or operant conditioning. I advocate that this term should be applied only to processes in which the organism learns to select, among the several behavior patterns in its repertory, the one fitting the immediate situation. In a vast majority of cases, the animal gains information by trying to apply *one* particular behavior pattern to different environmental situations and learns, by this activity, to choose the stimulus situation in which this particular activity affords a maximum of reinforcing feedback. Although the organism is active throughout, this is not a process of behavior selection but a process of stimulus selection. While this type of process—teaching the animal the teleonomically correct situation in which to discharge a phyletically programmed activity—is extremely common, the type of learning that really conforms to the accepted definition of type R conditioning is comparatively rare in nature.

This type R process is regarded by most learning theorists as the very essence of all learning, by some as the only one worthy of investigation, and by a few as the only important element of behavior altogether. Even Foppa (1965), in his brilliant exposition on the learning theories of important American psychologists, underrates the importance of the learning processes discussed in this chapter. He says: "For the natural process of behavioral adaptation, conditioning of the type R is much more important." In contradiction to this, I must state that even rather highly developed organisms, such as greylag geese, rely on learning processes with stimulus substitutions for practically all the necessary adaptive modifications of their behavior. Actually, I had some difficulty finding an example of operant conditioning in this species, and a rather doubtful one at that. When learning what to eat, the gosling does indeed apply different motor patterns while it is nibbling, in an exploratory way, on some new object, and it does indeed achieve a behavior selection of sorts, although there are only a few and closely related motor patterns to choose from. In corvid birds, in which exploratory behavior plays an incomparably more important role, this is quite different, as will be discussed in Chapter VI. Over-assessing the importance of operant conditioning and underestimating all other types of learning probably stems from a generalization of properties inherent in the learning processes of the rat *(Epimys norvegicus)* and of man *(Homo sapiens)*: both are extraordinarily exploratory creatures, and the importance of operant conditioning correlates directly with exploratory behavior.

Chapter IV
Learning Effected by the Consequences of Behavior

1. The New Feedback

Without any known exception, animals that have evolved a centralized nervous system are able to learn from the consequences produced by their own actions, success acting as a "reward" or "reinforcement," failure acting as a "punishment" tending to "extinguish" the animal's readiness to repeat the action just performed. This learning process cannot be explained even hypothetically on the basis of an association between two pre-existent neural systems. An "open program" with a much more complicated structure must be postulated. As discussed in Two/I/1, the system which Heinroth called the *arteigene Triebhandlung*, species-characteristic drive action, consists of several physiologically distinguishable components; a) appetitive behavior, b) achieving a stimulus situation to which an IRM responds and, finally, c) a consummatory act, in which a phylogenetically programmed action is performed, by which a teleonomic function is achieved and the "drive" or motivation of the action is stilled. This three-link chain of processes is the base on which the ability to learn by success or failure has evolved phylogenetically; also, it still remains an indispensable part of the system achieving this kind of learning. Wallace Craig had fully grasped this when, in his classic paper, "Appetites and Aversions as Constituents of an Instinct" (1914), he described the way in which the performance of the consummatory act induces the animal to seek a very special and complicated stimulus situation in which the act affords a maximum of satisfaction. The teleonomy of teaching the organism to do the right thing hinges on a *feedback* mechanism. The stimulus configuration giving satisfaction to the consummatory act must be characteristic enough of the situation in which this behavior achieves its teleonomic function in order to be able to afford a sufficiently *reliable* report on success or failure. This report must reach as far back as the mechanisms of precedent appetitive behavior, encouraging what has led to success and extinguishing that which has resulted in failure. Among behaviorist–learning theorists, it was only P. K. Anokhin (to the best of my knowledge) who postulated that, in the "conditioned reflex," a feedback cycle must be at work, a cycle in which the consummation and the adaptive success of the action is reported back and fed into the mechanisms of initial behavior (1961). As far as conditioning with behavior selection is concerned, he was perfectly right, though not with respect to all other learning processes conventionally but confusingly subsumed under that concept.

Obviously, feedback reporting the success or failure of a behavior pattern is highly teleonomic and the fact that so many kinds of metazoa have, independently of each other, "invented" learning mechanisms of this type, just as they have invented eyes, fins, and other analogous organs, is, therefore, not so surprising. In fact, all phyla have done so, as far as they achieved the evolution of a centralized nervous system. Platyhelminthes, annelids, gastropods, echinoderms, cephalopods, crustaceans, insects, spiders (Arachnomorpha), and vertebrates have done so.

As was explained in the last part of the previous chapter, two kinds of conditioning are distinguished according to behaviorist nomenclature. In the first, the animal is not faced with a problem which it actively tries to solve; it learns by a purely passive experience—that is, a certain, in itself irrelevant stimulus can be taken as a sign that another relevant stimulus will presently arrive for which certain preparations can be made. This is type S conditioning.

In sharp contrast to type S conditioning of stimulus selection, type R is defined as a process in which not a stimulus, but a behavior pattern is selected. The animal does not wait passively for a stimulus to arrive, but strives actively to master a certain stimulus situation which constitutes a *problem*. The animal learns, *by acting*, which of its several behavior patterns is adequate for the given situation. This is operant conditioning of type R. The distinction is, as Foppa has pointed out (1965), neurophysiologically legitimate, as it certainly makes a basic difference whether a central nervous excitation is caused by the organism's moving in space, or by something else doing so.

Although this clear and disjunctive conceptualization seems to brook no intermediates, we get into difficulties when we try to apply it to the learning processes we most often observe in wild animals living in natural surroundings. In all learning by success or failure the animal is *doing* something to get adaptive information; to this extent *all* of these processes conform to the definition of operant conditioning. However, it is extremely rare that they result in the selection of a behavior pattern. In a vast majority of cases it is a certain stimulus situation that is chosen, and to this extent the processes correspond to the definition of type S conditioning. The most common and quite certainly the biologically most important processes of learning by experience are those that form conditioned appetence (to be discussed in Section 3 of this chapter), and conditioned appetence for quiescence (Three/IV/4,5). Through both of these processes the animal learns from its own actions, but these actions remain the same throughout the process and it is a certain stimulus situation that is selected by learning.

In my opinion it is necessary to make a much sharper distinction than is generally done between the selection, by learning, of a behavior and the selection of a certain stimulus situation. Not all learning through the feedback of any activity undertaken is here considered operant conditioning. Operant conditioning is here equated with the selection, by "learning," of which behavior pattern, amongst many other ones, to choose in a given situation. It is not operant conditioning if, under the motivation of the appetite to perform *one* behavior, an animal learns by feedback which environmental situation is adequate. Nor is it exploratory behavior if the naive animal starts by performing this behavior pattern in an entirely "wrong" situation. A dog that "wants" to perform the behavior of burying a remnant of food (see One/II/5) first attempts to do so on the parquet flooring of the dining room, subsequently outdoors, and through a number of rewarding feedbacks it learns to choose the teleonomically correct place. It does not learn which behavior pattern to choose if it has an old bone left over; it learns to recognize the circumstances under which to carry out phylogenetically pre-adapted motor patterns. In the same way a bird that "wants" to carry out the beautiful motor pattern of nest building does not learn how to perform the movements (which will be described later), but learns to recognize the situation in which performing the nest-building movements gives the maximum satisfaction, and so on and so forth. In all these cases it is the *stimulus* that is selected and not the behavior that is programmed to function in a particular situation; nor is the behavior of the dog or the bird true exploratory behavior, although, in both cases, the organism gains information by its activity. Exploratory behavior is founded on a very particular and highly complex program and is the subject of Chapter VI.

Under laboratory conditions and, for instance, when constrained within a puzzle box, very many animals try to escape by going through the whole repertory of behaviors at their disposal and learn to prefer the one that has led to success. In this case one can speak of true operant conditioning, that is, of behavior selection as opposed to the selection of a stimulus situation fitting one particular programmed behavior pattern. In nature, operant conditioning in this strict sense is much rarer than is generally supposed.

Under normal conditions it is rare that an animal learns to choose, in a certain situation, a certain behavior pattern in preference to several others which are also at its disposal. Exploratory behavior is a highly distinctive process that occurs only in the most highly organized animals. It consists in the animal's responding to an unknown object by applying, tentatively, most or all of the programmed behavior patterns available to it. The motivation for this is absolutely autonomous and can, in subjective phenomenology, be described as curiosity. In exploration the animal treats any new environmental situation "as if" it were biologically relevant. When exploring a new object, a raven performs motor patterns of flight, predation, eating, and so forth. A rat in a new environment explores all the possible pathways and hiding localities. Information gathered through exploratory behavior is not immediately obvious to observation; it becomes apparent only if and when the animal has recourse to an object fulfilling some present need; hence the accepted term of "latent learning." Exploratory learning is very important in the life of many higher animals and quite particularly in that of humans.

For a long time the research interests of behaviorists have been confined to operant conditioning. In humans and in some other highly explorative animals such as the rat *(Epimys norvegicus)*, this type of learning does indeed predominate and is indeed worthy of the most thorough investigation. Any criticism directed at behaviorists cannot concern their brilliant analysis of operant conditioning, but only their neglect of the many other learning mechanisms in existence.

In their study of operant conditioning, behaviorists have discovered a number of laws which are valid for all learning by success or failure. One phenomenon is found to be true for all conditioning by success or failure: the association between the operant and the reinforcement does not endow the conditioned stimulus with an absolute and invincible releasing power, it only "facilitates" or "favors" the operant being performed, in other words, it makes its appearance more *probable*. This has been proved statistically by behaviorists and it is also understandable from the ethological point of view. As discussed in Two/II/7, the readiness to perform a fixed motor pattern fluctuates within wide margins, as do the threshold values of key stimuli releasing it and also the appetitive behavior directed at its performance. The rewarding and reinforcing effect exerted by the "satisfying" discharge of the action pattern is, of course, proportional to the present level of its ASP. This holds equally true when the action is represented by the "operant" in conditioning of type R, as when it is the appeted action pattern in the learning processes discussed in Chapter III.

Everything learned under the influence of a reward or a punishment is gradually forgotten again if either of these two unconditioned effects fails to occur a certain number of times; the conditioning must then be inforced again, hence the "re-" in "reinforce." Neither in English nor in German is there a word that describes this effect naturally. The first publication by I. P. Pavlov was written in German and the term he used was "verstärken" (as D. Kaltenhäuser very helpfully found out for me). In my opinion, the English expression most naturally describing the process under discussion would be "encouraging"—encouraging the animal to perform a rewarded action, or "discouraging" it if the "expected" result fails to be achieved. The conventionally accepted word "extinguishing" most unfortunately suggests a sudden disappearance of the learned effect.

2. Minimum Complication of the System

Unlike most behaviorists, ethologists persist in harping on the problem of how to explain the fact that, except in a very few illuminating dysteleological cases, learning always ends up *improving* the teleonomic effect of the behavior it modifies. An apparent exception consists in the seemingly neutral and redundant learning done by humans that continues through life and does not noticeably modify behavior. The process of this information gathering certainly comes under the heading of "latent learning." Humans as well as rats may, in the case of need, have access to some information that did not seem to be of any relevance at the time of its gathering. Those few other exceptions, when learning produces dysteleological changes, are always most instructive with regard to the mechanisms which usually achieve an improved adaptation: very often pathological functions reveal a great deal about the physiology of normal functions.

We know that an animal is encouraged by success to repeat a behavior and with increased vigor. We also know that repeated failures discourage an animal from initiating a behavior. But *how does an animal know* what is a success and what is a failure?

The three-link chain comprising appetence, the IRM, and the consummatory act can be found in many organisms as an entirely closed program devoid of any adaptive modifiability through learning. Most probably this was the original state of affairs when the evolution of the learning processes here under discussion began. Closed programs consisting of these three processes are frequently found in lower animals, particularly when an action is performed but once during the course of an individual animal's life. Modifiability of this system, on the other hand, is observed in rather more highly evolved organisms, so that modifiability can be regarded as an additional evolutionary achievement. But to the non-modifiable, purely linear arrangement of the three linked mechanisms, a fourth element is added. Its function is not to report on success or failure; its only message is that the consummatory act has been carried out and that this terminates the activity for the time being. It has already been mentioned in Two/I/6 that the end of an instinctive activity is but rarely brought about by the exhaustion of its ASP; the end of an instinctive activity is effected by a mechanism reporting the consummation of the act. As Frank Beach (1942) has shown for the male chimpanzee, the emptying of the seminal vesicle is reported by proprioceptors, whereupon copulatory activity is terminated.

The evolution of a regulating cycle in which the teleonomic success of an activity is fed back into the systems of initial behavior can hardly be visualized without assuming the pre-existence of a linear system composed of an initial appetitive behavior, an IRM, and an ending in a consummatory action, or, instead, in a specific state of quiescence (Two/I/ 10), or of positive affect, or reduction of a state of negative affect. Even on a purely theoretical, cybernetic basis, it is impossible to construct a model (of a regulatory cycle) that does not contain these three elements and, at the same time, simulates adaptive modification of the system's function by the influence of success or failure. Through observations and by means of experiments we can fully confirm this conclusion: *We do not know any behavior system modifiable by success or failure that does not include these three mechanisms.*

Certainly the animal must be supplied with some information concerning the effect the activity it has just performed has had on the external environment. It is clear that this information can only come from the external environment. Our built-in schoolmaster must, therefore, possess pertinent knowledge enabling him to recognize the outward signs that indicate success or failure. Without this knowledge he would not, in the case of success, be able to pat us on the back and say, "Do that again," or, in the case of failure, scold us. In order to be able to do this, he must possess quite a lot of phylogenetically acquired and genetically coded information. In fact, he must possess something very much like an IRM, a "detector," as I. P. Pavlov called it, which responds selectively to exteroceptor and proprioceptor reports signaling success or failure.

I am, admittedly, not a well-read man, and least of all am I well read in the literature of modern psychology. I will probably, therefore, give the wrong impression when I say that, to my limited knowledge, P. K. Anokhin has been the only behaviorist theorist of learning to ask the question, "What minimum complication must be assumed in a biocybernetic thought model constructed to simulate learning by success or failure?" Nor, as has already been pointed out, have behavior theorists ever raised the problem whether there might be more than one possible way of constructing a system which achieves this function. The reasons why both the behaviorists and the older ethologists neglected this problem have already been delineated in the Introductory History of this book. The first reason is that behaviorists persist in confusing teleonomy with teleology and refusing to have anything to do with either. The second reason is that they hope to be able to abstract, by statistical means, generally valid laws prevailing in *all* learning processes—if not in all behavior. In this way they hope to find a short cut to an understanding of animal and human behavior without going to the trouble of analyzing the immensely complicated physiological machinery whose function *is* behavior.

From the viewpoint of the cyberneticist, there seems to be little hope for gaining any insight into the functioning of a complicated, information-exploiting system consisting of a great number of very different parts of subsystems by controlling the input and by calculating the statistical probability of a particular output. H. Mittelstaedt has jocularly compared this to a procedure of trying to understand the function of an automatic dispenser of railway tickets by studying the coins put into its slot and the tickets coming out below. This may be a misrepresentation of the goal at which the scientists, thus satiricized, are aiming; yet they seem not to be trying to analyze the mechanism nor are they looking into the device. After all, in trying to concoct a flow diagram, the cyberneticist does the same thing—he alters the input, alters the feedback, and he establishes input-output rules under these varius conditions. The difference betweeen the procedure of the psychologist and that of the cyberneticist is only quantitative. The cyberneticist chooses a smaller subsystem for his study and has, thereby, in my opinion, much better chances for success. Provided one has some notion about the subsystems comprising a complicated system, and also some notion about the particular function performed by each of these subsystems, then an altogether different procedure is indicated. In One/II/2 it was explained that, in any attempt to describe a system, mere common sense dictates a method strictly analogous to that which cyberneticists call making a *flow diagram*: each subsystem, whose function is tolerably clear, is represented by a "black box" and the influence exerted by each of them on the next one is symbolized by an arrow, a positive and a negative sign indicating additive or subtractive influences.

B. Hassenstein has constructed flow diagrams of the different types of learning processes and has classified them according to these cybernetic models (1965, 1966). For the "black boxes" which symbolize functions he has chosen the concepts and terms that have been developed by the ethological approach. Our assumption that old ethological concepts correspond to very real physiological mechanisms is strongly confirmed by the unconstrained manner in which, without any mutual contradiction, they fit into his diagrams. Furthermore, the practical applicability of Hassenstein's theories in the education of children and even in the training of dogs and horses is an additional confirmation.

3. Conditioned Appetitive Behavior

As has already been explained, there are many learning processes which the animal achieves by actively doing something, but the result is not the selection of an action pattern but the selection of a stimulus situation.

In the particular type of conditioning I now propose to discuss, the selected (or conditioned) stimulus does not directly release the action by which it has been conditioned; instead, it releases an appetitive behavior directed toward that action. As has already been explained, the regulating cycle on which all learning by success or failure is based acquires information by "taking cognizance" of a rewarding or a punishing experience. As has also been explained earlier, in all regulating cycles of learning by means of the experienced consequences of initiated activities, the information acquired by a rewarding or a punishing experience is fed back to the mechanisms of precedent behavior. These mechanisms can be those of the action itself or, more commonly, those of the appetitive behavior directed at an IRM which has an unconditioned releasing effect. In the latter case we speak of conditioned appetitive behavior.

An impressive example has been published by Karl von Frisch in his short paper, "Ein Zwergwels, der kommt wenn man ihm pfeift"—"A Catfish That Comes If One Whistles For It" (1923). To investigate the auditory sensibility of this fish, Frisch whistled before giving the fish some food. At first the fish gave no reaction at all to the whistle, but after five trials made on five successive days the catfish responded to the whistle promptly by coming out of its little cave and by beginning to *search* for food. The remarkable thing is this: during the conditioning experiments, the food had been gingerly brought into contact with the barbs of the fish while it was lying quiescent. To this stimulation the fish had responded instantly by snapping and swallowing, in other words, with the consummatory acts of feeding behavior. What had been associated with the conditioned stimulus, however, was not the action elicited by the subsequent unconditioned stimulus. In other words, the direct elicitation of the IRM following the stimulus-to-be-conditioned led to an association with a behavior mechanism whose function *normally precedes* that of the IRM. It is not at all rare that the feedback to preceding behavior mechanisms thus skips one link, that is, the performance of the consummatory act, and the affects the next-to-last, that of appetitive behavior.

Another example of conditioned appetitive behavior has also been supplied by von Frisch (1965). A honeybee which has flown repeatedly to a blue flower and found no nectar but has found nectar when visiting a yellow flower will henceforth fly to yellow flowers only, although originally yellow as a color had no releasing effect. In other words, the insect searches for the situation which has proved rewarding. A simple experiment proves that it is indeed the bee's appetitive behavior which has become conditioned to the yellow color. An inexperienced bee is presented with a translucent food tray standing on yellow paper. The few seconds which elapse between the bee's alighting and its beginning to suck are utilized to exchange the yellow paper for a sheet of blue paper, so that sucking up the sugar solution, indubitably the consummatory act of the behavior sequence, is carried out while on the blue background. Nevertheless, the bee learns to fly to food trays with a yellow background in spite of having fed exclusively on trays with blue backgrounds. As Hassenstein points out, this process permits the conclusion that the organism has the capacity to *store information* for a span of time sufficient to associate a precedent sensory input with a subsequent rewarding stimulus situation that does not come into effect until some seconds later.

In his now famous experiments, I. P. Pavlov achieved a *quantification* of the conditioned salivating "reflex" of dogs by inserting a cannula into the salivary duct and counting the drops coming out of it. The ringing of a bell, originally non-releasing, becomes a conditioned stimulus after having been presented a few times shortly before the unconditioned stimulus of food was applied. Naturally this was—and still is—regarded as the prototype of a conditioned reflex. Nevertheless it is due to a process much more complicated than the "real" conditioned reflex as defined by Hassenstein and discussed in Three/III/3. It differs from the conditioned response of blinking, described in Three/III/4, in several respects: the conditioned salivation response can only be established while the dog is *hungry*; in other words, the conditioned response is dependent on a reinforcement which is effective only as long as the animal's appetitive motivation is operative. In most of Pavlov's experiments active appetitive behavior is made invisible by shackling the dog to a framework so that salivation is just about the only response which is *not* precluded. Howard Lidell has told me how he once conditioned a dog to salivate, using the conventional Pavlovian method, whenever a constantly ticking metronome was made to accelerate its beat. After Lidell had untied his dog, however, it ran up to the metronome at once, whined, wagged its tail violently and pushed against the metronome with its nose, salivating intensely all the while—even though the metronome had not changed its rhythm. What had really been conditioned in that dog was not a reflex at all, but a rather complex and specific system of appetitive behavior by which a dog *begs* food from its master, or a young wolf begs food from an older pack member. As Hassenstein points out, all these elements of behavior could not have been learned in the experimental situation because the fetters made that impossible. This example serves to clarify the difference between the true conditioned reflex and the conditioned appetitive behavior: in the first, the conditioned stimulus constantly releases the same motor pattern, as did the unconditioned stimulus, the differences which occur being only the strength in the response and the temporal sequence (ASP). In conditioned appetence, however, the conditioned stimulus elicits appetitive behavior with all its phyletically programmed variability (Two/I/10), independently of whether or not it has occurred during the learning process.

Obviously, this type of learning, as well as its biological counterpart, the conditioning of aversions, plays a very important role in the normal life of animals and is correspondingly common in the wild. At the beginning of any sort of spontaneous appetitive behavior, the animal acts in a way programmed to make *more probable* the encountering of the appeted stimulus situation (Two/I/10). The second phase consists primarily of the oriented approach to an object or a stimulus configuration by which the final act of the chain, the consummatory act, is released. The information about whether the environmental situation for its performance has been the "correct" one or not is, in many cases, received only during the course of this final act. In the case of failure, it is obviously impossible to change anything in the machinery of the well-proved but rigid phylogenetically programmed consummatory activity. What evidently should be adaptively modified is the appetitive behavior which, in the present case, landed the animal in a most disappointing situation. As Wallace Craig very clearly said as early as 1918, the mechanisms of appetitive behavior are obviously those in which modification has the best chance of becoming adaptive and of directing an organism's behavior toward the teleonomically correct situation. Thus it has become the main "locus of adaptive modifiability" in the chain of physiological mechanisms.

But in which other mechanisms, we must ask, should we look for the "built-in teacher" who "knows" what to reinforce and what to extinguish? One likely place to look for sources of information is the re-afference which the animal obtains from its own consummatory activities; these are *sensory* reports (the word "sensual" is derived from this fact) which may be derived both from proprioceptor and exteroceptor stimulation. In discussing the experiments made by I. Eibl-Eibesfeldt (One/II/9), we have already encountered the fact that the afference which the animal obtains while performing a certain motor pattern carries the information about whether the situation is "satisfactory," that is, teleonomic or not. In mentioning the bone-burying activity of dogs, we met with the same effect (One/II/5).

Another example serving to illustrate the point even better is furnished by a very widespread and, evidently, phylogenetically very old motor pattern of nest building in birds. In some songbirds (Oscines) and quite particularly in those with highly differentiated nest-building activities, the movements are coupled with a most selective IRM responding exclusively to one particular kind of nesting material. Our social weavers *(Philetairus socius)* failed to get into the right reproductive "mood," let alone into the mood for nest building, until we furnished them with the particular kind of African grass with which their nests are built in the wild; only later did we find "acceptable" substitutes. On the other hand, there are songbirds which possess practically no innate information about what their nesting material should be like. Inexperienced corvine birds, jackdaws *(Coloeus monedula)* as well as ravens *(Corvus corax)*, begin their nest-building activities by carrying all sorts of objects—pieces of tile, pieces of iron and even of ice, the metal parts of broken light bulbs, and many other things that have been noted in my records. The birds carry these objects to their prospective nesting places and there they perform—with the objects held tightly in their bills—the motor pattern which I have termed the "tremble-shove" *(Zitterschieben* in German).

When performing this fixed motor pattern, a bird stands in the center of its prospective nest and, pressing the object against the substratum, shoves it sideways while shaking it with a quick vibration. The bird holds its head slightly tilted so that an elongated object, such as a twig, would scrape against the ground. At first, however, no preference for twigs is observable in either jackdaws or ravens. It is only when they happen upon an object which, when treated in the way described, catches and gets stuck in some way, that the motor pattern increases its intensity. The object is then shoved and vibrated more violently; it is drawn back and shoved forward again in quick succession; when it remains really stuck, the action reaches a truly orgastic climax, after which there is a critical drop in intensity and, following that, a refractory period during which the bird has no interest in any kind of potential nesting material. We know quite a number of fixed motor patterns which end in the same manner, in an orgastic climax followed by a refractory period, and we know that these climaxes are usually the goal of a particularly intense appetite.

The point is that the information about the teleonomically "best" nesting material is *contained in the motor pattern itself*: the one and only consummatory situation which affords a maximum of satisfaction is reached when the bird tremble-shoves elongated objects with little projections that make them stick to the substrate as well as to one another. The probability, indeed, is very great that the bird, while trying to tremble-shove various objects at its nest site, will happen upon twigs with little, broken-off branches, and thus find the appropriate object for nest building.

The built-in teacher, checking on the exteroceptor and proprioceptor input coming in as re-afference of a fixed motor pattern, is a physiological mechanism in many ways comparable to an IRM. Like an IRM, it can be "taken in" by stimulus situations simulating the one for which it has been phyletically programmed. As has been described in Two/II/1, 2, IRMs are prone to dystelic functions if confronted with a "supernormal" stimulus situation. An analogous biological "error" can be made by the innate teaching mechanism of the tremble-shove. In the vicinity of human habitations pieces of soft metal wire are often left lying about and if a bird, by sheer bad luck, happens on some of these while driven by the motivation of tremble-shoving, it will find therein a superlatively rewarding object: nothing else gets stuck so well and so easily, and affords such satisfaction; the bird will henceforth refuse to use any other kind of building material. Otto Koenig possesses a collection of nests built by birds of various species, and all these nests have been made entirely of soft metal wire (1962). It would be worthwhile to replicate this unteleonomic learning process in captive birds and to test whether the addiction to a superlatively rewarding but biologically disastrous object can be corrected. I have used the word *addiction* intentionally and without quotation marks because this type of deception, the misguiding of a learning process, is exactly analogous to the formation of a vice.

4. Conditioned Aversion

In the same way as the conditioned appetence is functionally similar to the conditioned reflex, so the learning process now to be discussed shows some functional parallels to conditioned avoidance responses. In both cases, the difference lies in the nervous pathway taken by the learning process: In the classical conditioned reflex as well as in the conditioned avoidance response, a direct connection is formed between the conditioned stimulus and the response, while in the conditioned inhibition and in the conditioned aversion, which I intend to discuss in this section, adaptive information is derived from the feedback reporting success or failure of the animal's action. In both cases what is learned is the selection of a stimulus situation and not that of an action pattern.

As everyone knows, an appetite for a certain kind of food can be converted into a long-lasting and even permanent aversion if the eating of that food has ever caused severe suffering. This phenomenon is so unremarkable that nobody gave it any second thoughts until John Garcia's attention was drawn to it by a story told to him by his mother: As a child, she was given a big bar of chocolate just before the family boarded a ferryboat that made a crossing on a very rough sea; she became very seasick and vomited; the consequence was that she retained a lasting horror of any sort of chocolate, yet she clearly remembered having loved chocolate prior to her disagreeable experience. This story served as the basis for a series of very important experiments made by her son. The chocolate had not caused the seasickness. The conditioned stimulus associated with nausea, the chocolate, was clearly distinct from the unconditioned stimulus, the heaving of the ferryboat. But one important fact caught J. Garcia's attention; both the conditioned and the unconditioned stimulus had one criterion in common: both were able to cause intestinal trouble. An obvious teleonomy could be seen in this affinity of stimuli. Garcia then tried to effect a similar association between stimuli concerned with the intake of food and unconditioned stimulus situations *not* involving intestinal processes. In rats he attempted to create conditioned aversions to certain types of food by applying the worst possible kinds of punishing stimuli (electric shocks, swimming in cold water, and so forth) immediately after the food had been ingested. This did not influence in the least a rat's choice of foodstuff. If, on the other hand, he exposed the rat to an unconditioned stimulus producing nausea, such as a small dose of apomorphine or of x-rays, even a very mild dosage produced a lasting avoidance of the kind of food taken a short time before. By presenting his rats with a menu of different dishes at intervals, and by allowing the nauseating stimulus to impinge after one of them had been eaten, Garcia was able to show that Wundt's old laws of contiguity and succedaneity were perfectly valid in the learning process investigated, except for one interesting fact: if he inserted a *new dish* into the accustomed sequence of well-known dishes, the rat always associated the nausea with the hitherto unknown food irrespective of when, in the sequence, it was presented. The teleonomy of this particular learning mechanism is obvious.

Evidently conditioned responses to gustatory and olfactory stimulus situations can be conditioned only by association with proprioceptor reports coming from the vegetative system and from the intestinal tract. It is difficult to imagine a natural situation in which gustatory stimuli could bode ill with respect to non-intestinal consequences.*

These examples suffice to demonstrate the principle of conditioned aversion. If the perception of a neutral or even of an appetite-inspiring stimulus situation has been followed once or several times by a punishing experience, it becomes associated with a response of *avoidance* which can take the form of escape or of inhibition to approach. B. Hassenstein gives the following biocybernetic analysis with a flow diagram (Figure 32):

> The first question concerns the variables of input and output in the learning process that conditions an aversion. Input variables can be regarded as follows: first, the originally neutral and afterwards conditioned stimulus; second, the reports concerning punishing experiences, which, as the examples show, can be of a widely varying nature—fright, pain, isolation from a social group, and vegetative disturbances. Output variables are, at first, responses of avoidance or escape followed by the conditioned inhibition of approach to an originally "appeted" stimulus situation.
>
> *Input–Output Relationship*: a mathematical formulation is unnecessary because of the similarity to a formulation for learning processes. The response comprises avoidance, escape, and the inhibition of other behavior. At first it is directly released by the bad experience; then it is transferred to the conditioned stimulus after it has been followed once or several times by

---

*Polemics should not be included in a textbook, but it must be mentioned here that J. Garcia had difficulties getting his results published—just as the observations by H. Lidell were suppressed—because they clearly demonstrated that some learning processes are phylogenetically programmed. This was and is unacceptable to a certain type of ideology, and this same ideology motivated some scientists also to attempt, by unfair means, to suppress sociobiology.

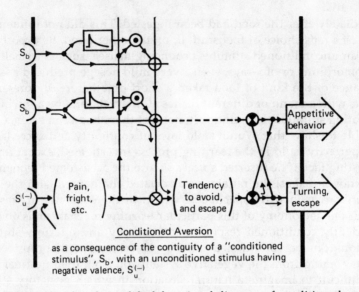

as a consequence of the contiguity of a "conditioned
stimulus", S_b, with an unconditioned stimulus having
negative valence, $S_u^{(-)}$

Figure 32. Idealized and simplified functional diagram of conditioned aversion.
The additional bent arrow going upward at the lower left is meant to indicate
that the negative conditioning factor need not be an external stimulus but may
be a purely vegetative state, for instance, nausea. To include a differentiating link
for conditioning by punishment, as has been done for conditioning by reward,
would have no functional meaning. The conditioned stimulus activating aversion
can, at the same time, be the former unconditioned stimulus releasing appetitive
behavior belonging to another system. This is indicated by the broken line. The
internal readiness for this other behavior is not represented. (From Hassenstein,
Verhaltensbiologie des Kindes.)

punishment. If an unconditioned appetitive behavior existed originally, this
is suppressed by the process.

Flow diagram: in Figure 33, the conduction of signals and the evaluation of
data are symbolized by a diagram which is able to represent the stimulus–
response relationships just described. On its right side, a subsystem of *mutual
inhibition* is represented; by virtue of their interconnections, the relationship
is unstable in the sense that, of the two signals coming from the left side,
the weaker one is completely suppressed while the stronger one passes
undiminished. (Translated from the German)

Conditioned aversions play a most important biological role in the
choosing of food, particularly in "eurytrophic" animals, those which
feed on many different kinds of nutrients. The pertinent experiments
made by Curt Richter were mentioned in One/II/9. In the wild, conditioning of avoidance indubitably occurs much more frequently than
learning by operant conditioning, even when one includes in the count
the behavior of the most intelligent and most exploratory animals.

5. Conditioned Action

The conditioning of an action is something other than operant conditioning, not only from the point of view taken by the cyberneticist, but equally so according to behaviorists' own definition. In operant conditioning (conditioning of the type R) learning selects, among a number of possible types of behavior, a particular one that, because it affords a reward, is retained while the others, having been tried in vain, are discarded. "Behavior selection" characterizes the operant, or stimulus R type of conditioning. What Hassenstein defines as conditioned action is the very opposite of this: a certain action that is a behavior pattern is chosen and immediately rewarded by a reinforcing stimulus situation after the animal has happened to perform it. The reward may stem from an altogether different behavior system, and nonetheless a functional connection is established between the motor behavior and whatever other motivation it is that has been satisfied by the reward. An extreme example of such a functional connection is the association between a motor pattern for defense against predation becoming associated with a piece of sugar, as in the example of Lipizzaner stallions performing the capriole motivated by their appetite for sugar. The result of this learning process, Hassenstein says, ". . . consists of a preference, on the part of the animal, to perform the 'rewarded' action whenever that other motivation is awakened. The conditioned action can be regarded as an appetitive behavior which, on the base of experience, has gained an additional new way of attaining satisfaction." The use of the word "action"—instead of reaction—is meant to indicate that the learning process concerns the *carrying out* of one particular motor pattern.

An almost unlimited number of behaviors, fixed motor patterns and their combinations, as well as any fortuitous sequence of movements, can be conditioned by the process under discussion. Many motor sequences are taught to circus animals by artificially producing a certain sequence and rewarding this immediately afterwards. Working with the Swiss Circus Knie, and with the kind help of the circus director, the processes of conditioning actions has been thoroughly analyzed by E. M. Dolderer (1975).

The important criterion of the learning process is that the reward is derived *from a behavior system entirely different* from the one to which the conditioned action originally belongs. As mentioned above, a horse learning to perform the capriole, on command, furnishes a striking example of a conditioned action. The movement begins as the horse first rears on its hind legs, then jumps high into the air and, at the culmination of the jump, kicks out with both hind legs. Pictures showing the horse high in the air with both hind legs stretched straight behind are apt to evoke, in the uninitiated, the impression that the horse is rushing forward. Therefore it must be mentioned that the animal comes down in exactly the same place from which it jumped upwards. The movement sequence can be repeated in swift succession while the horse wheels around a vertical axis so that the kicking is done in different directions. K. Zeeb has observed that, since the capriole is performed by completely untrained, semi-feral horses of the Duke of Croy in the park at Dülmen, it can be assumed that this is an innate fixed motor pattern of the horse (1964). Without any doubt the action serves to defend the horse against large carnivores; it is easy to visualize the effect of such kicking on a pack of wolves attacking a horse from all sides. Colonel Podhajsky, a former director of the Spanish Riding School in Budapest, told me in a personal communication in 1946 that the capriole, as a conditioned action, was intentionally used by armed knights in combat.

When conditioning the capriole, the horse is first taught to rear on its hind legs. Subsequently, and while the command to rear is continuously repeated, the horse's hocks and lower hindquarters are teased with a whip until the horse "loses patience" and kicks its heels. To do this it has to jump up high, because its forelegs are already off the ground. This "putting through" of a series of movements would hardly be effective unless the whole series were programmed as a single fixed motor pattern, which is indeed the case, as has been proved by Zeeb's observations.

It remains a marvelous achievement of learning that the horse is able to associate a motor pattern of self-defense, that is originally released by an immensely stressful stimulus situation, with a reward consisting of a caress or, at the utmost, a cube of sugar. But the power of association reaches even further. At the Spanish Riding School in Vienna, it was customary to enclose the tails of the Lipizzaner stallions in nets similar to those used by Sikhs for their beards, in order to prevent the kicking heels from tearing out the beautiful long tail hair. To an observer familiar with the motor pattern of the capriole, it was obvious that, even while the attendants were pulling the nets over the tails of the stallions, the "mood" for performing the capriole was already beginning to surge up in those noble beasts.

Another perfect example of a conditioned action was observed by Karl von Frisch in a Blumenau parakeet (Brotogerys tirica Gmelin), which he kept in a cage in his sitting room. From time to time the bird was allowed the freedom of the room in order to exercise. For obvious reasons, von Frisch chose for the bird's "constitutional" the moment immediately after it had dropped a dropping. The bird soon grasped the connection between this act and the gaining of temporary liberty, and when von Frisch approached the cage and requested the bird to "mach ein Batzi," the bird did its utmost to obey, often with only minimal and purely "symbolic" success. The scope and the power of association could hardly be demonstrated more impressively than by the harnessing of defecation—of all things!—to an appetitive behavior striving for free locomotion. (Swift locomotion, on the other hand, is frequently motivated by the urgent need to defecate.) Incidentally, this bird generalized the "hypothesis" that defecation merited a reward and used it also outside his cage, in a number of situations, to beg for food—or merely for attention.

If it has been said above that a great number of activities can be converted, by swift rewards, into conditioned actions, it seems necessary to emphasize here that there are also many that, even with unlimited patience and persistent endeavor, refuse to become conditioned to any kind of stimulation. What has been said in Three/III/4 concerning the true conditioned reflex, is equally true of the conditioned action. The prerequisite for all conditioning is, as postulated by Hassenstein, the pre-existence of a mechanism that is sensitive to the contiguity and succedaneity of stimuli (Three/III/4). Many authors underrate the number of existent unconditionable actions and reactions; even Foppa erroneously includes the tendon reflex in his list of conditionable responses. The neurological "tendon reflex," elicited by striking the patellar tendon or ankle or some other tendon with a hammer when the limb is in a certain position, is an artificial reflex such as one induced by electrical shock. So it would be trivial to say that one cannot get the same knee jerk to a conditioned stimulus. However, it is merely an exaggeration, by strong and synchronous stimulation, of the normal stretch reflex. The stretch reflex occurs in all degrees of strength and is highly labile, depending on many conditions including what one is thinking at the moment and what one is doing with his hands. It is doubtless quite conditionable by a number of circumstances, but certainly not by a reward pertaining to an altogether different behavior system.

The number of actions impossible to condition is likely to be even higher than the number of unconditionable reactions. Sexual action patterns, for instance, refuse to become conditioned to any kind of stimuli pertaining to other behavior systems—at least in non-human animals. It is impossible to teach a male pigeon, through food rewards, to utter his courtship coo, nor can female rats be conditioned through food or water rewards to assume the copulation posture, no matter how hungry and thirsty they may be. (No rat prostitutes are known to science.) W. Verplanck tried to condition a very common comfort activity of mallards, a sideways shaking of the bill, by rewarding a bird with a small piece of bread every time it performed this movement. A fluffing of feathers regularly precedes the bill shaking which is, therefore, so predictable that it was easy to present the reward immediately after the movement had taken place. The experimenter's gestures of preparation for throwing the reward acted as a signal that the ducks were quick to understand. They performed the association all right, but what they could not do was produce the motor pattern. Whenever Verplanck approached the pond and got ready to throw the pieces of bread, the ducks performed queer uncoordinated sideways contortions of the neck, somewhat reminiscent of convulsions. That was as near as they could get to the bill-shake through performing what may be regarded as voluntary movements. To my regret, Verplanck never published this very interesting finding.

Phenomena such as these raise the question of why some actions can be conditioned and some cannot. The fundamental prerequisite postulated by Hassenstein, e.g. the locus which is sensitive to temporal coincidence of stimuli (Three/III/4), forms a potential bridge which seems to exist more frequently between behavior systems that are rather closely allied to one another. The system of sexual activities is built rather firmly into the exclusive phyletic program of its own appetites, IRM's, and motor patterns. It is too self-sufficient to be receptive to environmental situations that represent unconditioned stimuli in other systems. Similarly, conditioned aversions against a certain kind of food (Three/IV/4) can only be formed to conditioned stimuli which stem from the intestinal tract and/or the vegetative nervous system. The chances of a conditioned action achieving a teleonomic function become obviously greater the closer is the normal interaction between the two systems to which the to-be-conditioned action and the conditioned stimulus belong.

Also, the possibility of forming conditioned actions is obviously correlated with the general evolutionary level of the organism—possibly to the mere size of its central nervous system, in other words, to the number of neurons available. It is not just a coincidence that the most striking examples of conditioned actions are furnished by higher mammals, Karl von Frisch's Blumenau parakeet being a surprising exception. There must be a vast number of freely available synapses if a horse is able to associate a predator-defense activity with patting and sugar!

Lastly, it seems that the formation of conditioned actions is made easier if the activity in question is a common, constantly available motor pattern, in other words, one with an abundant endogenous impulse production. All the multipurpose activities discussed in Two/I/12 are open to associations with impulses coming from other systems. Patterns of locomotion, in particular, are programmed in a manner which makes it easy to combine them into chains of conditioned actions. As will be discussed in Three/V/1, this is the origin and the most primitive form of motor learning. The biological importance of conditioned actions increases with that of motor learning and reaches its maximum level in humans.

6. Conditioned Appetitive Behavior Directed at Quiescence

The learning processes described in Section 4 of this chapter comprise the association of a stimulus situation, which was originally neutral or even constituted the goal of appetitive behavior, with an inhibition or even an avoidance. In the learning process now to be discussed, an unconditioned disturbing stimulus, the "primary annoyer" itself, motivates the most complicated and variegated kinds of learning. Both types, conditioning of the type S as well as of the type R, can occur.

In Two/I/10, purposive activities aimed at the avoidance of certain stimulus situations have been dealt with. As Monika Meyer-Holzapfel has suggested (1940), these can also be regarded as a kind of appetitive behavior striving for *quiescence*. In that section it was also explained why this term is particularly appropriate for all those activities that an organism initiates to attain certain *optima* of environmental conditions, such as those associated with humidity, temperature, illumination, and so on. Even internal "optima"—or values of reference—are kept constant by appetitive behavior; hunger and thirst are certainly disturbing stimuli since they do not permit the animal to rest.

That "state of quiescence" which the animal achieves by ridding itself of a disturbing stimulus must not be conceived of as anything like torpidity or sleep: the term is intended to indicate that the animal is delivered from a disturbing stimulus and exempt from the appetitive behavior evoked by this "annoyer." In other words, the animal is now free to do something else. A crustacean finding the environment "too" dry, a nocturnal rodent finding the illumination "too" strong, are both relentlessly driven to rid themselves of those disturbing stimuli and are thus prevented from doing anything else. Elimination of the annoyer allows the organism not to fall asleep, but to take up its everyday activities where they were interrupted by the annoyance. Habitat selection is almost exclusively accomplished through appetitive behavior directed at quiescence.

Almost all disturbing stimuli have one property in common: if their influence continues for any length of time, they can damage the organism to the extent of threatening its very existence. Averting this danger is, thus, of vital importance, and it is therefore easy to understand why the happy deliverance from a strongly disturbing stimulus situation acts as the most effective reinforcement known to science, more effective, in fact, than the strongest reward received through any consummatory action. Devouring the most tasty prey or copulating with the most attractive male or female are obviously less urgent than an escape from environmental conditions the continuation of which would endanger life.

Clark L. Hull developed a theory according to which the *relief of tension* is the most important reward or reinforcing factor of all learning (1943). This theory certainly holds true for all the processes of habitat selection mentioned above. There is no doubt that innumerable other learning mechanisms exist which conform exactly to Hull's theory, but there are just as many that do not. It seems somewhat forced to assume that the courtship and copulatory behavior of so many male animals is motivated by the disturbing—and that means annoying—stimulus emanating from a distended seminal vesicle, and that the reinforcing reward lies in getting rid of that tension. Still, the term *Detumeszenztrieb* (detumescence drive) has been coined on the basis of this assumption.

The existence of many other kinds of reinforcement does not detract from the importance of Hull's theory. In particular, it is important for an understanding of the motivation of *human* behavior because man, more than any other known species, is harassed by *stress* stemming from the multiplicity of his interests and the enormous probability of *conflict* among them. So man, and modern man more than any of his precursors, stands in need of relief from tension. Besieged by armies of annoying conflicts, he is exceedingly eager to welcome any relief of tension and—unfortunately—can find this all too easily in the pharmaceutical influence of drugs. The evolutionary construction of the human nervous system could not foresee the danger contained in the fact that a learning mechanism, whose teleonomic function lies in rewarding the successful mastering of conflicts and other stressful problems, would respond with equal satisfaction to the reinforcement afforded by tranquillizing drugs.

Stress is difficult to define because what is "still" normal and what is "already" pathological are next to impossible to separate by definition. A certain amount of nervous stimulation demanding activity is indispensable to the maintenance of a healthy state of general arousal. Any excess of stimulation, even if it remains qualitatively identical, leads to pathological phenomena, particularly to neuroses—or else to addiction.

Jules Massermann (1943) succeeded in simulating human alcoholism in cats. He put each experimental animal under steadily increased stress by making a discrimination problem gradually more and more difficult, and finally insoluble. Simultaneously he offered each cat, besides pure milk, a saucer with alcohol diluted in milk. This latter was refused at first, even when the alcohol was given as a minimal part of the whole. With increasing stress, however, a cat became more and more prone to accept the alcoholic drink. It is understandable that, having once discovered that alcohol affords relief from tension, they learned to resort to drink, but why they first tried it still remains an unsolved question. Relief from tension through the effect of alcohol was obvious. This was even accompanied, at first, by an improvement in a cat's discriminating powers, though soon afterwards these declined rapidly. Unlike humans, the cats were cured of their addiction immediately after the stress situation was removed. Interestingly enough, daily occupation with similar, but easier problems effected a more rapid cure than complete rest. This demonstrates that only a quantitative difference separates "healthy" stress from "pathogenic" stress.

The enormous motivating power exerted by the disturbing stimulus explains why conditioning of the type R, except in exploratory behavior, occurs almost exclusively in the context of appetitive behavior directed at quiescence. It seems that, except in exploration, a quite exceptional strength of motivation is necessary to impel an animal to try one behavior pattern after the other. One is almost tempted to say, anthropomorphically, that the animal must be in a state of desperation. The dog that tried several means of getting his bitch (Three/IV/1), is an exception which actually proves the rule: he was also in an exceptional state close to despair. The classical puzzle box represents to the cat enclosed in it an extremely alarming situation because it unambiguously forebodes death should the animal not succeed in getting out.

7. Operant Conditioning (In the Sense Here Advocated)

The term "operant conditioning" is generally used to identify two entirely different processes. If a pigeon is confined to a box in which there are "keys" of various colors, the bird will naturally peck at many different objects while it is in the box. Pecking randomly, and now and then striking the various keys, the pigeon will finally strike the one key intended by the experimenter as the rewarding one. Thereupon, by way of a chute, he lets a food pellet slide into the box. After a few such repetitions, the bird "grasps" that this one key is rewarding while the other keys are not, and it will cease to peck at the latter. The pecking has not changed, nor has the motivation of the pigeon; an appetite for food has remained the same throughout. "Pecking at a red key" is regarded as one behavior learned through operant conditioning; pecking at a blue key would be regarded as another.

As has already been explained in the section describing conditioned action, many movements can be reinforced by means of a reward presented immediately after the movement has been completed. If an experimenter waits until a pigeon happens to turn its head to the left, and then immediately drops a food pellet, the pigeon will "form the hypothesis," after surprisingly few repetitions, that turning to the left is rewarding. The pigeon will then learn that more pronounced turns to the left are even more rewarding and, in this way, it becomes possible for the experimenter to condition the bird to perform a circular dance in the desired direction. According to the old law of succedaneity formulated by Wilhelm Wundt at the turn of the century, the reinforcing effect is the stronger the quicker it follows the performance of the behavior that is to be conditioned. In her book, *Lads Before the Wind* (1975), Karen Pryor relates an amusing story illustrating this effect. A young porpoise trainer, an ambitious but also somewhat nervous young man, repeatedly blew the whistle—the expression of approval that is sufficient as a reward for these intelligent animals—just a fraction of a second too soon. The porpoise, most "logically," "formed the hypothesis" that it was supposed only *almost* to touch a certain key and, consequently, it indulged, as Karen expresses this, "in ecstasies of almostness."

It is also regarded as operant conditioning when a cat, confined in a puzzle box, tries many different behavior patterns—wedging its head between bars or into corners that might promise a way out, scratching at the floor, running aimlessly to and fro, uttering the distress call of its species, and so on—and finally (probably while performing the digging movements of scratching) trips the lever that unlocks the door.

It must be realized in what an enormously high state of general excitation the animal is when enclosed in such a box. If this situation were to occur within a natural setting, the inability to get out of such a confinement would mean certain death, and it is perfectly understandable, from the teleonomic viewpoint, that in such a situation the organism puts all it has into a bid for freedom. One can speculate that, physiologically, it is the very high general excitation that breaks out into several different pathways. This suspicion is confirmed by the occasional observation of senseless, "crazy" combinations of movements characteristic of the "state of despair" in which the experimental animal finds itself.

I would suggest that the two learning processes here described, the one in pigeons and porpoises, the other in cats, should be separated conceptually. The first type (which corresponds to many textbook paradigms of operant conditioning) cannot be regarded as type R conditioning insofar as it is not the behavior that is being selected. Furthermore, the behavior is not selected by the animal but by operations performed by the experimenter; the experimenter has selected the behavior as well as the stimulus. One might almost wish to call this "operated conditioning." Also, there are often extremely few behavior patterns to choose from; there is precious little a confined pigeon can do besides peck. No high, general excitation is needed and the result of this experimenter-operated conditioning is, in practically all cases, a gradual increase of the behavior-to-be-conditioned.

The second type of learning process certainly does conform more closely to the definition that includes selection of behavior. Not only are there more behavior patterns available to be selected from, but also the selection is done by the organism itself and not by the experimenter. There are additional essential aspects of the learning process that I should like to designate as characteristic of operant conditioning. One is the need for a high, general excitation that is *not* identical with the specific motivation of any one of the motor patterns released and which represents the material from which one pattern is finally selected by the process. Another is the immediate effect of true operant conditioning: a dog that, after days of unsuccessful attempts, has finally, and perhaps only once, succeeded in literally worming its way out of a detested kennel, will immediately resort to the same method if ever confined in the same kennel again.

From the cyberneticist's viewpoint (and here I am following Hassenstein's conceptualizations), operant conditioning of the type first discussed in this section should be regarded as a formation of chains of conditioned actions. This has been discussed in Three/IV/5. Such formations are to be found very frequently in nature, and it is my considered opinion that all motor learning is based on this learning process, as will be discussed in Chapter V.

Operant conditioning, in the strict sense here advocated, is rare under natural conditions. I had difficulty finding an example of appetitive behavior *not* being used in trying to get rid of a disturbing stimulus but aiming at the satisfactory discharge of a consummatory act, that is, appetitive behavior representing the motive of the behavior selection. One of my dogs, trying to get to a bitch in heat confined in a kennel, performed the following behavior selection. First he tried to jump over the kennel's slightly overhanging fence. Failing to get over the fence by jumping it, he tried to tear through the wire of the fence using his teeth, pushing and pulling alternately at the wire meshwork—a behavior he had learned in a successful attempt to get at rabbits in their hutch. Because the kennel wire proved to be too strong, the dog desisted, bleeding slightly at the mouth. After this he seemed to give up, and we also ceased to feel the need for any further guarding of the kennel. During the night, however, the dog succeeded in digging a tunnel under the wire fence, although this had been set quite deeply in the ground.

The most important function that operant conditioning performs in nature is closely linked with that of exploratory behavior. In exploratory behavior it is the stimulus situation that remains constant; the same situation or object elicits, in the exploring animal (or in man), a whole gamut of behaviors tried out one after the other. In this case, a *new motivating agent* comes into being that is *unspecific* with regard to the several behavior systems it is capable of motivating. This will be more thoroughly discussed in Chapter VI. For the present it suffices to say that the exploring animal can perform, through exploratory behavior, action patterns of attack, of fleeing, of eating, and such like, only as long as none of the specific motivations for these activities is aroused; the animal cannot continue its exploring when it really becomes furious, or afraid, or hungry. Similarly, play can only take place when all "serious" motivations remain silent, that is, within a "field devoid of tension"—*im entspannten Feld*, as Gustav Bally has put it, using the terminology of Kurt Levin.

It is only this kind of learning process for which I here suggest the term *operant conditioning*. Only this type of learning mechanism is ever functionally integrated with exploratory behavior. This integrated unit plays such an immensely important role in human behavior that this, alone, should be sufficient to justify the use of a special term.

8. Chapter Summary

1. **The New Feedback** A very particular process of learning is founded on the principle of feeding back, to the mechanisms of initial behavior, the final success or failure of the activity, and of adaptively modifying the activity accordingly. If we keep strictly to the behaviorists' definition of the type S and the type R of conditioning, the type of learning here under discussion does not fit either of the two categories. The definition of the type S, or classical conditioning, postulates that the organism remains passive and a given type of behavior is conditioned to a new stimulus. The definition of operant, or type R conditioning, demands that the animal choose, by trial and error, a pattern of behavior fitting the environmental situation. What actually happens most frequently is that the animal gains information by doing something, but what it does is perform, or try to perform, a given behavior pattern, and gain information not concerning this motor pattern, but concerning the stimulus configuration in which this same motor pattern attains a reinforcing reward. It is not the behavior that is selected to fit an environmental situation, but an environmental situation is chosen so as to afford optimal stimulation for a predetermined pattern of activity. Appetitive behavior can equally be aimed at the satisfactory accomplishment of a consummatory action (Wallace Craig 1918) or at a state of quiescence whose prerequisite is the *absence* of a certain disturbing stimulus. Craig termed this latter type of behavior "aversion," M. Meyer-Holzapfel (1940) described it as an appetite for quiescence.

2. **The Necessary Minimal Complication of the System** The prerequisite for learning by success or failure is a "feedback mechanism," in other words, a regulating cycle. This presupposes a relatively high minimal complication of the system. The best method for ascertaining the minimal complication of a system is an attempt to construct a flow diagram simulating a system's functions in the manner used in biocybernetics. As Hassenstein has shown, a flow diagram representing the process of learning by success or failure has to include, in the form of "black boxes," the mechanisms of appetitive behavior, of IRM, and of consummatory action. These three links are to be found in independently functioning and unmodifiable systems. The pre-existence of these systems must be postulated as a prerequisite in order that learning by success or failure could evolve.

   Even in unmodifiable systems there are feedback mechanisms reporting the accomplishment of a consummatory act and terminating the activity without, however, having furnished any information about its teleonomic effect. To achieve this latter function, it is necessary to supply information about the effect which the organism's activity has had on the *external environment*, hence an exteroceptor apparatus is needed which possesses sufficient phyletic information to distinguish success from failure. This apparatus is the "built-in teacher" rewarding or punishing the pupil.

3. **Conditioned Appetitive Behavior** In a majority of cases the rewarding effect is associated with the precedent appetitive behavior, less often with the consummatory act and still less often with a state of quiescence, representing the "goal of aversions" in Craig's meaning of the term. Even upon receiving a stimulus-to-be-conditioned simultaneously with the releasing of a consummatory act, the animal associates this not with the latter, but with the appetitive behavior phylogenetically programmed to precede that act.

Conditioned appetitive behavior has been confused with the classical conditioned reflex. In the latter, however, the conditioned stimulus releases exclusively that one response which previously was elicited by the unconditioned stimulus, while in conditioned appetitive behavior it releases appetitive behavior, irrespective of whether it has occurred within the training situation or not.

Very often the built-in teaching mechanism is situated in the fixed motor pattern of the consummatory action itself; its unmodifiable form furnishes rewarding reafferences only in the teleonomically correct environmental situation; in any other it acts as a punishment by being "disappointing."

4. **Conditioned Aversion** If a situation that is primarily neutral, or even eliciting appetitive behavior, is followed immediately by intense punishment, strong avoidance responses become associated with this situation, particularly if the punishing stimuli impinge immediately after appetitive behavior has begun to emerge and before the organism has had time to proceed to the subsequent consummatory act. Conditioned aversions play an extremely important role in the food selection of eurytrophous animals.

5. **Conditioned Action** Even an isolated action pattern, phyletically fixed or acquired, can be associated with a reinforcing stimulus derived from an altogether different behavior system, provided that the reward is presented immediately after the action. As a result of this, the action is dissociated completely from its original function and is performed when the appetitive behavior directed at the conditioned stimulus becomes activated. Thus a horse learns to kick its heels in order to get sugar as a reward; in other words, an action derived from a system of defense against predators is harnessed to an appetitive behavior aimed at getting food.

A conditioning by reinforcement of actions stemming from an altogether different system of behavior seems to occur only in very highly evolved organisms. On the other hand, conditioning an action by means of a reward stemming from a related system can lead to the formation of *chain* activities, of which each can be regarded as an appetitive behavior striving for the next. In this way the most primitive forms of *motor* learning are accomplished.

6. **Conditioned Appetitive Behavior Directed at Quiescence** As discussed in Two/IV/1, the unconditioned avoidance of disturbing stimuli, the "aversion" according to the conceptualization of W. Craig (1918), can also by conceptualized as an appetitive behavior aimed at becoming free from these "annoyers." Among all the rewards attained by appetitive behavior, deliverance from disturbing stimuli exerts the strongest reinforcing influence. Most disturbing stimuli signify a danger to survival if their influence endures for any length of time; therefore it is teleonomically understandable that the organism tries "by any means at its disposal" to rid itself of them; in other words, it tries different motor patterns, one after the other, and learns to employ the most successful one. Except in the course of exploratory behavior, to be discussed in Three/VI/7, operant conditioning under natural circumstances occurs almost exclusively under the excessively strong motivation of an appetite for quiescence.

7. **Operant Conditioning** The concept of operant conditioning is here confined to learning processes in which not the stimulus situation but the behavior pattern is selected, and from other patterns among those in repertory of the species concerned. Operant conditioning is not involved when an animal, by attempting to discharge a certain behavior pattern in different environmental situations, learns by trial and error which of these environmental situations affords a maximum of rewarding feedback. Nor is this trial and error behavior to be equated with exploratory behavior. Exploratory behavior is based on a much more complicated program. In nature, operant conditioning is much rarer than generally assumed and occurs mainly under the influence of disturbing stimulus situations, in other words, within a context of appetence directed at quiescence. Otherwise, operant conditioning functions mainly in cooperation with exploratory behavior.

Chapter V
Motor Learning, Voluntary Movement, and Insight

1. Motor Learning

All of the learning processes dealt with in Three/III/1, 2 accomplish an adaptive modification within the sensory sector only. Even in the mechanisms discussed in Three/III/3, 4, which function on the basis of a feedback of success or failure, no adaptive change is wrought in the motor pattern concerned. Motor learning becomes possible only by associating actions, as described in Three/IV/5. Simple and constantly available "multipurpose" motor patterns can be wrought into chains which can be correctly regarded as "new," that is, not phyletically programmed movements. To the best of my knowledge the Viennese zoologist, Otto Storch (1949), was the first to call attention to the fact that *Erwerbsrezeptorik*, "receptor learning" preceded *Erwerbsmotorik*, "motor learning" in evolution, and was much more common, especially among lower animals, than motor learning.

The most primitive form of a "new" motor pattern acquired through learning is the linking together of a chain of conditioned actions as described in Three/IV/5. If a reinforcing stimulus is made to follow immediately upon some readily available motor pattern, especially one of the multipurpose type activities, and if this process is repeated several times in quick succession, a long sequence can be formed of the repetition of this same motor pattern. For instance, the reinforcement of a slight turn to the left can teach a pigeon to repeat it as a kind of dance round and round in that direction. The pigeon has formed the "hypothesis" that turning to the left causes grain to fall out of a chute.

For reasons already discussed in Three/I/12 and Three/I/5, among all the fixed motor patterns, those of locomotion are the most easily welded into long sequences of conditioned actions. As the examples that were cited demonstrated, most of the conditioned actions produced during the training of horses are derived from this source. In laboratory experiments it is possible, by rewarding the first movement of a desired sequence and by reinforcing a second one when the animal happens to produce it, and by persevering in this procedure, to form amazingly complicated chains of conditioned responses, for instance, two pigeons "playing ping-pong," that is, driving a celluloid ball back and forth by pecking at it. Such chains of conditioned actions can, of course, be regarded as new motor patterns acquired by learning. Very striking examples of this process of "shaping" skilled movements are to be found in Karen Pryor's book, *Lads Before the Wind* (1975).

In the wild, this type of motor learning plays an important role in the acquisition of path habits. O. Koehler and W. Dingler demonstrated this process with a highly instructive film (1953). A mouse is put into a so-called high labyrinth, that is, a maze constructed with pieces of lath and elevated on stilts, high enough to discourage the animal from jumping down. At first, the mouse creeps along, step by step, very slowly feeling its way by groping about with its tactile vibrissae. After having moved through the maze two or three times in this painstaking way, the mouse begins to traverse certain stretches of the maze, at first very short ones, at a fast run, after which it balks again and returns to the vibrissae-palpating walk. The two methods of proceeding, first the slow walk steered by mechanisms of exploiting instant information, and second the fast run, which represents a learned or "skilled" movement, continue to alternate for a long time. The stretches mastered by skilled movement increase in length; they appear at new places along the course and fuse at their ends. Very often, though, the places of their fusing remain visible in the form of a slight hesitation made by the animal when passing those particular points—much like the way a child gets stuck again and again at certain places when reciting a poem or playing a piece of music. In the end, these remaining difficulties are smoothed over and disappear, so that henceforth running through the maze constitutes a single skilled flowing movement.

The telenomic value of this kind of path learning is obvious: An entire passage along a complicated route can be negotiated *without any retardation through reaction times*. For this reason the performance is very much faster than any analogous negotiation based on instant information-exploiting mechanisms could ever be. This is one—often forgotten—reason why animals confine themselves to a spatially limited territory: within it they have mastered all the possible contingencies of locomotion by skilled movements. The difference between the speed of skilled movements and those steered by instant information is brought home most impressively to anyone who has ever tried to catch a mouse, a lizard, a blenny, or any coral fish. Along its known pathways, the animal is much too quick to be caught, but if one can succeed in stampeding it out of its known territory, the odds are that one will catch it.

In his book, *Die Orientierung der Tiere im Raum* (1919), Alfred Kühn described a form of learning which he postulated as being a possibility, and which he called "mnemotaxis." He assumed an engram containing the entire sequence of motor patterns, which during an action was synchronized with the sequence of incoming stimuli, thus confirming the correctness of movement at every step. This he termed *mnemische Homophonie*. Critics argued that the process of orientation could only function if the animal, while running along a learned pathway, stepped exactly in the same places each time and thus received exactly the same "expected" reafference. In the second edition of his book, Kühn deleted "mnemotaxis" because no example was known of an animal behaving in the postulated manner. Since then, such animals have been discovered. The water shrew *(Neomys fodiens)* seems to achieve a fusing of single locomotor patterns into one skilled flowing movement of running along habitual paths by joining the elements, through conditioning, each to the stimulus situation, which not only provokes the next but also orients the animal and tells it that it is still on the right path. If this is true, then the animal must become disoriented and its skilled movements broken up, if only one step misses an appointed place. Contrary to the expectations of Kühn's critics, this is quite exactly what happens to the water shrew—and very probably to many other small mammals. If, experimentally, one causes a break in the shrew's "mnemic homophony" by changing a bit of the ground traversed by its habitual path, it will come to a complete stop, begin to explore its surroundings with palpating vibrissae, and run back along a stretch of the way it has come. Recognizing some landmark passed a few seconds before, it will reorient, resume the former course and, by "gathering momentum," attempt to overcome the difficulty caused by the changed bit of ground. When reciting poems, children do exactly the same thing. In one place, just before reaching "home," the path habit of my water shrews involved the necessity of jumping up onto the lid of their wooden nest box that was several inches high. After I removed this box, the shrews jumped up onto emptiness and, after falling down, continued to repeat the movement several times. Curiously enough, the shrews were demonstrably able to *see* the box—it contained their nest—because, when I put them onto the floor, they ran to the box at once, even when it was half a meter away. Thus the skilled and flowing movement of path running was actually able to overcome the influence of instant information!

As I mentioned in Three/III/2, little is known about the physiology of association. We do not know how the motor elements pertaining to skilled movements are linked together. Some researchers have assumed that proprioception takes part in the process of learning a sequence of movements "by heart," such as playing a musical instrument, reciting a poem, or running through a maze. The term "kinesthetic" (from the Greek *kinesis*, "the movement," and *aisthanomai*, "I feel") has been used in this context. Subjectively, when we "visualize" ourselves performing such a skilled movement, we seem to have some "feeling" of its perfor-mance. Also, in the process of acquiring a motor skill, proprioceptor action may play a role.

But two arguments oppose the kinesthetic hypothesis. As Erich von Holst has shown, skilled movements are subject to all the laws of relative coordination (Two/I/13) and of magnet effect that prevail in centrally coordinated movements; in centrally coordinated movements propri-oceptor processes play no part at all. Furthermore, it is known from the work done by J. Eccles that skilled motor patterns are formed in and con-trolled by the cerebellum. Self-observation, too, argues against the assumption that the faculty for performing skilled movements is based on a kinesthetic memory. If you ask someone who is so adept at driving an automobile that the motions of controlling the car have become "sec-ond nature," which foot is used on the brake and which on the clutch, it can be observed with predictable certainty that the person will move both feet alternately, in other words, the person has to activate the skilled movements in order to determine, by self-observation, which foot does what.

It is justified to assume that skilled movements more complicated than those of running along a known path are formed in the same way. There is no reason why simultaneously activated motor elements should not be associated by means of the same process that links successive ones.

Curiously enough, skilled motor patterns, particularly after they have been in use for some time and are well "ground in," develop some of the characteristics of centrally coordinated fixed motor patterns. As already mentioned, all the laws of central coordination prevail in skilled move-ments and tend to force the several motor elements into harmonious integral frequences. The better the possibilities for integration are, the more stable are the skilled movements. Conversely, the skilled move-ment is that much more unstable—and the more difficult to learn—the more the several frequencies of the elements resist such a harmonious integration. Everyone who, as a child, was taught to play the piano, will remember how hard it was to play triplets with one hand and quavers with the other. The harmonizing effects of central coordination endow skilled movements with forms at once economic and elegant, which have a strong appeal to our aesthetic sense.

A second property shared by the skilled movement and the fixed motor pattern is their strong resistance to any change. Karl Bühler's assumption that everything learned can be wiped out and forgotten (1922) holds true for all learning by reinforcement; it does not, however, hold true for imprinting (Three/VI/3), nor does it for the acquisition of skilled movements. The professional coach of sports such as tennis or

swimming knows very well that it is hopeless to attain maximum efficiency for a person who, through untutored training, has acquired self-
taught motor habits. These most perniciously block the way for learning
those motor habits indispensable to optimum skill.

The third and most amazing similarity between skilled movements
and fixed motor patterns is that, when not used for a certain period of
time, both give rise to appetitive behavior. As H. Harlow has shown,
rhesus monkeys take such pleasure in performing complicated movements, such as opening a lock, that they not only do this independently
of any reward, but even go to considerable trouble in order to be allowed
to do so. Karl Bühler was the first to notice this phenomenon and he
spoke about *Funktionslust*—pleasure in the function. The strength of the
motivation generated by this pleasure is evident from the avidity for
dancing, skiing, and other activities that we, ourselves, display. One
example can illustrate the blind striving for the performance of skilled
movements: if a military rifle is presented to a man who has seen military
service, he will predictably take it up and try to perform some learned
actions with this objectionable object, however much he may have hated
soldiering!

As we know from self-observation, the "smoothing out" which makes
the skilled movement so elegant and economically efficient affords a certain pleasure that is qualitatively unmistakable, and is the greater the
more complicated the movement and the more difficult the accomplishment is to attain. The teleonomy of the learning process thus motivated
is obvious, as every "smoothing," that is, removing any roughness,
means a saving of energy. In an earlier book I wrote about a "perfection-
reinforcing mechanism." It is my belief that this mechanism has become
liberated from its original teleonomic function in humans, and this "running free" has become the root of all human arts, the oldest of which is
dancing.

2. So-Called Voluntary Movement

One definition of the word "voluntary," which is going to be applied to
the processes now discussed, is that given in the *Concise Oxford Dictionary*:
"control exercised by deliberate purpose over impulse." An inclusion of
purposiveness in the definition of voluntary movements is admissible to
the extent that voluntary movements, with the few exceptions mentioned at the end of the last section, always form part of some sort of
appetitive behavior.

As was mentioned in Three/IV/5, an important physiological difference exists between those motor patterns which most easily form conditioned actions by becoming associated with some reinforcement and
those others which persistently refuse to do so. Examples of both have

been given in this section. We do not know what, physiologically, causes this difference, but we can make some suggestions about their teleonomy. Those fixed motor patterns which are easily built into skilled movements almost always belong to the "multipurpose" type of activity discussed in Two/I/11. An obvious part of their phylogenetic program is to serve as elements for the formation of skilled movements. The non-conditionable motor patterns are primarily those which normally appear only when driven by their own particular motivation. The elements out of which skilled movements are composed are predominantly common, easily "available" patterns such as pecking in pigeons, gnawing in rodents, and, more than any others, the movements of locomotion, including those of taxis-controlled turnings in every direction.

Regarding the patterns of locomotion, we are practically certain that their source is to be found in endogenous impulse production and that their form is determined by central coordination, as was assumed by Erich von Holst. This assumption implies that the motor patterns themselves are not susceptible to adaptive change through environmental stimulation. Whenever adaptive change becomes necessary, it is effected by a *superposition* of physiologically quite different motor processes which are directly controlled by external stimuli. Erich von Holst subsumed these under the concept of a "mantle of reflexes" which envelops the hard and immutable core of centrally coordinated fixed patterns. When a dog is trotting over an uneven surface, taxis-controlled movements are, at every step, interposed adaptively between the centrally coordinated movement and the irregularities of the ground.

The environment through which an animal moves often demands such radical and sudden acts of adaptation from an animal's locomotion that the "mantle of reflexes," in other words, the superposition of taxis-controlled movements, fails to cope with the situation. In this case, the central nervous system has to resort to the faculty that in Two/VI/11 was likened to the limited power exerted by a ship's captain who cannot change the movements of the ship's machinery but can command it to stop and to go ahead again. The phyletic adaptation of locomotor movements to extreme environmental conditions was not achieved, as some students of behavior believed, by "softening" fixed motor patterns so as to make them fit the requirements. Phylogeny found quite a different way to make an animal's locomotion adaptable to the ever-changing demands made on it by the circumstances of environments possessing complicated and irregular spatial structures, as do the crags of a rocky mountain or the branches of a tree. What actually happened during the evolution of locomotor patterns can be deduced from a comparison of closely related species, some of which live in spatially simple and regular biotopes, while others inhabit rocky habitats or trees. The more spatially homogeneous the biotope, the fewer are the demands made on instant adaptation of locomotion. The complete homogeneity of the open sea makes it unnecessary for some freely moving creatures, such as the jellyfish *Rhizostoma pulmo*, to react spatially to any sort of obstacle. Even in fast-swimming pelagic animals, the spatial responses helping to avoid solid obstacles need not be any greater than that of the ship's captain in our illustration who can command only deviations involving a rather large radius, and controls the engines only to the extent of moving forward, stopping and going into reverse. Among terrestrial habitats, the open steppe is somewhat similar to the open sea with regard to homogeneity, at least in two dimensions. The locomotion of steppe-dwelling animals is often surprisingly unadaptive as far as irregularities of the ground and unforeseen obstacles are concerned. The various gaits of walking, trotting, or galloping can only be "commanded" as unitary entities, each used at different speeds, the slower one being exchanged for the faster one at a predictably specified pace, much as the gears are changed by the automatic gear shift of a car. To a cantering horse or antelope, the flat ground gives very much the same support at every bound or leap, and even when it fails to do so, the obstacle can usually be seen far enough ahead so that swerving aside or stopping in time is possible. The *sudden* appearance of obstacles causes horses and other steppe-dwelling animals to stumble or fall.

Both open sea and steppe-dwelling organisms command only a rather poor capacity for superimposing taxis-controlled movements on their locomotor patterns. A horse walking uphill over uneven ground does not just struggle forward blindly; it does pay a modicum of attention to the ground it is traversing. But it succeeds only very inaccurately in putting its hooves on those places offering firm support.

In order to effect a more differentiated adaptation of locomotion to the substratum, the independently available elementary motor pattern must be *made smaller*. To aim one locomotor element exactly at a certain support, the "minimum separable unit" should not be a *series* of stepping or trotting or galloping movements, but *one* step or jump. That element must be independently available for the simple reason that an animal is often forced to aim its step or jump at a narrow goal, for instance, the summit of a rock, and to stop there. It is quite surprising how widely creatures closely related zoologically differ with regard to this ability. Horses as well as steppe-dwelling antelope are very bad at it; the donkey exceeds the horse, and certain species of mountain zebra are past masters of the art. The mule is proverbially surefooted because it has inherited some of the donkey's capabilities. The agility of the one antelope species specialized for living in rocky surroundings, the chamois of the Alps (*Rupicapra rupicapra*), excels even that of goats, which are adapted to mountain dwelling. Besides the faculty of disposing very freely of disjointed motor elements, these professional mountaineers possess an especially effective "mantle of reflexes," in other words, a very special ability to superimpose taxis-oriented movements on their locomotor patterns. A herd of chamois can pass over a slope covered with large and irregular boulders without interrupting the elegant and economic motor pattern of their gallop, which seems quite rhythmic and regular and in which, none the less, each step is aimed at a strictly determined spot. Only at intervals are slight "syncopes" observable; these show that, after all, the "captain" is sometimes forced to command a "stop," even if the interruption is but a very short one.

An element of locomotion that has become independently available to very many mammals is, so to speak, a half step forward performed with one front leg. In difficult situations, such as when being shut up in a puzzle box, but also quite generally in situations of stress, animals of the most diverse kind will "paw" with one front leg. They will do this long before they have learned through experience that this movement, when properly oriented, can open a latch. Conversely, researchers experimenting with animals are the ones who have learned to construe problem situations in such a way as to make the pawing movement applicable for the animal. Unlearned pawing is used by horses to beg for food and by dogs to beg forgiveness.

Among all possible habitats, the arboreal biotope makes the greatest demands on locomotion, both with respect to small independently available motor elements and to those capacities necessary for precise orientation. Among all tree-climbing animals, those with prehensile hands, such as chameleons, some marsupials, and many primates, are most dependent on the adaptability of locomotion. While a paw equipped with curved claws like those of a squirrel, or with adhesive pads like those of a tree frog, can catch hold even when hitting a support rather haphazardly, the prehensile hand does not afford any support at all unless it can close its grip at exactly the right place and at exactly the right moment. There is an interesting correlation between the functions of visual orientation and of clutching with prehensile hands: all mammals equipped with prehensile hands and able to move through branches in swift jumps, possess a "lemur-face," that is, eyes directed forward like those of humans, in other words, a visual apparatus specialized for stereoscopic orientation within space. It is easy to understand that man, in whose perceptual thought spatial visualization plays such a fundamental role, could only have descended from ancestors possessing prehensile hands.

The phylogenetic process of "cutting out" elements of general applicability from longer locomotor coordinations has very probably been the phyletic origin of all "voluntary movements." It must be kept in mind, though, that what we are accustomed to conceptualizing under this term is by no means the original, independently available element, but skilled movements built up by learning processes utilizing many such elements by linking them into most complicated chains and nets of conditioned actions. The elements themselves, programmed to be combined into skilled movements, are by no means basic neural elements. Each of them must be regarded as an autonomous, if small, fixed motor pattern that is a mechanism located on a very much higher level of integration than the elementary contractions of a muscle fiber—as represented on the lowest level of Tinbergen's diagram (Two/IV/3). The very minimum of a "voluntary element" implies the coordinated contractions of antagonistic muscles, such as occur when bending and stretching a finger.

Skilled movements are directed by our will only as far as their initiation is concerned. Their coordination, as we have seen, is subject to the workings of a rather rigid chain of associations which our will can change only gradually and by detours, and even then incompletely. What ought to be conceptualized as a voluntary movement is, in a strict sense, an *unlearned* movement, *only* commanded and coordinated by our "free will." If we try to coordinate our independently available motor patterns in a *new* way—that may be dictated by intelligence and insight—the resulting movements always look extremely *awkward*. A right-handed person trying to write with the left hand or anyone trying to make a drawing while looking at the paper and pencil in a mirror can be cited as examples. What we then observe in ourselves is strikingly reminiscent of the behavior of a mouse in an unfamiliar high maze.

3. Voluntary Movement and Insight

As was anticipated in Two/VI/1, a close connection exists between the evolutionary development of voluntary movements and the differentiation of mechanisms exploiting instant information. It was explained there that the function of these mechanisms results in what we call insight. Quite obviously the same environmental conditions favoring the highest development of spatial insight also favor movements that can be adapted to the smallest details of spatial exigencies. Generally, the faculty for gaining insight into complicated spatial structures and the ability to adapt movements to their requirements are so closely correlated in most organisms that the duality of receptor and motor functions is not immediately apparent.

All the more revealing are those few cases in which the spatial insight of an animal exceeds its ability to accomplish a complete adaptation by its motor control. A greylag goose *(Anser anser)* is able, with some exertion, to walk up and down a staircase. When walking upstairs, the bird is better able to adapt the length of its stride to the height of the risers and the depth of the treads than when it is walking downstairs. If the combined distance of height and depth exceeds the length of the goose's stride by any considerable extent, the phase difference between the goose's stride and tread distance will increase from tread to tread until the intercalation of one small step becomes necessary—and this is exactly what the goose is unable to do! Closely related species of Anatidae, otherwise by no means more intelligent than geese, but which are tree dwellers, such as muscovy ducks *(Cairina moscata)* or wood ducks *(Aix sponsa)* have no difficulty in taking the short step in between that brings them exactly to the edge of the tread on which they are standing and makes it easy to reach down to the next, but this our greylag cannot do. Gradually, the phase difference between its stride and the sequence of treads becomes so great that the bird is no longer able to reach the next tread below; the back side of its tarsus jams against the front edge of the tread on which it is standing. This situation is more than the goose can cope with. All it can do is reverse the attempted step and to try again and yet again. Finally, it resorts to the use of its wings and, fluttering, takes a one-legged jump to the lower tread. This brings the sequence of strides and treads back into phase, and the goose walks downwards until the process has to be repeated.

When a goose walking across a lawn meets an obstacle that is about as high as its breast (for instance, one of the usual wire or lath, less than knee-high fences bordering some lawns), while still a few yards away from this barrier the bird shows very clearly its complete insight into the presence of an obstacle and into the need to surmount it: quite a few steps before the obstacle is reached the goose, with lowered head, aims binocularly at the upper edge of the fencing. It "knows" exactly where the obstacle is situated, but its control over its own movements is so incomplete that a behavior as funny as it is unteleonomic results: even before arriving at the obstacle, the goose begins to lift its feet higher and higher, sometimes higher than the obstacle actually is. Rarely is the foot finally put exactly on the fence; more often than not it is aimed too short or too far and then the goose again resorts to the use of its wings. In exceptional cases geese respond to such an obstacle in a way that is usually used to surmount rocks or walls, that is, obstacles that obstruct the view. In order to negotiate these, the goose again aims binocularly at the upper edge of the obstacle, its neck often trembling with excitement. Then, at exactly the right distance, the goose takes a two-legged jump which lands it *exactly* on the visible edge of the obstacle. The bird can exert exact control over this jump, but not over its stride, although both jump and stride are obviously aimed by the same orienting mechanism.

In anticipation of a subject that will be discussed in the next chapter, the close interaction between voluntary movements and exploratory behavior must be mentioned here. When an animal performs exploratory behavior, the re-afferences gained from voluntary movements are what supply the most important information on which spatial insight is based.

Chapter VI
Exploratory Behavior or Curiosity

1. Choice of Behavior Patterns

As mentioned in Three/IV/3, stimulus selection through learning occurs much more frequently and in a greater number of organisms than does the selection of behavior patterns. Only in species with a very highly differentiated central nervous system, and even among these only in situations of utmost stress (Three/IV/6), does the animal perform a great number of behavior patterns in order to select the one that affords relief. Under normal circumstances, only within the context of *exploratory* behavior do we find learning processes agreeing strictly with a behaviorist's concept of operational conditioning or learning of the type R.

Exploratory behavior must not be equated with any other process that attains its teleonomic function by means of trial and error. This method is used by many other learning mechanisms, for instance, when an animal chooses the right object for one of its fixed motor patterns, as was illustrated in Three/IV/3 with the example of corvine birds learning to select the "correct" material for nest building. In this case the learning process is wholly motivated by the appetite for *one* special fixed motor pattern; the fixed motor pattern is unconditionally predetermined; only the stimulus situation is selected through learning.

Even in the classic puzzle box experiments conducted with cats, the animal does not go through its entire repertory of behavior patterns, but tries only a comparatively small number of them related to one another to the extent that all of them can serve the removal of solid obstacles. The cat scratches at the walls, bites at the bars, or wedges its head into any cleft that might provide a way out.

What is so unique about genuine exploratory behavior is that the animal really tends to direct at the object of its curiosity practically all of the behavior patterns it has at its disposal. A young raven *(Corvus corax)* confronted with an entirely new and unknown object treats it to a phyletically programmed sequence of behavior patterns whose functions are extremely varied. Caution being the better part of valor, the raven begins its exploration of an unknown object by treating it as if it were a dangerous predator, that is, something to be mobbed. The raven approaches the object edging sideways and even backward, crouched in preparation for flying off, delivers a very strong peck at it, and immediately, incontinently flees as fast as it can. If the object then follows in pursuit, the bird will try to get behind it and attack it from the rear; this develops frequently into the typical behavior patterns of mobbing a large predator. If, instead, the object flees, the raven takes up the pursuit immediately, delivering peck after peck and proceeding, if possible, to the motor patterns for killing large prey, that is, gripping the object with both feet and hammering fearful blows upon it. If the object does not respond and proves to be "dead already," the raven will grip it with one foot and try to tear it to pieces. During this process the object may prove to be tasty, whereupon the raven will eat some of it and proceed to hide the remnant. If the object is of no use at all for any of these functions, it gradually loses its attraction and may then be used to sit upon, or its pieces may be used to cover and hide more interesting objects.

As Arnold Gehlen has pointed out, this kind of exploration is "objective" in the strictest sense of the word. The object is "made familiar" with respect to its several inherent properties, and then either used or "laid ad acta"—in the original juridic sense of that expression, that is, stored in a place where it can, in case of need, be referred to.

2. The Autonomous Motivation of Exploratory Behavior

As Monika Meyer-Holzapfel has demonstrated (1956), exploratory behavior as well as play is activated by a specific motivation that differs from and is independent of those motivations that activate the sundry fixed motor patterns an animal performs while exploring or playing. In fact, the welling up of any of the latter motivations, for example, one of those which activate a motor pattern for its "serious," teleonomic function, will immediately suppress exploration as well as play. The motor patterns which appear during exploratory behavior and during play are derived from the most varied functions. A cat playing will perform successively the motor patterns of stalking and prey catching, of rival fighting, of escape, of defense against a large predator, and so on. Each of these patterns is a well-defined unit and perfectly recognizable for what it is.

One of the most cogent arguments for assuming a unitary and special motivation lies in the fact than an animal, when exploring or playing, goes through all of these functionally unrelated motor patterns in an extremely rapid sequence, one following the other within seconds. If one should elicit any of these behavior patterns through an IRM, releasing it in its teleonomic function, for instance, the provoking of a cat by confronting it with a large dog, so that it assumed the hunchbacked defense attitude, a half hour or more would be needed by the cat to quiet down enough to become interested in catching prey. As discussed in Two/V/4, the "inertia" of more highly integrated systems of behavior is much greater than that of the component activities on lower levels. In exploration and play the "inertia" of the several patterns is just as negligible as it is when they are artificially activated by patterns demonstrably belonging to altogether different systems. This phenomenon is equally characteristic of both exploratory behavior and play, and thus it cannot be used to separate them by definition.

A second and equally convincing argument for Meyer-Holzapfel's assumption of an autonomous motivation is that play, as well as exploratory behavior, can take place only in a "field devoid of tension"—as Gustav Bally (1945) has expressed it in terms of Kurt Lewin's field theory. Exploratory behavior, as well as play, disappears the instant that any other motivation arises, including any of those that activate "seriously" any of the patterns employed in play and exploration. The exploring raven in our example would immediately cease this activity the moment it became really frightened or really hungry. In the latter case, it would go to the food tray or approach the human foster parent with begging behavior. In other words, it would resort to behavior patterns whose hunger-assuaging funtions it *already knows*.

To assume that the motivation of exploratory behavior is any *weaker* than that of the "normal" or "serious" functioning of the same motor pattern would be an error. It is not due to a maximum selecting factor (*Extremwertdurchlaß*) when the arousal of any specific motivation precludes exploration and play, but to a very specific and obviously teleonomic program. The appetite for exploration can be overwhelmingly strong and, in the following example, stronger than hunger: when I wanted to lure my ravens into their aviary, and when the most enticing tidbits failed to bring them despite their very great hunger, the only inducement that invariably proved effective was my camera which, for obvious reasons, they had never been allowed to investigate. When I was still a child, my elder brother kept a mongoose and, to lure it into its cage, he used his doctor's diploma. Baiting by means of an object of curiosity is a practice well known to trappers, and the saying, "Curiosity killed the cat," bears witness to the power of this motivation.

3. Latent Knowledge

In its exploratory behavior, an animal treats every unknown situation *as if* it were biologically relevant. The rat investigates every hole with regard to its extent and penetrability and, when it has finished its exploration of a new locality, it knows the shortest way from every point to every other, wherever it happens to be, and it knows the shortest way to a cover of equally well-known security.

The everyday behavior of this rat reveals very little of this knowledge. The very considerable amount of information that has been acquired becomes apparent only in cases of need—when the animal can resort to what has been "laid ad acta," as Gehlen so graphically described it (1960). For this reason, what English-writing authors have termed *"latent learning"* is misleading; the learning is readily observable—if one deigns to observe an animal at all. What is latent—until a situation of need arises, is the *knowledge* already acquired through exploration. For this reason, *latent knowledge* is a more fitting term.

4. Objectivity

Acquiring latent knowledge through exploratory behavior is independent of any of the several motivations which activate the various motor patterns utilized during the learning process. What makes latent knowledge independent is exploration's very own special motivation. In human beings, *curiosity* is the subjective phenomenon accompanying exploration. Being independent of any of the "common" motivations, exploratory behavior acquires a kind of information that is in exactly the same sense *objective* as are the results of human scientific research. The exploring raven performing the motor patterns of eating is not hungry and does not, in any way, want to *eat* the object. Anthropomorphically speaking, he wants to *know* whether or not the object is edible *in principle*. The rat exploring all the existing cavities within its environment is not afraid and does not want to hide in them; it wants to know to what extent they can be used as a retreat in case of need. Jakob von Uexküll once said that all things in the "world" *(Umwelt)* of animals are "action things" *(Aktionsdinge)* (1909). This is particularly true of the objects with which an animal has made itself familiar through exploration, and has then "laid ad acta" for later reference. The information extracted through exploratory behavior concerns properties *inherent to the object and independent of an animal's present mood*. This is exactly what we call *objectivation* in science. Latent knowledge preserves this objective knowledge undisturbed by any possible changes in the organism's "moods," e.g., of the fluctuations in its several ASPs.

5. Specialization for Versatility

In all animals possessing highly developed exploratory behavior, the genetic program of *all* behavior patterns is, to the highest degree, what

Ernst Mayr terms an *open* program (1942). The IRMs in particular tend to be very *unselective:* as their response to the correct object is to be determined later through exploration, it is obviously teleonomic for them to be so! Arnold Gehlen has correctly regarded *Weltoffenheit*—being open to the world—as a specifically human property, but it is also characteristic to a lesser degree of all creatures in whose behavior exploration plays a considerable part. By responding to each single unknown object as if it were biologically relevant, these animals unavoidably discover those things which really *are* relevant. This endows them with the ability to adapt, through *individual* learning, to the most variegated biotopes. The raven can survive in the North African desert by behaving virtually like a vulture, soaring on thermal currents to discover carrion. It can live on islands in the northern seas, a parasite of bird colonies, eating eggs and young birds as does the skua *(Stercorarius).* It can live in European forests, where carrion is scarce, by hunting insects and small vertebrates much as the common crow *(Corvus corvus)* does.

For obvious reasons, an unspecialized morphological structure must correspond to the versatility of behavior: organs highly specialized for one particular function would preclude this. Therefore, all "versatility specialists" are species which represent the median or average morphological form of the taxonomic group to which they belong, such as the rat among rodents, or the raven among songbirds. Humans among the primates do, too, if we can forget their forebrains for the moment. The specialists in any of these groups will, in their own specialities, far excel the species specialized for versatility. A squirrel *(Sciurus)* can climb better than a rat, a beaver *(Castor)* can swim better, a gerbil *(Dipus)* runs better, the blind subterranean rodent *Spalax* can dig better, but the rat excels by far any of these in every function that is not the specialist's specialty.

Arnold Gehlen has called the human the "deficient" creature *(das Mängelwesen).* Even if, for the moment, one overlooks the extensive development of the human cerebral hemispheres, and even if one considers versatility based only on physical abilities, our species does not compare at all poorly with mammals of approximately the same size. To be able to walk 15 miles in a day, to swim a distance of 15 meters four meters deep under water and to fetch objects from that depth, and finally to climb up a thick rope for five meters—these are tasks which even an untrained human can accomplish, and no other mammal exists that is capable of doing the same.

6. Play

It is not easy to define what we mean when we say, naively and colloquially, that a man or an animal is "playing." Most of the activities usually described as play have one thing in common: actions recognizably belonging to a system of known function are performed without fulfilling that function. Furthermore, every naive observer would also add that they are performed "for the fun of it." He would probably be correct in many of the cases; see Three/V/2.

The most simple and, phylogenetically as well as ontogenetically, most primitive forms of behavior which a naive observer would describe as "play" are fixed motor patterns "going off in vacuo"—as discussed in Two/I/9. As was elaborated there, motor patterns of locomotion tend to merge at higher intensities into those of escape from, and defense against, predators. A foal jumping, bucking, and kicking in sheer exuberance is obviously enjoying itself—and I would have some doubts about the sanity of any hard-nosed scientist who, for epistemological reasons, denied such an assertion. If two colts or kids or puppies rush around a field chasing one another, the same impression is given, only more convincingly.

In these most primitive forms of play, it is not necessary to assume a special motivation; without doubt the autochthonous ASP for running and for the other motor patterns involved are responsible for their activation. If one rides a horse that has been confined too long in its stall, one becomes painfully aware that just these motor patterns are the ones which become "dammed up," as was discussed in Two/I/7. However, there are all kinds of possible transitions from such primitive forms of play to the more sophisticated and complicated ones in which motor patterns belonging to entirely different functional systems are produced in a haphazard succession, as was described in the preceding section. In those cases, M. Meyer-Holzapfel's assumption of an independent motivation (1956) is pertinent.

As was mentioned earlier in this text, exploratory behavior is impossible to distinguish from play by sharp definitions. One difference, if only one of degree, is to be found in the preponderance of the autochthonous motivation of movements in play. Many forms of play, such as running and chasing, playful fighting or prey catching, are certainly motivated by the enjoyment of the motor patterns themselves. In play-fighting, an important difference from the "serious" acting-out of the same patterns is the persistence of the social inhibition to bite or claw, an inhibition that disappears the very moment the fight becomes serious. A fully grown lynx (Lynx lynx) can enact the most alarming prey-catching and fighting play with the children of its owner. It performs all the movements characteristic of feline fighting, but always with "velvet paws" and without biting, so that hardly a scratch is sustained by even the most tender human skin. Dogs sometimes accompany their fighting play with extremely fearsome growls that still remain distinguishable from serious ones, even to the human ear. This is an example of what linguists call "meta-language." My wife and I react at once if we hear a playful bout of wrestling degenerating into a real dog fight. In dogs, such transitions are very rare, but when playing with adult tomcats, I have often experienced a gradual change from play to actual scratching and biting, yet in time to break off the contest. A tame and elderly male badger *(Meles meles)* taught me the hard way that, in this species, play can change very abruptly into fighting.

Still, the arousal of specific excitation does not always terminate play, but it certainly does terminate exploratory behavior, even when the motivation aroused belongs to one of the patterns performed while exploring—as was mentioned in the preceding section. The ASP of any motor pattern has a definite influence on the frequency, as well as on the intensity, with which it is acted out in play. P. Leyhausen demonstrated in some species of cats (Felidae) that captive animals fed on dead meat lack the opportunity of actually catching and killing prey; compensating for this lack, they tend to discharge the unused motor patterns in play. He observed these activities in cats that were otherwise not prone to play (1975).

An important difference between the performance of one and the same motor pattern during play and during the execution of its serious function was also observed by Leyhausen: during play the vegetative nervous system is not involved in the same way as during the "serious" function. While at play, an animal's fur remains smooth; when actually fighting with rivals or when defending itself against predators, the same motor patterns are regularly accompanied by a bristling of the fur on certain areas of the body.

A definite difference between play and exploratory behavior exists only with regard to their teleonomic functions: the latter serves to acquire objective, "latent" knowledge; the former indubitably serves to accomplish skilled movements. During play, therefore, the factors reinforcing the development of skilled movements (discussed in Three/V/2) contribute to the motivation, and it is just this that so often leads to the creative production of those very elegant movements that appeal to our sense of the aesthetic. There must be a special physiological mechanism that serves primarily to accomplish a maximum of teleonomic function with a minimum expenditure of labor. This has some very interesting consequences: some of the "purest" kinds of play, that is, those not containing any elements of exploration, tend to exploit external sources of energy. There is very little true play to be discovered among birds, but when in flight ravens and other birds learn to perform skilled movements of such great beauty and complication that their accomplishment seems to border on creative art, particularly because each individual bird develops its own lovely skills. Among mammals, too, the most differentiated forms of play are based on the exploitation of external, inorganic energy: sea lions and dolphins use the dynamics of waves and water currents in a way that is similar to the way in which ravens use thermal currents. Just as man has, these marine mammals have invented surfing; they jump onto the sloping front of a large swell and stay above water employing the principle of the aquaplane. Dolphins, moreover, use the pressure wave preceding a large swell or, for that matter, the bow waves created by a ship. Being driven along at a clip which they could never attain under their own power seems to give them enormous pleasure, and this appears to be the greater the faster a ship moves. Many observers unaware of the hydrodynamics of this process have been misled to assume that very high swimming speeds were attainable by Cetacea.

As early as 1933, K. Groos suspected that animals accomplish important learning processes while playing. He regarded play as an anticipation (*Vorahmung,* literally "pre-imitation"), a preparation for and a perfecting of later behavior. Some truth is contained in this hypothesis to the extent that, in certain species, the development of play behavior is clearly correlated with an ability to acquire skilled movements. Although it reads as if one were begging the question, I dare say that aquatic mammals, already mentioned with respect to the joy they take in playing, are particularly easy to train for circus performances involving the most complicated skilled movements. Even without any training sea lions and dolphins invent the most amazing tricks on their own initiative. Karen Pryor (1975), by rewarding a porpoise *(Steno bredanensis)* for every new movement it "invented" during play, succeeded in encouraging this animal's "creativity": once it had caught on to what was wanted, the porpoise produced so many new movements at such a rate that the human recorder found it hard to follow all of them.

As would be expected because of their prehensile hands, play is of the utmost importance to primates; they possess almost unlimited possibilities for developing skills (Three/V/2,3). Conversely, in the lowest animals and among insectivores such as hedgehogs *(Erinaceus)* or shrews *(Sorex),* play is, to the best of my knowledge, quite unknown. The brown rat *(Epimys norvegicus)* engages in true fighting play while still very young: two individuals grab one another with their front legs and kick at each other in very much the same way that cats do, but with only one hind leg. In mice *(Mus musculus)* there is, curiously, only a vestigial form of this kind of play. In fact, it would be unrecognizable to anyone unfamiliar with the play movements of the rat. Young mice in an exuberant mood perform the one-legged kicking movement exactly as the young rats do during their play, except for a sort of disjointed, haphazard jump, which also occurs while in the same mood and at the same ontogenetic phase of young mice. It can be assumed that this behavior should be regarded as vestigial, the mouse having lost a type of play behavior possessed by its ancestors.

Observations of the ontogeny of play make it appear probable that, even in forms as simple as that of the brown rat, elementary motor patterns which once were primarily independent are being joined into sequences of conditioned actions as was described in Three/V/1. This assumption has been confirmed as correct by Eibl-Eibesfeldt's study of the development of play in carnivores. The fighting play constituting a major part of the activities of young carnivores includes a number of multipurpose activities that find their place—and often their orientation—by the conditioning of actions that takes place during play. Polecats *(Putorius)* and other Mustelidae learn, when playing, to orient their biting at the neck of the partner. Reared in deprivation of the possibility of playing with siblings, a polecat will bite a prey or a rival anywhere, blindly and without any orientation. If the polecat is a male, it will also fail to grab the female at the back of her neck when attempting copulation, something every experienced male polecat would do. In this species, thus, the learned orientation of biting serves three different functions: prey catching, rival fighting, and copulation; all of these functions are learned during sibling play.

Rhesus monkeys *(Macaca rhesus)* are able to learn extremely complicated skilled movements by playing with objects such as locks, and afterwards they show—as H. F. Harlow has demonstrated (1950)—appetitive behavior aimed at the performance of these movements (Three/V/2). It is obvious that play can develop a very special teleonomic function when an animal is capable of achieving sufficient insight into and memory for the inventions which it has made fortuitously while playing, and to *apply* them later to "practical purposes," that is, in the service of some appetitive behavior. The classical example of this has been furnished by Wolfgang Köhler's chimpanzee, Sultan (1963). The ape was confronted with the task of reaching a banana with implements comprising two hollow sticks. One stick had to be inserted into the other in order to afford a tool of sufficient length. As long as the ape's interest remained centered on the banana, he failed to find a solution. He persisted in attempting to reach the fruit with the longer of the two sticks. Only when he had given up and had turned his back on the banana goal, and had begun aimlessly to play with the two sticks, did he succeed in inserting the one into the other. The moment this happened, he realized instantly that he now had the instrument required and he used it to get the fruit.

7. Curiosity, Play, Research, and Art

Exploratory behavior and play are indispensable elements of the human system of actions. The invention made by the chimpanzee, Sultan, is paradigmatic for the greatest part of applied science. It is quite typical of basic science that a discovery is made in a "field devoid of tension"—as Bally called it. Sultan was unable to find the solution to the banana problem as long as he was subject to the "tension" of his appetite for it. When Benjamin Franklin discovered that the wet line of a kite was conducting electricity from the clouds above, he was not intent on protecting human habitations from being struck by lightning; he was *playing* with the kite. The history of science abounds in examples of analogous processes of scientific discovery and practical subsequent applications.

A free play of innumerable factors, a play neither directed at any goal nor predetermined by any cosmic teleology, a play in which nothing is determined except the rules of the game has, on the molecular level, led to the origin of life. It has caused evolution and moved phylogenetic development in the direction from lower to higher organisms. Values cannot be defined in terms of rational science. All value judgments are based on emotional processes and it is a vain attempt to define what is a higher and what is a lower organism. Complication and differentiation are prerequisites but not the essence of the "upward" trend of evolution.

It would seem that this free play is the prerequisite for all truly creative processes, for those of human culture just as for those of evolution. The insatiable curiosity of Rudyard Kipling's elephant child and that of the human research worker is motivating in both a form of behavior which is clearly closely akin to, if not identical with, play; it is in no way astonishing that it can only accomplish its truly creative function when it is not biased and hampered by the setting of a predetermined end or goal. The great German poet, Friedrich Schiller, has said that man is wholly human only when he is playing. The great biologist, Alfred Kühn, expressed the same thought by saying that there is no such thing as applied science: if, occasionally, science bears golden fruits, it does so only for him who cultivates science for the sake of its flowers.

The research that humans do has its place somewhere along the ill-defined borderline between exploratory behavior and play. Human art, however, belongs more clearly within the realm of play. Colloquially, we say that a man plays the violin, or plays a role in the theater. The most important criterion of art is that it requires *skill*, a mastering of technique. The German word *Kunst* is derived from the verb *können*; the *Concise Oxford Dictionary* defines art as "human skill as opposed to nature." I should decidedly refuse, thus, to describe as true art some products of "modern art," made by people who believe skill to be dispensable.

As mentioned in the previous section, some skilled movements of animals, such as the flying play of ravens or the playful antics of dolphins on and in the waves, are apt to arouse our strongest aesthetic appreciation. They derive their elegance from a teleonomic process of economizing energy and scope of movement. This goal is reached, even on the lowest levels of motor coordination (Two/I/13), by achieving a *harmony* of impulses. We know that skilled movements are self-rewarding (Three/ V/1), and that they can become the goal of strong appetites, and we know by self-observation what immense pleasure they can give us. It is a rather obvious deduction that the most primitive and oldest form of human art, *dancing*, originated from this. It is possible that *all* human art has arisen from the motivation given by this joy of functioning for the sake of functioning and through a general preference for harmonies. Liberated from the bonds of teleonomy, these functions have been endowed with the character of the truly creative play in which nothing is predetermined except the rules of the game.

Afterword to Part Three

In Part Three I have tried to describe some of the processes involved in teleonomic modification of behavior, all of which I know from my own observations made under conditions that were as natural as possible for the animals being observed. Obviously, the processes chosen utilizing this perspective are different from those that an investigator working in a laboratory might choose for his research. It is suggested that the term operant conditioning as well as that of exploratory behavior should be applied only to learning processes through which animals "try out" *different* behavior systems in an attempt to gain information concerning *the same* stimulus situation. Operant conditioning by reinforcement, for instance, occurs in natural settings almost exclusively within the context of exploratory behavior. This type of learning is found in comparatively few mammals and in still fewer birds, and only among those representing the most highly developed stages of neural organization achieved by their class. If most psychologists continue to overassess greatly the biological importance of operant conditioning, this can be explained by the fact that learning theorists, more often than not, have investigated humans and rats—two species in which curiosity and exploratory behavior play a very much more important role than in a vast majority of other animals.

My hypothetical treatment of different learning mechanisms has been dictated primarily by biocybernetic considerations. For this reason I have sharply divided the small group of learning processes, in which the process of association does *not* participate, from the very much larger group in which association is essential. Among the groups of learning mechanisms for which the latter is the case, I have subsumed, under a concept, all those in which the feedback of success or failure modifies the mechanisms of precedent behavior. In most of my conceptualizations I have followed the biocybernetic hypotheses of Bernhard Hassenstein (1965, 1966).

I certainly do not presume to have given anything like a complete survey of the multiplicity of learning mechanisms which actually exists. Still less do I flatter myself with the belief of being able to describe the vast number of combinations in which the processes described can interact. Most important of all, I refrain from any assertion concerning the way in which the learning mechanisms here described can interact with conceptual thinking in man.

What I do hope to have demonstrated is that very different kinds of learning mechanisms, so-called open programs, have evolved independently of each other in various phyla and that, therefore, very different explanations have to be found for every case.There is no way of knowing how many such learning mechanisms are extant, nor in what manner each of them proceeds to exploit information in order to achieve an adaptive modification in the complicated machinery whose function is behavior. One assertion only can be made with certitude: Each of these open programs is based on vast quantities of information that have been phylogenetically acquired and that are genetically coded.

Appendix
Concerning Homo sapiens

1. Anthropologists' Allegations

One of the most customary and hackneyed objections to which ethologists have to listen is that humans are unique and that every attempt to understand human nature by the approaches of ethology is not only doomed to failure but shows a contemptible blindness for the august nature of humanity. In particular, we are wont to hear that we are drawing false analogies and that we are hugely underestimating the essential differences separating humans from the rest of organic creation. The answer is that we are not and we do not.

2. On Analogies

In fact, there is no such thing as a false analogy: analogy can concern only a greater or a smaller number of characteristics and thereby endow the deduction of a common function with a greater or smaller probability. As has been explained in One/IV/5-7, the mere ascertainment of a reliable analogy, and therewith of a function common to two behavior patterns in two taxonomically widely distant forms, is of extreme value. We are fully aware, though, that the finding of the analogy neither tells us wherein this common function lies nor what the physiological nature of the two analogous behaviors may be. What is strictly determined by a genetic program in the greylag may well be fixated by cultural tradition in human beings. It is important to keep in mind what has been said about functional, phylogenetic and physiological conceptualization.

Do ethologists underestimate the differences between the highest animals and human beings? The counterquestion is: Do anthropologists correctly assess this difference? Some ontological reductionists such as Earl W. Count (1958, 1959) regard "the distinction between a kingdom of insects and a society of human beings . . ." only as " . . . that between a culture with a large instinct-component and insignificant learning-component on the one side, and one with a high learning-component on the other." Other anthropologists such as M. J. Adler (1967) and G. Dux (1970) deny the validity of all conclusions drawn from analogies between animal and human behavior; such conclusions are described as a "relatively harmless form of careless thinking." Dux also regards the principle of adaptation as an "epistemological monstrosity which survives only because it appears to be of some use to ethologists." These extremes should not cause one to forget that there are many more sophisticated anthropological opinions on a continuum between these two!

These quotations are used here only to show how completely some anthropologists of repute fail to understand the process of creative evolution. The fallacy of ontological reductionism has been extensively discussed in One/I/3, with the particular intent to make quite clear that *every* major step in evolution creates *unprecedented* systematic characteristics, in other words, a difference in *essence*, not only in degree.

3. The Difference of Homo sapiens

With the same intent, that is to say, with regard to the origin of the essential specific properties in human beings, I have enlarged on the fact that new, unprecedented systemic properties come into being through the merging of two or more pre-existing subsystems into one well-integrated unit. This process can be simulated even in a simple electronic model, as represented in Figure 1.

Creation can do without miracles. The immense gap which once seemed to yawn between inorganic nature and life is well on the way to being bridged, and I contend that the same is true of the second great "hiatus"—as Nicolai Hartmann would call it—which yawns between beasts and human beings.

To appreciate the dimensions of this chasm, even when viewed from the purely functional, biological side, one must call to mind one essential fact: the primal method of gathering and storing information—that is, the hoary trial-and-success procedure of random genetic change and natural selection—has remained virtually unaltered from the virus-like predecessors of living organisms up to and including our own closest primate ancestors.

Saying this I do not forget that, with the increasing complexity of central nervous systems, the importance of individual experience and learning also grew, but the knowledge gained by it was short-lived; it was extinguished with the death of the individual—it was not inheritable. The passing on of individually acquired knowledge by means of tradition could perpetuate, even among the highest primates, only a very minute amount of information, an amount which is negligible when compared to that stored and transmitted by means of genes. Even in the lowest organisms known, the latter type of information could, and indeed does, fill volumes when expressed in written words.

We are neglecting only what is really negligible when we state that, during the immense periods of our planet's history, during which life worked its way from self-reproducing chain molecules to anthropoid primates, the mechanisms responsible for the gathering and storing of information remained virtually the same.

Then, suddenly, towards the end of the tertiary period, an unprecedented system came into existence which accomplished these very same primal functions of life by altogether different means—and faster by some powers of ten.

If asked to define life, a modern biologist, aware of the results of molecular genetics, would certainly include as one of the most essential characteristics in the definition the function of acquiring and perpetuating information as it is performed by the double-chain molecules of the genome. The biologist's definition would probably leave out of consideration the specifically human way of gathering and transmitting knowledge that is performed by conceptual thought. It is hardly an exaggeration to say that conceptual thought—with syntactic language accompanying it—constitutes a new kind of life.

Except for the one great evolutionary step leading from non-life to life, the coming into existence of conceptual thought certainly creates the most essential distinction known to science. Yet it is no miracle, no more than is any other of the great creative events in evolution. Like all other evolutionary events, it consists of integrating pre-existing and independently functioning systems to form a new, superordinated one which possesses unprecedented and previously unpredictable systemic properties.

We have fairly well-founded notions about which of these subsystems were involved. In my book, *Behind the Mirror*, I have discussed the cognitive mechanisms that were integrated to achieve conceptual thinking. Every one of these mechanisms is found in animals; every one has evolved independently and under the selection pressure of its own separate function. If one knew these functions only from the study of animals, it would not be at all obvious that they could be integrated into one unitary system of a higher order because it is, on principle, as impossible to infer the possibility of a superordinated system from studying the characteristics of its potential components as it is impossible to predict the evolution of a more advanced organism on the strength of the most exhaustive knowledge about its predecessors. However, recognizing the result of creative evolution through systematized afterthought, a stringent deduction can be made concerning the way along which evolution must have proceeded.

Although the pre-existing subsystems become integrated into a new superordinated whole, it must not be supposed that in doing so they then lose their characteristics as well-knit units, or that they lose their own previous functions. Quite the contrary, these functions of the subsystems not only remain indispensable but actually gain in importance for the entire organism.

Learning mechanisms of all types have already been mentioned among the pre-existing subsystems that are combined in the integrated system of conceptual thought. These mechanisms are a good example of such subsystems because they are demonstrably extant and found in exactly the same forms in animals that are still very far from conceptual thinking. One type of learning, however, assumes an especially important role: it is probable that learning through exploratory behavior and, quite particularly, through self-exploration played a decisive part in the genesis of conceptual thought. Where all sources of certain knowledge fail, speculation is permissible. Exploration is closely akin to play, and it is perfectly possible that self-exploration and, with it, reflection, arose out of a playful exploration of a fellow member of the species. It is perfectly possible that the evolving human first saw his own hand gripping that of his playmate; it may first have dawned on him that his own hand was as real an object in the same real world as was the hand of his fellow which he was grasping. At this momentous moment, our ancestor may have had an inkling of the relationship between his own grasping appendage and the things it grasped—the gripping of an individual thing may have turned into the grasping of a concept. Incidentally, the Latin word *concipere* means "to grasp."

The process of conceptualization is, of course, closely connected with, and also dependent on, a number of other cognitive processes already discussed. The functions of *abstraction* performed by perception, and especially by gestalt perception, enable the animal to recognize an object which it has explored as being the same even under extremely varying conditions. Abstraction is indubitably one of the basic elements of conceptual thinking and abstraction is indivisibly linked with perception.

Likewise, most or all of the mechanisms exploiting instant information (Two/VI) and in particular the mechanisms providing a central representation of space (Two/VI/12), with all the subservient functions that go to make it, including the knowledge derived from the reafferences of voluntary movements (Three/V/3), are all indispensable parts and functions of conceptual thinking.

4. Conceptual Thought and Syntactic Language

Conceptual thought and syntactic language apparently came into being together. In Noam Chomsky's opinion, conceptual thinking evolved under the selection pressure of dealing with the external world rather than under that of intraspecific communication. On the whole, I share Noam Chomsky's opinion that syntactic language is based on a phylogenetic program evolved exclusively by humans. At present, some doubts have been cast over the results obtained by A. and B. Gardner, D. Premack, and others in their experiments with anthropoid apes which, under the normal conditions of their life in the wild, give no indication of possessing syntactic language. It is purely speculation on my part that the forming of conceptions and associating them with symbols may be possible for apes while syntax remains absent. I remember a story Cathy Hayes told me many years ago. She did not include the episode in her book, *The Ape in Our House* (1951); she was saving it for a second volume that has not appeared. The story is this. Cathy had trained her chimpanzee, Vickey, to bring objects on command: "Bring the brush"; "Bring the potty"—and such like. Vickey also responded to commands such as, "Kiss Mama," "Kiss Papa." "Give me your hand," and "Give me your foot" were commands used during cleaning operations, and Cathy Hayes had used them repeatedly when grooming Vickey. Once during such a grooming session and on an unpremeditated impulse, Cathy Hayes said to Vickey, "Kiss your foot." Vickey looked up surprised, and then questioningly, but on repetition of the command she kissed her own foot. Then she looked up again at her mentor with an expression that could only be interpreted as astonishment. I give this anecdote for what it is worth, but I must add that I was strongly and strangely moved by its telling, just as much as Mrs. Hayes was moved by the experience. It would mean arguing in a circle, of course, if one were to say that apes would have developed culture if they did have the capacity for syntactic language.

In humans, the new way of communicating by means of syntactic language opened unprecedented possibilities not only for spreading and sharing knowledge among contemporaries but also for transmitting it from one generation to the next. All of this means nothing less than something comparable to the much-discussed *inheritance of acquired characters.* Knowledge became heritable! If a man invented a bow and an arrow, not only he and his kin were henceforward in possession of these invaluable tools, but so was his tribe and possibly the whole of humanity. The likelihood that this acquisition should be forgotten again is as small as the probability that a physical organ of equal teleonomic value should become vestigial.

The realization that a certain event or process does *not* usually occur is often brought home to our conscious observation by that exceptional case in which it does indeed occur. There is hardly anything that could afford so cogent a proof that, in the general way of evolution, the inheritance of acquired characteristics does not play a role as do the far-reaching consequences which the arising of inheritance of learned knowledge has had for the evolution of human behavior, especially for that of human social behavior.

5. Consequences

The basic consequence of verbal communication was an immense strengthening of tradition through the quantity of information transmitted and especially with regard to a perpetuation of knowledge. It is still an open question why, in animals, tradition *does not accumulate from generation to generation,* which it does not, not even in most highly intelligent primates, though tradition does play a role in their behavior. One possible explanation, which I have pointed out in my book *Behind the Mirror,* is that the transmission of traditional knowledge is dependent, among animals, on the presence of the object which the knowledge concerns. A jackdaw cannot convey to its progeny that cats are dangerous if there is no cat at which to discharge a "rattling attack," nor can a brown rat transmit the knowledge that a certain food is poisonous if it is not there to be urinated upon. Among the primates that are demonstrably able to learn skilled movements by tradition, it is rather an enigma why they do not form a cumulating tradition. When observing wild chimpanzees shivering in a cold rain, one cannot help wondering why these highly intelligent apes, although they build beautiful sleeping nests, have not hit on the notion of constructing similar shelters against the rain. So it would seem as if a much better ability for conceptual thinking is still necessary as a prerequisite for accumulating knowledge. The hoard of knowledge thus accumulated is the joint possession of a society. Common knowledge unavoidably forms a bond among human beings that is unprecedented in the animal world. It gives rise to common abilities to act and to act in common, it creates a common will to act for common aims in the interest of common values. The community of many human beings united by these bonds, all of which arise out of a common store of accumulated tradition, is what we call *culture.*

The most revolutionizing consequence of accumulating information was an *acceleration* of the evolutionary process by some powers of ten. The humanities do not identify the following process as evolution but as history. Because the fundamental processes of evolution, based on genetic changes, are not accelerated by the invention of conceptual thought, the two processes, though by no means independent of each other, tend to *diverge.* The historical development of a culture is apt to overtax the genetically limited capacities of its constituent members; this divergence, in itself, may explain why, as Oswald Spengler has pointed out, cultures regularly disintegrate once they have reached a certain degree of differentiation.

6. Cultural Ethology

A culture is a living system like any other. Although it is by far the most complicated one extant on our planet, it is still subject to all the laws of nature prevailing in the organic world. Since conceptual thought is the basic human function that makes culture possible, it seems an obvious assumption that conceptual thought and human insight are able to determine the direction in which a culture is developing—evolving. This is one of the fundamental errors committed by many humanists who repudiate the very idea that biological, ethological approaches can be applied to human cultures.

If, with an open mind, one compares the phylogeny of various species of animals with the history of different cultures, the two kinds of processes appear, in spite of their very different levels of integration, to be akin to one another in very many aspects. In both we find the same vacillating equilibrium, the same state of balance between "conservative" factors tending to advocate for a retention of what has been proved successful and of "revolutionizing" tendencies urging the trial of what is as yet unproved but might imply an advance. And what is most important: in both, in the comparison of species and in the comparison of cultures, we find the same two types of similarities; those which are caused by common descent from a mutual ancestral form, as well as those which were brought about by convergent adaptation to the same external factors.

The comparative study of languages has, for a long time, been using exactly the same methods to disentangle the history of the etymon of a word that comparative morphology has been using to determine the phylogenetic history of an organ or an organism. And Otto Koenig has recently demonstrated that the cultural development of any man-made object obeys exactly the same laws (1970). He concentrated on the historical development of military uniforms—a truly inspired choice of study object. In Austrian army museums there is a well-ordered and extremely complete collection of uniforms, together with all the historical regulations controlling their details. In very much the same way that Erwin Stresemann, many years earlier, delved into the vast ornithological collections and exploited them to an end never dreamt of by their collectors (1951), so Otto Koenig used the amassed stock of old uniforms hoarded in the museums to new ends. What he found was surprising enough. The interactions between historically induced similarities and resemblances caused by parallel or convergent evolution were strictly analogous to those with which we are familiar in phylogeny. In other words, the con-

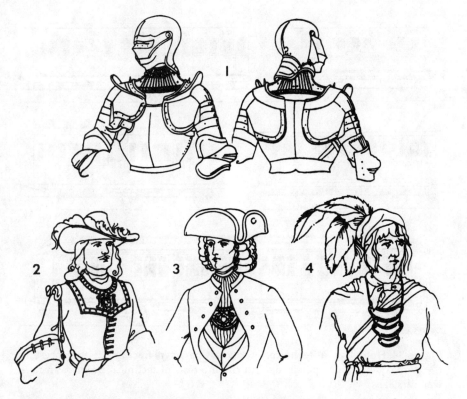

Figure 33. Change of function in a piece of medieval armor which, losing its protective function, becomes a status symbol of officers.

cepts of homology and analogy must be applied in the comparative study of cultural products.

Figure 33 illustrates the existence of cultural homology in products which are the result of a typical change of function. A certain piece of armor that was originally designed to protect the throat and chest was gradually turned, by a change of function, into a status symbol. In his book, *Kulturethologie,* Otto Koenig has adduced many other examples of persistent, historically induced similarities of characteristics to which the adjective "homologous" can legitimately be applied.

Ritualization and symbolism play an important role in traditional clothing and particularly in military uniforms throughout their historical changes, so that the appearance of historically retained similarities is, perhaps, not very surprising. It is, however, surprising that the same retention of historical features, not only independently of function but in clear defiance of it, is observable even in that part of human culture that one would suppose to be free of symbolism, ritualization, and sentimental conservatism—namely, in technology. Figure 34 illustrates the development of the railway carriage. The ancestral form of the horse-

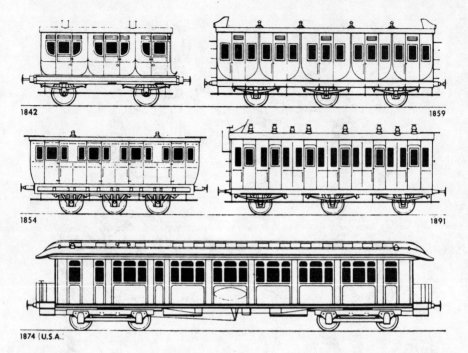

Figure 34. Homology of technical products. Characters traceable to the ancestor, the horsedrawn coach, persist against the interests of technical progress in railway carriages.

drawn coach stubbornly persists in spite of the very considerable difficulties that this entails, such as the necessity of constructing a running board the length of the train along which the conductor must clamber from compartment to compartment, exposed to every kind of weather and to the obvious danger of falling off. The advantages of the alternative solution, the building of a longitudinal corridor within the carriage, are so obvious that they serve as a demonstration of the amazing power exerted by the factors tending to preserve historical features in defiance of expediency.

The existence of these cultural homologies is of extreme theoretical importance because such homologies prove that, in the passing on of cultural information from one generation to the next, processes are at work that are entirely independent of rational considerations and that, in many respects, are functionally analogous to the factors maintaining invariance in genetic inheritance.

References

Abel, O.: Lehrbuch der Paläozoologie. Jena: G. Fischer, 1920.

Adler, M. J.: The Difference of Man and the Difference It Makes. New York: Holt, Reinhart and Winston, 1967.

Anokhin, P. K.: A New Conception of the Physiological Architecture of Conditioned Reflex. *In:* Brain Mechanism and Learning, Oxford: Blackwell, 1961, pp. 189–229.

Aschoff, J.: Circadian Clocks. Proc. Feldafing Summer School, September 1964. Amsterdam: North Holland Publ. Co., 1965.

Baerends, G. P.: Fortpflanzungsverhalten und Orientierung der Grabwespe Ammophila campestris. Tijdschr. Ent. **84,** 68–275 (1941).

Baerends, G. P.: On the Life-History of Ammophila campestris Jur. Nederl. Akademie van Wetenschappen, Proceedings **44,** 1–8 (1941).

Baerends, G. P.: Aufbau tierischen Verhaltens. *In:* Handb. d. Zool. (Kükenthal, W., Hrsg.), **8,** 10, 1–32 (1956).

Baerends, G. P.: Moderne Methoden und Ergebnisse der Verhaltensforschung bei Tieren. Rheinisch-Westfälische Akad. Wiss. Vortrag, **218.** Opladen: Westdeutscher Verlag, 1973.

Baerends, G. P., Drent, R. H.: The Herring Gull's Egg. Behaviour **17** (Suppl.) (1970).

Baeumer, E.: Lebensart des Haushuhns. Z. Tierpsychol. **12,** 387–401 (1955).

Baeumer, E.: Verhaltensstudie über das Haushuhn—dessen Lebensart, 2. Teil. Z. Tierpsychol. **16,** 284–296 (1959).

Bally, G.: Vom Ursprung und den Grenzen der Freiheit. Eine Deutung des Spielens bei Mensch und Tier. Basel: Birkhäuser, 1945.

Batham, E. J., Pantin, C. F. A.: Muscular and Hydrostatic Action in the Sea-anemone Metridium senile (L.). J. Exp. Biol. **27,** 264–289 (1950).

Batham, E. J., Pantin, C. F. A.: Inherent Activity in the Sea-anemone Metridium senile (L.). J. Exp. Biol. **27**, 290–301 (1950).

Beach, F. A.: Analysis of factors involved in the arousal, maintenance and manifestation of sexual excitement in male animals. Psychosom. Med. **4**, 173–198.

Becker-Carus, Ch., Schöne, H.: Motivation, Handlungsbereitschaft, „Trieb". Z. Tierpsychol. **30**, 321–326 (1972).

Beebe, W.: Zaca Venture. London: John Lane, The Bodley Head, 1938.

Bertalanffy, L. v.: Theoretische Biologie. Bern: Francke, 1951.

Bierens de Haan, J. A.: Die tierischen Instinkte und ihr Umbau durch Erfahrung. Leiden: E. J. Brill, 1940.

Bol, A.: *See* Sevenster-Bol.

Brehm, A. E.: Brehms Tierleben. Leipzig & Wien: Bibliographisches Institut, 1890.

Brehm, A. E.: Gefangene Vögel. Leipzig & Heidelberg: C. F. Winter'sche Verlagsbuchhandlung, 1872.

Bridgeman, P. W.: Remarks on Niels Bohr's Talk. Daedalus, Spring, 1958.

Brunswick, E.: Wahrnehmung und Gegenstandswelt. Psychologie vom Gegenstand her. Leipzig & Wien: 1934.

Brunswick, E.: Scope and Aspects of the Cognitive Problem. *In:* Contemporary Approaches to Cognition (Bruner et al., Ed.). Cambridge: Harvard Univ. Press, 1957.

Bubenik, A. B.: The Significance of the Antlers in the Social Life of the Cervidae. Deer **1**, 208–214 (1968).

Bühler, K.: Handbuch der Psychologie, I. Teil: Die Struktur der Wahrnehmung. Jena: 1922.

Bullock, Th. H.: Introduction to Nervous Systems. San Francisco: Freeman & Co., 1977.

Butenandt, E., Grüsser, O. J.: The Effect of Stimulus Area on the Response of Movement Detecting Neurons in the Frog's Retina. Pflügers Archiv **298**, 283–293 (1968).

Buytendijk, F. J. J.: Wege zum Verständnis der Tiere. Zürich & Leipzig: Max Niehaus Verlag, 1940.

Chomsky, N.: Sprache und Geist. Frankfurt: Suhrkamp, 1970.

Chomsky, N.: Language and Mind. New York: Harcourt, Brace, Jovanovich, 1972.

Count, E. W.: Eine biologische Entwicklungsgeschichte der menschlichen Sozialität. Homo **9**, 129–146 (1958); **10**, 1–35 and 65–92 (1959).

Craig, W.: Appetites and Aversions as Constituents of Instincts. Biol. Bull. Woods Hole **34**, 91–107 (1918).

Darwin, C.: The Expression of the Emotions in Man and Animals. New York & London: D. Appleton, 1872.

Dethier, V. G., Bodenstein, D.: Hunger in the Blowfly. Z. Tierpsychol. **15**, 129–140 (1958).

Dewey, J.: Experience and Nature. Chicago & London: Open Court Publishing Co., 1925.

Dewey, J.: Reconstruction in Philosophy. New York: North Holland & Co., 1936.

Dobzhansky, T.: Genetics of Natural Populations XVI. Genetics **33**, 158–176 (1948).

Dobzhansky, T.: Genetics of Natural Populations XVIII. Genetics **33**, 588–602 (1948).

Dobzhansky, T.: Genetics of Natural Populations XX. Evolution **6**, 234–243 (1952).

Dobzhansky, T.: Mankind Evolving. Yale Univ. Press, 1962.

Dolderer, E. M.: Lernverhalten von Pferden aus der Sicht der modernen Verhaltensbiologie. Zulassungsarbeit f. d. Wiss. Prüfung f. d. Lehramt an Gymnasien, Univ. Freiburg, 1975.

Drees, O.: Untersuchungen über die angeborenen Verhaltensweisen bei Springspinnen (Salticidae). Z. Tierpsychol. **9**, 169–207 (1952).

Driesch, H.: Philosophie des Organischen. Leipzig: Quelle & Meyer, 1928.

Dux, G.: *See* Plessner, H.

Eccles, J. C.: The Neurophysiological Basis of Mind: The Principle of Neurophysiology. London: Oxford Univ. Press, 1953.

Eccles, J. C.: Brain and Conscious Experience. Heidelberg & New York: Springer-Verlag, 1966.

Eccles, J. C.: Uniqueness of Man (Roslansky, J. B., Ed.). Amsterdam: North Holland, 1968.

Ehrenfels, C. v.: Über Gestaltqualitäten. Vierteljahresschrift für wiss. Philosophie **14**, 249–292 (1890).

Eibl-Eibesfeldt, I.: Zur Biologie des Iltis (Plutorius plutorius L.). Zool. Anz. Suppl. **19**, 304–314 (1956).

Eibl-Eibesfeldt, I.: Versuche über den Nestbau erfahrungsloser Ratten. (Wiss. Film B 757.) Göttingen: Inst. wiss. Film, 1958.

Eibl-Eibesfeldt, I.: Grundriß der vergleichenden Verhaltensforschung. München: Piper, 1967.

Eigen, M., Winkler, R.: Das Spiel. München: Piper, 1975.

Fisher, R. A.: The Genetical Theory of Natural Selection. Oxford: Clarendon Press, 1930.

Fletcher, R. A.: Instinct in Man. London: George Allen & Unwin, 1957.

Foppa, K.: Lernen, Gedächtnis, Verhalten. Köln & Berlin: Kiepenheuer & Witsch, 1965.

Fraenkel, G. S., Gunn, D. S.: The Orientation of Animals. Oxford: Clarendon Press, 1961.

Franck, D., Wilhelmi, U.: Veränderungen der aggressiven Handlungsbereitschaft männlicher Schwertträger Xiphophorus helleri, nach sozialer Isolierung. Experientia **29**, 896–897 (1973).

Franzisket, L.: Untersuchungen zur Spezifität und Kumulierung der

Erregungsfähigkeit und zur Wirkung einer Ermüdung in der Afferenz bei Wischbewegungen des Rückenmarksfrosches. Z. Tierpsychol. **34,** 525–538 (1953).

Freud, S.: Three Essays on the Theory of Sexuality. 1905.

Freud, S.: Introductory Lectures on Psycho-analysis. 1916–1917. Part III General Theory of Neuroses (1917). Lecture XVIII Fixation to Traumas—The Unconscious.

Freud, S.: Gesammelte Werke. London: Imago Publ., 1950.

Frisch, K. v.: Ein Zwergwels, der kommt, wenn man ihm pfeift. Biol. Zbl. **43,** 439–446 (1923).

Frisch, K. v.: Erinnerungen eines Biologen. Heidelberg & New York: Springer-Verlag, 1957.

Frisch, K. v.: Tanzsprache und Orientierung der Bienen. Heidelberg & New York: Springer-Verlag, 1965.

Frisch, K. v., Lindauer, M. and Daumer, K.: Ueber die Wahrnehmung polarisierten Lichtes durch das Bienenauge. Experimentia **16,** 289–302 (1960).

Gadow, H.: Vögel. *In:* Bronn's Klassen und Ordnungen des Tierreichs, Anat. Theil, **6,** 1–1008. Leipzig: 1891.

Garcia, J. & Ervin, F. R.: A Neuropsychological Approach to Appropriateness of Signals and Specifity of Reinforcers. Proc. of Intern. Neuropsychology Society Meeting, 1967.

Garcia, J. & Koelling, R. A.: A Comparison of Aversions Induced by X-Rays, Drugs and Toxins. Radiation Res. Suppl. **7,** 439–450 (1967).

Garcia, J., Hankins, W. G. & Rusiniak, K. W.: Behavioral Regulation of the Milieu Interne in Man and Rat. Science **185,** 824–831 (1974).

Gardner, R. A. & Gardner, B. T.: Acquisition of Sign Language in the Chimpanzee. Univ. Nevada Progr. Report. (Ms.) (1967).

Gardner, R. A. & Gardner, B. T.: Teaching Sign Language to a Chimpanzee. Science **165,** 664–672 (1969).

Gardner, R. A. & Gardner, B. T.: Two-Way Communication with an Infant Chimpanzee. *In:* Schreier, A. and Stollnitz, F. (Eds.) Behavior of Nonhuman Primates, **4,** 117–184. New York & London: Academic Press, 1971.

Gehlen, A.: Der Mensch, seine Natur und seine Stellung in der Welt. Berlin: Junger und Dürrhaupt, 1960.

Grey Walter, W.: The Living Brain. London: Gerald Duckworth & Co., 1953.

Groos, K.: Die Spiele der Tiere, 3. Aufl. Jena: 1933.

Gunn, D. S., Fraenkel, G. S.: The Orientation of Animals. Oxford: Clarendon Press, 1961.

Haldane, J. B. S.: The Inequality of Man. London: Chatto & Windus, 1932.

Haldane, J. B. S.: The Philosophy of a Biologist. Oxford: Clarendon Press, 1936.

Harlow, H. F.: Primary Affectional Patterns in Primates. Amer. J. Orthopsychiat. **30** (1960).

Harlow, H. F., Harlow, M. K.: The Effect of Rearing Conditions on Behavior. Bull. Menninger Clinic **26**, 213–224 (1962).

Harlow, H. F., Harlow, M. K., Meyer, D. R.: Learning Motivated by a Manipulation Drive. J. Exp. Psychol. **40**, 228–234 (1950).

Harlow, H. F., Harlow, M. K.: Social Deprivation in Monkeys. Scient. American **207**, 137–146 (1962).

Hartert, E.: zitiert nach Stresemann: Die Entwicklung der Ornithologie, (1899).

Hartline, H. K., Wagner, H. G., Rattcliff, F.: Inhibition in the Eye of Limulus. J. of General Physiology **39**, 651–673 (1956).

Hartmann, M.: Allegemeine Biologie. Jena: G. Fischer, 1933.

Hartmann, M.: Die philosophischen Grundlagen der Naturwissenschaften. Jena: G. Fischer, 1948, 1959.

Hartmann, N.: Der Aufbau der realen Welt. Berlin: Walter de Gruyter, 1964.

Hartmann, N.: Teleologisches Denken. Berlin: Walter de Gruyter, 1966.

Hassenstein, B.: Abbildende Begriffe. Zool. Anz. Suppl. **18**, 197–202 (1955).

Hassenstein, B.: Biologische Kybernetik. Heidelberg: Quelle & Meyer, 1965.

Hassenstein, B.: Kybernetik und biologische Forschung. Handb. d. Biol. **1**, 631–719. Frankfurt: Athenaion, 1966.

Hassenstein, B.: Verhaltensbiologie des Kindes. München: Piper, 1973.

Hassenstein, B.: *In:* Biologie: Ein Lehrbuch für Studenten der Biologie. Herausgegeben von G. Czihak, H. Langer, H. Ziegler. Heidelberg & New York: Springer-Verlag, 1976.

Hayes, C.: The Ape in Our House. New York: Harper & Row, 1951.

Hebb, D. O.: The Organization of Behaviour. New York: 1940.

Hebb, D. O.: Heredity and Environment in Mammalian Behaviour. Brit. J. Anim. Beh. **1**, 43–47 (1953).

Hebb, D. O.: A Textbook of Psychology. Philadelphia: W. B. Saunders Co., 1958.

Hediger, H.: Zur Biologie und Psychologie der Flucht bei Tieren. Biol. Zbl. **54**, 21–40 (1934).

Hediger, H.: Wildtiere in Gefangenschaft. Basel: Benno Schwabe & Co., 1942.

Hediger, H.: Skizzen zu einer Tierpsychologie im Zoo und im Zirkus. Zürich: Gutenberg, 1954.

Heilbrunn, L. V.: Grundzüge der allgemeinen Physiologie. Berlin: Dtsch. Verl. d. Wiss., 1958.

Heiligenberg, W.: Uraschen für das Auftreten von Instinktbewegungen bei einem Fische (Pelmatochromis subocellatus kribensis). Z. vergl. Physiol. **47**, 339–380 (1963).

Heiligenberg, W.: Ein Versuch zur ganzheitsbezogenen Analyse des Instinktverhaltens eines Fisches (Pelmatochromis subocellatus kribensis, Boul., Cichlidae). Z. Tierpsychol. **21**, 1–52 (1964).

Heiligenberg, W.: Der Einfluß spezifischer Reizmuster auf das Verhalten der Tiere. *In:* Grzimeks Tierleben, Ergänzungsband Verhaltensforschung. Zürich: Kindler Verlag AG, 1974, pp. 234–254.

Heinroth, O.: Beiträge zur Biologie, insbesondere Psychologie und Ethologie der Anatiden. Verh. 5, Int. Ornithologen-Kongr., Berlin (1910), pp. 589–702.

Heinroth, O.: Über bestimmte Bewegungsweisen der Wirbeltiere. Sitzungsber. Ges. naturforsch. Freunde: Berlin, 1930.

Heinroth, O., Heinroth, M.: Die Vögel Mitteleuropas. Berlin & Lichterfelde: Behrmüller, 1928.

Heinroth-Berger, K.: Beobachtungen an handaufgezogenen Mantelpavianen. Z. Tierpsychol. **16**, 706–732 (1959).

Heinroth-Berger, K.: Über Handaufzuchten. Der Zool. Garten **39**, 1/6 (1970).

Heisenberg, W.: Der Teil und das Ganze. Gespräche im Umkreis der Atomphysik. München: Piper, 1969.

Helmholz, H. L. F. v.: Handbuch der Physiolog. Optik. 1856–1867.

Helmholz, H. L. F. v.: Das Denken in der Medizin. (1877).

Helmholz, H. L. F. v.: Ueber die Tatsachen in der Wahrnehmung (1878).

Helmholz, H. L. F. v.: Abhandlungen, 3 Bände. (1882–1895).

Helmholz, H. L. F. v.: Zählen und Messen erkenntnistheoretisch betrachtet. (1887).

Helmholz, H. L. F. v.: Vorlesungen über theoretische Physik, 5 Bände. (1897–1898).

Helmholz, H. L. F. v.: Schriften zur Erkenntnistheorie. (1921).

Herrick, F. H.: Instinct. Western Res. University Bulletin 22/6.

Herrick, F. H.: Wild Birds at Home. New York & London: D. Appleton-Century Comp., 1935.

Herter, K.: Beziehungen zwischen der Ökologie und der Thermotaxis der Tiere. Biol. Gen. **17**, 243–309 (1943).

Herter, K.: Der Temperatursinn der Säugetiere. Beitr. Tierkunde-Tierzucht **3**, 1–171 (1952).

Herter, K.: Der Temperatursinn der Insekten. Berlin: Duncker & Humblot, 1953.

Hess, E. H.: Space Perception in the Chick. Scient. American **195**, 71–80 (1956).

Hess, E. H.: Imprinting, an Effect of Early Experience. Science **130**, 133–141 (1959).

Hess, E. H.: Imprinting: Early Experience and the Developmental Psychobiology of Attachment. New York: van Nostrand. 1973; Deutsche, Übersetzung: Prägung. München: Kindler, 1975.

Hess, W. R.: Das Zwischenhirn, 2. Aufl. Basel: Schwabe, 1954.

Hess, W. R.: Die Formatio reticularis des Hirnstammes im verhaltensphysiologischen Aspekt. Arch. Psychiatr. Nervenkr. **196**, 329–336 (1957).

Hinde, R. A.: The Nestbuilding Behaviour of Domesticated Canaries. Proc. Zool. Soc. London **131**, 1–48 (1958).

Hinde, R. A.: Unitary Drives. Anim. Behavior **7**, 130–141 (1959).

Hinde, R. A.: Animal Behaviour. New York: McGraw-Hill Book Company, 1966.

Hoffmann, K.: Versuche zu der im Richtungsfinden der Vögel enthaltenen Zeitschätzung. Z. Tierpsychol. **11**, 453–475 (1954).

Hoffmann, K.: Experimental Manipulation of the Orientational Clock in Birds. Cold Spring Harbor Symp. Quant. Biol. **25**, 379–387 (1960).

Hogan, J. A., Adler, N.: Classical Conditioning and Punishment of an Instinctive Response in Betta splendens. Anim. Behav. **11**, 351–354 (1963).

Holst, E. v.: Zur Verhaltensphysiologie bei Tieren und Menschen. (Gesammelte Abhandlungen, Band I und II.) München: Piper, 1969/70.

Hückstedt, B.: Experimentelle Untersuchungen zum "Kindchenschema." Zeitschrift für experimentelle und angewandte Phychologie XII, **3**, 421–450 (1965).

Hull, C. L.: Principles of Behavior. New York: 1943.

Huxley, J. S.: The Courtship of the Great Crested Grebe. Proc. Zool. Soc. London, 1914.

Huxley, J. S.: Courtship Activities in the Red-Throated Diver (Colymbus stellatus PONTOPP); Together With a Discussion of the Evolution of Courtship in Birds. J. Linn. Soc. London Zool. **53**, 253–292 (1923).

Huxley, J. S.: Evolution, the Modern Synthesis. New York: Harper, 1942.

Huxley, J. S.: A Discussion on the Ritualization of Behaviour in Animals and Man. Philosoph. Trans. Roy. Soc. (London) **B 251** (1966).

Iersel, J. J. J. v.: An Analysis of the Parental Behavior of the Three-Spined Stickleback (Gasterosteus aculeatus). Behaviour, Suppl. 3 (1953).

Iersel, J. J. J. v.: Some Aspects of Territorial Behavior of the Male Three-Spined Stickleback. Arch. Neerl. Zool. **13**, 383–400 (1958).

Iersel, J. J. J. v. & Bol, A. C. A.: Preening of two tern species. A study on displacement activities. Behaviour **13**, 1–88 (1958).

Immelmann, K.: Prägungserscheinungen in der Gesangsentwicklung junger Zebrafinken. Naturwiss. **52**, 169–170 (1965).

Immelmann, K.: Zur Irreversibilität der Prägung. Naturwiss. **53**, 209 (1966).

Jarvik, E.: The systematic position of the Diproi. *In:* T. Ørvig (Ed.), Current problems of lower vertebrate phylogeny. New York: Wiley-Interscience, 1968, pp. 223–245.

Jarvik, E.: Aspects of vertebrate phylogeny. *In* T. Ørvig (Ed.), Current problems of lower vertebrate phylogeny. New York: Wiley-Interscience, 1968, pp. 497–527.

Jennings, H. S.: The Behavior of the Lower Organisms. New York: 1906; Deutsch: Berlin & Leipzig: 1910.

Jordan, H. J.: Vergleichende Physiologie wirbelloser Tiere. Jena: S. Fischer, 1913.

Jordan, H. J.: Allgemeine vergleichende Physiologie der Tiere. Berlin: Walter de Gruyter, 1929.

Jung, R.: Selbstreizung des Gehirns im Tierversuch. Med. Wochenschr. **83**, 39: 1716–1721 (1958).

Kaltenhäuser, D.: Über Evolutionsvorgänge in der Schwimmentenbalz. Z. Tierpsychol. **29**, 481–540 (1971).

Kant, I.: Werke (Cassirer, E., Hrsg.), 11 Bde. Berlin: Bruno Cassirer, 1912–1918.

Kaup, J. J.: Classification der Säugethiere und Vögel. J. Orn., 1854.

Kear-Matthews, J.: Mündliche Mitteilung.

Knoll, F.: Insekten und Blumen. Abhandl. Zool.-Bot. Ges. Wien **12** (1926).

Koehler, O.: Die Ganzheitsbetrachtung in der modernen Biologie. Verh. d. Königsberger gelehrten Gesellschaft, 1933.

Koehler, O.: Die Analyse der Taxisanteile instinktartigen Verhaltens. Symp. Soc. Exp. Biol. **4**, 269–302 (1950).

Koehler, O.: Vom unbenannten Denken. Zool. Anz. Suppl. **16**, 202–211 (1952).

Koehler, O., Dinger, W.: Orientierungsvermögen von Mäusen, Versuche im Hochlabyrinth. (Wiss. Film B 635.) Göttingen: Inst. wiss. Film, 1953.

Koenig, O.: Ungewöhnliches Nistmaterial. Die Pyramide **10**, 4 (1962).

Koenig, O.: Kultur und Verhaltensforschung. Einführung in die Kulturethologie. München: Deutscher Taschenbuch Verlag, 1970.

Kogon, Ch.: Das Instinktive als philosophisches Problem. (Kulturphilos., philosophiegeschichtliche u. erziehungswissenschaftl. Studien, Heft 16.) Würzburg: K. Triltsch, 1941.

Köhler, W.: Intelligenzprüfungen an Menschenaffen. Heidelberg & New York: Springer-Verlag (Neudruck, 1963).

Kortlandt, A.: Eine Übersicht über die angeborenen Verhaltensweisen des mitteleuropäischen Kormorans. Arch. neerl. Zool. **4**, 401–442 (1940).

Kortlandt, A.: Aspects and Prospects of the Concept of Instinct. Arch. neerl. Zool. **11**, 155–284 (1955).

Kramer, G.: Untersuchungen über die Sinnesleistungen und das Orientierungsverhalten von *Xenopus laevis*. Zool. Jb. Abt. Phys. **52**, 629–676 (1933).

Kramer, G.: Macht die Natur Konstruktionsfehler? Wilhelmshavener Vorträge, Schriftenreihe d. Nordwestdtsch. Universitätsges. **1**, 1–19 (1949).

Kramer, G.: Ueber individuell und anonym gebundene Gemeinschaften der Tiere und Menschen. Stud. Gen. **3**, 564–572 (1950).

Kristiansen, K. and Courtois, G.: Electroencephalog. and Clin. Neurophysiol. **1**, 265 (1949).

Krueger, F.: Lehre vom Ganzen. Bern: Huber, 1948.

Kruijt, J.: Ontogeny of the Social Behaviour in Burmese Red Jungle Fowl (Gallus gallus spadicus). Behaviour, Suppl. 12 (1974).

Kruijt, J.: Early Experience and the Development of Social Behaviour in Jungle Fowl. Psychiatr. Neurol. Neurochir. **74**, 7–20 (1971).

Kuenzer, P.: Die Auslösung der Nachfolgereaktion bei erfahrungslosen Jungfischen von Nannacara anomala (Cichlidae). Z. Tierpsychol. **25**, 257–314 (1968).

Kühn, A.: Die Orientierung der Tiere im Raum. Jena: G. Fischer, 1919.

Kummer, H.: Soziales Verhalten einer Mentelpavian-Gruppe. Beih. 33 zur Schweiz. Z. Psychol. u. ihre Anwend. Bern: Huber, 1957.

Kummer, H.: Social Organization in Hamadryas Baboons—a Field Study. Biblioth. Primat. Basel: Karger, 1968.

Kummer, H.: Primate Societies, Group Techniques of Ecological Adaptation. Chicago: Aldine, 1971.

Kummer, H.: Sozialverhalten der Primaten. Heidelberg: Springer-Verlag, 1975.

Kuo, Z. Y.: Ontogeny of Embryonic Behavior in Aves I and II. J. Exp. Zool. **61** (1932).

Lawick-Goodall, J. v.: In the Shadow of Man. Boston: Houghton-Mifflin; London: Collins, 1971.

Lawick-Goodall, J. v., & Lawick, H. v.: Innocent Killers. Boston: Houghton-Mifflin, 1971.

Lehrman, D. S.: A Critique of Konrad Lorenz's Theory of Instinctive Behavior. Quarterly Rev. Biol. **28**, 337–363 (1953).

Leong, C. Y.: The Quantitative Effect of Releasers on the Attack Readiness of the Fish Haplochromis burtoni (Cichlidae). Z. vgl. Physiol. **65**, 29–50 (1969).

Lettvin, J. Y., Maturana, H. R., McCulloch, W. S., & Pitts, W. H.: What the Frog's Eye Tells the Frog's Brain. Proc. Instit. Radio Engineers **47**, 1940–1951 (1959).

Leyhausen, P.: Verhaltensstudien an Katzen. Berlin & Hamburg: Parey, 1975.

Leyhausen, P., & Lorenz, K.: Antriebe tierischen und menschlichen Verhaltens. Gesammelte Abhandlungen. München: Piper, 1968.

Lidell, H. S.: The Conditioned Reflex. *In:* Comparative Psychology (Moss, F. A., Ed.) New York: Prentice-Hall, 1934, pp. 247–296.

Lidell, H. S.: Conditioned Reflex Method and Experimental Neurosis. *In:* Personality and the Behavior Disorders (Hunt, J. McV., Ed.), Vol. I. New York: Ronald, 1944, pp. 389–412.

Lissmann, H.: Die Umwelt des Kampffisches Betta splendens. Z. vgl. Physiol. **18–65** (1932).

Lorenz, K.: Beobachtungen an Dohlen. J. Orn. **75**, 511–519 (1927).

Lorenz, K.: Über den Begriff der Instinkthandlung. Folia biotheoretica, **B 2**, Instinctus, 17–50 (1937).

Lorenz, K.: Vergleichende Verhaltensforschung. Verh. Dt. Zool. Ges., Zool. Anz. Suppl. **12,** 69–102 (1939).

Lorenz, K.: Vergleichendes über die Balz der Schwimmenten. J. Orn. **87,** 172–174 (1939).

Lorenz, K.: Kants Lehre vom Apriorischen im Lichte gegenwärtiger Biologie. Blätter für Deutsche Philosophie **15** (1941).

Lorenz, K.: Die angeborenen Formen möglicher Erfahrung. Z. Tierpsychol. **5,** 235–409 (1943).

Lorenz, K.: The comparative method in studying innate behaviour patterns. Symposia of the Soc. for Experimental Biology, IV. Cambridge: 1950.

Lorenz, K.: Ausdrucksbewegungen höherer Tiere. Die Naturw. **38,** 113–116 (1951).

Lorenz, K.: Die Entwicklung der vergleichenden Verhaltensforschung in den letzten 12 Jahren. Zool. Anz. (Suppl.), 36–58 (1952).

Lorenz, K.: Moralanaloges Verhalten geselliger Tiere. Universitas **11,** 691–704 (1956).

Lorenz, K.: Über das Töten von Artgenossen. *In:* Die Natur, das Wunder Gottes (Dennert, E., Hrsg.), **6.** Aufl., 262–281. Bonn: Athenäum. 1957.

Lorenz, K.: Phylogenetische Anpassung und adaptive Modifikation des Verhaltens. Zeitschrift für Tierpsychologie **18,** 139–187 (1961).

Lorenz, K.: Das sogenannte Böse. Zur Naturgeschichte der Aggression. Wien: Borotha-Schoeler, 1963.

Lorenz, K.: Zur Naturgeschichte der Aggression. Neue Sammlung **4,** 296–308 (1965).

Lorenz, K.: Über tierisches und menschliches Verhalten. (Gesammelte Abhandlungen, Band I und II.) München: Piper, 1965.

Lorenz, K.: Innate Bases of Learning. *In:* On the Biology of Learning (Pribram, K. H., Ed.). New York: Harcourt, Brace & World, 1969.

Lorenz, K.: The Enmity Between Generations and Its Probable Ethological Causes. *In:* The Place of Value in a World of Facts. Nobel Symposium 14, Stockholm, 1970, pp. 385–418.

Lorenz, K.: Fritz Knoll als vergleichender Verhaltensforscher. Verh. d. Zool.-Bot. Ges. Wien, 1974.

Lorenz, K.: Die Rückseite des Spiegels. München: Piper, 1973.

Lorenz, K.: Analogy as a Source of Knowledge. Les Prix Nobel en 1973. The Nobel Foundation: 1974, pp. 185–195.

Lorenz, K., & Rose, W.: Die räumliche Orientierung von Paramaecium aurelia. Die Naturwiss. **19,** 623–624 (1963).

Lorenz, K., & Saint-Paul, U. v.: Die Entwicklung des Spießens und Klemmens bei den drei Würgerarten Lanius collurio, L. senator und L. excubitor. J. Orn. **109,** 137–156 (1968).

McDougall, W.: An Outline of Psychology. London: Methuen & Co. Ltd., 1923.

MacKay, D. M.: Freedom of Action in a Mechanistic Universe. Cambridge: Univ. Press, 1967.

Magoun, H. W.: The Waking Brain. Springfield, Illinois: Chas. C. Thomas, 1958.

Makkink, G. F.: An Attempt at an Ethogram of the European Avocet (Recurvirostra avosetta L.) With Ethological and Psychological Remarks. Ardea **25**, 1–60 (1936).

Marler, P., & Hamilton, W. J.: Mechanisms of Animal Behaviour. New York: John Wiley & Sons Inc., 1966.

Massermann, J. H.: Behavior and Neurosis. Chicago: University of Chicago Press, 1943.

Matthaei, R.: Das Gestaltproblem. München: J. F. Bergmann, 1929.

Mau, H.: Zum Einfluß von Testosteron auf Balz-, Kopulations- und aggressives Verhalten erwachsener weiblicher Stockenten (Anas platyrhynchos L.). Inaugural-Dissertation zur Erlangung des Doktorgrades für Biologie der Ludwig-Maximilians-Universität zu München, 1973.

Mayr, E.: Systematics and the Origin of Species. New York: Columbia University Press, 1942.

Mendel, G.: Versuche über Pflanzenhybriden. *In:* W. Ostwalds Klassiker der exakten Wissenschaften (von Tschermak, E., Hrsg.). 1901.

Metzger, W.: Psychologie. Darmstadt: Steinkopff, 1953, 4. Aufl.: 1968.

Meyer-Holzapfel, M.: Triebbedingte Ruhezustände als Ziel von Appetenzhandlungen. Die Naturwiss. **28**, 273–280 (1940).

Meyer-Holzapfel, M.: Das Spiel bei Säugetieren. Handb. Zool. **8**, 1–36 (1956).

Mittelstaedt, H.: Prey Capture in Mantids. Recent Advances in Invertebrate Physiology. University of Oregon Publications, 1957, pp. 51–71.

Morris, D.: "Typical Intensity" and Its Relation to the Problem of Ritualization. Behaviour **11**, 1–12 (1957).

Moynihan, M.: Hostile and Sexual Behavior Patterns of South American and Pacific Laridae. Behaviour, Suppl. 8 (1962).

Nelson, J. S.: Fishes of the World. New York: John Wiley & Sons, Inc., 1976.

Neweklowsky, W.: Untersuchungen über die biologische Bedeutung und die Motivation der Zirkelbewegung des Stars (Sturnus v. vulgaris L.). Z. Tierpsychol. **31**, 474–502 (1972).

Nice, M. M.: Studies of the Life History of the Song Sparrow. Transact. Linn. Soc. (New York) **4**, 57–83 (1937).

Nicolai, J.: Elternbeziehung und Partnerwahl im Leben der Vögel. (Gesammelte Abhandlungen.) München: Piper, 1970.

Pallas, S. P.: zitiert nach Stresemann, Die Entwicklung der Ornithologie.

Pantin, C. F. A.: *See* Batham, E. J., Pantin, C. F. A.

Pavlov, I. P.: Conditioned Reflexes. Oxford: 1927.

Pelkwijk, J. J. Ter & Tinbergen, N.: Eine reizbiologische Analyse einiger Verhaltensweisen von Gasterosteus aculeatus L. Z. Tierpsychol. **1**, 193–201 (1937).

Pittendrigh, C. S.: Perspectives in the Study of Biological Clocks. *In:* Perspectives in Marine Biology. La Jolla: Scripps Inst. Oceanogr., 1958.

Plessner, H.: Philosophische Anthropologie. Herausgegeben und mit einem Nachwort von Günter Dux. Frankfurt am Main: S. Fischer Verlag, 1970.

Popper, K. R.: Scientific Reduction and the Essential Incompleteness of All Science. *In:* Studies in the Philosophy of Biology (Ayala, F. J., Dobzhansky, T., Hrsg.). London: Macmillan Press Ltd. 1974, pp. 259–284.

Popper, K. R.: Studies in the Philosophy of Biology (Ayala, F. J., Dobzhansky, T., Hrsg.). London: Macmillan Press Ltd., 1974.

Portielje, A. F. J.: Dieren zien en leeren kennen. Amsterdam: Nederlandsche Keurboekerij, 1938.

Porzig, W.: Das Wunder der Sprache. München-Bern: 1950.

Prechtl, H. F. R.: Zur Physiologie angeborener Auslösemechanismen I. Quantitative Untersuchungen über die Sperrbewegung junger Singvögel. Behavior **5**, 32–50 (1953).

Prechtl, H. F. R.: Die Entwicklung der frühkindlichen Motorik I–III. (Wiss. Filme C 651, C 652, C 653.) Göttingen: Inst. wiss. Film, 1955.

Prechtl, H. F. R., Schleidt, W.: Auslösende und steuernde Mechanismen des Saugaktes I. Z. vgl. Physiol. **32**, 252–262 (1950).

Prechtl, H. F. R., Schleidt, W.: Auslösende und steuernde Mechanismen des Saugaktes II. Z. vgl. Physiol. **33**, 53–62 (1951).

Prechtl, I.: Auslösende und steuernde Mechanismen der Sperrbewegung einiger Nesthocker. Dissertation, Univ. Wien, 1949.

Premack, D.: Language in the Chimpanzee? Science **172**, 808–822 (1971).

Premack, D.: Intelligence in Ape and Man. New York: Wiley, 1976.

Prosser, C. L., & Brown, F. A., Jr.: Comparative Animal Physiology, 2. Aufl. Philadelphia: W. B. Saunders & Co., 1961.

Pryor, K.: Lads Before the Wind. New York: Harper & Row, 1975.

Pumphrey, R. J.: Hearing. Symp. Soc. Exp. Biol. **4**, 1 (1950).

Rasa, O. A. E.: Appetence for Aggression in Juvenile Damsel Fish. Beiheft zu Z. Tierpsychol. Hamburg: Parey, 1971.

Regen, J.: Über die Orientierung des Grillenweibchens nach dem Stridulationsschall des Männchens. Sitz. Ber. Akad. Wiss. Wien, math.-naturw. Kl. **132** (1924).

Remane, A.: Die Grundlagen des natürlichen Systems der vergleichenden Anatomie und Phylogenetik. Leipzig: 1952.

Remane, A.: Die Geschichte der Tiere. *In:* Die Evolution der Organismen (Heberer, G., Hrsg.), 2. Aufl., 340–419. Stuttgart: G. Fischer, 1959.

Remane, A., Storch, V., & Welsch, U.: Kurzes Lehrbuch der Zoologie. Stuttgart: Gustav Fischer Verlag, 1971.

Rensch, B.: Evolution Above the Species Level. New York: Columbia Univ. Press, 1960.

Richter, C. P.: Animal Behavior and Internal Drives. Quart. Rev. Biol. **2**, 307–343 (1927).

Richter, C. P.: Total Self Regulatory Functions in Animals and Human Beings. Harvey Lectures Series **38**, 63–103 (1942–43).

Riess, B. F.: The Effect of Altered Environment and of Age on the Mother-Young Relationships Among Animals. Ann. N.Y. Acad. Sci. **57**, 606–610 (1954).

Roeder, K.: Spontaneous Activity and Behavior. The Scientific Monthly **80**, 362–370 (1955).

Roeder, K., Tozian, L., & Weiant, E. A.: Endogenous Nerve Activity and Behaviour in the Mantis and Cockroach. J. Ins. Physiol. **4**, 45–62 (1960).

Rose, W.: Versuchsfreie Beobachtungen des Verhaltens von Paramaecium aurelia. Z. Tierpsychol. **21**, 257–278 (1964).

Ruiter, L. de: The Physiology of Vertebrate Feeding Behavior; Toward a Synthesis of the Ethological and Physiological Approaches to Problems of Behavior. Z. Tierpsych. **20**, 489–516 (1963).

Saint-Paul, U. v., & Lorenz, K.: Die Entwicklung des Spießens und Klemmens bei den drei Würgerarten Lanius collurio, L. senator und L. excubitor. J. Orn. **109**, 137–156 (1968).

Schindewolf, O. H.: Paläontologie, Entwicklungslehre und Genetik. Kritik und Synthese. Berlin: 1936.

Schleidt, M.: Untersuchungen über die Auslösung des Kollerns beim Truthahn. Z. Tierpsychol. **11**, 417–435 (1954).

Schleidt, W. M.: Reaktion von Truthühnern auf fliegende Raubvögel und Versuche zur Analyse ihrer AAMs. Z. Tierpsychol. **18**, 534–560 (1961).

Schleidt, W. M.: Die historische Entwicklung der Begriffe „Angeborenes auslösendes Schema" und „Angeborener Auslösemechanismus". Z. Tierpsychol. **19**, 697–722 (1962).

Schleidt, W. M.: Wirkung äußerer Faktoren auf das Verhalten. Fortschr. Zool. **16**, 469–499 (1963).

Schleidt, W. M.: Über die Spontaneität von Erbkoordinationen. Z. Tierpsychol. **21**, 235–256 (1964).

Schleidt, W. M.: How „Fixed" Is the Fixed Action Pattern? Z. Tierpsychol. **36**, 184–211 (1974).

Schleidt, W. M., Schleidt, M., & Magg, M.: Störungen der Mutter-Kind-Beziehung bei Truthühner durch Gehörverlust. Behaviour **16**, 254–260 (1960).

Schutz, F.: Sexuelle Prägung bei Anatiden. Z. Tierpsychol. **22**, 50–103 (1965).

Schutz, F.: Sexuelle Prägungserscheinungen bei Tieren. *In:* Die Sexualität des Menschen, Handb. d. Med. Sexualforschung (Giese, H., Hrsg.). Stuttgart: F. Enke, 1968, pp. 284–317.

Schwartzkopff, J.: Vergleichende Physiologie des Gehörs. Fortschr. Zool. **12,** 206–264 (1960).

Schwartzkopff, J.: Vergleichende Physiologie des Gehörs und der Laut-äußerungen. Fortschr. Zool. **15,** 214–336 (1962).

Seitz, A.: Die Paarbildung bei einigen Cichliden I. Z. Tierpsychol. **4,** 40–84 (1940).

Seitz, A.: Die Paarbildung bei einigen Cichliden II. Z. Tierpsychol. **5,** 74–100 (1941).

Sevenster-Bol, A. C. A.: On the Causation of Drive Reduction After a Consummatory Act. Arch. neerl. Zool. **15,** 175–236 (1962).

Sevenster, P.: A Causal Analysis of Displacement Activity, Fanning in Gasterosteus aculeatus. Behaviour, Suppl. 9 (1961).

Sevenster, P.: Motivation and Learning in Sticklebacks. *In:* The Central Nervous System and Fish Behaviour (Ingle, D., Ed.), 223–245. Chicago & London: Univ. Press. 1968, pp. 223–245.

Sherrington, C. S.: The Integrative Action of the Nervous System. New York: Scribner's, 1906.

Sherrington, C. S.: Quantitative Management of Contraction in Lowest Level Coordination. Brain **54,** 1–28 (1931).

Sjölander, S.: Sexual Imprinting on Another Species in a Cichlid Fish, Haplochromis burtoni. Rec. Comp. Animal T. **7,** 77–81 (1973).

Sjölander, S.: Effects of Cross-Fostering on the Sexual Imprinting of the Female Zebra Finch Taeniopygia guttata. Z. Tierpsychol. **45,** 337–348 (1977).

Skinner, B. F.: Conditioning and Extinction and Their Relation to Drive. J. gen. Psychol. **14,** 296–317 (1936).

Skinner, B. F.: The Behavior of Organisms. New York: Appleton-Century-Crofts, 1938.

Skinner, B. F.: Reinforcement Today. Amer. Psychologist **13,** 94–99 (1958).

Skinner, B. F.: Beyond Freedom and Dignity. New York: Knopf, 1971.

Spitz, R.: The First Year of Life. New York: International Universities Press, Inc., 1965.

Stellar, E.: The Physiology of Motivation. Psychol. Review **61,** 5–22 (1954).

Stellar, E.: Drive and Motivation. *In:* Handbook of Physiology (Field, J., Ed.), Sec. 1, Vol. III. Washington: Amer. Physiol. Soc., 1960, pp. 1501–1527.

Stellar, E., & Hill, J. H.: The Rat's Rate of Drinking as a Function of Water Deprivation. J. comp. Physiol. **45,** 96–102 (1952).

Stensiö, E. A.: The Downtonian and Devonian Vertebrates of Spitzbergen. I. Skrift im Svalbard, No. 12 (1927).

Stensiö, E. A.: On the Head of Macropetalichthyids With Certain Remarks on the Head of the Other Anthrodires. Field Mus. Nat. History, Chicago (1925).

Storch, O.: Erbmotorik und Erwerbsmotorik. Anz. Math. Nat. Kl., Öst. Akad. Wiss. 1, 1–23 (1949).

Storr, A.: Human Aggression. London: Allen Lane, The Penguin Press, 1968.

Stresemann, E.: Die Entwicklung der Ornithologie. Von Aristoteles bis zur Gegenwart. Berlin: F. W. Peters, 1951.

Thorndike, E. L.: Animal Intelligence. New York: Macmillan, 1911.

Tinbergen, N.: Die Übersprungbewegung. Z. Tierpsychol. 4, 1–40 (1940).

Tinbergen, N.: An objectivistic study of the innate behaviour of animals. Biblioth. biotheor. 1, 39–98 (1942).

Tinbergen, N.: Social releasers and the experimental method required for their study. Wilson Bull. 60, 6–52 (1948).

Tinbergen, N.: The Study of Instinct, 1. Aufl. Oxford Univ. Press, 1951.

Tinbergen, N.: Das Tier in seiner Welt. München: Piper, 1977.

Tinbergen, N., Lorenz, K.: Taxis und Instinkthandlung in der Eirollbewegung der Graugans. Z. Tierpsychol. 2, 1–29 (1938).

Tinbergen, N., Meeuse, B. J. D., Boerma, L. K., Varossieau, W. W.: Die Balz des Samtfalters (Eumenis semele L.). Z. Tierpsychol. 5, 182–226 (1943).

Tolman, E. C.: Purposive Behavior in Animals and Men. New York: Appleton, 1932.

Twarog, B. M., & Roeder, K. D.: Properties of the Connective Tissue Sheath of the Cockroach Abdominal Nerve Cord. Biol. Bull. (Woods Hole) 111, 278–286 (1956).

Uexküll, J. v.: Umwelt und Innenleben der Tiere. Berlin: 1909 (2. Aufl. 1921).

Verplanck, W.: Mündliche Mitteilung.

Washburn, S. L., & DeVore, I.: The Social Life of Baboons. Scient. Americ. 204, 62–71 (1961).

Weiss, P. A.: Hierarchically Organized Systems in Theory and Practice. New York: Hafner Publishing Co., 1971.

Wells, M. J.: Brain and Behavior in Cephalopods. London: Heinemann, 1962.

Wells, G. P.: Spontaneous Activity Cycles on Polychaete Worms. Symp. Soc. exp. Biol. 4, 127–142 (1950).

Whitman, C. O.: Animal Behavior. Biol. Lect. Mar. Biol. Lab. (Woods Hole, Mass.) 1898, 285–338.

Whitman, C. O.: The Behavior of Pigeons. Publ. Carnegie Inst. 257, 1–161 (1919).

Wickler, W.: Mimikry—Signalfälschung in der Natur. München: Kindler, 1968.

Wickler, W.: Sind wir Sünder? Naturgesetze in der Ehe. München: Droemer, 1969.

Wickler, W.: Stammesgeschichte und Ritualisierung. München: Piper, 1970.

Wickler, W., Seibt, U.: Vergleichende Verhaltensforschung. Hamburg: Hoffman und Campe, 1973.

Wilson, E. O.: On Human Nature. Cambridge, Massachusetts: Harvard University Press, 1978.

Wright, S.: Statistical Genetics and Evolution. Bull. Amer. Math. Soc. **48**, 223–246 (1942).

Wright, S.: Evolution and the Genetics of Populations, Vols. I and II. Univ. Chicago Press, 1968, 1969.

Wundt, W.: Vorlesungen über die Menschen- and Tierseele. Leipzig: Verlag von Leopold Voss, 1922.

Zeeb, K.: Zirkusdressur und Tierpsychologie. Mitt. Nat. forsch. Ges. Bern, (N. F.) **21** (1964).

Zimen, E.: Wölfe und Königspudel. Ethologische Studien (Wickler, W., Hrsg.). München: Piper, 1971.

Index